Women and recession

Women and recession

Edited by Jill Rubery

Routledge & Kegan Paul
London and New York

First published in 1988 by
Routledge & Kegan Paul Ltd
11 New Fetter Lane, London EC4P 4EE

Published in the USA by
Routledge & Kegan Paul Inc.
in association with Methuen Inc.
29 West 35th Street, New York, NY 10001

Set in Monophoto Times Roman
and printed in Great Britain
by Butler & Tanner Ltd
Frome & London

© Routledge & Kegan Paul 1988

No part of this book may be reproduced in
any form without permission from the publisher
except for the quotation of brief passages
in criticism

Library of Congress Cataloging in Publication Data

Women and recession.
(International library of economics)
Includes index
1. Women——Employment. 2. Married women——Employment.
I. Rubery, J. (Jill)   II. Series: ILE (Series)
HD6053.W6375   1988   331.4'12   87-20626

British Library CIP Data also available
ISBN 0-7102-0701-8 (c)
    0-7102-1337-9 (p)

Contents

List of contributors   vii
Preface   ix
Acknowledgments   xiii

Part One

WOMEN'S EMPLOYMENT

Introduction   3

1 Women's employment in restructuring America: the changing   20
  experience of women in three recessions
  Jane Humphries

2 Female labour reserves and the restructuring of employment   48
  in booms and slumps in France
  Patricia P. Bouillaguet–Bernard and Annie Gauvin

3 Sex-typing of occupations, the cycle and restructuring in Italy   74
  Francesca Bettio

4 Women's employment in declining Britain   100
  Jill Rubery and Roger Tarling

Part Two

WOMEN, THE STATE AND THE FAMILY

Introduction   135

5 Women, the state and the family in the US: Reaganomics and   140
  the experience of women
  Marilyn Power

6 Women, the state and the family in France: contradictions of   163
  state policy for women's employment
  Patricia Bouillaguet-Bernard and Annie Gauvin

7 Women, the state and the family in Italy: problems of female   191
  participation in historical perspective
  Francesca Bettio

8 Women, the state and the family in Britain: Thatcher econ-   218
  omics and the experience of women
  Jill Walker

Part Three

**WOMEN AND RECESSION: A COMPARATIVE
PERSPECTIVE**
9 Women and recession: a comparative perspective   253
  Jill Rubery

Index   287

List of contributors

Francesca Bettio is a researcher in economics at the University of Rome. She completed a PhD. dissertation at the University of Cambridge on the sexual division of labour in Italy which is shortly to be published as a book. She is also the co-author of a report on women in Italy for the EEC expert group on women in the labour force.

Patricia Bouillaguet-Bernard is a CNRS researcher at the *Seminaire d'Economie du Travail* at the University of Paris I, and has been working recently, on secondment, at the Ministry of Labour. A specialist in labour economics, she has published a book with Annie Gauvin on women in prosperity and crisis, and has acted as co-ordinator of the EEC expert group on women in the labour force.

Annie Gauvin is a lecturer at the University of Paris I and a researcher attached to the *Seminaire d'Economie du Travail*. A specialist in labour economics, she has published a book with Patricia Bouillaguet-Bernard on women in prosperity and crisis, acted as co-ordinator of the EEC expert group on women in the labour force, and recently completed a project on the implementation of new working-time arrangements in France.

Jane Humphries is a lecturer in the Faculty of Economics, University of Cambridge and fellow of Newnham College. She has published both historical work on women, including articles on the origin of the family, the working-class family and real wages, protective legislation and women's employment and on the sexual division of labour, as well as work on current trends, including the changing role of female labour reserves in the 1970s and 1980s in the US, and with Jill Rubery on the relative autonomy of social reproduction.

Marilyn Power is an associate professor at Saint Olaf College, Northfield Minnesota. She has published articles on feminist theories of class and gender, on women as a reserve army in the transfer from home production to wage labour, and is currently researching on black women clerical workers and on the impact of government anti-discrimination policies on women workers in the US.

Jill Rubery is a senior research officer in the Department of Applied Economics, University of Cambridge and fellow of New Hall. As a member of the DAE Labour Studies Group, she has published work on low pay and minimum wages, women's employment and payment structures in small firms, segmented labour market theory, home-working and flexibility in the labour market. She has also published previous work on women in the recession with Roger Tarling, and on the relative autonomy of social reproduction with Jane Humphries.

Roger Tarling is a managing partner at PA Cambridge Economic Consultants. As a former member of the DAE Labour Studies Group, he has published work on low pay and minimum wages, employment functions and segmented labour markets, labour supply, inflation and collective bargaining, and edited a book on flexibility in the labour market. An article on women in the recession was published with Jill Rubery in 1982.

Jill Walker is a post-doctoral research fellow in the Urban Research Unit, at the Australian National University. She completed a PhD dissertation at the University of Cambridge on central government policy and local authority labour markets and is currently researching into employment in community services, home-based work, spatial divisions of labour and women's life-cycle employment.

Preface

The current world recession interrupted a long period of relatively steady expansion within advanced countries, a boom in which the employment of female labour played an unprecedented role. The sharp reduction in the rate of growth, associated first with the oil crisis in 1973, and later with the more intense recession of the 1980s, led immediately to speculation over the impact of such a turnaround on the general upward trend in women's employment. If the increase in female employment had occurred simply because of the shortage of male labour, and the simultaneous extension of marketed and non-marketed substitutes for domestic labour which released women from household tasks, then these advances for women might be expected to be halted or even reversed when, with the onset of recession, welfare provision was cut back, and excess supplies of male labour became available. Alternatively, if permanent structural changes, associated with the integration of women into the wage economy, had taken place in both the system of production and in the social and family system, then the higher participation for women could be expected to be a persistent and potentially still increasing trend in advanced countries. However, a continuation of the upward trend in women's employment could be the result either of progress towards the homogenisation and equalisation of the male and female employment roles, or be caused by the persistence of differences in sex roles on the labour market, with demand for female labour protected by rigid patterns of sex segregation or by the effects of employers' more intensive search to reduce costs under recessionary conditions.

This book is concerned with making sense of these apparently contradicting pressures on women under the current recession in four advanced countries, the US, Britain, Italy and France. However current pressures and trends cannot be considered in isolation from past patterns and experience. This observation determines the first aspect of the methodology that has been followed in this volume: each chapter adopts an historical perspective, and where appropriate, tries to develop an appropriate theoretical framework for analysing the role of cyclical factors in longer-term trends. Empirical questions, such as whether women's participation has risen or fallen in the recession, can be relatively easily answered, provided national data sources exist; a much more difficult task is the development of an appropriate framework in which to analyse and understand these empirical facts.

The second area of common methodology is the rejection of a neoclassical framework for the analysis of labour markets. All the authors have been actively involved in the new developments in labour market analysis, associated with the rebirth of interest in models of labour market segmentation in the 1970s. The contributions to this book are based on independent research work in individual countries.[1] However the authors have all had opportunities to confront each other with their theoretical and empirical methodologies, either through the forum of the International Working Party on Labour Market Segmentation (see Wilkinson, 1981; Tarling, 1987), or within the Cambridge Department of Applied Economics and Faculty of Economics.

The fundamental characteristic of the 'labour market segmentation' approach as adopted here is the rejection of the notion of a competitive, homogeneous labour market as an appropriate starting point for analysis. Divisions within the labour force should not be treated as imperfections or deviations from an 'ideal type' labour market as labour markets always have been and always will be inherently structured or segmented. These labour force divisions, such that labour is employed on different terms and conditions and under different forms of labour organisation, arise from divisions in the industrial structure (from within the hierarchical and complex systems of large firms, and between different types of firms and industries); from systems of labour market regulation control (including the legal and institutional controls over the employment contract); and from the organisation of the system of social reproduction, which structures the conditions under which labour is supplied. The system of social reproduction cannot be treated simply as either an exogenous factor or as a pure dependent variable adjusting smoothly to the demands of the production system. It thus requires analysis in its own right as a central structuring influence on labour market organisation, which develops along a path which is *relatively autonomous* of changes in the production sphere (Humphries and Rubery, 1984). This perspective lies behind the division of the book into two main sections. The first deals directly with the changing patterns of women's employment related to changes in industrial organisation and in systems of labour market regulation. The second section focuses on the role of the state and the family in structuring women's position in and out of the labour market.

In the concluding chapter we switch the focus from the internal country analysis of women's experience compared both to their own past and to the current experience of men, to comparisons between countries. The methodological approach used for this comparative analysis has direct parallels to the labour market segmentation approach outlined above. Just as the latter rejects the existence of tendencies to convergence of systems of labour organisation *within* labour markets, and of the notion of 'one best way' of organising production and labour, so the methodology adopted for the inter-country comparison, rejects the search for a universal model across countries and accepts the notion of different 'societal' systems with different patterns of social coherence and integration (Maurice et al., 1984, 1986; Wilkinson, 1983). This 'systems' approach means that it is important for comparative analysis to locate the position of women within the overall structure and functioning of the social and economic system, that is to undertake the types of detailed country-specific and historical analysis that are presented in Sections 1 and 2 of the book. This perspective highlights the differences in women's position within societies, which in other analyses become obscured by simple one-dimensional comparisons of, for example, levels of job segregation or trends in participation rates. The application of similar measures of job segregation across countries may have no real meaning if the structure of labour force divisions are fundamentally different between countries; nor are trends in participation very informative without detailed knowledge of how women's pattern of employment over the family formation phase are interrelated with, on the one hand, the pattern of recruitment and job tenure, and the system of childcare provision on the other. This type of approach to comparative analysis requires a much more extensive research programme than a conventional comparison of statistical series across countries, which makes the implicit assumption that the units of analysis represent sufficiently significant and comparable categories across countries to yield interesting results.

These differences *between* the countries are explored in the last chapter, but not at the expense of identifying some major common trends with major significance for women's prospects in the next decade. Thus we identify both the variations in the forms by which women's employment is used to differentiate the labour force and the employment contract between countries, and also the common trend towards an increased importance of this process of differentiation or deregulation in the 1980s. These tendencies towards deregulation cut across another common tendency observed in the four countries, towards higher and more permanent participation by women and towards an increasing proportion of women entering higher level jobs through attainment of qualifications. Expansion of deregulated employment on the one hand, and individual opportunity for mobility on the other hand, must result in an increasing *divergence* in the employment opportunities between women, a divergence which might reduce the pressure to improve women's position *in general*, through collective action and regulation, and lend increased support to policies which stress advancement through individual effort and attainment.

NOTE

1 Reference to earlier work on these issues by the authors of this volume include Bouillaguet-Bernard et al. 1981; Bettio, 1984; Humphries, 1983; Rubery and Tarling, 1982; Walker, 1985; Power, 1983.

REFERENCES

Bettio, F., (1984), 'The sexual division of labour: the Italian case', doctoral dissertation, University of Cambridge.

Bouillaguet-Bernard, P., Gauvin-Ayel, A. and Outn, J. L., (1981), *Femmes au Travail Prospérité et Crise*, Serie: Sciences Economiques, Recherches Panthéon-Sorbonne, Université de Paris 1, Economica.

Humphries, J., (1983), 'The "emancipation" of women in the 1970s and 1980s: from the latent to the floating', *Capital and Class*, no. 20, Summer.

Humphries, J. and Rubery, J., (1984), 'The reconstitution of the supply side of the labour market: the relative autonomy of social reproduction', *Cambridge Journal of Economics*, vol. 8, no. 4.

Maurice, M., Sellier, F. and Silvestre, J. J., (1984), 'The search for a societal effect in the production of company hierarchy: a comparison of France and Germany', in P. Ostermann (ed.) *Internal Labor Markets*, Cambridge, Mass., MIT Press.

Maurice, M., Sellier, F. and Silvestre, J. J., (1986), *The Social Foundations of Industrial Power*, Cambridge, Mass., MIT Press.

Power, M., (1983), 'Falling through the "safety-net": women, economic crisis and Reaganomics', paper presented to the 1983 International Working Party on Labour Market Segmentation Conference, Aix-en-Provence, France.

Rubery, J. and Tarling, R., (1982), 'Women in the recession', in D. Currie and M. Sawyer (eds), *Socialist Economic Review 1982*, London, Merlin Press.

Tarling, R. (ed.), (1987), *Flexibility in Labour Markets*, London, Academic Press.

Walker, J., (1985), 'Central government policy and local authority labour markets in England and Wales 1979–84', doctoral thesis, University of Cambridge.

Wilkinson, F. (ed.), (1981), *The Dynamics of Labour Market Segmentation*, London, Academic Press.

Wilkinson, F., (1983), 'Productive systems', *Cambridge Journal of Economics*, vol. 7, no. 3/4.

Acknowledgments

The people I would most like to thank for their help in the preparation of this book are my co-authors. The idea for such a volume emerged out of discussions and joint work with friends and colleagues in Cambridge and members of the International Working Party on Labour Market Segmentation. Although I alone take responsibility for the editing, this task would have been impossible without my co-authors' active support and advice; particularly that of Francesca Bettio, Jane Humphries and Roger Tarling. I should also record my thanks to Shirley Dex, Peter Elias, Bennet Harrison, Bob Rowthorn and David Marsden for helpful comments and assistance, to Andrew Wilson for translating the two chapters on France, to Sara Horrell for preparing the index and the many members of the computing, secretarial and administrative staff of the Department of Applied Economics who helped at different stages of the preparation of this volume.

Part One
Women's Employment

Introduction

1 COMPETING OR COMPLEMENTARY HYPOTHESES?

There are three basic hypotheses that have been put forward to predict the impact of recession on women's employment. These are the flexible reserve or 'buffer' hypothesis; the job segregation hypothesis; and the substitution hypothesis (Bruegel, 1979; Rubery and Tarling, 1982). At a simple level they offer very different predictions about the relationship of women's employment and the cycle (for a summary of these predictions see Humphries, Table 1). According to the *buffer* hypothesis women are a flexible reserve, to be drawn into the labour market in upturns and expelled in downturns; women's employment moves thus *pro-cyclically*. According to the job segregation hypothesis, there is rigid sex-typing of occupations (Milkman, 1976): hence demand for female labour is dependent on demand in female-dominated sectors: employment trends will thus be related more to secular trends in sectoral and occupational structures than to cyclical factors. Finally, the *substitution* hypothesis predicts *counter-cyclical* trends for women's employment for, as the recession intensifies, the search for cost-saving induces substitution towards cheaper forms of labour, such as women.

As well as providing different employment predictions, these hypotheses have been associated with different theoretical perspectives on women's employment. The flexible reserve hypothesis is associated with human capital labour market theories including some dual labour market theories (Doeringer and Piore, 1971); lower human capital endowments, and in particular lower levels of job-specific skills reduce the incentive for firms to hoard women workers in a downturn (Oi, 1962). This tendency for women to be displaced from jobs where they are currently employed is only one part of the 'buffer' mechanism. In addition women voluntarily withdraw or, under the 'discouraged worker' hypothesis, fail to re-enter the labour market because their labour supply decisions are influenced by the overall level of labour demand. (Mincer, 1962; Bowen and Finegan, 1969). Some Marxist theorists have also identified an incentive for capital to displace women from the labour market: to supplement declining real wages of the breadwinner through domestic labour (see review of debate by

Himmelweit and Mohun, 1977), or to minimise political and social responses to unemployment.

Job segregation cannot be adequately accounted for by differences in biologically-determined skills and attributes of men and women workers. Theories of job segregation thus point to the existence of 'ideological' or socially constructed boundaries between jobs. These boundaries serve to reinforce women's socially subordinate position, condition the types of skills that woman acquire and according to some theorists, serve to link sexual division in the household with sexual division in the labour market (Barron and Norris, 1976).

The starting point for the substitution hypothesis is that women are a relatively cheap form of labour: this cheapness may derive from their position as dependent adults, so that their 'supply price' is related to the need to supplement household income and not to the full consumption needs of the individual (Beechey, 1978). In this version of the substitution hypothesis women essentially form part of the Marxist reserve army of labour which is used to check the rise in the real wage rate. In more neoclassical approaches, women's low wages may arise from so-called 'imperfections' in the labour market which exclude women from specific areas of employment and crowd them into others (Bergmann, 1974). In periods of recession employers have greater incentives and greater opportunities to break down these labour market 'barriers'.

Despite their different theoretical origins and predictions, these apparently 'competing' hypotheses can, in closer examination, be shown to be potentially compatible once women's employment patterns are analysed within an historical and country-specific perspective. For example, the job segregation hypothesis can be related to both the buffer hypothesis and the substitution hypothesis. Segregation may in fact be associated with the concentration of women in relatively unstable jobs or unstable firms: the buffer mechanism then operates through job segregation and not in opposition to it (Bruegel, 1979). Indeed part of the buffer mechanism might operate through the different patterns of labour turnover of women. Firms may concentrate women in areas where they wish frequently to adjust the numbers employed, with the aim of using 'natural wastage' as an alternative to costly and disruptive redundancies.[1] To the extent that women become a more stable and a more dominant part of the labour force this buffer mechanism is likely to diminish in importance as only a minority of women will be concentrated in unstable jobs or participate voluntarily in labour market flows.

This prediction of diminishing importance of unstable jobs needs to be qualified if the recession leads to an increase in the share of employment in unstable jobs or firms. Under these conditions women's employment is likely to decline in the initial phases of the recession as the less protected jobs disappear (for example as firms cut temporary workers or part-timers before making their permanent labour force redundant). As the recession deepens firms may be encouraged to convert some of their stable and higher paid jobs into less stable and lower paid jobs, to reduce costs or increase flexibility of labour costs. More importantly firms setting up or taking on more labour may wish to do so on a temporary basis to minimise risk. These practices may even lead to a substitution of women for men, to the extent that women are more willing to accept jobs on these types of terms and conditions.

Moreover, if the incentive for 'substitution' is the reduction of labour costs, then the process of substitution is likely to be limited to the reconstruction of the system of job segregation. Reductions in wage costs usually require a lowering of the rate for the job which is more difficult to achieve if men continue to be employed alongside women. Thus the process of substitution can often be more properly interpreted as the first stage in the creation of a new, but still sex-segregated, division of labour, so that substitution may lead not to mixed occupations but to a new set of feminised occupations. Cost reduction is not the only incentive to substitution, and male labour shortage or technical change, both more likely to be associated with the upturn than the downturn, may be equally important incentives. However, on either count it is plausible to suggest that boundaries between male and female jobs are influenced by cyclical factors. The job segregation hypothesis in its pure form fails in fact to provide a theory of how these boundaries do change over time: case-study evidence reveals a continual reconstruction of male and female segregation around technically and socially different job structures, so that the simple hypothesis of rigidity in the sexual division of labour is insufficient to explain labour demand patterns. Nevertheless 'flexibility' with the cycle may be only in one direction, with females substituting for males either under cost or labour shortage pressures. The downgrading of the terms and conditions resulting from substitution, and the relatively rapid identification of these jobs as inherently female jobs may restrict any reversal of this substitution process even when excess supplies of male labour become available, as occurs in a recession.

The different hypotheses can also be interpreted as focusing on different aspects of women's relationship to the wage labour market. The buffer and the substitution hypotheses are concerned with labour market flows, or more specifically with the mobilisation of women as a reserve army of labour, while the job segregation hypothesis is concerned with the allocation of women within the job structure and not with flows into or out of the labour market. These two perspectives can be compatible if job segregation is considered a constraint on the mobilisation of female labour reserves, Moreover, mobilisation of female labour reserves takes place in particular time periods, and these historical conditions will determine the types of sectors and occupations in which women are concentrated.

The notion of assymetry or non-reversible historical change can also be applied to the analysis of the reserve army of labour, which guards against simplistic hypotheses that women form a completely flexible and malleable supply of labour. Thus, even if women in certain historical periods form a flexible labour reserve, that is, move readily from the 'latent' part of labour reserves to the labour market and back again, over time it is probable that these reserves will become mobilised on a relatively permanent basis, thus making a permanent transition to at least the 'floating' part of the reserve army (Humphries, 1983). If within firms the buffer mechanism was still in operation, women would tend to be displaced from jobs into unemployment and the 'discouraged worker' effect would fail to materialise. This prediction of decreasing importance of women's flows into and out of the labour market is qualified to the extent that women still quit the labour market for childbearing and may be prevented from re-entering due to shortage of vacancies. Under these conditions the discouraged worker effect is purely 'involuntary' and may exist simply because of the lack of financial incentives for women to register their desire for work. The conversion of women from a 'flexible' reserve to a permanent part of the wage labour force reduces differentiation between male and female labour on labour supply behaviour, but the permanent mobilisation of female labour may be associated with 'deskilling' or cost reducing strategies which require a differentiated labour force. Homogenisation of male and female labour on one dimension may not therefore imply homogenisation across other dimensions of the labour market.

To summarise, it is possible to construct a more sophisticated analysis of women's employment in which the three basic hypotheses are taken as complementary, from an historical perspective. Women may be particularly vulnerable to job loss in particular firms or industries or to the exclusion from the labour market because they withdraw from the labour market over the family formation phase. At the same time they may be relatively protected from job loss by the pattern of job segregation, which may not be easily changed to absorb more of the excess male labour supplies both because of lower wage levels, and the 'feminisation' of jobs. Substitution is restricted by job segregation if feminisation is essential for employers to take advantage of cost reductions associated with female labour; but these cost pressures may induce substitution and changes in the boundaries of the sexual division of labour. These 'demand-side' pressures for change may also be conditioned by the 'supply-side' responses of women which may change their relationship to labour market flows as they become more stable and continuous workers, or which may put pressure on established patterns of job segregation as women acquire the appropriate qualifications and characteristics to compete with men in a wider range of occupations and industries.

2 COUNTRY-STUDIES

In the chapters that follow these theoretical issues are confronted by historical and empirical evidence from four advanced industrialised countries, namely the US, France, Italy and Britain. Each chapter, however, stresses those issues of greatest empirical importance for the country and of greatest theoretical significance for the author or authors. The impact is thus both to reveal the diversity of conditions affecting women's employment and to contribute to the continuing debate on the determinants of women's employment. For example, for the authors of the French paper, the starting point for the analysis of women's employment is the role of female labour reserves in the restructuring of the French economy in the post-war period. For the author of the Italian paper, the prime determinant of the demand for female labour is the sex-typing of occupations: this segregated demand structure does not simply limit or constrain the role of the reserve army of labour but also calls into question the validity of the concept for analysing women's role in the economy. Comparing the chapters in the US and Britain, we find the former is primarily concerned with evidence of increasing diffusion of women throughout the employment system, associated with continuing trends towards higher and more permanent participation. In the chapter on Britain the number of women employed is also found to be expanding relative to the number of men but the main cause is the growth of part-time jobs and the relative expansion of female employment sectors, whereas in the US there is more evidence of substitution of women for men within all employment sectors.

All the chapters, however, situate the trends in women's employment within a broader analysis of the effects of the restructuring taking place in the production system, in employment relationships and in the family economy. In the US, women's participation growth is related directly to the changing structure of employment, towards service sector and lower-paid employment on the one hand, and to the changing family economy brought about through the *decline* in male real earnings (caused not only by job displacement but also by declines in real pay for those in jobs) and through the rapid breakdown of the standard nuclear family model. In the French paper similar developments are linked to the changing 'rapport salarial', that is the system of wage relations which characterise a particular phase of capitalist development. These changes are being brought about primarily by the displacement of male jobs in typically higher paid sectors and by the growth of part-time and temporary work for women. However, the effectiveness of the use of women as a 'floating reserve' to undermine the 'rapport salarial' has so far been contained by the implementation of strong minimum wage protection and by the increasing permanence of women's participation in the labour market.[2] In Britain, in contrast, government policy has been to increase the effectiveness of the 'reserve' through, on the one hand, deflationary policies which have exacerbated the decline in total job opportunities and in male manufacturing employment in particular, and on the other hand through reducing employment and pay protection to stimulate the growth of both low paid and part-time employment. In Italy the forces towards a change in the 'rapport salarial' have been much more constrained by government and trade union policy which has restricted the rate of job loss and maintained real income levels in the formal economy. Women's role in restructuring employment relationships and the structure of wage income has consequently been much less in Italy. Even the informal sector, which has grown relative to the formal sector and absorbs some of the pressures towards change in the aggregate employment and income system, has relied on both male and female workers for its expansion. It is not simply changes in the economic structure which determines women's employment opportunities. These changes are conditioned by the system of state and institutional regulation of the labour market, and by the organisation of social reproduction, themes to which we return in Section 2 of the book.

3 EMPIRICAL ISSUES AND METHODOLOGIES

In this last section of the introduction we discuss some of the empirical issues that have arisen from these country studies and present some of the common methodologies adopted in the chapters.

It has become clear from the above discussions that it is not essential to assume that trends in women's employment are affected by only one mechanism, whether it is the substitution mechanism, the job segregation mechanism or the buffer mechanism. It is therefore useful to develop methodologies for distinguishing between different influences on women's employment instead of trying to identify a single causal explanation. The first distinction we need to make is between secular trend influences on women's employment and cyclical influences. The former are likely to be related to job segregation influences: secular trends in sectoral or occupational structures will have a secular trend impact on women's employment under rigid sex-typing of occupations. Moreover, if there are longer term trends in substitution of women for men within occupational categories, unrelated to cyclical influences, then these influences on women's employment should also be captured by the trend element.

The model used to distinguish between cyclical and trend influences on women's employment in the chapters on the US, Italy and Britain[3] is

$$\log F_t - \log F_{t-1} = \alpha + \beta (\log T_t - \log T_{t-1}) + \gamma t$$

Where F = female employment
      T = total employment

The trend elements are captured by α and γt and the cyclical elements by β. More specifically, if β is significantly different from 1, the rate of change in female employment is significantly different from the rate of change in total employment, in which case it is also significantly different from that of male employment. If β is not significantly different from 1, there is similarity in male and female employment patterns over the cycle.

This is not an ideal test for although it can be used to estimate the direction and likely magnitudes of the relationships, there are difficulties in testing for significance because changes in female employment may not be determined independently of changes in male employment. The results should thus be interpreted only as providing evidence that is consistent or inconsistent with the hypothesis that women's employment is more volatile than that of total employment. Moreover the higher the employment share of women the less likely it is that the β coefficient will be significantly greater than one. One of the striking findings of the results for all three countries is that those with low shares of female employment tended to have β coefficients close to unity even though the scope for their employment to change at different rates from the total is considerable.

The estimation of the trend element has been decomposed into a constant trend element and a time trend element. Only a constant term was included in the earlier model, developed by Rubery and Tarling (1982) in response to an article by Bruegel (1979) and applied by Humphries (1983) and Bettio (1984). This revised specification captures any structural changes in the trend element in women's employment share over time. The net trend depends on the two terms taken together: if both bear the same sign, the constant will then be accelerated exponentially by a significant time trend, but if they bear opposite signs, the net trend will depend on the relative magnitudes of the two terms, with the time trend progressively offsetting the constant trend. In the empirical investigations, if time trends were not found to be significant the original model was applied. For formal specification of the two models and their relationships see appendix 1.

The results from the previous application of these models, together with the developments in theoretical analysis of the problem, as described above, suggested the need to apply this model at a disaggregated level. The 'buffer' mechanism was more likely to be identified at the individual industry level, associated with industry-specific patterns of job segregation. At the aggregate level, changes in the composition of occupations and industries which affect female employment through job segregation are likely to reduce the likelihood of identifying a 'buffer' mechanism, except if there is a strong 'discouraged' worker effect influencing the total level of women employed, and not just the registered unemployment rate.

These expectations were confirmed by the results; in all three countries where the model was applied there was evidence consistent with a buffer mechanism in manufacturing but not generally in services, and even within manufacturing its incidence was industry- and also country-specific. Whereas the separation of the trend from the cycle allowed the identification of, on the one hand, quite different trend elements between countries, and changes in trends over time, and on the other hand quite similar 'buffer' mechanisms, the interpretation of these results revealed some further interesting conceptual and empirical issues. Firstly, evidence at a case-study level suggested that displacement of women workers in the recession may be the result of cyclical forces instigating a longer run trend towards labour displacement and rationalisation. Under these conditions trend and cycle are not analytically separable, as the cycle plays a direct role in determining the trend. However, the inclusion of a time trend in the model provides some means of picking up systematic change in the trend over time. There was in fact little evidence that the recent recession had systematically changed the relationship between changes in female employment to changes in total employment: even in Britain where the impact of the recent recession has been most severe on total employment, the equations estimated up to 1978 provided predictions in female employment up to 1983 which were close to actual changes. Secondly, it was clear that the existence of a buffer mechanism within an industrial sector did not differentiate between volatility arising out of women's employment in cyclically sensitive individual industries, or arising out of women's employment in cyclically sensitive firms or from relatively higher rates of displacement within actual firms. Indeed, in Italy and Britain at least, the evidence suggested that the first effect might be more significant than the latter two effects in explaining the pattern of volatility found in manufacturing and industry orders.

These problems of distinguishing empirically between structural change and changes in the sex segregation of employment apply also in tackling two other main foci of the empirical investigations: namely, first the extent to which the change in female employment and participation rates can be explained by changes in the structure of demand (with sex segregation constant) or by changes in occupational or industrial sex segregation (with the structure of demand constant). Second we are interested in measuring and explaining changes in indices of sex segregation of employment over time. The index of dissimilarity (Duncan and Duncan 1955; Joseph 1983) gives a value of 100 if men and women are employed in completely different occupations and a value of zero if they are distributed across the occupational structure in the same proportions relative to the total male and the total female labour forces respectively. Changes in the index can be decomposed into those that have come about through changes in 'sex representation' within occupations and those brought about by changes in the relative weights of either male or female dominated occupations compared to more mixed occupations. In the papers shift-share type analyses decompose the trends in female employment into *growth* and *share* effects, and changes in sex segregation into *structural* and *sex-composition* effects (see appendix 2 for definitions). A further distinction is introduced by Humphries. The *growth* effect which measures the impact of changes in the structure of demand can be decomposed into the *scale* effect which measures the effect of change in aggregate employment and the *weight* effect which measures the impact of the industrial or occupational composition. (See appendix 2.)[4]

One of the general findings of the research is that to make sense of the aggregate changes in women's employment, we not only need to disaggregate national data sources by industry and occupation but we also need to supplement this information by more detailed sectoral or case-study material as it is at the level of the workplace that the important divisions between male and female labour are often constructed. Reliance on national data sources gives the impression both of homogeneity within the industry or occupation, and of stability. The British and French papers stress the existence of diversity within industries in the utilisation and pay of female labour, and the Italian study emphasises the continual process of reconstruction of the sexual division of labour around changing technologies, a process which is obscured at the national level by the relative stability of male and female shares. Macro and micro approaches to the study of labour market trends are thus found to be complementary, and the authors in this volume make reference to case-study and sectoral material, some of which they have assembled themselves, to interpret aggregate trends.

APPENDIX I

The model for the equation used in the estimation is:

(1) $\dfrac{F_t}{F_{t-1}} = (1+g)e^{\gamma t}\left(\dfrac{T_t}{T_{t-1}}\right)^{\beta}$ where F = female employment
T = total employment

Transforming (1) into logs gives

(2) $\log F_t - \log F_{t-1} = \alpha + \beta(\log T_t - \log T_{t-1}) + \gamma t.$

where $\alpha = \log(1+g)$

for $\beta = 1$ and $\gamma = 0$, g is the constant rate of growth of the share of female employment: i.e.

$$g = \log\left(\dfrac{F_t/T_t}{F_{t-1}/T_{t-1}}\right)$$

APPENDIX 2

(i) *Decomposition of changes in employment*

Let F_t be female employment in year t

$F_t = \sum_i T_{it} p_{it}$ where T_{it} = total employment in industry/sector i in year t

p_{it} = proportion of female: male employment in industry/sector i in year t.

Then $\Delta F_t = F_t - F_{t-1} = \sum_i (T_{it} - T_{it-1})p_{it-1}$ [the growth effect]

$\qquad\qquad + \sum_i (p_{it} - p_{it-1})T_{it-1}$ [the share effect]

$\qquad\qquad + \sum_i (p_{it} - p_{it-1})(T_{it} - T_{it-1})$ [the interaction effect]

Also as $T_{it} = W_{it}\tau_t$ where W_{it} = weight of employment in industry/sector i in year t; i.e. $\dfrac{T_{it}}{\sum T_{it}}$ and

T_t = total employment in year t,

Then the growth effect =

$\sum_i (W_{it}T_t - W_{it-1}T_{t-1})p_{it-1} = \sum_i (T_t - T_{t-1})W_{it-1}p_{it-1}$ [the scale effect]

$\qquad\qquad + \sum_i (W_{it} - W_{it-1})T_{t-1}p_{it-1}$ [the weight effect]

$\qquad\qquad + \sum_i (W_{it} - W_{it-1})(T_t - T_{t-1})p_{it-1}$ [the residual effect]

The effects can be presented as percentage of the total change in female employment: $F_t - F_{t-1}$.

(ii) Decomposition of changes in the Index of Dissimilarity

$$S_t = \tfrac{1}{2}\Sigma_i |f_{it} - m_{it}|$$

Where S_t = Index of Dissimilarity

$$f_{it} = \frac{F_{it}}{\sum_i F_{it}} \quad (100)$$

where F_{it} = female employment in occupation/industry i in year t

$$m_{it} = \frac{M_{it}}{\sum_i M_{it}} \quad (100)$$

where M_{it} = male employment in occupation/industry i in year t

then

$$f_{it} = \frac{F_{it}}{T_{it}} \cdot \frac{T_{it}}{\sum_i F_{it}}$$

where T_{it} = total employment in occupation/industry i in year t

and

$$m_{it} = \frac{M_{it}}{T_{it}} \cdot \frac{T_{it}}{\sum_i M_{it}}$$

so

$$S_t = \tfrac{1}{2}\Sigma_i \left| \frac{F_{it}}{T_{it}} \cdot \frac{T_{it}}{\sum_i F_{it}} - \frac{M_{it}}{T_{it}} \cdot \frac{T_{it}}{\sum_i M_{it}} \right|$$

define

$$S_t^s = \tfrac{1}{2}\Sigma_i \left| \frac{F_{it}}{T_{it}} \cdot \frac{T_{it+n}}{\sum_i F_{it+n}} - \frac{M_{it}}{T_{it}} \cdot \frac{T_{it+n}}{\sum_i M_{it+n}} \right|$$

then the structural effect = $S_t^s - S_t$

define

$$S_t^c = \tfrac{1}{2}\Sigma_i \left| \frac{F_{it+n}}{T_{it+n}} \cdot \frac{T_{it}}{\sum_i F_{it}} - \frac{M_{it+n}}{T_{it+n}} \cdot \frac{T_{it}}{\sum_i M_{it}} \right|$$

then the sex-composition effect = $S_t^c - S_t$

then $S_{t+n} - S_t = (S_t^s - S_s) + (S_s^c - S_s) + R$

where R is the residual or interaction effect.

NOTES

1 These considerations could explain the relationships between sex
segregation, labour turnover and employment instability predicted by the
Doeringer and Piore (1971) dual labour market model.

2 This chapter is concerned with the period before the election of a conservative government in 1986; the adoption of a policy of deregulation in the French labour market occurred after the chapter was completed.

3 In France, it was found impossible to apply this model over the relevant time period because of the lack of a continuous series of industry employment data by sex (see Bouillaguet-Bernard and Gauvin, this section).

4 However, although these techniques allow a separation of sex-segregation effects from substitution effects for time series within a specific country, the differences in the units, whether industries or occupations, between countries precludes comparison of the relative importance of these effects between countries. Similar problems exist with indices of sex segregation which as a result can only be used to distinguish trends within countries and not levels between countries.

REFERENCES

Barron, R, D. and Norris, G. M. (1976), 'Sexual divisions and the dual labour market', in D. L. Barket and S. Allen (eds), *Dependence and Exploitation in Work and Marriage*, London, Longman.

Beechey, V., (1978), 'Women and production: a critical analysis of some sociological theories of women's work', in A. Kuhn and A. M. Wolpe (eds), *Feminism and Materialism*, London, Routledge & Kegan Paul.

Bergmann, B. R., (1974), 'Occupational segmentation, wages and profits when employers discriminate by race or sex', *Eastern Economic Journal*, vol. 1, nos. 2–3.

Bettio, F., (1984), 'The sexual division of labour: the Italian case', doctoral dissertation, University of Cambridge.

Bowen, W. and Finegan, A., (1969), *The Economics of Labour Market Participation*, Princeton, New Jersey, Princeton University Press.

Bruegel, I., (1979), 'Women as a reserve army of labour: a note on recent British experience', *Feminist Review*, no. 3.

Doeringer, P. and Piore, M., (1971), *International Labour Markets and Manpower Analysis*, Lexington, Mass., D. C. Heath.

Duncan, O. and Duncan, B., (1955), 'A methodological analysis of segregation indices', *American Sociological Review*, vol. 20.

Himmelweit, S. and Mohun, S., (1977), 'Domestic labour and capital', *Cambridge Journal of Economics*, vol. 1, no. 1.

Humphries, J., (1983), 'The "emancipation" of women in the 1970s and 1980s: from the latent to the floating', *Capital and Class*, no. 20, Summer.

Joseph, G., (1983), *Women at Work: the British Experience*, Oxford, Philip Allan.

Milkman, R., (1976), 'Women's work and economic crisis: some lessons of the Great Depression', *Review of Radical Political Economy*, vol. 8, no. 1.

Mincer, J., (1962), *Aspects of Labor Economics*, a report of the National Bureau of Economic Research, Princeton, New Jersey, Princeton University Press.

Oi, W., (1962), 'Labour as a quasi-fixed factor', *Journal of Political Economy*, December.

Rubery, J. and Tarling, R., (1982), 'Women in the recession', in D. Currie and M. Sawyer (eds), *Socialist Economic Review 1982*, London, Merlin Press.

1 Women's employment in restructuring America: the changing experience of women in three recessions

Jane Humphries

1 INTRODUCTION

What recession means for women workers is a controversial issue. Hypotheses abound, which if not directly competitive, coexist only with tension. For example, some authors argue that the concentration of women workers in certain industries, occupations and types of enterprise, specifically ones which are relatively insulated from cyclical variation in output and employment, affords them some relative protection in the downswing (Milkman, 1976; OECD, 1976; Milkman, 1980; Johnson, 1983; Miller, 1986). Emphasizing, as it does, a 'silver lining' of the dual labour market, the argument is denoted here as *the segmentation hypothesis*. In contrast, other authors propose that as marginal and often recently hired workers, women are especially vulnerable to cyclical unemployment. Women who leave the work-force temporarily may be trapped by the downswing into a protracted job search, or conceptually if not statistically equivalent, a longer than planned spell of non-participation (Niemi, 1974). Furthermore, seniority rules and social attitudes may mean that women are disproportionately represented among layoffs (Humphries, 1976; Yanz and Smith, 1983). Women thus bear the brunt of cyclical variations in employment, being shed disproportionately in the downswing and recruited intensively in the upswing: summarized here as *the buffer hypothesis*. Yet other commentators hold that recession opens up new opportunities for women workers as employers, pressed to cut costs and increase the flexibility of production, substitute women for men within their workforces (Humphries, 1983): a position depicted here as *the substitution hypothesis*. The implications of each of these hypotheses for the behaviour of key economic variables describing women's labour market experience during the downswing are summarized in Table 1.1.

Since it is not possible to ascertain *a priori* which pressures will be dominant in any particular instances, these arguments are necessarily explored empirically. The context is that of post-World War II America.

There are two main conclusions of the paper. First, these hypotheses can be simultaneously valid descriptions of the experience of women workers if they are applied to particular subsectors of the economy.

Table 1.1 Summary of hypotheses

Hypothesis	Predictions regarding behaviour of variable during downswing				
	Women's employment	Women's unemployment rates	Women's participation rates	Women's relative share of employment	Employment segmentation
Segmentation	relatively stable due to concentration of women in less cyclically sensitive sectors	reduced relative to men's	no prediction	rises in aggregate due to changing composition of total employment stable within sectors	declines due to declining weights of predominantly male occupations
Buffer	relatively unstable as women are disproportionately shed	rises relative to men's: but rise not equal to fall in employment as 'discouraged' workers leave the labour force	may fall as 'discouraged' women leave the labour force	rises in boom: declines in slump across all industries	relative rise in segmentation due to declining relative numbers of women in one or more occupations as women workers are disproportionately shed
Substitution	relatively stable and may even increase as women are disproportionately retained	reduced relative to men's though may be partly offset by rise in participation rate	may rise as households 'respond' to substitution by 'adding' female workers	increases through time, especially in recession	if substitution possibilities vary inversely with the proportion of women, segmentation will fall due to sex composition change

Thus American data suggest that while women workers' concentration in certain currently 'trade exposed' industries and plants – a crowding which clearly derives from their historical experience as disadvantaged workers – has made them especially vulnerable to redundancy associated with plant closures, simultaneously women's relative absence from *heavy* industry, which has been particularly adversely affected by recent recessions exacerbated by the oil price increases and new conservationist public policy, has worked to protect their industrial jobs. The same diversity of experience is also reflected if broader employment categories are considered, for women's disproportionate presence in the fast-growing and buoyant service sector can be shown to have played a key role in the continued expansion of female employment.

Second, but related to the first point above, it is clear that the experience of women workers in recession, as in boom, depends upon both the organization of the family and the organization of the economy, as the former will generate supply side pressures and constraints for potential and actual female workers, and the latter will influence the demand for women's paid work. Elsewhere (Humphries and Rubery, 1984) it has been argued that neither social reproduction (the family) nor production (the economy) can be seen as absolutely autonomous: their influences will be dialectically and historically related. Hence it is inappropriate to try to identify the impact of recession on women workers in the *abstract*: how workers and employers respond to recessionary conditions will vary with their national, industrial, technological, trade union, public policy and family circumstances. In particular the longer run economic context of a recession is crucial in determining the specific implications for women workers. The sensitivity of American women's employment experience in recession to the secular trend in the absorption of female labour illustrates this point. The particular context of the American economy in the early 1980s was that of a permanent and irreversible mobilization of female labour into the wage economy, and an increasing dependence of both two adult and single adult families on women's earnings. Under these conditions a simple 'buffer' hypothesis could not capture the experience of the majority of women workers. Both these conclusions are echoed in other contributions to this volume.

2 THE EMPIRICAL EVIDENCE: EMPLOYMENT, UNEMPLOYMENT AND LABOUR FORCE PARTICIPATION IN THREE POST-WORLD WAR II US RECESSIONS

As any understanding of the impact of recent American recessions on women requires the location of that experience in a longer run context, Table 1.2 summarizes post-World War II trends in employment,

Table 1.2 Employment, unemployment and participation rates, by sex, 1950–82 [thousands, %]

Year	Civilian employment*		Civilian labour force participation rates**		Unemployment rate†	
	men	women	men	women	men	women
1950	39394	15824	88.4	33.3	4.7	5.1
1951	39626	16570	88.2	34.0	2.5	4.0
1952	39578	16958	88.3	34.1	2.4	3.2
1953	40296	17164	88.0	33.9	2.5	2.9
1954	39634	17000	87.8	34.2	4.9	5.5
1955	40526	18002	87.6	35.4	3.8	4.4
1956	41216	18767	87.6	36.4	3.4	4.2
1957	41239	19052	86.9	36.5	3.6	4.1
1958	40411	19043	86.6	36.9	6.2	6.1
1959	41267	19524	86.3	37.1	4.7	5.2
1960	41543	20105	86.0	37.6	4.7	5.1
1961	41342	20296	85.7	38.0	5.7	6.3
1962	41815	20693	84.8	37.8	4.6	5.4
1963	42251	21257	84.4	38.3	4.5	5.4
1964	42886	21903	84.2	38.9	3.9	5.2
1965	43422	22630	83.9	39.4	3.2	4.5
1966	43668	23510	83.6	40.1	2.5	3.8
1967	44294	24397	83.4	41.1	2.3	4.2
1968	44859	25281	83.1	41.6	2.2	3.8
1969	45338	26397	82.8	42.7	2.1	3.7
1970	45581	26952	82.6	43.3	3.5	4.8
1971	45912	27246	82.1	43.3	4.4	5.7
1972	47130	28276	81.6	43.7	4.0	5.4
1973	48310	29484	81.3	44.4	3.3	4.9
1974	48922	30424	81.0	45.3	3.8	5.5
1975	48018	30726	80.3	46.0	6.8	8.0
1976	49190	32226	79.8	47.0	5.9	7.4
1977	50555	33775	79.7	48.1	5.2	7.0
1978	52143	35836	79.8	49.6	4.3	6.0
1979	53308	37434	79.8	50.6	4.2	5.7
1980	53101	38492	79.4	51.3	5.9	6.4
1981	53582	39590	79.0	52.1	6.3	6.8
1982	52891	40086	78.7	52.7	8.8	8.3

* Employed civilians twenty years and over in thousands.
** Per cent of the civilian non-institutional population in the civilian labour force.
† Unemployment rate calculated as a per cent of the civilian labour force.
Source: Bureau of Labour Statistics.

Table 1.3 Changes in unemployment rates, employment and labour force participation from periods of low to periods of high unemployment by sex: three post-World War II US recessions

Peak year	Trough year	Absolute change in unemployment rate		% change in unemployment rate		Absolute change in numbers employed		% change in numbers employed		Absolute change in participation		% change in participation	
		M	F	M	F	M	F	M	F	M	F	M	F
1969	1971	+2.3	+2.0	+110	+54	+574	+849	+1.3	+3.2	-0.7	+0.6	-0.9	+1.4
1973	1975	+3.5	+3.1	+106	+63	-292	+1242	-0.6	+4.2	-1.0	+1.6	-1.2	+3.6
1979	1982	+4.6	+2.6	+110	+46	-417	+2652	-0.8	+7.1	-1.1	+2.1	-1.4	+4.2

Definitions of variables: as Table 1.2.
Source: Bureau of Labour Statistics.

unemployment and labour force participation by sex. The first point to note is that all register a secular rise except for the male participation rate. There has been a major increase in numbers of jobs, although not sufficient to match the increased supply of labour, but in the case of men the increased supply nevertheless represents a smaller share of the male population. The second point to note is the secular and increasing trend towards higher female participation: all studies of this movement emphasize that it is relatively independent of short run demand-side variables, and is partly at least related to changes in family organization and to changes in the demographic characteristics and educational qualifications of women (Shapiro and Shaw, 1983).

Turning to the secular increase in the unemployment rate,[1] three 'trough years' can be identified, 1971, 1975 and 1982. Comparing these years of high unemployment with the nearest previous year of low unemployment (1969, 1973 and 1979 respectively) pinpoints downswings. Comparisons can then be made of the changes in unemployment, employment and labour force participation of men and women from peak to trough, as shown in Table 1.3.

Until very recently the female unemployment rate exceeded the male unemployment rate in all post-World War II years except 1958. Factors which have been cited as responsible for the relatively high unemployment rate of women include: the definition and methodology used in deriving unemployment statistics (Johnson, 1983); women's greater movement into and out of the labour force which makes them more vulnerable to unemployment or enforced non-participation when hard times come (Niemi, 1974); a susceptibility to cyclical layoffs and unemployment; and occupational and geographic immobility resulting in a high level of structural unemployment also exacerbated in recession conditions (Yanz and Smith, 1983). These factors, which are clearly associated with the buffer hypothesis, must be set against a fourth point, emphasized in the segmentation hypothesis: the differing industrial distributions of the male and female labour forces. Women's concentration in the more cyclically robust sectors works in the opposite direction, lowering the unemployment rate of women relatively to that of men.

If the burden of recession falls disproportionately on women workers then their unemployment should have risen more than the male unemployment rate. In none of the three periods reviewed did this occur. Rather it appears that, in agreement with the historic experience reported in Niemi (1974; see also Johnson, 1983; and Podgursky, 1984) the unemployment situation deteriorated much less for women than for men during these downswings. Moreover the relative deterioration of the male unemployment rate seems particularly acute in the most recent recession, when the ratio of male/female unemployment rates jumped by 37 per cent leaving the male unemployment rate above the female for the first time in recent American experience. In short if changes in unemployment rates are used to indicate the impact of recession it appears that in all three downswings the unemployment situation of women deteriorated less than that of men.

But obviously the unemployment rate is a very imperfect measure of the impact of recession because employment and unemployment may be simultaneously changing in the same direction, as happened in the United States in this period, where there was both a rising unemployment rate and increasing employment. A significant indicator of the position of women is therefore how their employment gains, absolute and relative, compare with those of men.

In the 1969–71 recession both female and male employment expanded, but female employment gained relatively. Subsequently female employment continued to advance in the downswings but male employment declined. Thus it seems that employment opportunities for women as a group were less severely affected when compared with the changing employment opportunities for men. Moreover while the negative impact of recession on male employment seems to intensify over time, women's employment seems to gain in resilience. Changes in the labour force participation will also affect the employment situation of both men and women. The buffer hypothesis suggests that the 'discouraged' worker effect will dominate in the recession and the 'added' worker effect in the boom. Both factors can of course be present but the work of Bowen and Finegan (1969) as well as historical studies (summarized by Joseph, 1983, p. 41 ff.) suggest that under high unemployment the added worker effect has usually been swamped by a 'discouraged' worker effect. Table 1.3 shows sex specific changes in participation rates during the three downswings. The male participation rate does indeed decline in all three recessions and with increasing amplitude. But for women the participation rate increased through all three recessions which conflicts with the evidence from historical studies and most current cross section analysis (Joseph, 1983, p. 60). This increase in measured participation rates was also accompanied by an increase in hidden unemployment. Bureau of Labour Statistics (BLS) data report an increase of over 60 per cent in the 1973–5 recession and of over 100 per cent in the 1979–82 recession in people out of the labour force who want a job now but are not looking because they think they cannot get one (Bureau of Labour Statistics, 1983). The rate of increase was the same for both men and women but there were about twice as many women as men in this position in 1973 and about 1.7 times as many in 1979. It remains possible that the recession reduced the rate of growth that the female participation rate would otherwise have attained and *ceteris paribus* reduced the available labour force below its potential.

Various possible estimates of potential labour are available. The BLS figures are based on estimates of future participation rates obtained by simply extrapolating the series observations, after adjusting for changes in age-sex distributions. These projections make no allowance for the accelerating participation rates of prime age females and have under-estimated the size of the female labour force in both low and high unemployment years[2]. If differences between projections and actual labour force figures are attributable to added/discouraged worker effects then persistent shortfalls in the projections suggest that the former is dominant in boom and slump. Accelerating secular trends provide a more convincing explanation particularly when it is recognised that the shortfall was often even greater in slumps, for example, 20.4 per cent of the actual labour force in 1982 compared with 17.6 per cent in 1979.

Econometric models of female participation rates are also problematic, in part because the time series models which explain changes in participation of married women do not seem to fit the behaviour of single or divorced women. But also although there is considerable theoretical agreement on the main determinants of female labour supply, and as suggested above on the dominance of discouraged worker effects, studies have not generated a consistent set of parameter estimates (Cain, 1977)[3]. While the inability of such simplified models to predict female participation derives partly from omitted variables. In particular the continuing rise in women's educational attainment, and the decline in the number of women living with their spouses have undoubtedly boosted participation rates through the last recession, and it is also clear that the parameters derived by modelling earlier experience may not capture women's response in 1973–5 or 1979–82. Moreover even if we could develop a model with considerable explanatory power it is difficult to isolate the impact of recession. While the negative effect of a rising unemployment rate is obviously cyclically related, many other variables such as income, fertility and educational attainment also vary over the cycle. What part of the increase in the number of women with husbands absent can be attributed to marital breakup caused by increased unemployment and declining income?

In short then this evidence suggests that the labour supply behaviour of men and women has changed over the three downswings with women's behaviour becoming less and men's becoming more cyclically sensitive. This accords with earlier work comparing 1950–62 with 1963–76 which found that the cyclical sensitivity of women workers was greater than that of men but declined while that of men increased between the two periods (Bednarzik and Klein, 1977), results which echo the suggestions of other well known studies (Fields, 1976). Indeed Bowen and Finegan (1969) had themselves found evidence that wives were becoming less sensitive to key labour market variables. These developments are clearly linked to other significant socioeconomic trends. The rapid rise in two-earner families and the accompanying increase in women's aggregate earnings have permitted greater flexibility among men but demanded more commitment from women.

Moreover other changes such as more equal employment opportunities, higher educational attainment and postponed childbearing have been expected to make women's worklife patterns more like those of men. Thus the declining cyclical sensitivity of women workers suggested in the descriptive material here, relates to their increased participation in paid work. Whatever the specific links, whether it is that with women workers by 1982 comprising 44 per cent of the civilian labour force they were more thoroughly assimilated into a broad range of occupations and industries (Humphries, 1983), whether it is because their higher profile in paid work has had its own logrolling effect on aspirations and attitudes (Waite, 1977), or whether it relates to the impact of a key group of more experienced work oriented wives (Bowen and Finegan, 1969), it is not surprising to find women workers behaving more like men workers, or at least like men workers used to behave.

3 THE CYCLICAL SENSITIVITY OF FEMALE EMPLOYMENT

Using a simple model, initially developed by Rubery and Tarling (1982), it is possible to confront directly the alleged greater cyclical sensitivity of female employment. Regressions of the percentage change in female employment on the percentage change in total employment provide a direct test of the hypothesis that the former is relatively more cyclically sensitive. If the hypothesis is correct then the coefficient on total employment, $\hat{\beta}$, should be significantly greater than one, in which case the share of women would rise in boom and fall in recession. In contrast $\hat{\beta}$ significantly less than one corresponds to the possibility that female employment is actually sheltered. The model is formally described in Appendix I to the introduction and the results by major industrial divisions, and concentrating on manufacturing, by major industrial groups are presented in Table 1.4a and 1.4b.

The results reported in Table 1.4a, analysing the relationship at the level of industrial divisions, confirm earlier findings (Rubery and Tarling 1982; Humphries 1983). Greater cyclical volatility of female employment is evident in manufacturing, both in the aggregate and in durable and non-durable manufacturing divisions. Women's employment changes were also significantly more volatile in wholesale trade. The data did not however confirm Rubery and Tarling's findings of $\hat{\beta}$ significantly greater than one in finance, insurance and real estate, nor in aggregate employment on non-agricultural payrolls (see also Humphries 1983). The time trend,[4] which if positive, indicates an acce-

Table 1.4a Changes in female employment on non-agricultural payrolls by industry division, 1960–82

equation: $\log F_t - \log F_{t-1} = \alpha + \beta (\log T_t - \log T_{t-1}) + \gamma t$

Sector	Subperiod	$\hat{\alpha}$	$\hat{\beta}$	$\hat{\gamma}$	R^2
Total employment	1964–82	0.0158* (9.48)	0.9300 (−1.31)	0.0002* (0.08)	0.95
Goods producing total	1964–82	0.0097* (3.97)	1.1432 (2.45)		0.96
Services producing total	1964–82	0.0091* (3.38)	1.0804 (1.01)		0.92
Mining	1960–82	0.0004 (0.03)	1.0174 (0.09)	0.0033* (2.44)	0.89
Construction	1964–82	0.0444* (6.42)	0.4636*(−) (−4.32)		0.47
Manufacturing	1960–82	0.0012 (0.32)	1.1784* (4.00)	0.0006* (2.23)	0.97
Manufacturing durable goods	1960–82	0.0004 (0.05)	1.3273 (4.73)	0.0012* (2.16)	0.95
Manufacturing non-durable goods	1960–82	0.0042* (4.58)	1.2879* (7.60)		0.98
Transportation and public utilities	1964–82	0.0174* (4.03)	1.1956 (1.11)		0.74
Wholesale trade	1960–82	−0.0137 (−3.92)	1.3056* (3.67)	0.0012* (5.30)	0.94
Retail trade	1960–82	0.007* (2.61)	0.9959 (−0.05)		0.88
Finance, insurance and real estate	1960–82	−0.0052 (−1.14)	1.1028 (0.91)	0.0008* (3.53)	0.86
Services	1964–82	0.010 (1.76)	0.9683 (−0.25)		0.79
Government: total	1964–82	0.0061 (1.55)	1.2069* (1.81)		0.87
Government: federal	1964–82	0.0179* (3.25)	1.2255 (1.09)		0.69
Government: state and local	1964–82	0.0050 (1.02)	1.1054 (0.84)		0.83

For α, t ratio tests $H_0: \alpha = 0; H_1: \alpha \neq 0$
For β, t ratio tests $H_0: \beta = 1; H_1: \beta > 1$;
For t, t ratio tests $H_0: t = 0; H_1: t \neq 0$;
* indicates value is significant at 95 per cent probability level.

Table 1.4b Changes in female and total employment on manufacturing payrolls, by major industry group, 1960–82

Industry group	$\hat{\alpha}$	$\hat{\beta}$	$\hat{\gamma}$	R^2
Durable goods				
Lumber and wood	0.0352	1.2470*		0.82
	(4.32)	(1.88)		
Furniture and fixtures	0.0241*	1.2075*		0.89
	(4.32)	(2.16)		
Stone, clay and glass	0.0002	1.1179	0.0011*	0.93
	(0.03)	(1.65)	(2.08)	
Primary metal	0.0266*	0.8507		0.67
	(2.76)	(−1.11)		
Fabricated metal products	0.0097*	1.3434*		0.94
	(2.39)	(4.69)		
Machinery except electrical	−0.0076	1.2240*	0.0021*	0.92
	(0.81)	(2.80)	(3.11)	
Electrical and electronic equipment	0.0012	1.4027*		0.98
	(0.46)	(9.44)		
Transportation equipment	−0.0263	1.2524	0.0036*	0.84
	(−1.62)	(2.01)	(2.88)	
Instruments and related products	0.0021	1.3313*		0.96
	(0.66)	(5.23)		
Miscellaneous manufacturing	0.0063*	1.2508*		0.98
	(3.81)	(6.24)		
Non-durable				
Food and kindred products	0.0054	1.5331*	0.0007*	0.81
	(1.63)	(3.88)	(2.54)	
Tobacco	−0.0099*	1.3996*		0.81
	(−2.03)	(2.65)		
Textile mill products	0.0056*	1.1460*		0.97
	(3.08)	(3.31)		
Apparel, etc.	0.0044*	1.0051	−0.0003*	0.99
	(3.07)	(0.26)	(−2.23)	
Paper and allied products	0.0166*	1.3537*	0.0016*	0.94
	(−3.47)	(4.68)	(4.30)	
Printing and publishing	0.0144*	1.1377		0.89
	(6.87)	(1.50)		
Chemicals and allied products	−0.0069*	1.3965*	0.0015*	0.97
	(−2.13)	(6.77)	(6.79)	
Petroleum and coal	−0.0109	0.7049	0.0034*	0.76
	(−1.08)	(−2.02)	(4.46)	
Rubber and miscellaneous	0.0026	1.2373*		0.94
	(0.57)	(3.34)		
Leather and leather products	0.0082*	1.0790		0.94
	(3.24)	(1.35)		

For α, t ratio relates to H_0: $\alpha = 0$
$\qquad\qquad\qquad H_1$:|$\alpha \neq 0$
For β, t ratio related to H_0: $\beta = 1$
$\qquad\qquad\qquad H_1$: $\beta > 1$
For t, t ratio relates to H_0: $t = 0$
$\qquad\qquad\qquad H_1$: $t \neq 0$
* value is significant at 95 per cent probability level.

lerating female share of employment, was found to be significant and positive in all manufacturing, durable goods manufacturing, wholesale distribution and finance, insurance and real estate; these findings provide support for the hypothesis that the dominant force structuring women's employment in the US has been integration into the wage economy and not cyclical responses to demand changes.

At this level of aggregation then the results provide only limited support for the buffer hypothesis, greater cyclical volatility being confined primarily to the manufacturing sector. These results, however, relate as much to the simplistic assumptions of the buffer hypothesis as to the actual role of women in the employment structure. As Rubery and Tarling suggest, even if women are employed in cyclically sensitive areas, they are also employed in relatively stable ones, and moreover in employment sectors where women predominate they must necessarily constitute the core labour force as well as fill the secondary jobs (Rubery and Tarling, 1982, pp. 53–4), considerations which prompted a move to a less aggregated level of analysis. Table 1.4b reports the results of estimating the same equation at the more disaggregated level of major industrial groups (and see also Humphries, 1983).

These results, while confirming earlier indications that the buffer hypothesis is relevant to women's experience in certain divisions of manufacturing, can also be interpreted as rather striking evidence that a sex differential in the cyclical instability of employment simply indicates that the absorption of female workers is incomplete. If, after estimating the equations relating changes in female employment to changes in total employment and testing for the significance of the coefficient, industry groups are ranked according to the proportion of women employees relative to total employees in 1982, as reported in Table 1.5, the ranking correlates with the results of the hypothesis testing. In durable goods industries, in all groups where women comprised more than approximately one fifth of the labour force the null hypothesis was rejected. The interpretation is that where women are less than 20 per cent of total employment they have not yet attained a wide range of production jobs, but are likely to be concentrated in clerical work, cleaning, packing, etc. Whatever else may be said about such segregation it does afford some relative protection in the business cycle. Where women comprise more than 20 per cent of employment they have obviously penetrated beyond their traditional enclaves. As production workers, and often recently recruited production workers, their employment pattern is consistent with the buffer hypothesis.

The results for non-durable industry divisions are even more suggestive. Here there are two industries, apparel and leather, which are substantially feminized, and where women must have moved beyond their marginal status and become more fully integrated. Consequently women's employment is not more affected by the cycle than total

Table 1.5 Ranking of industry according to the share of women in total employment in 1982

	Share of women workers $\beta > 1$ (per cent)	
Durable		
Miscellaneous manufacturing industries	45.7	*
Instruments and related products	42.3	*
Electric and electronic equipment	42.2	*
Furniture and fixtures	30.1	*
Machinery except electrical	21.2	*
Fabricated metal products	21.1	*
Stone, clay and glass products	19.9	
Transportation equipment	16.5	
Lumber and wood products	15.0	*
Primary metal products	11.3	
Non-durable		
Apparel and other textile products	80.6	
Leather and leather products	59.8	
Textile mill products	47.6	*
Printing and publishing	40.5	
Tobacco manufactures	35.4	*
Rubber and miscellaneous plastic products	34.6	*
Food and kindred products	30.3	*
Chemical and allied products	26.0	*
Paper and allied prodicts	23.1	*
Petroleum and coal products	15.5	

* If β significantly greater than 1, see Table 1.4.

employment. In the middle range of industries as defined by share of women's employment, that is 20 to 40 per cent (with textile mill products as an exception), the evidence was consistent with the buffer hypothesis.

Thus the buffer hypothesis is only found to be supported at an intermediate stage of absorption of women's employment: when they have penetrated beyond the clerical and ancillary tasks they tend to occupy the more cyclically volatile operative jobs, but once they constitute a major share of the work-force in an industry their employment cannot be substantially more cyclically volatile than total employment. Women's role as a cyclical reserve emerges as a characteristic feature of their transition from a latent labour reserve into a more homogenous proletariat. To understand this process more fully attention must be returned to the process of substitution.

4 SUBSTITUTION AND SEGMENTATION: THE DECOMPOSITION OF CHANGES IN FEMALE EMPLOYMENT

The demonstrated resilience of female employment during the downswing could derive from either: 1 the relative concentration of women workers in certain sectors of the economy which were not only less cyclically volatile but continued to grow throughout the recession; or 2 the substitution of (cheaper) female workers for (more expensive) male workers in some/all sectors; or 3 some combination of both effects. In other words, so far, the empirical evidence has not discriminated between the segmentation and the substitution hypotheses. It is clear that the second source of growth in female employment is conceptually distinct involving greater dissonance between sex role stereotypes and women's actual experience, and implying different pressures on female earnings.

Using multiple standardization techniques (Kitagawa, 1955) it is possible to decompose aggregate changes in female employment by industry division (see Table 1.5a) identifying: 1 the change which derives from changes in total employment in each industry holding the proportions of women in each industry constant; 2 the change which derives from changes in the proportions of women workers in each industry holding the total employment in each industry constant; 3 the change which derives from the interaction between changing industrial employment and changing proportions of women. These sources of growth are termed: 1 *the growth effect*; 2 *the share effect*; and 3 *the interaction effect*. In turn the growth effect can be further decomposed into: a. the change which derives from changes in the total numbers employed holding the relative weights of the sectors/industries constant; b. the change which derives from changes in the relative weights of the sectors/industries holding total employment constant; and c. the change which derives from the interaction between changing total employment and changing weights. These sources of growth are termed: (a) *the scale effect*; (b) *the weight effect*; and (c) *the residual effect*. The model is described more formally in Appendix 2 to the introduction.

Any of these effects could of course be negative, as it is only the net effect which determines the direction of change of total employment, and which must therefore be positive in each time period as we know that female employment grew throughout the period 1964–82 even in the downswings. Division by the growth in female employment in each period allows identification of the proportion of that growth which came from each source.

Table 1.6 gives the change in the number of female employees on non-agricultural payrolls by industry division for all booms and slumps from 1969 to 1982, and the decomposition of the change in employment according to its growth, share, scale, weight, interaction and residual components. The last two factors are sufficiently small that they can be ignored in the discussion which follows. Grouping the booms and the slumps together allows the identification of patterns in the sources of growth over the cycle in employment. These patterns can then be related to the main predictions of the hypothesis on trial. The segmentation hypothesis anticipates a positive and substantial weight effect in recessions as the distribution of female employment works to reduce job loss. In the upswings a relatively minor, perhaps even negative weight effect is expected, given women's alleged disproportionate representation in sectors which are unresponsive to short-run variations in demand. The substitution hypothesis predicts that a positive share effect, especially marked in downswings, is the primary mechanism safeguarding women's jobs. In contrast the buffer hypothesis suggests a negative share effect in downswings and a positive one in recoveries. A weaker version of this hypothesis would involve a *relatively* strong share effect in booms compared with slumps.

Table 1.6 Growth in female employees on non-agricultural payrolls, by industry division, booms and recessions, 1964–82

	Booms			Slumps		
	1964–9	1971–3	1975–9	1969–71	1973–5	1979–82
$F_t - F_{t-1}$ (thousands)	5933	2522	6918	871	1190	1896
%						
Contribution of the share effect	21	17	23	15	40	63
Contribution of the growth effect	74	82	73	83	57	37
Contribution of the scale effect	69	76	73	35	5	− 5
Contribution of the weight effect	5	6	0	48	50	43
Contribution of the interaction effect	5	1	4	2	3	0
Contribution of the residual	0	0	0	1	2	0

Note: $F_t - F_{t-1}$ = Share effect + growth effect + interaction effect
Growth effect = Scale effect + weight effect + residual.

Comparing the booms with the slumps: in the former the picture is one of stability in the relative contributions of the different effects, whereas in the latter the pattern changes from recession to recession. In all upswings the growth effect was overwhelmingly important accounting for some three-quarters of the aggregate change. In the recessions although the growth effect accounts for some 83 per cent of the continued expansion of female employment in 1969–71 its contribution falls dramatically in subsequent slumps. Within the growth effects, changing scale was most significant in the upswings, but in the downswings, as to be expected, the contribution of scale advance was limited at best, contributing 35 per cent in 1969–71 and even turning negative in the most recent downturn. To some extent the weight effect compensates. In the booms, though never negative, it is small in two cases and zero in the third whereas its solid positive contribution of around half the growth in female employment is one consistent element across recessions. This pattern is strongly supportive of the segmentation view that women's employment is protected in the downswing but restricted in the upswing by their concentration in sectors which are relatively unresponsive to changes in demand.

Turning to the contribution of women's changing share of employment within sectors; this is relatively stable in the booms at around 20 per cent, though it fell to 17 per cent in 1971–3. Comparing these booms with the subsequent recession it emerges that the share effect was relatively large in 1964–9 compared with 1969–71 though it remained positive in these three slump years. At this juncture extra female employment originating in increased representation for women was both relatively and absolutely small, and of decreased importance *vis-à-vis* the long boom of the 1960s, suggesting that women found it easier to increase their relative share of employment in periods of expansion and tight labour markets. Widespread substitution was not occurring. Indeed where the recession really bit, actually forcing reductions in employment, women were shed disproportionately. Significantly in two of the three sectors where women lost ground relative to men (durable and non-durable manufacturing) employment declined from 1969 to 1971, and in the third sector (wholesale trade) it was relatively static. Thus this period provides limited support for the buffer hypothesis but it is important to underline the fact that these losses were more than offset by gains described above. We will look in more detail at the manufacturing sector subsequently.

Although the contribution of the share effect was normal for the booms at 17 per cent in 1971–3, the subsequent slump marked a real break in the previous pattern as the share effect jumped to account for some 40 per cent of the increase in female employment. This positive contribution was somewhat obscured by the decline, as in the previous recession, in the share of women in both divisions of manufacturing. At the time this prompted many commentators to argue that the recession discriminated against women workers, a characteristic which they linked to the historical specificity of female labour market gains, in particular their recentness: 'last hired, first fired' (*Newsweek*, 2 December 1974). These losses were considerable accounting for over half a million female jobs, but were more than offset by the gains elsewhere both in terms of the restructuring towards female intensive sectors and from the increase in the share of women employees which characterized all sectors except manufacturing and government.

Significantly in the final upswing the share effect, though falling back from the level achieved in the preceding slump, was larger than hitherto experienced in booms. Moreover in the recent recession the pattern established in 1973–5 reappeared, the share effect accounting for more than half the growth. Women increased their representation in all industry divisions including those where employment fell: construction, durable and non-durable manufacturing, transportation and public utilities and both state and local and federal government. When work-forces contracted women were no longer disproportionately shed. Although the weight effect was also substantial and critical if women's employment was to continue to advance, in a period when the scale effect was actually negative, gains from this course were quantitatively less than from the increased proportions of women in all major divisions.

From being relatively more important in the upswing the share effect has moved to become the dominant effect in recession which provides powerful evidence against the buffer hypothesis. Of course the relatively smaller share factor in 1975–9 still generated more total jobs for women, that is some 1,609,000 over the four years, than the relatively larger share effect of 1979–82, which provided some 1,191,000 over the three years, but without these extra jobs in the latter period the rate of growth of female jobs in the recession would have fallen to 0.6 per cent. Nor was the share effect concentrated in already female intensive industries. Women did increase their share of the labour force in services and finance, insurance and real estate where they were already represented in higher proportions than they were in the aggregate, but they also increased their relative standing in manufacturing, mining and transport and public utilities where they were under-represented. In fact the latter two sectors registered the largest jumps in the proportion of women workers.

Thus the factors underpinning the robustness of female employment appear to vary from recession to recession. In the earlier years women reaped the benefits of the continued growth particularly of certain sectors where they were strongly represented and, indeed, of the cylical exaggeration of such sectors. In the most recent recession however significant gains have derived from female penetration of employment across the all industry divisions. This transition from *extensive* to *intensive* growth in female employment relates to their aggregate gains in the labour market and associated changes in political and social attitudes to their employment.

Increased female representation can be viewed as a substitution of female for male labour: substitution for *potentially* male labour if employment in the sector is growing and for *actual* male labour if employment in the sector is declining. In the 1960s and early 1970s substitution was of minor importance, and intensified in the upswing when labour markets were tight and growth in total employment meant that only potentially male workers were being replaced. However in the recent downswings a new pattern appears to have become defined, involving a widespread substitution of women, which in the last context of declining employment in several sectors must have involved, at least in those sectors, disproportionate shedding of male labour.

As in the case of the direct test of the buffer hypothesis, for a closer look at the manufacturing sector, the analysis can be replicated by major industrial groups. The results are reported in Table 1.7. Note that in contrast to female employment on non-agricultural payrolls which continued to grow through the recession, in manufacturing female employment grew only in booms and declined in recession. As in aggregate female non-agricultural employment, in manufacturing the booms exhibit remarkable stability in the sources of growth.

Table 1.7   Growth in female employees on manufacturing payrolls, by major industry group, booms and slumps, 1964–82

	Booms			Slumps		
	1964–9	1971–3	1975–9	1969–71	1973–5	1979–82
$F_t - F_{t-1}$ (thousands)	+1129	+636	+1209	−438	−608	−459
%						
Contribution of the share effect	+33	+35	+38	−14	−6	+27
Contribution of the growth effect	+62	+62	+56	−88	−96	−123
Contribution of the scale effect	+67	+66	+64	−99	−88	−146
Contribution of the weight effect	−6	−5	−7	+12	−10	+24
Contribution of the interaction effect	+6	+3	+6	+2	+1	−2
Contribution of the residual	−1	0	−1	−1	+2	−2

Note: $F_t - F_{t-1}$ = share effect + growth effect + interaction effect
growth effect = scale effect + weight effect + residual

In the upswings the growth effect consistently contributed between 62 and 56 per cent of the total growth. The scale effect was slightly larger in each subperiod but offset by changes in the weights of the industrial groups which were unfavourable to female employment. The restructuring away from the female intensive sectors had a negative impact of between 5 and 7 per cent across the upswings: evidence which supports the segmentation hypothesis.

In the slumps, the growth effect is universally negative. The relative contributions of the scale and weight effects are asymmetric *vis-à-vis* their configuration in the booms. The scale decline exceeds even the negative contribution of the growth factor in two out of three cases. In these two instances the difference originates in a positive weight effect, thus as predicted by the segmentation hypothesis, the changing weights within the manufacturing sector offered some relative protection to women's jobs, without which the decline in female employment would have been 12 per cent greater in 1969–71 and 24 per cent greater in the most recent recession.

The 1973–5 downswing breaks the usual pattern in that the weight effect is negative: textile mill products and apparel and other textile products, two significant female employers, were particularly hard hit in this recession partly due to import substitution. Why did this pattern not recur in 1979–82 when we have seen the weight effect not only become positive again but increase in importance? One reason is that reduced by their secular and periodic cyclical declines, and enjoying some protection from overseas competition, the textile and apparel sectors were more resistant than previously. Moreover the stability exhibited by food and kindred products was shared in this recession by certain durable goods industries which were by now substantial employers of women: electric and electronic equipment and instruments and related products (42.5 and 42.6 per cent female in 1979 respectively). In contrast primary metals and fabricated metal products, both relatively parsimonious employers of women (10.7 and 20.9 per cent female in 1979) were particularly adversely affected.

Moreover if the relative sizes of the share effects in boom and slump at the higher level of aggregation above, supported a buffer hypothesis for the first cycle, then the evidence is strengthened here by the signs of the share effects, which move from strongly positive in 1964–9 to quite significantly negative in 1969–71. The same pattern is replicated in the next cycle though the negative contribution is smaller in the 1973–5 recession. Over this period of time in manufacturing American women were disproportionately shed in slumps and found it easier to increase their relative numbers when times were good. The mitigation of the buffer effect in 1973–5 perhaps reinforces the argument that employers' capacity to use women workers as a buffer labour reserve declined over time as they became an increasingly significant part of the work-force in a wide range of industries. The dramatic change in the sign of the share effect in the most recent downturn is further support for this theme. Without the positive contribution from women's increased representation in 1979–82 the decline in female employment would have been 27 per cent larger. During this period the proportion of women rose in 14 out of 20 manufacturing industries, 12 of which suffered declines in their work-forces. Major gains were registered in several sectors where women comprised a small minority of employees in 1979. For example, stone, clay and glass products, transportation equipment, machinery except electrical, chemicals and allied products, and petroleum and coal products, as well as in industries where they were already within reach of proportional representation, such as printing and publishing. It is significant perhaps that in this most recent recession the positive impact of the increased representation of women exceeded that of the cyclical variation in weights. Thus within the manufacturing sector, in microcosm, there is evidence that substitution is becoming an increasingly important phenomenon. The importance of this process for the pay and employment conditions of women workers will be taken up subsequently, but first we must look at the evidence on segmentation by occupation.

5 THE SEGMENTATION OF THE LABOUR FORCE BY SEX

How does the business cycle impinge on the segmented distribution of male and female workers by occupation? A useful summary index of segmentation is the 'index of dissimilarity', a measure of the absolute difference in the percentage distribution of males and females employed across occupations (Duncan and Duncan, 1955). More precisely:

$$S_t = \tfrac{1}{2} \sum_i |f_{it} - m_{it}|$$

Where f_{it} and m_{it} are percentages of the female labour force and the male labour force employed in occupation i at time t respectively and $i = 1, 2 \ldots n$ represents the occupational categories, here the broad occupations categories deployed by the Bureau of Labour Statistics (BLS).[5]

S_t lies between 0 and 100 where 0 represents a distribution of females across occupational categories which is exactly identical to the male distribution, that is there is no occupational segmentation by sex and 100 represents complete segmentation with men and women being employed in strictly separate categories (Duncan and Duncan, 1955; Joseph, 1983).

One obvious problem in the use of S_t to make inferences about changes in segmentation overtime is that an observed change in S_t could indicate either a change in the occupational structure being studied and/or a change in the proportion of women (men) in one or more occupational categories, that is a sex composition change. For example a decline in S_t may be a result of a fall in the relative numbers in predominantly male or female occupations with sex composition within occupations remaining unchanged, of a change in sex composition with relative numbers unchanged, or of a simultaneous change in both sex composition and occupational structure.

The different hypotheses of how recession affects women workers carry different implications for segmentation (for an analysis of the relationship between the sex-differential in unemployment rates and S_t see Miller, 1986). The segmentation hypothesis predicts that the segmentation of women would decline in the downswing due to the structural effect described above, that is the fall in the relative numbers in predominantly male occupations. The substitution hypothesis anticipates a fall in segmentation too but deriving from an increase in the relative numbers of females in several occupations including those where women were previously under-represented, that is a sex composition change. In contrast the buffer hypothesis implies a rise in segmentation during the downswing as the relative numbers of women within one or more occupations would be expected to decline as women workers were disproportionately shed from mixed or male dominated sectors. However, if the buffer mechanism worked through the feminization of cyclically volatile occupations, then segmentation would decline as jobs are destroyed in these feminized parts of the labour process.

Using the same multiple standardization technique as before it is possible to *decompose* changes over time in S_t into 1 structural effects; 2 sex-composition effects; and 3 interaction effects. The process of decomposition is explained in more detail in Appendix 2.ii to the Introduction (page 13) (see also Joseph, 1973, p. 146 ff.).

In Table 1.8 below, estimates of S_t for 1964–82 are given: the tendency is for a slow and not uninterrupted decline in segmentation (see also Beller, 1982). Table 1.9 decomposes the change in the index using the periodization previously developed in order to try and identify the impact of the business cycle.

Table 1.8 Estimates of sex segmentation across broad occupational categories, 1964–82

Years	1964	1965	1966	1967	1968	1969	1970	1971	1972	1973
Index of dissimilarity (S_t)	44.2	44.0	43.6	43.5	43.4	43.6	44.2	43.5	43.5	43.1

Years	1974	1975	1976	1977	1978	1979	1980	1981	1982
Index of dissimilarity (S_t)	43.6	43.4	42.8	42.6	42.3	42.1	41.5	40.8	40.2

Source: Bureau of Labour Statistics.

The earlier downswings interrupted the decline in sex segmentation slowing the negative trend and in 1973–5 it actually reversed and segmentation increased temporarily. More recently recession appears not to interrupt a now accelerating decline: between 1979 and 1982 the index dropped dramatically relating to the rapidity of growth in the female labour force in the 1970s and 1980s and to the increased penetration not just of already feminized jobs, which would exacerbate segmentation, but of a wide range of occupations as suggested in the earlier industrial survey. The decomposition of changes of S_t adds credence to this interpretation.

In the long boom of the 1960s the slow decline of segmentation was largely due to changes in occupational structure, in particular the decline of two heavily segregated employments: farm labouring and private household service. Significantly the sex-composition effect was positive in this period, that is changes in the proportions of men and women within occupations holding the structure constant would have led to increased segmentation by sex.

During the 1969–71 downswing changes in the occupational structure put upward pressure on sex segmentation partly due to the increased weights of the feminized service sector and the male dominated 'managers and administrators' which were sufficient to offset the falling importance of other segregated sectors such as 'farm labourers and supervisors'. Negative sex-composition and interaction effects just stopped segmentation from increasing.

Table 1.9 Decomposition of changes in the index of dissimilarity: select periods, 1964–82

Years	1964–9	1969–71	1971–3	1973–5	1975–9	1979–82
Actual change in S_t	− 0.6	− 0.1	− 0.4	+ 0.3	− 1.3	− 1.9
Structural effect	− 2.1	+ 0.4	+ 0.3	− 0.5	− 1.0	− 1.4
Composition effect	+ 1.4	− 0.1	+ 0.2	+ 1.1	− 0.3	− 0.5
Interaction effect	+ 0.1	− 0.4	− 0.3	− 0.3	0.0	0.0

Source: Bureau of Labour Statistics.

In the next upswing similar factors and a simultaneous positive contribution from intra-occupation changes in sex composition meant that only a negative interaction effect stopped the index from rising.

In the 1973–5 downswing the index did increase but increased segmentation was not caused by structural change, the falling weight of household service workers and non-farm labourers being enough to offset the increased weight of managers and administrators. However composition changes were strongly positive, the rising female share of clerical work being a major factor. Thus the increased segmentation was more associated with further feminization of occupations than with the disproportionate shedding of women from mixed occupations, as is predicted by the buffer hypothesis.

In the following upswing the decline in segmentation derived both from negative structural and sex-composition effects, the former being stronger. The declining weights of feminized sectors such as private household service work were major contributors. But there was also increased homogenization of the distribution of male and female workers holding the employment structure constant.

Both factors continued to have a negative influence in the next downswing with mixed occupations such as 'professional and technical' increasing their relative weights, whereas segregated occupations such as clerical work and craft and kindred work continued to decline. The negative sex-composition effect evident in the most recent downturn, the strongest in recent experience, means that women's increasing penetration of the employment structure has extended beyond already feminized sectors to include mixed and hitherto male dominated employments and constitutes some support for the substitution hypothesis.

6 THE EARNINGS EXPERIENCE

Each of the working hypotheses employed in this paper would take as data the existence of an earnings gap between men and women explainable by the historic interaction of supply and demand side forces including both pre- and in-market discrimination. But the hypotheses have different implications for the variation in relative female wages over the cycle.

The segmentation hypothesis may involve a relative rise in female earnings as male earnings decline due to the impact of falling demand in male dominated industries, particularly if this results in displacement of men from relatively high paying jobs. Earnings may also fall independently of wages if hours of work decline. Similarly the substitution hypothesis could be compatible with a relative rise in female earnings over the slump as women are substituted for men in a wider range of occupations and industries. But added worker effects may drown the positive impact of relatively robust female opportunities, and substitution may be associated with the extension of particularly low paid and insecure work even compared to the average standard of women's terms and conditions of work. In contrast, the buffer hypothesis implies a decline in women's relative pay as they are more prone to cyclical layoffs, less likely to be organized, and so on.

Table 1.10 summarizes the relative experience of women workers (both year long full-time and part-time) in terms of median incomes in constant 1981 dollars. In all cases the earnings differential closes during the downswing. Table 1.11 presents additional evidence at the level of median weekly earnings of full-time wage and salary earners for the last recession. Again the evidence suggests a relative increase in women's earnings: There is thus no support for the buffer hypothesis, nor for substitution based on particularly low-paid forms of female employment, and the relatively stronger demand for female labour does appear to have been associated with improvements in relative pay.

But what part have the increased participation and aggregate earnings of women workers played in the evolution of the average earnings and incomes of the American working class? One important development in the literature here has been to link the changes in the role of women workers to the 'deindustrialization' (or at least de-traditional industrialization) of the American economy.

Table 1.10 Median earnings of persons 14 years and over (1981) dollars

	1969	1971	1973	1975	1979	1981	1969–71	1973–5	1979–81
(i) *Full-time year round workers*									
males	21504	21628	23470	21856	21901	20692	+124 (+0.58%)	−1614 (−6.88%)	−1209 (−5.52%)
females	12595	12803	13278	13044	13195	12457	+209 (+1.65%)	−234 (−1.76%)	−738 (−5.59%)
ratio female/male earnings	58.57%	59.19%	56.57%	59.68%	60.25%	60.20%	+0.62%	+3.11%	−0.05%
(ii) *All workers*									
males	15950	15502	16487	14960	14759	13473	−448 (−2.81%)	−1527 (−9.26%)	−1286 (−8.71%)
females	5289	5408	5722	5720	5453	5458	+119 (+2.25%)	−2 (0%)	+5 (0%)
ratio female/male earnings	33.16%	34.89%	34.71%	38.24%	36.95%	40.51%	+1.73%	+3.53%	+3.56%

Source: Economic Report of the President 1983.

Table 1.11 Median weekly earnings of full-time wage and salary workers 1979–82 (current dollars)

	1979	1982	1979–82
	(i) *16 years and older*		
males	298	371	+73 (+24.5%)
females	186	241	+55 (+29.6%)
ratio female/male earnings	62.4%	65.0%	+2.6%
	(ii) 16–24 years		
males	201	231	+30 (+14.9%)
females	154	194	+50 (+32.5%)
ratio female/male earnings	76.6%	84.0%	+7.4%
	(iii) 25 years and older		
males	322	403	+81 (+25.2%)
females	197	257	+60 (+30.5%)
ratio female/male earnings	61.2%	63.8%	+2.6%

Source: US Department of Labor.

The main features of the deindustrialization hypothesis are well known (for a good introduction to the issue see Bluestone and Harrison, 1982; the special issue of the *Annals of the American Academy of Political and Social Science*, 1984: Vol. 475; for a sceptical view see Lawrence, 1983). The slowdown in US investment in the 1970s retarded the growth in capital per worker and labour productivity and contributed to the erosion of international competitiveness in many traditional manufacturing sectors including steel, automobiles, rubber, and apparel (Appelbaum, 1984). Employment growth in these branches has been curtailed and in some industries there has even been job loss. As traditional manufacturing in the north east and north central has declined employment has grown in the service sector generally and in both services and manufacturing in the south and west, less due to migration to the sunbelt than to the growth industries already located there, in particular, electric and electronic equipment, defence and space related sectors. By 1982 services alone accounted for more jobs in America than did manufacturing. Similarly wholesale and retail trade generated some 20.4 million jobs in 1982 far exceeding the 18.9 million in manufacturing. McDonald's fast food chain now employs more people than US Steel (Tippet, 1983 quoted in Appelbaum, 1984, p. 30). Moreover the absolute growth in finance, insurance, and real estate employment from 1973 to 1982 matched the absolute decline in manufacturing. These kinds of trends it is argued are illustrative of the shifting nature of a post-industrial society (Gershuny, 1983; Sternleib and Hughes, 1984).

The powerful relationship between these changes and the earnings of Americans is illustrated in Table 1.12 below which compares changes in employment, with levels and changes in average weekly earnings in current dollars by industry division for selected years. It is the fastest growing sectors which have the lowest earnings both historically and currently; and conversely it is the highest earning sectors (construction, and manufacturing) which involve the smallest absolute growth in jobs over time. Thus as Sternleib and Hughes suggest, 'just as a function of changes in what Americans do for a living, weekly earnings for the *average* working American would have gone down' (1984, p. 78; see also Appelbaum, 1984, pp. 31–2) though they hastily caution against too superficial an analysis of cause and effect here. Not surprisingly then most indices of real earnings suggest that growth was curtailed in the mid 1970s and register deterioration in recent years (Sternleib and Hughes, 1984; Currie, Dunn and Fogarty, 1980).

Women, of course, fit into this analysis because many of the relatively poorly paid but fast growth sectors have involved stereotypically female work, historically employed high proportions of women, and afforded significant numbers of new jobs for women workers in the 1970s and 1980s as can be seen in Table 1.12. Hence women's employment gains are associated with, though cause and effect is again complicated, a restructuring which several authors see as threatening the standard of living of the American working class. This is not only because wages in the growing sectors tend to be below those in the declining, traditional, male-dominated industries, but also because as Appelbaum, for example, emphasizes, of the *indirect* effects. A recent BLS study, for instance, has shown that for workers whose pay is strongly influenced by local labour market conditions, factors such as location, degree of unionization, and presence or absence of high paying manufacturing industries are all important influences on wages (US Department of Labour, 1979, quoted in Appelbaum, 1984, p. 32).

In some respects the deindustrialization argument can be interpreted as an extension of the segmentation hypothesis, only in deindustrialization the reweighting of the sectors is caused by longer run changes in technology and shifts in demand. The emphasis is not so much on the variation in the composition of employment over the cycle, as on the pressures on average earnings with the increased employment of women workers understood as a facilitating intermediate variable.

If the deindustrialization thesis is interpreted in this way, our findings provide an important qualification. As emphasized earlier, in 1979–82 women increased their representation in *all* industrial divisions whether

Table 1.12 Proportion of women in the labour force, average weekly earnings, and change in total employment by industry division, 1964–82

Industry	Proportion of women			Weekly earnings			% Change in total employment 1964–73	% Change in total employment 1973–82
	1964	1973	1982	1964	1973	1982		
Total	33.7	37.8	43.5	$91.33	$145.06	$267.26	31.8	16.7
Mining	5.4	6.7	11.9	$117.74	$201.40	$459.88	1.3	78.0
Construction	4.9	5.9	9.6	$132.06	$235.89	$426.82	32.3	-4.5
Manufacturing	26.3	29.1	31.9	$102.97	$166.46	$330.26	16.7	-6.5
Transportation and public utilities	18.3	21.2	26.3	$125.14	$203.31	$402.48	17.8	9.1
Wholesale trade	22.1	23.1	26.4	$102.56	$160.34	$309.85	28.2	23.5
Retail trade	44.0	46.2	50.6	$64.75	$96.32	$163.85	39.7	22.7
Finance, insurance & real estate	50.3	52.8	59.9	$85.79	$129.20	$245.44	39.0	32.0
services	51.0	54.6	59.4	$73.60	$117.29	$225.59	48.5	48.3

Source: Bureau of Labour Statistics. Private non agricultural production or non-supervisory workers.

fast or slow growing, high or low wage. Therefore the increased importance of women workers is not bounded by the increased importance of
female intensive industrial divisions and is, partially at least, independent of the restructuring. What role women workers have been
playing in some of these traditional sectors awaits micro-level analysis,
but a pessimistic position would associate their increased proportions
with the slowdown in the growth of earnings experienced.

The identification of the *causal* contribution of women's increased
participation to the restructuring of the American economy bristles
with complexities. While it is clear that women's role is neither a
fortuitous coincidence, nor, simply a response to price and income
effects, which would be a pure demand side interpretation, it is also
apparent that exogenous change in the supply of women workers has
not in isolation motivated the shifts in the behemoth of American
productive potential. The intervening variables mentioned earlier,
including declining incomes and employment in traditional blue collar
jobs, perhaps themselves caused by shifting international comparative
advantage (Magaziner and Reich, 1983) have had added-worker effects.
These became more potent by the 1970s and 1980s associated with
changes in the organization of the family. Undoubtedly too there have
been feedback effects from increased female involvement in particular
traditional industries, slowing earnings growth there, and in certain
industries displacing male labour in the downswing and potential male
labour in the upswing.

Thus while it would be farfetched to see women's increased participation as the key factor motivating the shifts described, it is interesting that in search of new bastions of international comparative
advantage, the US has developed sectors which use intensively, and
increasingly intensively, their own indigenous source of low cost labour,
and increased markedly the use of such labour even in traditional
industries. Perhaps this is the pattern of post-industrial countries'
response to international competition with the relatively low-wage
newly industrializing nations.

However viewed from the perspective of the individuals and families
caught up in this process, increased female participation has been
primarily a response to labour market conditions, albeit one conditioned by historically-specific, educational and attitudinal conditions.
Put bluntly, increased involvement of working-class American women
has been the major way in which American families have tried to
maintain their living standards in the teeth of declining pay levels and
secular increase in unemployment (Currie, Dunn and Fogarty, 1980;
Sternlieb and Hughes, 1984). This point is illustrated by the relatively
slower decline in real median family income compared with real earnings
since 1964: a testimony to the increasing number of Americans at work
within the family unit, even though their impact is muted by the lower

increments in weekly earnings per worker (Sternleib and Hughes, 1984; Klein 1984; Power, this volume).

By their work efforts then women have prevented even larger numbers of families from sinking below the poverty standard. Contrary to initial speculation (Thurow, 1975), their increased participation has also mitigated the impact of the tendency towards increasing inequality of distribution in household income minus wives' earnings (Smith, 1979; Danzinger, 1980; Betson and Van der Gaag, 1984). In the process of trying to protect family income standards their efforts might have aggravated the tendencies towards earnings decline, higher male unemployment, and increasing inequality of family income before wives' contribution.

It is not clear that increased female participation will continue to be successful in keeping the wolves from the doors of many American families. Since, as emphasized above, a job gained does not match or in net compensate for a job lost, the number of new jobs created must stay ahead of the jobs lost if there is to be scope for a household's move to two earners to cope with the threat of poverty. If the rate of job attrition should run ahead of employment gains, the resulting net decline in the wage bill must injure some working families and spread deprivation beyond those existing pockets associated with geographical and industrial decay (see also Klein, 1984).

It is also possible as Bergman et al. (1980) have demonstrated, that in the future increased female participation may augment rather than dampen inequality in household income distribution. Nor should it be forgotten that for many American families whose demographic circumstances or geographic location are inappropriate, and households headed by women are a major component of this group (Johnson and Waldman, 1984), the move to two-earner status is impossible. The evidence presented here suggests that such families remain in serious danger of real decline in both their standards of living and the wellbeing of all those who live within them.

7 CONCLUSION

According to the argument developed here increasing cyclical stability has accompanied American women's remarkable secular gains in employment in the last twenty years: gains which though unevenly distributed have carried women workers beyond their traditional locations in both the broad industrial structure and within manufacturing itself.

But the 'gains' of women workers discussed in this paper are unambiguously gains only in a narrow quantitative sense. Evaluation of their welfare implications requires closer attention to their attendant circumstances. As suggested in the previous section, if the increased involvement of women workers is inextricably linked to a loss in income, employment and bargaining power for some men workers, who may incidentally be the husbands, fathers or sons of the women concerned, then for many families total income must decline despite the efforts of their women members. True, the increased economic importance of women may enhance their status and relative consumption within the family – but against this must be set the family's loss of income and social standing from which women would find it difficult to insulate themselves.

Work itself may enhance women's wellbeing but care should be exercised in generalizing the middle class's positive attitude to the interesting and rewarding jobs that they enjoy. While college educated women have been shown to be happier if they have jobs, presumably because they have *satisfying* jobs, married women without college educations are not found to be necessarily less happy if they do not do paid work, presumably because the jobs available to them are less enjoyable (Richardson, 1973).

Finally attention must also be paid to the allocation of the necessary labour in the home associated with cooking, cleaning and, most significantly, childcare. If the traditional division of housework by sex has responded sluggishly or not at all to the increased time that women are spending in paid work, whatever the implications of the latter for the wellbeing of the working class as a whole, the impact of the double shift on the women concerned must be adverse.

Thus though the changes in the economic status and involvement of women contain the seeds for positive social change, in and of themselves they do not ensure such progress. Indeed without simultaneous innovations in public policy geared to guiding and controlling the current economic restructuring and protecting the vulnerable from the hardship that must come in its wake, and in traditional attitudes within families to the division of housework, these changes could be retrograde for large numbers of both American families and American women.

NOTES

1 The American unemployment rate is not comparable with unemployment rates for other countries which are differently estimated, nor is it strictly comparable through time due to minor changes in the definition of unemployment. The American unemployment rate is derived from the Current Population Survey (CPS) which is conducted by the Bureau of the Census for the Bureau of Labour Statistics (BLS) and involves monthly surveys using a scientifically selected sample of 60,000 households designed to represent the civilian non-institutional population. The rigorous definition of the unemployed is all civilians who had no employment during

the survey week, were available for work, and (1) had made some specific efforts to find employment sometime during the prior four weeks, or (2) were waiting to be recalled to a job from which they had been paid off, or (3) were waiting to report to a new job within thirty days.

2 In both a recent low (1979) and high (1982) unemployment year BLS projections of the female labour force fell significantly below *actual* employment levels, giving rise to estimates of added worker effects of 7.8 million for 1979 and 9.7 million for 1982.

3 To illustrate take R. E. Smith's (1977) model based on the earlier empirical work of Cain and Dooley (1976) and Ashenfelter and Heckman (1973). When only wages and unemployment are used, that is making the heroic assumption that all other relevant factors cancel out, the equation for predicting the participation rate of prime age women is:

$$(L/P_{25-54}) = 0.86 \, W_{25-54)} - 0.35 \, H_{25-54)} - 0.6 \, u$$

where the first two variables are the projected growth in median incomes of year round full time female and male workers (in hundreds of 1975 dollars) and the third variable is the projected change in the aggregate unemployment rate (percent). The equation predicts a 0.02% decline in prime-aged women's participation between 1973–5 from actual trends in the independent variables, whereas the relevant rate actually rose by 2.8%. During the 1979–82 downswing the results are even worse with the equation predicting a 0.88% decline confronted by a 3.5% increase.

4 The time trend was included in the initial specification of the model for all sectors but was omitted if found not to be significant (see introduction to section).

5 These consist of: 1 Professional and technical; 2 Managers and administrative except farm; 3 Sales workers; 4 Clerical workers; 5 Craft and kindred workers; 6 Operatives; 7 Non-farm labourers; 8 Private household workers; 9 Farmers and farm managers; 10 Farm labourers and supervisors.

6 Mining, a high earnings industry, did expand relatively fast but accounted for a very small share of aggregate employment growth.

REFERENCES

Appelbaum, E.. (1984), 'High Tech and the Structural Employment Problems of the 1980's', in *American Jobs and the Changing Industrial Base*, edited by E. Collins and L. Dewey Tanner, Ballinger, Cambridge, Mass.

Ashenfelter, C. and Heckman, J. (1974), 'The Estimation of Income and Substitution Effects in a Model of Family Labor Supply', *Econometrica*, vol. 42.

Bednarzik, R. and Klein, D. (1977), 'Labour Force Trends: a Synthesis and Analysis', *Monthly Labor Review*, vol. 100, no. 10.

Beller, A. (1982), 'Occupational Segregation by Sex: Determinants and Changes', *Journal of Human Resources*, vol. XVII, no. 3.

Bergmann, B. et al. (1980) 'The Effect of Wives Labour Force Participation on Inequality in the Distribution of Family Income', *Journal of Human Resources*, vol. XV, no. 3.

Betson, D. and Van der Gaag, J. (1984), 'Working Married Women and the Distribution of Income', *Journal of Human Resources*, vol. XIX, no 4.

Bluestone, B. and Harrison, B. (1982), *The Deindustrialisation of America*, Basic Books, New York.

Bowen, W. and Finegan, A. (1969), *The Economics of Labor Force Participation*, Princeton University Press, Princeton, New Jersey.

Cain, G. (1977), 'Comment', in *Women in the Labour Market*, edited by C. Lloyd, E. Andrews and C. Gilroy, Columbia University Press, New York.

Cain, G. and Dooley, M. (1976), 'Estimation of a Model of Labor Supply, Fertility, and Wages of Married Women', *Journal of Political Economy*, vol. 84, no. 4, pt II.

Currie, E., Dunn, R. and Fogarty, D. (1980), 'The New Immiseration: Stagflation, Inequality and the Working Class', *Socialist Review*, vol. 10, no. 6.

Danziger, S. (1980), 'Do Working Wives Increase Family Inequality', *Journal of Human Resources*, vol. 15.

Duncan, O. and Duncan, B. (1955), 'A Methodological Analysis of Segregation Indices', *American Sociological Review*, vol. 20.

Fields, J. (1976), 'A Comparison of Inner-city Differences in the Labour Force Participation Rates of Married Women in 1970 with 1940, 1950 and 1960', *Journal of Human Resources*, vol. 11.

Gershuny, J. (1983), *Social Innovation and the Division of Labour*, Oxford University Press, Oxford.

Hakim, C. (1978), 'Sexual Divisions within the Labour Force: Occupational Segregation', *Department of Employment Gazette*, November.

Hakim, C. (1981), 'Job Segregation: Trends in the 1970's', *Employment Gazette*, December.

Humphries, J. (1983), 'The Emancipation of Women in the 1970's and 1980's: From the Latent to the Floating', *Capital and Class*, no. 20.

Johnson, B. and Waldman, E. (1984), 'Most Women Who Maintain Families Receive Poor Labour Market Returns', US Department of Labor, Bureau of Labor Statistics, *Bulletin* 2209.

Johnson, J. (1983), 'Differentials in Unemployment Rates: A Case of No Concern', *Journal of Political Economy*, vol. 91, no. 1.

Joseph, G. (1983), *Women at Work: The British Experience*, Philip Allan, Oxford.

Kitagawa, E. (1955), 'Components of a Difference Between Two Rates', *Journal of the American Statistical Association*, vol. 50.

Klein, D. (1984), 'Trends in Employment and Unemployment in Families', in *Families at Work: The Jobs and the Pay*, US Department of Labor, Bureau of Labor Statistics, Bulletin 2209.

Lawrence, R. (1983), 'Is Trade Deindustrializing America? A Medium-Term Perspective', in *Brookings Papers on Economic Activity*, edited by W. Brainard and G. Perry, Brooking Institution, Washington, D.C.

Magaziner, I. and Reich R. (1983), *Minding America's Business*, Vintage Books, New York.

Milkman, R. (1976), 'Women's Work and Economic Crisis', *Review of Radical Political Economies*, vol. 8, no. 1.

Milkman, R. (1980), 'Organising the Sexual Division of Labor: Historical Perspectives on "Women's Work" and the American Labor Movement', *Socialist Review*, vol. 10, no. 1.

Miller, R. (1980), 'Women's Unemployment Pattern in Post-War Business

Cycles: The Gender Segregation of Work and Deindustrialization', Paper presented at the Eastern Economics Association Meetings held on April 12, in Philadelphia, PA.

Newsweek (1974), 'Last Hired–First Fired', 2 December.

Niemi, B. (1974), 'The Female–Male Differential in Unemployment Rates', *Industrial and Labor Relations Review*, vol. 27, no. 3, reprinted in *The Economics of Women and Work*, edited by A. Amsden, Penguin, Harmondsworth, Middlesex.

Organisation for Economic Cooperation and Development (1976), *The 1974– 1975 Recession and the Employment of Women*, OECD, Paris.

Pogursky, M. (1984), 'Sources of Secular Increase in the Unemployment Rate, 1969–82', *Monthly Labor Review*, vol. 107, no. 7.

Power, this volume.

Richardson, E. (1973), *Work in America*, MIT Press, Boston, Mass.

Rubery, J. and Tarling R. (1982), 'Women in the Recession', *Socialist Economic Review*, Merlin, London.

Shapiro, D. and Shaw, L. B. (1983), 'Growth in the Labor Force Attachment of Married Women', in *Southern Economic Journal*, vol. 50, no. 2.

Smith, J. (1979), 'The Distribution of Family Earnings', *Journal of Political Economy*, vol. 87, no. 5, part 2.

Smith, R. (1979), 'Projecting the Size of the Female Labor Force: What makes a Difference?', in *Women in the Labor Market*, edited by C. Lloyd, E. Andrews and C. Gilroy, Columbia University Press, New York.

Sternlieb, G. and Hughes, J. (1984), *Income and Jobs, USA: Diagnosing the Reality*, Center for Urban Policy Research, Rutgers, the State University of New Jersey.

Summers, G. Special Editor (1984), *Deindustrialization: Restructuring the Economy*, The Annals of the American Academy of Political and Social Science, vol. 475, Sage, New York.

Thurow, L. (1975), 'Lessening Inequality in the Distribution of Earnings and Wealth', Unpublished.

Travis, S. (1970), 'The US Labor Force Projections to 1985', *Monthly Labor Review*, vol. 93, no. 5.

US Department of Labor (1979), *Annual Earnings and Employment, Patterns of Private Nonagricultural Employees, 1973–1975*, Bureau of Labor Statistics, Bulletin 2031, Government Printing Office, Washington, DC.

US Department of Labor (1983), *Handbook of Labor Statistics*, Bureau of Labor Statistics; Bulletin, 2175, Government Printing Office, Washington, DC.

Waite, L. (1977), Projecting Female Labor Force Participation from Sex-Role Attitudes', Working Paper Draft for the Urban Institute, Washington, DC.

Yanz, L. and Smith, D. (1983), 'Women as a Reserve Army of Labor: A Critique', *Review of Radical Political Economics*, vol. 15, no. 1.

2 Female labour reserves and the restructuring of employment in booms and slumps in France

Patricia Bouillaguet-Bernard and Annie Gauvin: France

1 INTRODUCTION

The restructuring of the productive system in France since the 1960s has been based to a large extent on the use of reserves of female labour. Two of the basic characteristics of the development of women's work outside the home have been the entry of large numbers of women into the wage-earning class and the extent to which women have become permanent members of the economically active population. These developments are related to changes in the productive system and to the conditions under which the labour market operates.

There is, nevertheless, no necessary reason to expect that the earlier trends in women's work should persist through the current economic crisis that began in the early 1970s. However, despite rising unemployment, the growth of women's participation in the labour force has continued. Between 1975 and 1982, participation rates for adult women increased at a higher rate than that for the period 1968–75. In March 1982, 63.5% of women aged between 25 and 55 were economically active, compared with 53.1% in March 1975 and 44.6% in March 1968 (Marc and Marchand, 1984).

The number of female wage-earners is continuing to rise, even though the rate of increase in the number of wage-earners in the working population as a whole is probably slowing down. In March 1984, 41% of wage-earners were women, compared with 38% in March 1975 and 35% in March 1968. The fall in waged employment since 1975 has mainly affected manufacturing industry. The continued creation of jobs in the service sectors (particularly in market services), even if at a slower rate, is still of greater benefit to women than to men. In March 1982, 75% of female wage-earners were employed by firms in the service sector, compared with 50% of male wage-earners.

More and more jobs are now being taken by women, partly as a result of favourable sectoral change. These developments are also indicative of a *relative transformation of some of the conditions under which the labour market operates*. Although women still remain at a disadvantage in the labour market, with the female unemployment rate in March 1984 standing at 12.1% compared with 7.6% for men, nevertheless, *male unemployment is rising more rapidly than female unemployment*, largely as a result of the reductions in employment in manufacturing and in building and public works. The continuous rise in the number of redundancies and, more particularly, in the number of temporary or unprotected jobs which have disappeared, has had only a slow and moderated effect on women's unemployment, largely because of their concentration in sectors less affected by job losses. Indeed there has been no significant change in the numbers of women leaving the labour market in response to declining employment.

At the same time, the worsening situation in the labour market has greatly increased the rate of unemployment among young people (Cezard, 1984) resulting from a sharp reduction in the number of young people being hired, either for stable or for insecure jobs. Between 1982 and 1984, the unemployment rate for young people in the 20 to 24 age group rose from 9.5% to 14.2%, and for young women from 13.7% to 17.7%. Moreover, the various training schemes and other measures set up to help young people have not necessarily led to the creation of new jobs and often merely lengthen the period between entry into the labour market and the subsequent acquiring of more permanent employment. The measures taken by the government to reduce the number of older workers seeking employment have been more effective: this was especially true in 1982–3, but less so in 1984.

This summary of recent conditions indicates that although female participation rates have not fallen at all during the recession, there have, nevertheless, been changes over this period in the functioning of the employment system and in the conditions under which the various categories of labour are utilised.

Our analysis of the employment situation of women in the recession in France will comprise two stages. The first stage examines the incorporation of women into the employment system during the period of growth. The second part studies how recessionary conditions and structural changes in the labour market over the past ten years have led to the restructuring and redefinition of the criteria for the stratification of the labour force and jobs. In particular, we shall formulate the hypothesis that the ways in which women have been incorporated into the wage-earning class since the end of the Second World War have introduced rigidities into labour management policies. Attempts are now being made to circumvent these rigidities by experimenting with more flexible ways of using the female labour force. This argument requires the separate but interrelated analyses of changes in the productive system and changes in the labour market.

2 THE MASS MOBILISATION OF FEMALE LABOUR IN A PERIOD OF PROSPERITY

The path of development of the capitalist economies in the post-war period created favourable conditions for the mass mobilisation of female labour. An understanding of these changes under 'prosperity' is essential for any analysis of why the increasing female participation has been sustained throughout a period of prolonged economic crisis.

2.1 The forces behind the increased participation of women in the labour market

The causes of the increased participation of women are complex and multidimensional, including changes in the economic, demographic, institutional and social structures of the capitalist system. The conjunction of these various forces has led to women becoming wage-earners in greater numbers and in a more permanent way than ever before (Bouillaguet-Bernard, Gauvin-Ayel and Outin, 1981). In March 1982, 84.4% of economically active women were wage-earners, compared with 74.5% in March 1968.

It is not possible to establish any very strong direction of causation between structural changes and the increase in female participation rates as these two processes have had a mutual influence on each other. Nor is it easy to determine which of these structural changes has been the driving force, since they all interact.

Nevertheless, it is possible to suggest a framework for analysis: the development of the social structure in France since the 1960s has created conditions favourable to the increase in the number of female wage-earners, firstly through the greater availability and then through the increased mobilisation of this section of the labour force. The main factors that have increased availability of potential reserves of female labour are:

- demographic changes (lower birth rate and changes in the way women plan their families);
- changes in the way families are organised (the socialisation of domestic work and the increased instability of marriages);
- changes in consumption patterns (increase in the number of domestic appliances bought by families, rising levels of indebtedness, particularly for housing needs).

Changes in the productive system, particularly since the mid-1960s, have also been based to a large extent on the widespread mobilisation of the reserves of female labour. Three interrelated changes seem to have been the driving force behind this process of mobilisation:

(i) *The rapid development of the service sector* (market and non-market). In the market service sector, this development has been in both producer and consumer services. Part of this expansion is due to the 'externalisation' of some activities previously carried out within manufacturing firms (maintenance, engineering, etc.). sometimes involving use of contract labour. The non-market service sector has expanded with the development of public services, particularly health and education.

(ii) *The restructuring of the productive system*: internal restructuring in the capitalist sphere, particularly in manufacturing industry, but also including an extension of the capitalist mode of production to the pre-capitalist sectors (agriculture, commerce).

(iii) *Attempts by the managers of firms to reduce costs*, which have resulted on the one hand in the decentralisation and the transfer of activities to rural areas, thus encouraging the hiring of female labour, and, on the other, in the adoption of stricter labour management policies (fixed term contracts, the use of contract labour, part-time work).

In such a context, and in a period of prosperity, it is obvious that the increased use of the reserves of female labour reflected a need for new sources of labour and new labour management policies. *The fundamental role of the female labour force was therefore to make possible the restructuring of the productive system.*

2.2 The expansion of the market sphere and the increase in the number of female wage-earners

Between 1949 and 1983 the number of wage-earners as a percentage of the economically active population has grown from 61.8% to 83.7% (source: *Les Comptes de la Nation*). Thus behind the processes by which the reserves of female labour became increasingly available and mobile lies a more general historical trend towards the expansion of the wage-earning class. The necessary capitalist accumulation leads both to the expansion of the wage-earning class and to the transformation of the conditions under which it exists and thus of the ways in which the labour force is reproduced. The development of modern capitalism has been based on the spread of market relationships: in particular, consumption norms have become increasingly dependent on capitalist products. 'With Fordism, the spread of market relationships is reflected in their domination over patterns of consumption' (Aglietta, 1976).

The reproduction of the labour force, which was previously an essentially non-market process, has been transferred from the 'private' sphere of the family to the 'public', socialised sphere.

These processes of socialisation have enabled new reserves of labour to enter the wage-earning class. Women, who are generally responsible for domestic production, have transferred their labour from domestic work to paid work outside the home as the market has gradually absorbed a whole range of activities formerly carried out within the home.[1] Moreover, non-market domestic work has been transformed both into waged work in non-market sectors and into waged work in market sectors. Female wage-earners are concentrated in particular in such sectors as education, health, social services and distribution, which are extensions of the traditional responsibilities allocated to women within the family.

2.3 Women as latent and floating reserves during the period of growth

In the course of the long period of prosperity from 1950 to 1974, women came to form both the latent and floating reserves of labour: as they took over the latent reserve the conditions were created under which they began to form the floating reserve as well.

As the productive system was restructured, women began to play an important role in the processes of adjusting supply to demand. The large number of jobs created in France from the mid–1960s onwards attracted a surplus of women into the labour market. The expansion of the service sector and the transfer of factories to declining rural or industrial areas were the main forces behind the mobilisation of these labour surpluses.

The work force for the service activities that provided many new jobs in the 1960s and 1970s was drawn to a large extent from new entrants to the labour market. Between March 1968 and March 1974, all net job creation in the distribution sector, 97% of that in the transport, telecommunications and services sectors and 78% of that in financial institutions and the civil service was carried out through the use of previously inactive people. This was the main method by which firms in the service sector reproduced and expanded their labour force (Bouillaguet-Bernard, Gauvin-Ayel and Outin, 1981). The expansion of tertiary activities thus helped to increase the size of the economically active population rather than to absorb unemployment. Moreover, this economically active population was swelled by the mainly female surplus labour entering the labour market and thus contributing to the rise in unemployment.

Macro-economic models drawn up on the basis of data collected in the 1954, 1962 and 1968 censuses confirm the importance of variations in the participation rates of female adults. For every 100 jobs created during this period, 70 additional people were attracted into the labour market, of which 45 to 50 were women (Salais, 1971). According to these estimates, the supply of female labour is more sensitive in the short term to variations in tertiary employment than to variations in employment in manufacturing industry.

Surveys carried out in local labour markets found (Thelot, 1975) that the setting up of new production units led to the creation of new jobs, but was accompanied at the same time by a three-stage process leading to a rise in unemployment. The existence of a large pool of potentially available labour was a decisive criterion in the selection by firms of new sites and the new jobs created as a result attracted into the labour market a large number of potential workers, mainly women, some of whom obtained jobs and some of whom joined the ranks of the unemployed. Finally, in the event of redundancy, these new wage-earners remained in the labour market, their behaviour having been determined by their work experience, which had made their entry into the wage-earning class an irreversible process.

In the short term, therefore, employment demand structured the movements of the labour force and thus the functioning of the employment system itself. By mobilising latent reserves, the demand for labour created a supply of labour which led in turn to the creation of a surplus or floating reserve. This dynamic is indicative of the movements in the female labour force during the period of prosperity and partly explains the apparent paradox of a simultaneous increase in both employment and unemployment (1961–74) (Salais, 1977). Another explanation of this paradox lies in the link between mobility and unemployment, with the former process creating a greater supply of labour than can be absorbed.

Between 1965 and 1974, therefore, there was an increase in the mobility of both male and female workers as a result of sectoral and geographical restructuring and of changes in firms' management practices. The search by firms for increased flexibility in the management of their work forces was reflected in an increase in redundancies, in temporary jobs and also in the level of temporary unemployment.

It is not possible unreservedly to attribute a fundamental role in all these changes to the existence of abundant reserves of female labour. The segmentation of women's employment (cf. below) is indicative of the specific use of male or female labour according to the nature of the vacancies to be filled. The use of women as a reserve of labour is not by any means a 'mechanical' process, and may only occur under certain circumstances.

Nevertheless, segmentation of the employment structure is not always a binding constraint. At the local level, firms may prefer to use women for unskilled manual jobs in order to make up for shortages of male labour or to avoid pressure to increase wages. Thus within the same sector, the proportion of women in unskilled manual jobs can differ widely from area to area. In France the relative share of women in this type of job is relatively higher in factories set up in employment areas in which the traditionally male manufacturing activities predominate and where there is a high level of female underemployment (Gaspard, 1975). In this context, a high level of sustained growth in manufacturing industry favours the hiring of women.

More generally, it would seem that the characteristics of the local labour market (in particular the available labour supply and the scarcity or abundance of reserves of labour) influence not only firm's wages policies but also their selection, recruitment and labour management strategies (Pommier-Pennef, 1975).

Women may also be used as a reserve of labour in sectors in which vulnerability to fluctuations in the general economic situation makes it impossible for firms to implement stable labour management policies (Michon, 1975).

For example, the increase in labour turnover rates in some of the sectors in which large numbers of jobs were created for women between 1968 and 1974 (distribution and market services) seems to be linked to the abundance of available female labour (Eymard-Duvernay and Salais, 1975).

2.4 The structuring of the reserves of female labour: the changes of the 1960s

From the end of the 1960s onwards, the ways in which women entered and left the labour market began to change, which introduced a certain degree of rigidity into the functioning of the employment system. As wage employment increased, women entered the labour market in increasing numbers, while fewer of them interrupted their labour market participation. Exit rates thus tended to fall, particularly for adult women aged between 25 and 54 (see Table 2.1). The movements of women into and out of the labour market provided a less and less important source of flexibility in the functioning of the employment system.

This rigidifying of the supply of female labour was the result of two major changes, which were indicative of the irreversibility of the entry of women into the labour market. First, the lower level of discontinuity in women's economic activity (Labourie-Racape et al., 1977) reduced the level of voluntary movements into and out of the labour market by adult women and, as a consequence, the flexibility that these movements gave to firms' strategies for managing their female labour. The entry of large numbers of young women into the labour market on a permanent basis changed the demographic composition of labour market flows to a younger age composition increasing the similarities between male and female labour force flows.

Second, female participation rates became less sensitive to the general economic situation. The supply of secondary workers, such as young

Table 2.1   Rate of flows out of the labour force for women by age (Census data)

Ages	Years 1970–1971	1971–1972	1972–1973	1973–1974	1975–1976	1976–1977	1977–1978	1978–1979	1979–1980	1980–1981
15–19	3,9	3,0	3,1	2,5	3,3	3,8	3,0	2,6	15/17 yrs 87,5	86,0
20–24	9,8	8,0	7,3	7,3	5,4	6,3	6,6	5,1	18/24 yrs 2,4	19,0
25–29	10,5	8,9	9,7	7,8	6,3	6,3	6,4	5,8 ⎫		
30–34	6,7	7,0	6,6	6,4	6,9	6,6	5,8	5.1 ⎬	6,7	6,4
35–39	6,3	6,1	5,8	5,8	5,4	4,4	5,2	4,1 ⎭		
40–44	6,0	5,9	5,1	4,8	5,5	4,7	4,8	3,9 ⎱	6,2	5,7
45–49	6,2	4,9	5,2	4,7	5,1	5,2	4,6	3,2 ⎰		
50–54	7,9	6,6	6,9	7,0	5,4	5,4	6,7	4,8 ⎱	4,4	3,8
55–59	8,3	7,7	7,2	7,4	8,3	9,6	9,0	9,1 ⎰		
60–64	14,6	14,0	14,1	16,2	16,3	16,7	25,8	23,4 ⎫		
65–69	⎱34,5	40,1	42,8	43,3	39,6	51,5	50,5	48,5 ⎬	6,3	5,8
70–74	⎰	29,2	40,3	32,5	24,5	43,5	35,4	25,7		
75 et +		30,3	29,7	34,9	31,7	44,7	21,3	27,4 ⎭		
Total	9,1	8,2	8,2	7,8	7,0	7,3	7,4	6,4	6,6	6,7

(a) = number leaving economic activity between 2 enquiries
     active population at the time of the first enquiry.
Source: Enquête sur l'emploi (March), INSEE.

people and married women, is generally considered in France and elsewhere to vary with conditions in the labour market (Woystinsky, 1942), thereby cushioning the effects of variations in employment on the level of unemployment. A certain degree of flexibility in female participation rates has been observed in France during the economic turnarounds of 1958–9, 1963–5 and 1967–8 (recessions) and of 1968–70 (resumption of growth) (Michal, 1973). However, from 1968 onwards, the short-term sensitivity of movements in the economically active population to the slowing down of economic growth, began to decrease. An asymmetrical relationship was established between short-term fluctuations in economic activity and levels of employment and unemployment. Unemployment began to fall less in periods of vigorous economic activity (the movements in the economically active population increasingly absorbed the changes in employment) and to increase proportionally more in periods of recession (surplus labour tended to become unemployed rather than inactive) (Salais, 1977). This asymmetrical relationship reflected the emergence of resistance to the reduction of employment, which primarily affected women.

During the 1970s, therefore, there was a gradual change in the structure of the reserves of female labour. Instead of the two pole model, in which women moved back and forth between participation and non-participation, there emerged a three pole structure in which women moved from non-participation to employment but subsequently moved only between employment and unemployment so that unemployment took on an increasingly important role in the processes of reallocating and recirculating the female labour force among jobs (Bouillaguet-Bernard and Germe, 1981).

two poles   non participation↔participation
three poles   non participation→employment↔unemployment

The dual function of latent and floating reserves fulfilled by the female labour force, together with the increasing importance of unemployment as a means of forming and allocating those reserves, explain why there was such a high proportion of women among the unemployed in periods of prosperity. Moreover, women's vulnerability to temporary and long-term unemployment increased in periods when economic growth was slow and not sustained. Women remained at a disadvantage in the labour market, and their position improved only during long and sustained periods of either vigorous economic activity or recession (Ledrut, 1966 and Michon, 1975). This disadvantage also extended to the terms and conditions under which they were employed.

2.5 Employment conditions and the mobilisation of women in the period of prosperity

The entry of large numbers of women into the labour market during the period of prosperity was not accompanied by any significant change in the occupational structure of this category of labour.

Men and women are not employed in the same jobs and developments in the employment structure and in methods of personnel management have both encouraged a more intensive utilisation of female labour.

Different methods of management are used for male and female workers; this is reflected in a marked degree of concentration in the jobs open to women and greater insecurity in the particular forms of their employment contracts. Men and women do not have equal employment rights (Huet, 1984). Thus it cannot be assumed that there is any real competition between male and female workers for access to jobs and even less that there is any large-scale substitution of female for male labour.

Turning first to manufacturing during the so-called period of prosperity, the female labour force was diffused throughout manufacturing industry, particularly in those sectors where there were few women workers. Until 1975, in fact, women became integrated into those sectors of manufacturing industry which played leading roles in the growth of wage employment: the electrical and electronics industries, agriculture and food processing, the chemical industry, primary metal processing, etc. However, this process has not changed the fact that women are allocated to unskilled jobs. Indeed, women tended to be allocated to production jobs in sectors in which the development of mechanisation and automation was increasing the number of unskilled and semi-skilled jobs. Between 1968 and 1975, women provided 53% of the increase in the basically unskilled labour force. In 1980, 28% of semi-skilled workers and 47% of unskilled workers were women compared to 25% and 37% for 1968 respectively.

Thus within manufacturing industry, the different work situations affected the extent to which women were integrated into the various sectors. These various work situations include:

(i) The production process. Until the mid-1970s, women tended to enter those sectors of manufacturing industry dominated by large batch, highly automated production.

(ii) The type of work done. There are more unskilled workers in packaging, cleaning and transport, and there are more skilled workers in maintenance and production. Women manual workers are often employed on the production line and in packaging jobs, whereas men are more likely to be employed in maintenance and supervisory jobs.

(iii) Conditions of work. It has been observed that women's jobs are more frequently subject to time constraints and to high work rates (linked to automation or production norms and repetitive work), whereas men's jobs more frequently involve considerable physical effort, poor work environment and risk of injury and accident (Molinie and Volkoff, 1980).

(iv) Wage levels. Female workers are more highly concentrated in those parts of manufacturing which pay the lowest wages for equal qualifications. For women, wages are more frequently linked to output levels.

Certain types of work organisation and work situations seem to encourage greater use of female labour. Constraints, linked of course to the nature of the productive system, influence the use but cannot be considered binding. Decisions on work organisation (that it should be Taylorist, broken down into individual operations and automated) and on the general conditions for labour force utilisation include whether or not to use a less skilled, more malleable and therefore female work force in the more vulnerable jobs. The situation of female manual workers is qualitatively different from that of their male counterparts.

Studies concerned more directly with female manual workers (Dutoya and Gauvin-Ayel, 1982) have shown that one of the unifying characteristics in the female manual labour force is its 'capacity to stick to repetitive and very constraining jobs, both in terms of discipline and work rates, in which skill levels are either very low or non-existent'. Moreover, there are virtually no opportunities for promotion or career development (Kergoat, 1982).

Even though the compartmentalisation of men's and women's jobs often reflects social stereotypes about the position of women outside of the work context (they are seen primarily as assistants) and their 'natural' qualities (dexterity, attention to detail), these stereotypes are used by employers mainly to justify discrimination in the allocation of jobs. In fact, the differentiation between male and female manual workers is based more on the types of jobs occupied by women than on the specific characteristics of female workers.

As already noted, the rapid growth of the service sector was based largely on the mobilisation of the female labour force. Even though there are more women than men employed in the service sector, a certain degree of job segregation still persists. Sixty-four per cent of women in the service sector are employed in administrative or clerical jobs and in management (but not in technical or senior management), which accounts for 37% of jobs in the sector. Sixty per cent of these jobs are occupied by women. This concentration of women in service jobs reflects the training that they receive. The lowest concentrations of women are to be found in management and technical occupations, whereas those with the highest concentrations of women are clerical and office workers, whether skilled or unskilled.

More detailed studies have also shown that the differentiation between male and female clerical and office workers involves both access to managerial jobs and other positions of responsibility and also the type of job (Battagliola, 1984). In this survey of male and female clerical staff in social security offices, it was shown that the jobs held mainly by women were 'the jobs most subject to the technical division of labour, to pressures to increase output and to the weight of the hierarchy'. The jobs occupied mainly by men 'are characterised by a certain degree of autonomy, little or no pressure from the hierarchy, more flexible work rates and frequently higher pay'. This differentiation according to sex cannot be explained simply by the specific characteristics of the female labour force. The functioning of the institution in question is to a large extent responsible for such differentiation. Once again, it is a question of different methods of managing the jobs typically held by women. The sexual division of labour actually arises out of a division in employment conditions (hiring, methods and level of pay, allocation to jobs, content of tasks, promotion prospects).

Thus the entry of women into the labour market has not been accompanied by any change in the types of jobs occupied by women. The majority of women have entered jobs which have certain characteristics in common. Moreover, the leading role played by certain vulnerable sectors, such as distribution, and by small and medium-sized firms with high turnover rates, together with the concentration of women in unskilled and often insecure jobs, make it possible to describe these jobs as 'reserve jobs'. The flexibility desired by employers relates more to the jobs occupied by women than to women as a category in the labour force. The need for flexibility can be satisfied by allocating women to these jobs.

The question to be examined in the next part of this paper is whether the current recession has been accompanied by any change in the conditions under which women enter the labour market.

3 THE EFFECTS OF THE RECESSION ON THE UTILISATION OF THE FEMALE LABOUR FORCE

The break with the period of prosperity that took place in 1974 did not halt the changes taking place in the use of female labour. On the contrary, it seems to have brought about even greater changes: women have entered waged employment on a permanent basis, they have benefited from the creation of jobs in the service sector, and have been relatively sheltered in the current period of continuously rising unemployment, even though they are still at a disadvantage in the labour market.

These observations will lead us to examine the effects of the recession on women's employment conditions; our analysis will comprise the following three stages:
(i) examination of the nature of the present crisis with reference to economic history: this will reveal the implications of a period of economic crisis for the use of female labour;
(ii) analysis of the sensitivity of women's employment to the change in the economic situation in manufacturing industry during the current period;
(iii) study of the changes in women's employment conditions since 1974 – and more particularly since the beginning of the 1980s.

3.1 Does the current crisis mark a break with earlier ways of using female labour?

The economic crisis that France has been experiencing for the past ten years is not a simple accumulation of periods of recession (1974–5, 1979–80, 1893–4) interspersed with brief periods of respite or economic recovery, similar to the downturns that interrupted the thirty years of rapid growth after the Second World War. The present crisis is fundamentally structural, like those experienced by France between 1880 and 1890 and in the 1930s, which brought to a head all the obstacles to the continuation of the previous accumulation regime.

Large-scale crisis, like wars, are crucial periods for the redefinition of the 'rapport salarial'. This is a term used by economists of the French 'regulation' school to denote, in the words of Boyer (1979), 'the set of conditions that govern the use and reproduction of the labour force, including the organisation of the work process, the hierarchy of qualifications, the mobility of the labour force and the determination and utilisation of wage income'. In periods of crisis, it is argued, there tends to be a regression towards competitive forms of the 'rapport salarial'.

We are concerned here with whether or not an historical link can be established between the way in which capitalism is extended and the way in which female labour is used. In order to do this, we shall examine the evolution of the 'rapport salarial' in order to distinguish two major phases in the historical development of French capitalism.

The period that ended with the outbreak of the Second World War was dominated by a 'rapport salarial' of the competitive type (Boyer, 1979) and was characterised in particular by large-scale adjustments of employment and wages to the economic situation in manufacturing industry. This initial phase was characterised by the alternation between predominantly extensive accumulation regimes (increase in surplus value by extension of productive capacities and the wage-earning class) during the first part of the nineteenth century and between 1896 and 1914 and predominantly intensive accumulation regimes (increase of surplus value through increased productivity gains linked to radical changes in the organisation of production and work) during the periods between 1848 and 1873 and 1920 and 1930.

The second period, which began in 1945, has been dominated by a 'rapport salarial' of the monopolistic type and characterised by the increasing institutionalisation of the 'rapport salarial' and of the forms of competition and by increased state intervention. This phase is characterised by greater reluctance on the part of the workers to submit to market conditions with respect to both job and wage determination. The growth in production has been dependent on a regime of extensive and intensive accumulation based on the development of mass consumption which made possible the increased application of scientific methods of work organisation through which significant productivity gains were realised.

Indeed the restructuring of the productive system that accompanied the periods of radical change in the capitalist economies depended largely on the mobilisation of new supplies of labour. At the same time, the sphere of production was continuously extended to include new activities; the use of new supplies of labour was a decisive factor in creating the flexibility of the productive system and its capacity to reproduce itself, if only because it made it possible to overcome the resistance and rigidities characteristic of the forms of wage labour (Bouillaguet-Bernard and Germe, 1981).

The use of female and child labour developed in France from the end of the eighteenth century onwards on the basis of home work in the textile and clothing industries. During the first half of the nineteenth century, the development of French industry was characterised by dispersion (small firms set up in rural areas). Among the obstacles to the formation of an urban wage-earning class was the strengthening in the aftermath of the French Revolution of the position of small peasant landowners. The use of women and children as supplies of labour was one way of overcoming labour shortages, which were aggravated by strong resistance on the part of agricultural workers to entering manufacturing industry. Women and children thus played an important role in the establishment of an industrial wage-earning class. The use of this new supply of labour made it possible to extend the sphere of capitalist production by making use of the traditional mode of production in agriculture and of the method of family organisation to which it gave rise. Technical progress in production techniques and the mechanisation of certain activities in the textiles industry led to the concentration of production in large units. Home work began to decline from the 1850s onwards. There then emerged a work cycle specific to women, characterised by alternation between periods of staying at home and working in factories. This new work pattern, which made women's paid employment subordinate to their role in the reproduction of the labour force, was an obstacle to the entry of women into the urban wage-earning class.

The crisis of the period between 1880 and 1890 marked a turning point in the development of industrial capitalism in France and the use of female labour. Industrialisation was based on large production units in the cities. The extension of the wage-earning class depended to a large extent on the mobilisation of surplus supplies of male agricultural labour migrating to the cities and on the use of foreign labour. During this phase, women were discarded from the labour market and returned to the home. The widespread use of female labour to replace men during the First World War (700,000 women were employed in armaments factories alone) was only a temporary phenomenon. However, it was to play a leading role in the extension of Taylorism. As early as 1918–1920, the female labour mobilised during the war was beginning to return to the home.

Nevertheless, it was only from 1936 onwards that the reduction in the number of women in manufacturing industry became apparent. Before this date, the entry of women into the agricultural, food, metal processing and chemical industries had offset the sharp fall in the number of women employed in the textile and clothing industries, where they had traditionally been employed. During the first thirty years of the twentieth century, therefore, there was a sectoral redistribution of female labour in manufacturing industry.

The development of tertiary activities (public services, banking and insurance, distribution) was accompanied by recruitment of women on a large scale. Significantly, the creation of these kinds of jobs led to the increase in the number of female wage-earners from the end of the 1950s onwards. Social and family structures and the forms of the extension of the capitalist sphere encouraged the use of new supplies of female labour made up of married women from the middle and upper classes living in urban areas.

Thus this brief historical survey shows that the emergence of women as wage-earners was only one manifestation of the extension of wage employment in general. The periods of capitalist development dominated by an extensive accumulation regime encouraged the entry into the wage-earning class of new supplies of labour, including women. But women were not the only element in these new supplies. At certain times, young people, migrant workers and non-wage-earners have been able to provide alternative or simultaneous sources. In periods of change, it is essentially through the interrelationships between the state and the evolution of the productive system on the one hand, and of socio-familial structures on the other, that the norms governing women's work emerge and are transformed (Bouillaguet-Bernard and Germe, 1981).

Will the current crisis lead to changes in women's employment patterns? As far as family structures are concerned, strategies aimed at preserving gains already made (particularly in terms of consumption) in a context of job insecurity and a fall in real wages have led to an increase in the number of dual wage families. The 1982 census showed that for the first time families with two wage-earners have now become the dominant form of the family in France. In this sense, the present crisis, as a result of its impact on standards of living, has helped to strengthen the irreversibility of women's entry into the labour market.

As far as the productive system is concerned, possible future changes in the utilisation of the labour force make it necessary to analyse these changes on both the quantitative (analysis of the sensitivity of female labour) and the qualitative level (changes in women's employment conditions).

3.2 The cyclical sensitivity of women's employment compared to men's employment

Evidence suggests that women no longer form a special category of labour on which the productive system depends in order to adapt the supply of labour to the requirements of the production process. In the 1970s studies of women's employment and unemployment did find support for the argument that female employment in manufacturing industry was relatively sensitive to turnarounds in the economic situation during the period of prosperity (cf. above). Women were the first to be affected by job losses and the last to benefit from the effects of a strong and lasting recovery. Thus women did form a floating reserve supply of labour for manufacturing industry during the post-war period of rapid economic growth.

However, the present crisis seems to have changed the way in which the job market functions. For the first time, it is no longer women, but men, both young and adult, who have been the first to suffer the effects of the recession that were first felt at the end of 1974 and that until the beginning of the 1980s amplified fluctuations in unemployment levels, both upwards and downwards. The adoption from 1981 onwards of an active employment policy focused particularly on young people and older workers has stabilised the increase in unemployment (see Figure 2.1). The rate of increase of unemployment among adult males is now persistently higher than that for other categories in the labour force, as is indeed observed in most of the industrialised economies (Paukert, 1984).

It is as if the most protected categories in the labour market have, as a result of the recession, lost the relative advantage that they had acquired during the thirty years of prosperity. In this sense, the crisis seems to be bringing the various elements of the labour force into competition with each other, to be destroying divisions that existed previously and to be destructuring the market (Michon, 1975).

The effects of the current recession have been felt most strongly in those areas central to the structure of the industrial wage-earning class (Silvestre, 1980), i.e. in large, highly concentrated firms in which employers' strategies for regulating the labour force, on the one hand, and workers' struggles on the other have led to the establishment of very institutionalised forms of the 'rapport salarial'. Women are an insignificant part of the labour force in these sectors and firms (iron and steel, coal, shipbuilding, motor industry). In fact, those most affected by the rise in unemployment since 1975 are male manual workers and women have been relatively sheltered by their concentration in the tertiary sector and in non-manual jobs.

This relative protection could be the result of strict sectoral effects or these sectoral effects may be reinforced by the system of labour force management. Under the first hypothesis women may still occupy the most vulnerable jobs within each industry and are protected only because industries where men predominate are worst affected. Under the second hypothesis, men may lose out relative to women within sectors, either because of concentration of female labour in administrative jobs or as a result of a deliberate policy of retaining female manual workers, because they are less expensive and more malleable.

Unemployment statistics for the depression of the 1930s show that, in France at least, women were not more severely affected than men by job losses, although it took longer for female unemployment to be

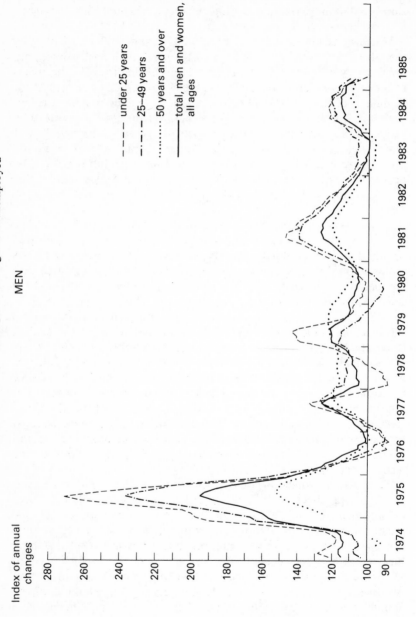

Figure 2.1 Annual changes in the registered unemployed

MEN

Index of annual changes

- - - - under 25 years
- · - · - 25–49 years
········· 50 years and over
———— total, men and women, all ages

Figure 2.1 (cont'd)   Annual changes in the registered unemployed

WOMEN

Index of annual changes

– – – – under 25 years

– – · – · 25–49 years

············· 50 years and over

——— total, men and women, all ages

reduced. In his survey of the unemployed, Letellier (1938) found some evidence that women were being substituted for men in manufacturing industry, which he used to explain why women's employment was relatively protected. However, this practice was uneven and far from being widespread.

For example in some sectors, such as the metallurgical and food industries, married women were often dismissed first in order to limit the number of unemployed. On the other hand, policies aimed at retaining women workers and substituting women for men in jobs left vacant were observed in sectors with a high proportion of female labour (textiles, hosiery, men's clothing) or in which the proportion of female labour was rising (distribution, banking). Even in sectors with a predominantly male labour force (metallurgy), this practice was observed in some departments with a relatively high proportion of female labour (cutting, stamping, small tools).

Thus the dismissal of male manual and clerical workers and their replacement by women seem to have been strategies restricted to sectors or departments in which the use of female labour was well established before the crisis; these strategies were too limited in their scope to have had a major influence on the structure of women's unemployment in the 1930s. Their relatively low share in the rise of unemployment can in fact be explained by other circumstances linked more to the method of registering and compensating the unemployed (Salais, 1983) and to the number of women leaving the labour market (Ledrut, 1966).

Even though women have maintained their employment levels relative to men overall in the current recession, this protection could have occurred simply through sectoral change, and women could still be more vulnerable within individual sectors. Other countries have revealed selective vulnerability of women's employment, particularly within manufacturing industries. Lack of data at the sector or industry level on male and female employment caused by the changeover in the industrial classification system in 1975 precludes a full investigation of whether there has been any change in women's role as a flexible reserve, pre and post recessions.[2] However, previous investigations into the rate of change in women's employment relative to total employment for the periods 1969–74 and 1975–9 found a similar pattern of diversity of vulnerability to those revealed in the studies of the US, Italy and Britain. In services, the rate of change in women's employment tended to be consistently higher than that of total employment, but in service sectors the rate of growth was always positive so that the tendency for women to be displaced relative to men in downturns could not be investigated. In manufacturing the industries could be divided into two main groups: those where the rate of change in women's employment tended to support the flexible reserve notion and those where it did not. In the former cases women's employment increased faster than total employment in the later stages of an upturn and decreased faster than total employment in the downturn. In the latter, either women's employment increased faster than total employment in the upturn and decreased more slowly in the downturn, or the rate of growth of women's employment remained relatively constant, unaffected by the rate of change in total employment. The industries coming into each of these two categories in the two time periods are listed in Table 2.2. The first category, indicating the use of women as a flexible reserve, is smaller than the second category where women's employment appears to be relatively protected in downturns; these findings fit with those in the other three countries but suggest a relatively weak incidence of the flexible reserve mechanism in the French case.

Table 2.2   Variations in women's employment relative to total employment

A. *Industries where the 'flexible reserve' hypothesis is supported*
(Women's employment increases faster than total employment in the later stages of the upturn; decreases faster than total in the downturn)

1969–74 (Code BCND)		1975–9 (Code Sect 38)	
08	Glass	10	Glass
09	Extraction of ferrous metals and minerals	07	Ferrous metals and minerals
10	Extraction of non ferrous metals and minerals	08	Non ferrous metals and minerals
16	Chemicals and rubber	11	Basic chemicals, man-made fibres
17	Textiles	12	Chemical by-products and pharmaceuticals
23	Plastics processing and other industries	23	Rubber and plastics

B. *Industries where the 'flexible reserve' hypothesis is not supported*
(i) (Women's employment increases faster than total in the upturn, decreases more slowly than the total in the downturn)

1969–74 (Code BCND)		1975–9 (Code Sect 38)	
12	Mechanical engineering	10	Mechanical engineering
14	Motor vehicles	16	Vehicles etc. for land transport
15	Shipbuilding and aircraft construction	17	Shipbuilding and aircraft construction
19	Leather	19	Leather
21	Paper	21	Paper box
22	Printing and publishing	22	Printing and publishing

(ii) (Women's employment changes are independent of changes in total employment)

1969–74 (Code BCND)		1975–9 (Code Sect 38)	
02	Food processing	02	Meat and milk
07	Building materials	03	Other food processing
		09	Building materials, other minerals

Source: Bouillaguet-Bernard et al., 1981, pp. 224, 233.

The relative protection enjoyed by female employment until now is essentially the result of structural factors, namely their concentration in tertiary sectors, which are the only sectors in which the number of jobs is continuing to increase. The high turnover rate in some sectors (distribution, personal services) also tends to create vacancies and facilitates the mobilisation of female reserves. Tertiary occupations and unskilled shop and office jobs have been relatively spared since 1975. Employment in all service activities has increased rapidly, which reflects the increased use of subcontracting in producer services. But the market service activities in which growth has been highest already had the highest proportion of female workers and the most rapid rate of increase in the proportion of female workers (retail food distribution, services to firms and individuals, hire and credit services and property leasing).

This underlines once again the particular role played by the female labour force in the development of the productive system. In manufacturing industry, at least until 1979, female employment was slow to show the effects of the job losses that followed the first oil price shock, and was less affected than male employment. Since 1975, recruitment policies in those industrial sectors where jobs are still being created (the dairy and meat industries, electricity, gas and water, non-ferrous metals, printing, publishing and the press) have continued to favour the hiring of women (Bouillaguet-Bernard, Gauvin-Ayel and Outin, 1981).

Until 1979, the fall in manufacturing employment in those industries with a relatively high proportion of female workers (textiles and clothing, leather goods) was less than in other sectors where jobs had been lost. Since 1979, the position has been reversed. However, in all the other sectors where there have been job losses (with the exception of the glass, paper box, rubber and plastics and electrical equipment industries), female employment has been less affected than male employment (Huet, 1982). There may be three factors at work here:

(i) The employment structure

Until 1979, those made redundant were mainly skilled workers, adult males between 20 and 45 years old with a certain degree of seniority within the firm. Women are concentrated to a very high degree in unskilled manual and shop and office jobs.

(ii) The size of the firm

Most redundancies have taken place in large firms (UNEDIC); there have been fewer job losses in small and medium-sized firms, and waged employment in small firms has even continued to increase. Women are concentrated to a greater extent than men in small firms.

From 1979 onwards, women began to lose the relative advantage that they had retained since 1974. The second oil price shock (1979–1980) resulted in massive job losses in manufacturing industry; women in unskilled manual jobs were the worst affected.

(iii) The rise in the number of closures

From 1979 onwards, the stricter adjustment of the work force to the requirements of a permanent slow-down in production (Marchand, 1984) explains these massive movements.

Men and women employed in manufacturing industry have been affected by different types of job loss. Women are more vulnerable to job losses to the extent that the sectors in which they are most likely to be employed are those in which job reductions are more likely to lead directly to redundancy for the job holders. Men tend to be employed in highly concentrated and capital intensive industries (iron and steel, engineering, the motor industry, shipbuilding, mining) in which compulsory redundancy is a last resort after all other methods of shedding, particularly early retirement, have been exhausted (Cezard, 1984).

3.3 The questioning of the dominant employment norm

As a result of job losses and the threat to the gains made in terms of employment and wages, the present recession has had a major impact on the industrial wage-earning class in those sectors that were the driving force in the growth of the French economy in the post-war period. And it was the same sectors that helped to form the dominant wage norm, based on a system of rules drawn up collectively and which determine the management of the labour force (Eymard-Duvernay, 1981) and also its reproduction. It is also this dominant wage norm, established in the key sectors of economic growth, which forms a main characteristic of the monopolistic 'rapport salarial'.

What is at stake in the current crisis is the destruction of the monopolistic 'rapport salarial' and the establishment of new production relationships, new patterns of consumption and new labour management methods, and, eventually, of a new 'rapport salarial' (Margirier, 1984). The exclusion of large numbers of workers (adult male manual workers of French origin) – the hard core of the industrial wage-earning class – from hitherto sheltered sectors of manufacturing industry is one of the ways in which the 'rapport salarial' is being dismantled. Another way, which appears to us to be fundamental, is the increasingly apparent rise in the use of more flexible and more insecure job forms.

The destabilisation of job forms, by breaking up and thus weakening collective labour, has given rise to a trend towards the greater individualisation of employment contracts. This leads in turn to a more competitive form of 'rapport salarial'.

It would appear from the important role played by female labour in the implementation and development of non-standard job forms, such as contract work, fixed-term contracts and part-time work, that female labour has been used to test these new job forms. The development of these job forms is intended to reduce wage costs by introducing greater flexibility into employment contracts. This greater degree of flexibility operates on two levels; the jobs on offer are more insecure and working hours tend to be rearranged (Huet, 1984). Some examples of this process are given below.

The majority of workers on fixed-term contracts are women. The use of such contracts had been spreading since the early 1970s and in March 1984 women accounted for 52% of all workers on such contracts (INSEE – French Government Statistical Service). Young people are also disproportionately represented with under 25s accounting for 45% of the people on short term contracts. Contract labour arrangements based on agencies affect women less, since mostly male manual workers are involved. At the end of 1983, women represented 35.9% of wage earners working for contract agencies, but 38.2% of all employees in the private sector. However, the majority of the first contract workers in the early 1960s were women.

According to the Employment Survey of March 1984, the loss of temporary or unprotected jobs was responsible for 24.2% of entries by women into unemployment, compared with 21.9% for men. For the first time, this was the main reason for women becoming unemployed, ahead of redundancy (22.8%).

Part-time work, in which women were already disproportionately involved, is developing at an increasingly rapid rate and women are the main participants in this increase. In 1984, 21% of women in employment (1,850,000 women) had part-time jobs. The use of this job form increased by 58% for wage-earners between 1978 and 1984 (Huet, 1985). Part-time work has increased at roughly the same rate in both government departments and private firms.

The increasing use of female labour by firms and the continuously increasing importance of women in the productive system can be explained, once again, by the ability of female labour to adapt better to the present needs of firms.

4 CONCLUSION

The recession has led to a restructuring of employment and of the conditions under which the whole of the labour force is used. In France, the female labour force has played a central role in the changes in the dominant norms of waged employment. Firstly changes in the employment structure have been accompanied by the continued growth in tertiary jobs occupied by women and by the decrease in jobs in manufacturing industry occupied by men. Secondly, the more flexible and more insecure job forms occupied by women and the individualisation of work rates and working hours, which has been tested out on the female labour force, help to undermine the employment norm that dominated during the period of economic growth.

The recession has thrown back on to the labour market categories of labour hitherto considered to be sheltered from unemployment. This raises the question of whether the reintroduction of competition between the various categories of labour might tend in the future to slow down the growth in the employment of women. Examination of the structure of unemployment may lead to the existence of these competitive processes being confirmed. However, our analysis of the extension of female employment does not show that women are being substituted for men in jobs, but rather that the jobs traditionally occupied by women are continuing to increase in number. We cannot necessarily conclude that there will be substitution in the opposite direction, with men taking over women's jobs, even if the unemployment position for men deteriorates, as the different categories of labour tend to occupy distinct positions in the employment structure, reinforced by differences in employment conditions.

This suggests that it is essential to situate the consideration of the employment prospects for any segment of the labour force in the general analysis of changes in the system of work organisation and employment conditions, and not to concentrate attention solely on supply-side factors as the determinants of employment change.

NOTES

1 This has not led to the abolition of domestic labour for women, but rather to a change in the nature of that labour. 'On the contrary, the more the production and consumption sectors have developed and the more products have multiplied and diversified, the more the tasks associated with shopping, transport and the transformation and finishing of products have been increased in number and often made more complex according to family responsibilities, income and the requirements of social representation' (Vandelac, 1985).

2 The same regressions of changes in women's employment against changes in total employment as those described in the introduction to this section and estimated in the other three chapters in this section were estimated for manufacturing industries in France from 1975 to 1983. However, significant results were found for only 9 out of 37 sectors. Four of these indicated that women were relatively more vulnerable to employment variations than men, and five that they were relatively less vulnerable. In view of the unreliability of the results with the small number of observations, it was decided not to present these results in detail. Nevertheless they tend to confirm the view that the flexible reserve mechanism was not particularly strong in French manufacturing for women employees.

REFERENCES

Aglietta, M. (1976), *Régulation et crise du capitalisme*, Calmann-Lévy.

Battagliola, F. (1984), 'Employés et employées. Trajectoires professionnelles et familiales' in *Le Sexe du Travail*, PUG.

Bouillaguet-Bernard, P., Gauvin, A. (1984), *L'évolution de l'activité et de l'emploi des femmes en France*, Rapport pour la Commission des Communautés Economiques Européennes.

Bouillaguet-Bernard, P., Germe, J. F. (1982), 'Incidence de la situation conjoncturelle sur la structuration des réserves de main-d'oeuvre en France', *Cahier de l'ISMEA*, Série AB.

Bouillaguet-Bernard, P., Gauvin-Ayel, A., Outin, J. L. (1981), *Femmes au travail, prospérité et crise*, Ed. Economica.

Boyer, R. (1979), 'La crise actuelle: une mise au point en perspective historique, quelques reflexions à partir d'une analyse du capitalisme français en longue période', *Critiques de l'Economie Politique*, nos. 7–8.

Boyer, R. (1981), 'Les transformations du rapport salarial dans la crise, une interprétation des aspects sociaux et économiques', *Critiques de l'Economie Politique*, nos. 15–16.

Cezard, M. (1984), 'Enquête-Emploi: 2 240 000 chômeurs en Mars 1984', *Economie et Statistique*, nos. 171–2.

Dutoya, C. Gauvin-Ayel, A. (1982), 'Assignment of women workers to Jobs and Company strategies in France' in *Flexibility in the Labor Market*, R. Tarling, ed., Academic Press, London, 1987.

Eymard-Duvernay, F., Salais, R. (1975), 'Une analyse des liens entre emploi et chômage', *Economie et Statistique*, no. 69.

Eymard-Duvernay, F. (1981), 'Le secteur de l'industrie et leurs ouvriers', *Economie et Statistique*, no. 138.

Gaspard, M. (1975), 'Comment se déterminent les structures d'emploi des établissements industriels', *Economie et Statistique*, no. 67.

Huet, M. (1982), 'L'activité féminine est-elle irreversible?', *Economie et Statistique*, no. 145.

Huet, M. (1984), '*La gestion de l'emploi féminin et masculin obéit-elle à des logiques différentes?*' Communication au colloque, 'Les hommes et la sexisme'.

Huet, M. (1985), 'Evolution de la situation professionnelle des femmes depuis la crise', *Cahiers de l'APRE*, no. 1.

Humphries, J. (1983), 'The emancipation of women in the 1970s and 1980s. From the Latent to the Floating', *Capital and Class*, no. 20.

Kergoat, D. (1982), *Les ouvrières*, Le Sycomore.

Labourie-Racape, A., Letablier, M. T., Vasseur, A. M. (1977), 'L'activité féminine: enquête sur la discontinuité de la vie professionnelle', *Cahier du CEE*, no. 11, PUF.

Letellier, G. (1938), *Le chômage en France de 1930 à 1936*, Sirey, Paris.

Ledrut, R. (1966), *Sociologie du chômage*, PUF, Paris.

Marc, N., Marchand, O. (1984), 'La population active de 1975 à 1982 les facteurs d'une forte croissance', *Economie et Statistique*, nos. 171–2.

Marchand, O. (1984), 'L'emploi en 1982–1983: simple répit dans la divergence entre demande et offre', *Economie et Statistique*, no. 166.

Margirier, G. (1984), 'Quelques aspects des transformations récentes du rapport salarial', *Critiques de l'Economie Politique*, nos. 26–7.

Michal, M. G. (1973), 'Les femmes jeunes travaillent de plus en plus fréquemment', *Economie et Statistique*, no. 51.

Michon, F. (1975), *Chômeurs et chômage*, PUF, Paris.

Molinie, A. F., Volkoff, S. (1980), 'Les conditions de travail des ouvriers et ouvrières', *Economie et Statistique*, no. 118.

Paukert, L. (1984), *L'emploi et le chômage des femmes dans les pays de l'OCDE*, OCDE.

Pommier-Pennef, F. (1975), 'Emploi et politique de personnel', *Revue Française des Affaires Sociales*, no. 1.

Rault, D. (1984), 'Secteur d'activité: l'évolution des structures de la main-d'oeuvre', *Economie et Statistique*, nos. 171–2.

Rubery, J., Tarling, R. J. (1982), 'Women in the Recession', *Socialist Economic Review*.

Salais, R. (1971), 'Sensibilité de l'activité par sexe et âge aux variations du chômage', *Annales de l'INSEE*, no. 8.

Salais, R. (1977), 'Une analyse des mécanismes de détermination du chômage', *Economie et Statistique*, no. 93.

Salais, R. (1978), 'Les besoins d'emploi: contenu et problèmes posés par leur satisfaction', *Revue économique*, no. 1.

Salais, R. (1983), 'La formation du chômage moderne dans les années trente', *Economie et Statistique*, no. 155.

Silvestre, J. J. (1983), *Crise de l'emploi et formes de régulation du marché du travail. France 1968–1980*, L.E.S., CNRS.

Thelot, J. C. (1973), 'Mobilité professionnelle plus forte entre 1965 et 1970 qu'entre 1959 et 1964', *Economie et Statistique*, no. 51.

Thelot, J. C. (1975), 'Le fonctionnement du marché de l'emploi, l'exemple des Pays de la Loire', *Economie et Statistique*, no. 69.

Vandelac, L. (1985), *De travail et de l'Amour*, St Martin's – Montreal.

Woystinsky, W. S. (1942), *Three Aspects of Labor Dynamics*, Washington, DC.

3 Sex-typing of occupations, the cycle and restructuring in Italy

Francesca Bettio

1 INTRODUCTION

Both the chapters on Italy in this book analyse female employment through the perspective of job segregation by sex. The present chapter explores the implication of sex-typing for the distinctiveness of the pattern of women's employment relative to the male pattern, particularly over the cycle. It focuses primarily, though not exclusively, on demand and considers the post-war period. Chapter 7 assesses the implication of sex-typing for the pattern of female participation, including unemployment. It takes a longer term perspective and explores the interaction between demand and supply.

Traditional views of female labour see women as an inherently vulnerable segment, more easily attracted and dismissed in response to the needs of the economy. The question posed by this chapter is not whether these views are proving obsolete in the light of the increasing integration of women into the labour force, but instead, whether they ever adequately fitted the behaviour of female employment.

Recent literature has seen sex-typing as a constraint on women's role as buffer which is otherwise intrinsic to the female supply. This perspective is reversed here. It is argued that sex-typing makes the comparative contribution of women to the pattern of employment contingent upon economic circumstances. Thus, women may suffer disproportionately from cyclical instability, but this is just one of the possible outcomes.

The Italian experience is used to support this view. The case of Italy also underlines the importance of institutional factors in blurring or sharpening differences between male and female vulnerability to employment loss. A very distinctive system of industrial relations in Italy has blurred the female/male divide but sharpened the divide between the flexible informal sector and the rigid official sector, a division which cuts across sex lines.

The argument is organized as follows. The first section tests the comparative vulnerability of female employment and the trends in the share of women. The second section relates the statistical findings to the characteristics of sex-typing and its pattern of change. The third section discusses the role of the informal sector in determining the comparative patterns of instability for male and female labour.

2 THE PATTERN OF FEMALE EMPLOYMENT OVER THE CYCLE: A STATISTICAL INVESTIGATION

The idea of women as some kind of flexible reserve is shared by several conflicting perspectives. On the one hand, Marxists consider it as a broad conceptualization of female labour and stress the permanent precariousness of the employment status of women (the floating and latent reserves), more than its role as a cyclical buffer (Furnari, 1975; Humphries, 1983; Simmeral, 1978). On the other hand, the human capital and segmentation schools focus more narrowly on the greater vulnerability of female labour to cyclical fluctuations (Doeringer and Piore, 1971; Oi, 1962). The reasons given also differ: lower skills and/or seniority are proposed by the human capital and strands of the segmentation approach. Marxists and radical segmentationists (Edwards, 1975) prefer to emphasize the greater 'disposability' of women on social grounds.

This idea has been challenged both factually and theoretically on the grounds that it neglected the protection afforded by the resilience of sex-typing (Milkman, 1976). However, the challenge provided a qualification rather than an alternative, partly because empirical results were mixed (Bruegel, 1979). This section tests the comparative cyclical vulnerability of employment for women in Italy as the first step towards providing such an alternative.

One of the problems that beset empirical investigations of the cyclical pattern of female labour is confusion between trend and cycle. In Italy, in particular, pronounced negative trends in the share or amount of female employment in most industries until the late 1970s were often mistaken for higher vulnerability to the cycle since they entailed a higher rate of job losses for women in the down turn.[1] We shall argue instead that such trends stemmed from restructuring that, even if often catalysed by the cycle, nonetheless protracted into long term structural developments.

The model proposed by Rubery and Tarling (Chapter 4, this volume) overcomes this difficulty. Estimation of the trends in the share of female employment is broken down into a constant growth rate factor measured by α and a factor of exponential acceleration measured by γ. The trend path charted by α is accelerated exponentially if γ and α bear the same sign; it is moderated or reversed if γ bears a different sign from α. In this latter case the respective magnitudes of α and γ determine whether the reversal of the trend occurs within or after the estimation period. β measures comparative instability of female employment. Estimated values of β significantly greater than unity indicate a higher degree of volatility for female employment than for aggregate (hence, a fortiori, male) employment. The opposite holds for values lower than unity, while values not significantly different from unity indicate similarity in cyclical patterns across the sexes.

Initially all independent variables were included in the estimation. The results were retained only for those cases where γ was found to be statistically significant. In the remaining cases the estimation was repeated after dropping the variable t. Two different sets of data have been used. At an aggregate level, ISTAT series from 1959 up to 1983 were used for estimation on the three broad sectors, namely agriculture, the industrial sector (which includes mining, construction and manufacturing) and services (including public administration). ISTAT data consider all employees. For less aggregate estimations we have reconstructed series for single industries based on Ministry of Labour data for a sub-sample of manufacturing industries over the period 1955–77. Data by the Ministry of Labour consider only production workers, including technical personnel on the shop floor. The series cannot be extended beyond 1977 due to insurmountable problems of standardization.[2] However, data after 1977 were inspected to detect any major change of trend in the share of women. With a few exceptions that will be mentioned later, no major change was detected.

The results of the estimation must be situated in context. Women began to increase their share of the labour force as well as their rate of activity in the early 1970s, after almost a century of decline. The 1970s also witnessed a change in the features of the cycle. Following the formidable post-war recovery that lasted unabated until 1963, aggregate employment experienced the most severe slump of the post-war period that lasted until the early 1970s. Since then fluctuations have been modest around an equally modest rising trend. If only one estimation, covering the whole period, was carried out it would be possible to detect changes in trends in the share of female employment but only one value would be estimated for the β coefficient. Thus in order to investigate whether there were any changes in behaviour estimations were repeated for the 1970–83 sub-period for the three broad sectors and for 1965–77 for manufacturing and its component industries. Results are summarized by Tables 3.1 and 3.2.

Agriculture and the industrial sector showed distinctly higher cyclical instability for female employment in contrast to the services. Separate investigation of the sub-period 1970–83 revealed two changes. First, the negative trend in the share of female employment in services and the industrial sector both became positive during the 1970s; but, whereas in the services the reversal of the initial negative trend came early in the 1970s, with the constant α taking a positive value as well as the time trend coefficient over the recent sub-period, this reversal took place

Table 3.1 The relationship between percentage changes in female employment and percentage changes in total employment: by sector

$$\log F_t - \log F_{t-1} = \alpha + \beta(\log T_t - \log T_{t-1}) + \gamma t$$

	1959–1983				1970–1983			
	$\hat{\alpha}$	$\hat{\beta}$	$\hat{\gamma}$	R^2	$\hat{\alpha}$	$\hat{\beta}$	$\hat{\gamma}$	R^2
Agriculture	.0292*	1.5987*		.70	.0316*	1.5215*		.80
	(.0095)	(.2228)			(.0079)	(.2297)		
Industry	−.0316*	1.4133*	.0023*	.72	−.0145	2.0026*	.0036*	.77
	(.0101)	(.1947)	(.0007)		(.0105)	(.3503)	(.0014)	
Services	−.0135*	1.1861	.0014*	.80	.0071	1.4172		.77
	(.0056)	(.1745)	(.0004)		(.0069)	(.2305)		

Key: $\hat{\alpha}$* $\hat{\gamma}$* : estimate significantly different from ø (5%, two-tailed test)
 $\hat{\beta}$* : estimate significantly greater than 1 (5%, two-tailed test)
 $\hat{\beta}$*(−) : estimate significantly lower than 1 (5%, two-tailed test)
 Standard errors in brackets
Source: Based on ISTAT data.

later in the industrial sector with the negative constant α being progressively off-set by the positive time trend coefficient.[3] In contrast, agriculture displayed a positive but steady trend in the share of women throughout.

The second change concerns the comparative instability of female employment over the cycle. In the recent sub-period (1970–83) the value of β increased in both the services and the industrial sector, considerably in the former case and less so in the latter case, suggesting that the instability of female employment outside agriculture was actually higher in recent years. However, this is only a possibility as in services the β coefficient was still not significantly higher than 1, and in industry the variance of the β coefficient also increased in the 1970–83 period, so that it was not found statistically to be significantly higher than the coefficient for the whole period.

Aggregate results are, however, difficult to interpret in so far as higher (or lower) vulnerability of female employment in any statistical aggregate can be due to the higher (or lower) instability of total employment in those component activities that account for the bulk of female employment and/or to greater (or lower) vulnerability of female positions within most component activities, each taken separately. Hereafter, the former shall be referred to as *growth effect* and the latter as *share effect*. The β coefficient in equation (1) is influenced by both and not necessarily in the same direction, but the lower the statistical aggregation the closer β identifies the share effect. To interpret aggregate results we therefore need to investigate what is happening within single component industries, but this can only be done for manufacturing.

In contrast to the industrial sector as a whole, manufacturing did not reveal disproportionately volatile female employment for the period

Table 3.2   The relationship between percentage changes in female employment and percentage changes in total employment: by manufacturing industry

Industry	1955–1977				1965–1977			
	$\hat{\alpha}$	$\hat{\beta}$	$\hat{\gamma}$	R^2	$\hat{\alpha}$	$\hat{\beta}$	$\hat{\gamma}$	R^2
All manufacturing industries ($\neq$)	−.0139* (.0032)	1.0836 (.0983)		.86	−.0142 (.0041)	1.3259* (.1445)		.89
Grain milling	.0598 (.0459)	3.0442 (1.1558)		.27	.1561 (.0961)	4.9710 (2.0560)		.37
Confectionery	−.0123* (.0019)	1.0153 (.0525)		.95	−.0130* (.0025)	.9537 (.0767)		.94
Sugar	−.0774* (.0172)	.3193 (.1965)		.12	−.0613* (.0161)	.1196 (.1782)		.04
Pasta	.0037 (.0040)	1.2318* (.1098)		.87	−.0076 (.0097)	1.0166 (.2216)		.68
Silk-twining	.0065 (.0074)	1.0643 (.0342)		.98	.0108 (.0107)	1.0100 (.0500)		.98
Silk-spinning	−.0078* (.0016)	.9300*(−) (.0231)		.99	−.0079 (.0043)	.9293 (.0703)		.95
Cotton	−.0135* (.0023)	.9291 (.0513)		.95	−.0100* (.0031)	1.0360 (.0631)		.96
Wool	−.0093* (.0022)	1.0966 (.0584)		.94	−.0118* (.0040)	1.0722 (.0940)		.93
Man-made fibres	−.0386* (.0075)	1.0208 (.1320)		.76	−.0461* (.0113)	.9906 (.2012)		.71
Knitwear	.0071* (.0023)	.9470*(−) (.0185)	−.0006* (.0002)	.99	−.0030 (.0010)	.9528*(−) (.0171)		1.00
Linen textiles	−.0122* (.0028)	.9503 (.0417)		.97	−.0179* (.0051)	.8513 (.0754)		.93
Shoes	.0059 (.0030)	1.0363 (.0499)		.96	.0042 (.0038)	.9900 (.0768)		.94
Hats	.0132* (.0024)	1.1034* (.0429)		.97	.0121* (.0044)	1.1040 (.0700)		.96
Paper	.0026 (.0098)	1.1898 (.9242)	−.0032* (.0008)	.82	−0.0480* (.0090)	1.3064 (.3266)		.62
Printing	−.0166* (.0028)	1.1986 (.0971)		.89	−.0178* (.0032)	.9891 (.1671)		.78
Leather	.0290* (.0086)	.8369 (.1059)	−.0019* (.0007)	.83	−.0031 (.0072)	.8551 (.1719)		.71
Rubber	−.0217 (.0070)	.7953 (.1257)		.68	−.0258 (.0137)	.8174 (.2916)		.44
Chemicals	.0110 (.0084)	.9173 (.1434)	−.0019* (.0006)	.83	−.0213* (.0051)	1.0003 (.3290)		.48
Ceramics	−.0049 (.0042)	1.0617 (.0804)		.90	−.1114* (.0037)	1.1400 (.0790)		.95
Bricks	−.0525 (.0383)	.9745 (.6860)		.10	−.0445 (.0877)	.9999 (1.3912)		.05
Glass	−.0179 (.0061)	1.1247 (.1714)		.69	−.0242 (.0071)	.9088 (.3115)		.46
Cement	−.0402 (.0372)	2.6638 (1.0714)		.25	−.0566 (.0530)	.2806 (1.8438)		.00

Industry	1955–1977				1965–1977			
	$\hat{\alpha}$	$\hat{\beta}$	$\hat{\gamma}$	R^2	$\hat{\alpha}$	$\hat{\beta}$	$\hat{\gamma}$	R^2
Chalk	−.0491	−.8085		.03	−.0039	−.8542		.01
	(.0672)	(1.1473)			(.1386)	(2.6493)		
Iron and steel	.0080	.3347		.10	−.0031	.2874		.20
	(.0150)	(.2285)			(.0141)	(.1819)		
Metal casting	.0004	.6923		.41	.0098	.4754		.14
	(.0090)	(.1925)			(.0115)	(.3702)		
Electrical	−.0012	1.2486*		.94	−.0424*	1.6143*	.0040*	.99
engineering	(.0053)	(.0735)			(.0111)	(.0866)	(.0012)	
Automobiles	.0317	.5513		.02	.0318	.8868		.06
	(.0386)	(.8432)			(.0508)	(1.0862)		
Miscellaneous	.0179	.9050		.50	.0272	1.0463		.56
	(.0161)	(.2092)			(.0463)	(.2830)		

Key: $\hat{\alpha}*\ \hat{\gamma}*$: estimate significantly different from ø (5%, two tailed test)
$\hat{\beta}*$: estimate significantly greater than 1 (5%, two-tailed test)
$\hat{\beta}*^{(-)}$: estimate significantly lower than 1 (5%, two-tailed test)
$\neq$: Comprises all manufacturing industries including those that could not be separately tested because of problems of standardisation of the series
Standard errors in brackets.
Source: based on data from Ministero del Lavoro.

1955–77 as a whole. One explanation may be that the industry data extends to 1983, and both industry and manufacturing reveal greater volatility in the later subperiods. A second explanation may be that industry data have been adjusted to take account of irregular employment, and in the absence of systematic independent evidence, these adjustments in practice build in to the data set an element of cyclical instability.

The results for single manufacturing industries over the period as a whole fit the aggregate manufacturing pattern. Out of the 23 industries yielding significant estimates of β (i.e. different from 0) 14 recorded a value greater than one and 9 a value lower than one. However, β was found to be *significantly* higher than one in 3 cases only – pasta, hats and electrical engineering. Ten industries had a β coefficient of less than one, but only two were found to be significantly different from one (knitwear and silk spinning). Thus the hypothesis of a distinctive cyclical pattern of female employment was borne out by a minority of industries, with the case of comparatively higher volatility receiving marginally greater support than the converse possibility of comparatively lower instability. The findings for the recent sub-period – 1965 to 1977 – contrast with the results for aggregate manufacturing. The instances of β significantly different from one fell to 2 only: electrical engineering and knitwear. The reduction in the instances of comparatively higher volatility from 3 to 1 is especially puzzling given that volatility increased in aggregate manufacturing.

The distinction between growth and share effects comes into play here. The year 1970 divides a period of mild increase in manufacturing employment starting in 1965 from one of decline/stagnation ending in 1977. Using shift-share analysis, we found that, if the proportion of female labour in each manufacturing industry was kept constant over each of the two sub-periods, respectively, female employment would have displayed an accentuated pro-cyclical pattern on account of the growth effect. If instead total employment in each industry was kept constant and the share of female labour allowed to vary in line with actual changes in the two periods, female employment would have decreased consistently on account of the share effect, along a negative trend only mildly accelerated by the downturn (Table 3.3). That is, the accentuated pro-cyclical volatility of aggregate female manufacturing employment since 1965 is attributable to the higher growth elasticity of total employment in industries with a higher than average share of female labour rather than to the higher vulnerability of feminized jobs within each manufacturing activity.[4]

Table 3.3   Variations in employment and its components of change: Manufacturing 1965–1977

	Women		Men	
	No.	%	No.	%
1965–70				
Total	+ 134785	+ 18.22	+ 310375	+ 19.75
Share effect	− 21707.4	− 2.94		
Growth effect	+ 153683.2	+ 20.78		
Residual effect	+ 2809.2	+ 0.38		
1970–77				
Total	− 126436	− 14.46	+ 31908	+ 1.7
Share effect	− 48138.3	− 5.50		
Growth effect	− 82706.8	− 9.46		
Residual effect	+ 4409.1	+ 0.50		

Source: Based on data from Ministero del Lavoro, See Appendix 2 in the Introduction for the decomposition of changes in employment.

The shift-share exercise (Table 3.3) draws attention to the role of trend factors in increasing the female rate of job losses in the downturn. The estimations for the whole period reveal significant negative constants in 11 cases with no significant time trends. In only one case, electrical engineering, was there evidence of a reversal of the negative trend in the recent subperiod through a positive time trend. In contrast only 3 cases had positive significant trends, two of which weakened or became negative in the recent subperiod.

Thus higher cyclical vulnerability was not the dominant characteristic of the pattern of female employment throughout the post-war period. Moreover, even though there were sufficient instances of greater volatility at sector or single industry level for these not to be dismissed as exceptions, the randomness of the results even at a fine level of disaggregation and the complexity of the trends in shares of female employment suggests that attempts to repair or modify this hypothesis are misplaced.

3 SEX-TYPING THE CYCLE AND RESTRUCTURING

3.1 The relevant features of job segregation

Under rigid sex-typing comparative employment instability necessarily depends upon the distinctive characteristics of feminized versus male jobs. However, the pattern of change in sex-linked job allocation becomes equally relevant if, as we shall argue, the cycle is a catalyst in restructuring and the latter engenders change in the sexual division of labour.

Table 3.4 Index of dissimilarity. 1901–1981

Year	no. of occupational categories	$S_t (\times 100)$
1901	270	78
1936	335	75
1971	235	56
1981	235	52

Source: Population Censuses.

Sex-typing is both widespread and persistent in Italy. One possible measure is the index of dissimilarity (see Appendix 2(ii) this volume), which stands for the proportion of male (or female) employees that ought to change occupation for the distribution of the sexes between occupations to be the same. The value of the index of dissimilarity for census occupational distributions of the active population has remained relatively high to date (52% in 1981) despite having declined from the beginning of the century (Table 3.4). The extent of the decline recorded in Table 3.4 is, however, deceptive. Only by isolating the importance of changing sexual composition within occupations from that of changing structure of occupations can the scope of actual progress away from sex-typing be assessed. We have done this elsewhere, adopting the same methodology as other contributors to this volume (see Introduction to this section Appendix 2(ii)) and results show that changes in the structure of occupations and industries were more important for declining levels of segregation than the relaxing of sex-typing within occupations.[5] Women have made significant inroads into several male-dominated occupations over the last decade but the gains have so far been modest and also counteracted by increasing segregation on account of further feminization of female-dominated service occupations.

The characteristics of occupational segregation by sex have been studied in detail elsewhere with reference to Italian manufacturing (Bettio 1984), but the implications are wider. The findings suggest that a crucial feature is the relatively higher labour/output ratio of feminized occupations or tasks. For example, within a typical pasta-producing firm, the share of the labour force in the four main production stages are: 10% for the milling of wheat, 11% for the processing of flour into the final format of pasta, 52% for packaging and 9% for storage.[6] Women are confined almost exclusively to packaging, i.e. to tasks with a relatively high labour/output ratio.

Though the proportions are not always so striking, the differentiation between feminized and male positions on this score holds throughout the manufacturing industries surveyed, independently of the industry's share of female labour. Even in a highly feminized industry such as clothing, the stages with the highest labour input are more feminized than others. Higher labour/output ratios does not rule out substantial capital intensity for feminized jobs or production stages. Indeed, although female jobs tend also to be comparatively less automated or mechanized within each individual production process, the same does not apply across different production processes or industries; that is women are not necessarily encountered within the least automated firms or industries. Moreover there are exceptions within the same production process, e.g. in the case of repair and maintenance positions that are high in human, not physical, capital and are regularly male.

As a second distinctive feature, feminized occupations tend to have less impact on production outcomes. This partly stems from the asymmetry in the labour/output ratio, since the performance of individual workers necessarily impinges on higher (lower) amounts of output per unit time in stages with lower (higher) labour/output ratios. Thus any malfunctioning is more costly in typically male jobs, both in terms of output loss and potential damage to the equipment. However, the impact over production outcomes also depends on the level of skill required and on the location of occupations in the flow of production, irrespective of the labour/output ratio. For example, repair and maintenance personnel hold key positions in so far as the prevention or limitation of stoppages depends on the quality of their performance (accuracy, timing). So do, say, machine operators in the pasta making stage of a pasta firm, i.e. where the flour is processed into final pasta, since it is there that the consistency and the shape of the final product is obtained.

Mastery of the respective skills matters in both cases. Yet key jobs do not necessarily entail high conventional skill, i.e. skills acquired through a long period of formal or on-the-job training. Taking the typical pasta firm, repair and maintenance is often skilled in conventional terms, but this is less true for many jobs in the pasta making stage. The general findings on levels of conventional skill reveal less than dramatic differences between the sexes throughout manufacturing. While it is true that women's positions were often found to require only several weeks of on-the-job training, the bulk of men's positions did not need much more than six months' training. Moreover, skilled female jobs were not as uncommon as is often suggested. Part of the problem is also that skill is less readily recognized in the case of women – e.g., when it is acquired through housework – although undue weight cannot be assigned to this factor since processes of socialization influence the pre-market acquisition of skill of both sexes.

In contrast, the marked asymmetry in terms of impact over outcomes of the respective occupations gives rise to an equally marked asymmetry in what can be termed 'unconventional' skills such as authority and, in particular, 'responsibility' for quantity of output, for equipment and for materials. Occupations are not weighted simply according to the demands made upon the worker like knowledge, speed, attention, etc., but also according to their importance in the labour process as a whole: *ceteris paribus*, responsibility is higher where mistakes have greater consequences. It is the reserving of jobs requiring responsibility/ authority for men that not infrequently results in women being prevented from gaining access to conventional skills. This is particularly evident in the Italian case where women's (voluntary) turnover has only a modest bearing on their opportunities to acquire skills, for their seniority within firms is not much lower generally and even higher in several instances than that of men.

Two distinctive characteristics of female labour matter above all others for the sexual division of labour. The first is their lower wage demands which can be shown to derive from women's role as secondary income earners within the family and which potentially allows employers to hire and/or retain them in positions offering relatively poor pecuniary and non pecuniary conditions. The second is their subordinate social position. The social hierarchy matches the job hierarchy to a considerable degree. While male positions require higher responsibility/authority, feminized positions demand patience, endurance of monotony or sustained visual concentration. Feminized jobs also tend to have a larger share of total labour inputs, which constitutes grounds for preferring cheaper women. In contrast not only do men's occupations tend to involve lower labour costs but they also confer on the workers greater bargaining power over pay because of the responsibility, authority and conventional skill associated with the jobs. At least part of the explanation of job segregation is thus that employers use segregation to match the differential wage demands of men and women with the pay structure and at the same time use this pay structure to control total labour costs, allocating labour intensive jobs to low pay female labour and rewarding by higher remuneration the skill or responsibility involved in men's jobs. However this is not a sufficient explanation. Wages only buy labour time, not performance and the latter depends upon workers' cooperation. If key jobs and higher wages were not allocated on a sexual basis, the sexual hierarchies which sustain the social and material reproduction of the labour force would be overturned, putting workers' cooperation in jeopardy. This possibility places a major restraint in employers' opening up the job structure to competition from female labour.

Because the extent to which women, qua cheaper labour supplies, enter in competition with men is ultimately restricted by social factors, there is nothing deterministic about the sexual division of labour and the precise boundaries are influenced by the pressure on labour costs of the product market conditions of each firm or industry. Such influence is felt when industries first develop or job restructuring occurs, sexual divisions at any moment of time being the outcome of a series of cumulative changes made upon an initial pattern. The evolution of product demand conditions over time thus matters in this context, whereas static, dualistic dichotomies in terms of secondary/primary jobs or industries are largely inadequate.

Other factors such as sex-related differences in physical attributes, differences in working time availability, etc. also play some part, though on a far less consistent basis than those just discussed. The nature of industrial relations can be important. In this respect the specifities of Italian labour history, and especially of its industrial relations, put into a different perspective certain crucial aspects of sex-typing compared to its development in the Anglo-Saxon world. Unlike in other countries, Italian unions have not pursued the kind of restrictive practices aimed against women that have elsewhere reinforced job segregation. In fact unions have favoured wage parity. Differentials in the official sector of the economy have been decreasing over a long period and are currently lower than in most industrialized countries. In the industrial sector hourly earnings of female production workers stood at 85.4% of their male counterparts in 1984. Relative monthly earnings of female full timers equalled 81.4% for production workers and 73.5% for clerical employees in 1978 (latest available figure). The corresponding figures for service activities in 1978 were 79% in the distributive trades, 81.4% in banking and 82.7% in insurance (Eurostat data).[7] Aiming for wage parity could be seen as an alternative strategy on the part of unions to reinforcing segregation in order to counteract the threat of cheaper labour. However, this was neither the intention nor fully the result of unions' policies. If wage competition between men and women was an issue, then women would still have remained competitive in Italy, if only because they are still willing to take on and put up with unrewarding job conditions without asking for wage compensation. But the threat of competition was selective at best, as we shall argue later on, and wage parity between men and women was for unions a by-product of a wider wage strategy rather than a goal in itself. Finally, whatever the level of female pay, the Italian case stresses that lesser willingness on the part of women to acquire conventional skill may not explain it. The security of tenure successfully pursued by unions prompted, in fact, a strategy of strong firm attachment from men and women alike, as noted. Yet, apparently, this was not sufficient to open up access to a wider range of skilled work for female labour.

3.2 The cycle restructuring and change in sex-typing

Does the process of industrial restructuring tend to break down or to reproduce, albeit in a different form, the pattern of sex-typing of occupations which we have described above? And how does it all relate to the cycle? These issues can only be substantively investigated by studies of the processes of change within specific firms and industries.[8] The findings will throw fresh light on our estimation results which we will reconsider in the next section.

Our first four examples are of restructuring which has resulted in net declines in the female share of employment. In a large baking firm the female labour force fell from 47% to 36% of the total when the firm was closed in 1977, restructured and reopened; and in a large chocolate factory, the female labour force fell from 72% to 45% over the period 1951 to 1971.[9] The first instance of restructuring occurred in the context of deteriorating prospects in the firms' product market, the second was a response to a booming market. A close examination of the data showed that the changes in female shares were associated mainly with the process of restructuring and rationalization which had a much more severe impact on job categories with high labour/output ratios. For the baking firm the rate of rehiring was very variable between occupations and was not systematically related to the share of women within each occupation. The overall reduction in the female share was largely the result of the greater reduction in labour-intensive jobs. In the case of the chocolate firm both substitution of men for women and rationalization curtailed the female share of employment. Substitution occurred in key departments; rationalization affected primarily traditionally feminized departments which still account for a large share of the total labour force. Women's jobs were thus mainly lost through rationalization even in this instance.

In cotton, in other textile industries and in clothing restructuring has reduced the share of female labour. The process has been at work since the 1950s and is still under way, but its pace was accelerated by the recession of the early and middle 1970s. In textiles, substitution of men for women in key occupations took on a greater importance in explaining the decline of female employment shares, particularly in the

1970s. However, in cotton especially, this effect was compounded by the destruction of labour-intensive female jobs and the creation of jobs in the male-dominated repair and maintenance sections as a result of the introduction of automated open-end spinning rings and other equipment. It was the operating jobs on this new equipment that were often transformed into male jobs. Early interpretations suggested that it was the need to introduce shift work, including night work and weekend work in order to amortise the machines more quickly that prompted this move; and similar explanations were offered for the substitution of men for women in the cutting rooms in clothing upon the introduction of laser and other automated cutting machines. Recent studies have, however, shown that this substitution occurred even in cases when no such work schedules were introduced; and in the case of clothing night shifts were often introduced after the change in the workforce, and sometimes involved feminised departments. Moreover this substitution process also involved the upgrading of the new occupations. The need for manual dexterity had been removed but these jobs were described as more skilled because of the greater responsibility and control over production which arises from the reunification of previously Taylorised occupations.[10]

In our remaining four examples the share of women has remained stable or has even increased. These net changes again resulted from a complex pattern of job destruction and job creation, and in these instances two-way processes of substitution, with men substituting for women in some instances and women for men in others. There appear to be a variety of forces behind this pattern of substitution. On the one hand there are the changes in the nature of the jobs as the result of the automation of different processes, but these changes in job content were not always sufficient to overcome the tradition or inertia with which the existing pattern of sex-typing of occupations is endowed. At the same time there is some recent evidence of women making inroads into traditional male occupations, without necessarily associated changes in job content. Whilst in the case of substitution by men the nature of the change in job content was of primary relevance, in the converse case other factors were also at work. The underlying force was probably the price incentive of employing female labour: men would accept female type positions on a temporary basis, if at all. It is also the case that trade unions' opposition to redundancies may have led to the redeployment of women displaced from labour-intensive jobs into more tradition-ally male jobs. Finally legislation put pressure on employers to hire women by requiring them to fill vacancies by the person at the top of the unemployment register, who in practice would also often be a woman. Pressure from unions or legislation produced a better response in cases where there was a shortage developing in the male labour supply.

We need to take all these forces into account if we are to explain the uneven pattern of substitution that took place in the ceramic tile industry under the impact of innovations introduced in response to the downturn in demand in the 1970s.[11] In quantitative terms feminization prevailed over substitution for women and counteracted the impact of restructuring on female jobs. Without changes in occupational sex-typing, the new technology of the 1970s would have reduced the share of women in the labour force. Instead overall stability characterized the industry since the mid 1970s.[12] Feminization occurred in two main areas; one where there was considerable deskilling (e.g. press work), and one which had always been a menial job (e.g. extraction of tiles from their firing cases). But feminization has not occurred in other areas where work has been made lighter (for example, at the kilns) or where indeed physical strength has never been a barrier (for example in glazing). A few women have recently been employed in male occupations, thanks to the pressure of radicalized unions in some plants, but the incidences remain limited. These occupations are crucial to production outcomes, some of them also being highly skilled in conventional terms (glazing). Men have substituted for women on the newly mechanized loading of the sorting line but have not entered other newly mechanized areas such as sorting where the pace of work is still very fast and tasks are routinized. Tradition or inertia are clearly important in explaining the constraints on the substitution process but the impact of tradition, or conversely of change in job content, on sex-typing of occupations, appears to be highly selective.

In the electronics industry adoption of mass production methods designed to meet the expansion of the market in the early part of the post-war period increased the share of women in typically labour intensive tasks such as assembly. The automation of assembly which has been under way since the middle 1970s threatens to reverse the trend. However, its impact has been more than offset by substitution of women for men in those electronics industries that are currently experiencing the fastest growth such as the computer industry and telecommunications, with the result of stabilizing the female share in the electronics industry as a whole.[13]

The production of television sets provides an example of a mature electronic industry where the share of women is currently decreasing on account of automation. By the end of the 1970s a typical factory with advanced assembly methods had a female share of 64.5% compared to 69.5% in a more backward factory.[14] The cases of a firm producing computers and of a telecommunication firm stand in contrast.[15] In the former the share of female labour increased slightly between 1977 and 1982 (22.1 to 22.7%) despite destruction of female assembly jobs. This increase was found amongst technical and clerical as well as amongst production workers, with substitution for men occurring within both categories of employees. Women were displaced from assembly jobs by automation but recruited to test plates in the new automated assembly processes, a job reserved for men under the old technology. Similarly they were introduced into software design to meet growing demands. In both cases the stimulus for substitution was the increasing difficulty of retaining men of equivalent qualifications at the going rates. Nevertheless women are still employed in lower positions relative to men with equivalent qualifications. Women in software design fill ancillary positions and hardware design remains a male preserve, while plate testing has become the bottom occupation in automated assembly.

In the case of a large firm in the telecommunications industry feminization was favoured by union and state policy. Here women have retained their share of employment between 1977 and 1982 despite cuts that are estimated to involve 30 to 40% of production workers, primarily in assembly, when restructuring plans are fully implemented. The main factor counteracting restructuring has been the successful demand by the union for voluntary rather than selective redundancies, a goal which was easier to achieve because of the firm's links with the public sector. In the same context as above of favourable prospects of mobility for men within advanced electronics voluntary redundancy attracted men, rather than women and women have been reallocated from assembly to plate-testing.

Relative scarcity of men for lower positions also encouraged women's entry into previously all male areas in a different instance, despite the absence of restructuring. In the largest Italian car manufacturer women have recently increased their share of employment largely because of the company's use of the unemployment queue to hire new workers, which discourages discrimination against women. This factor was just as important in raising women's employment share as the shrinkage in the supply of male labour from the south. But again, women have been largely placed in low grade jobs.[16]

These examples illustrate that there is no systematic connection between restructuring and either phase of the cycle. Brisk demand can favour the spread of innovations, e.g. in chocolate production or advanced electronics, as can recession, e.g. in the case of ceramic tiles or textiles. Furthermore, whatever phase first acts as a catalyst, the effects of restructuring are often felt for much longer.

The second point to emerge concerns the direction of change in the sexual division of labour following restructuring. Selective two-way substitution emerges as the salient feature in this respect. In the case of feminization, labour costs normally provide the incentive. In Italy, where wage differentials are narrow, direct wage savings are currently marginal, but women are still cheaper to retain in the kind of positions they normally occupy. And of course the incentive is greater the higher the labour/output ratio. Selectivity arises when direct or indirect considerations of labour costs are overridden by other considerations. Sexual disparities in physical strength or inability to fit in with certain time schedules may occasionally play a role, but considerations of skill are dominant, with unconventional skills such as responsibility and authority taking on at least as much importance as conventional skills. Defeminization is, in fact, often accompanied by wage rises to elicit 'responsibility', more so when costly equipment is involved. In short, change in sex-based job allocation occurs in a way that recreates the basic features of the existing sexual division of labour when innovations or other disruptive circumstances call for a redrawing of previous boundaries. Tradition may hamper or slow down the process, but does not change its direction.

If, then, substitution is selective and not uni-directional, its ultimate impact on the share of women's (and men's) jobs is necessarily industry-specific. This is all the more true because it occurs in association with job destruction and job creation, whose ultimate effect on the sexual composition of employment cannot be fitted into predefined patterns. Although the main result of the restructuring process in the latter part of the post-war period in Italy has been a disproportionate destruction of female jobs, in industries such as electronics, leather manufacturing or woodwork, the converse was more common during the first wave of mass production. Nor does a growing labour supply (see Chapter 7 this volume) necessarily guarantee an increased female share as it does not overcome the industry-specific forces determining sex-typing, nor necessarily break down the social hierarchies that sustain sex-typing.

4 INTERPRETATION OF THE STATISTICAL RESULTS

4.1 Comparative cyclical instability of female labour

This discussion of the restructuring of sex-typing provides a basis for interpreting the estimation results we obtained for both the broad sectors and for single industries.

For single industries, it is important to distinguish between mere fluctuations in output and employment and fluctuations accompanied by restructuring. If in the former case, as we have argued, stability of sex-typing is a reasonable assumption two contradictory tendencies can be expected to operate within each process of production. On the one hand, the rigidity of segregation prevents the burden of flexibility from falling solely onto female labour. On the other hand, feminized jobs are more exposed to fluctuations on account of their higher labour/output ratio, provided that no technical indivisibility holds. The more female labour is spread along different stages of the process of production or placed in overhead sections of the labour force, the greater the likelihood of indivisibilities in its favour. To the extent that skilled personnel are hoarded, higher skill levels for men will tend to protect their employment, but it is conventional skills that are the most likely to be hoarded and male-female differences are less marked in conventional-type skills.

Thus, the net overall outcome depends on the specific features of each production. Matters are complicated by the possibility that restructuring accompanies cyclical employment variation. Moreover, if the impact of restructuring is confined within either cyclical phase, the coefficient β (Table 3.1) would be sensitive to the outcome of restructuring. But, as argued earlier, the comparative impact of restructuring on female jobs is indeterminate in principle; hence nothing can be added a priori to the expectations in the absence of restructuring. In practice, however, the overall result of restructuring was a disproportionate loss of feminized jobs in Italian manufacturing during the post-war period. Yet, since this loss took place during slumps and booms equally, it may have reduced women's volatility (in the boom) as much as it may have increased it (in the slump).

On balance we should have expected to find even more manufacturing industries displaying greater vulnerability for female production workers because of their employment in jobs with a high labour-output ratio. This expectation is even greater as the data used refer only to production workers.[17]

In the case of agriculture and services we were not able to investigate single component industries. However, aggregate results are in line with a priori expectations and may well reflect consistency of behaviour on the part of single component industries. Volatility of employment in agriculture could be expected to be high because women tend to be confined to occupations demanding more labour in relation to output, e.g. picking, sorting, harvesting. The opposite could be expected for service employment and indeed for the clerical segment of female labour throughout the economy. Both clerical occupations and a large part of service occupations are in the nature of overheads, the former with respect to individual activities, the latter with respect to the whole economy. Limited sensitivity to the cycle on the part of service and clerical employment would also tend to weaken male–female differences in employment instability. Furthermore, because the division of labour within the services is still less Taylorized than elsewhere in the economy, fluctuations in employment have a less selective occupational impact.

The key to the puzzling results for manufacturing industries lies in industrial relations. As noted, Italian unions fought successfully for security of tenure throughout the post-war period both on the shop floor and at government policy level. Perhaps the single most important achievement is the institution of the Cassa Integrazione. Negotiations between firms, unions and government can avoid mass redundancies through the state fund called Cassa Integrazione. While a firm undergoes restructuring, employees out of work are paid 80% of their wages by the Cassa and retain their job position and their status as employees. The Cassa was instituted in 1945 but became important in the 1970s.

Official estimates indicate that some 9.6% of all manufacturing employees benefitted from the Cassa Integrazione for at least some time in 1984, the peak year in the expansion of this fund, as compared to a proportion between 2 and 3% throughout the 1970s. Employees benefiting for longer than one year were, however, much less numerous, their proportion of manufacturing employment being lower than 2% even in 1984.[18] Figures by sex are not available but the distribution of subsidies by the Cassa among industrial activities suggests that, overall, women are beneficiaries in proportion to their incidence among industrial employees. The protection that union and government action afforded to women in industry did not redress the disproportionate burden of restructuring on female jobs but lessened the impact on women by reducing employment instability for both sexes.

When considering sectoral levels it must be recognized that the growth effect can dampen or boost employment fluctuations for women independently of the pattern in each component industry. The direction and strength of the growth effect depends on the characteristics of each cycle. In the case of manufacturing, the severity and length of the cycle are especially relevant. A relatively mild cycle can be expected to affect mainly income elastic industries where women predominate, e.g. consumer goods manufacturing; whereas protracted and marked fluctuations also affect non-income elastic industries where men predominate, e.g., intermediate goods manufacturing. We have found that, since 1965, female labour in Italy has displayed higher cyclical volatility in the manufacturing sector as a whole, but not in many of its component industries. This is probably accounted for by the fact that cycles in this period were mild in contrast to the pre-1965 pattern.

The growth effect is likely to be less important in agriculture. Sex-based segregation here is, in fact, found more within than between component industries. Also, the composition of agricultural employment tends to be less sensitive to the cycle. Therefore, the findings of higher vulnerability for women in the aggregate should mainly relate to the nature of their occupations and the fact that female agricultural wage labour is primarily seasonal or temporary.[19]

Relative stability of female employment in services as a whole may have been enhanced by employment policy responses to cycles, because of the weight of the public sector. Unlike elsewhere, in Italy the recent recession did not induce cuts in public expenditure such as to adversely affect female service employment (see Chapter 7, this volume). On the contrary, the government remained committed to security of tenure for its employees throughout the post-war period.

4.2 Trends in female employment shares and sex-typing

An overall picture of the direction of sex-typing emerges from the estimations of trends in the share of female labour and from case study analysis. The increase in the share of women in the whole of the labour force recorded since the 1970s as well as the preceding decline hide contradictory trends both between and within sectors. The trend was markedly negative in the industrial sector until the middle 1970s and spared few components industries, as revealed by the estimates of α. Case studies suggest that the disproportionate loss of feminised jobs was the underlying cause rather than any major change in sex-typing. From the mid 1970s onward more industries experienced stable or positive trends, a development not accounted for by our estimations. The most important examples are ceramic tiles, electronics and motor vehicles, as already mentioned, together with light engineering. While it appears that the reversal of the trend in these instances ensued primarily from substitution for men, it is doubtful whether this signals the beginning of a breakdown of segregation in industry as opposed to a redesign of its boundaries in a context of decreasing male supply.

The same ambiguity attaches to developments in the services. Here the gradual feminization of employees in the 1970s and after (both α and γ were found to be positive in the recent sub-period) was accompanied by an increase in the share of men in self-employment which in Italy can be considered the top of the employment pyramid. At the same time women gained further access to traditionally male areas and to career paths especially in banking and public administration.[20] Finally, there was an earlier and more marked growth in the share of female labour in agriculture (α was found positive and significant throughout), but the implications for women were, however, no less ambiguous. In this sector the tendency for women was to stay behind and fill positions that men abandoned in pursuit of better opportunities elsewhere in the economy.

The strength of aggregate employment expansion is likely to be most important in determining the outcome of these feminisation processes. If prospects remain uncertain, these trends towards substitution may not get women far beyond the lower and middle ranks of the employment pyramid.

5 THE VULNERABLE SEGMENT OF FEMALE EMPLOYMENT

There is a widespread belief in Italy that, despite the protection afforded by unions in the official sector, women may still conform to the buffer hypothesis on account of their disproportionate representation in the informal sector. The large segment of inherently precarious labour in the 'informal' sector, which we have so far largely ignored because of the problems with data, owes part of its post-war expansion to the very strength and strategy of trade unions. Not only did unions defend the stability of full-time employment, they also opposed part-time work. Only recently (1984) has this contractual form been regulated and its application liberalized (see Chapter 7, this volume). In 1983, the share of part-timers among employees was 6.6% for women and 1.2% for men, practically the same as in 1977.[21] The negligible incidence of the phenomenon limits its significance for the pattern of female employment both in the past and in the near future, even though part-time working is on the increase.

The restraints imposed by unions on labour flexibility favoured the expansion of the informal sector. A second contributory factor was the income and institutional protection that non wage earners, irregular employees or the self-employed can receive from the family in the absence of a generalized income support system from the state (see Chapter 7, this volume).

Manufacturing is well represented in the informal sector though the share of the service sector is thought to be even larger as well as growing faster. However, more is known about manufacturing, so that the following discussion will focus on manufacturing even though its implications are wider. Here lack of unionization and of legal restraints on dismissals for firms with less than 15 employees compounds larger scope for evading social security on the part of small firms in general and give the latter a central role in the informal network. This network acts as a flexibility valve for medium and large firms and also for employees who in the official sector are prevented from increasing their supply of hours and their earnings by union-imposed ceilings on overtime and wage differentials. As noted, unions have fought to level all differentials, including sex-related ones. In the wage indexation system (scala mobile) low paid workers have received higher percentage rises than higher paid workers so that the high rates of inflation experienced since the late 1960s have helped to make the unions' strategy a dramatic success.

Due to the increasing penetration of foreign markets by industries that rely especially on the informal network, employment there has not so far faced widespread cutbacks. Its inherent instability has manifested itself only in high rates of new openings and closures of firms and pronounced inter-firm mobility within the labour force. However, even if domestic demand remains steady, protectionism or saturation of foreign markets will continue to pose a threat.

When the scale of the informal economy within manufacturing was first recognized, it was expected that women were disproportionately involved. Allegedly they were perfect candidates for employment there, combining lower wage demands with higher 'disposability'. In short, a dualist perspective was proposed in which the 'primary' male labour was preferred in the 'structured' official sector, while the 'secondary' qualities of female labour became an advantage in the unstructured segment.[22]

This perspective appears simplistic in the light of two extensive studies of the engineering and the knitwear industries in one of the regional centres of the submerged economy. Simple dichotomies between the formal and the informal sector based on primary/secondary workers or advanced (mechanized) versus backward (less mechanized) processes were not found to apply. Nor is it possible to identify the informal sector as simply a means to exploit either the flexibility of female labour supply or women's lower wage demands. Both strategies would require use of female labour in traditional male occupations.[23]

Instead, both studies found that female and male activities were equally represented in the informal sector. In both industries, workers in the informal segment have frequently learnt their trade within official establishments: firms usually rely on former employees for outwork. The result is that the sexual division of labour is reproduced outside the official network of firms. Moreover, subcontracted production involves both skilled and unskilled operations, not infrequently in advanced technological processes. The decision as to which production stages are contracted out is determined neither by the prevailing sex of the workers nor by the quality of the work. The decisive factor is rather the absence of any significant economies of scale inherent in the technology of a particular operation or in the production of specialised short run items. Nor is the opportunity for wage cutting a necessary factor (though labour costs are often reduced by avoiding social security payments), but it does carry much greater weight in the case of homework.[24] If the dualism of the industrial structure is far from clearly divided along sex lines, a larger number of women are nevertheless affected by potential instability. In manufacturing, men are predominantly involved as second job holders or on a full-time basis in the subcontracting network of the informal sector and thus, presumably, in lower numbers, whereas women are employed predominantly in homework on a more discontinuous basis.[25]

The respective magnitudes of male and female involvement are open to speculation, but there is no doubt about the high incidence of homeworkers among female labour.[26] The incidence of homework is linked to the resilience of the Italian family, as is the secondary importance of wage income for a still larger number of women compared to their commitments to reproduction. For this reason female labour is more prepared to enter unstable employment in the informal sector as well as to accept a less than full working week. Male workers in the informal sector also suffer from potential job instability, but they more often use the extensive informal network to secure full-time employment and trade off its risks against the scope for increasing earnings through extending their hours of work and their earnings.

6 CONCLUSION

The experience of Italy in the post-war period challenges the view that women act as a buffer against fluctuations in employment. This is particularly true because the sharp division within its economy between a protected or official sector and an informal segment cuts across sex lines. The Italian case suggests rather that, because of sex-typing, the relative vulnerability of employment depends on the specificities of the cycle.

In the official area of the economy sex-typing has afforded selective protection to female labour. At the aggregate level the bulk of women's employment has not been disproportionately hit by cyclical fluctuations but the evidence of volatility in agriculture throughout the period and the emergence of volatility in manufacturing over the later subperiod (1965–77) suggests that protection is contingent upon the features of the cycle and in particular its differential impact on activities with different income elasticities. However, greater cyclical volatility was found in only a minority of cases at the finest level of aggregation: the rigidity of sex-typing combined with strong opposition to dismissals from unions has counteracted the comparative vulnerability arising out of the higher labour/output ratio of feminized positions.

In the informal area flexibility is sought equally in male and feminized positions but there has been no breakdown of sex-typing to take advantage of the higher disposability of women. Thus segments of female and male employment were and remain equally exposed to the threat of instability, although this is a permanent rather than a cyclical feature of their employment. The difference between men and women here is one of degree, since women are over-represented in the informal area on account of homework.

Homework illustrates the contradictory implications for comparative employment stability of women's position in the family, especially their role as secondary earners. On the one hand, this position underpins a relatively rigid sexual division of jobs that can protect female labour from fluctuations in demand. On the other hand, it exposes women to precarious work arrangements to a higher degree.

Women are increasingly becoming primary income earners or co-earners. So far, however, there has been a slow and ambiguous response to this change in terms of desegregation, due in part to the modest level of overall employment growth in recent years. The prospects for the future are thus contradictory. Should the pressure of rising female supply be insufficient to break down segregation and thus reduce the current disparity in unemployment rates, the area of precarious female employment may expand as a consequence. At the same time, the growing incidence of feminized service jobs will enhance the stability of female employment within the official, 'protected' sector.

NOTES

1 See Bruno (1979) for a review of earlier interpretations of the pattern of female employment over the cycle in Italy. Some contributions did stress the importance of structural trends, in particular those by Pazzi, Jannaccone and Frey.

2 Alterations were introduced in 1965 and 1977 to the code and the coverage of the survey for the data collected by the Ministry of Labour on manufacturing industries. The first series of alterations could be overcome for a sample of 28 out of the 73 industries specified for manufacturing. The sample is representative since in 1977 it accounted for 55% and 53% of total and female manufacturing employment respectively. Because residual discontinuity may have remained in the reconstructed series owing to the alterations introduced in 1965 the observation corresponding to 1964/1965 was dropped from the estimation. Since the model tested considers rates of change, this was a simple and effective method to eliminate the random disturbance.

3 The time trend coefficient for the later period is higher than that for the period as a whole.

4 Also, note that the shift and share exercise considers total variations in employment, i.e., those due to both the trend and cyclical components. Thus the results are not immediately interpretable in terms of the β coefficient which isolates the cyclical component. However, the trend has been consistently negative in the majority of industries over the period analysed. Thus, if it has accentuated the decrease in female employment in the downturn, it has correspondingly moderated its growth in the upturn (relative, that is, to male or total employment). Consequently, it is justifiable to presume that results would not change significantly if the trend component was discounted.

5 See Bettio (1984, chapter 8) for earlier results and Bettio (forthcoming) for an extended version. Note that occupations in agriculture were excluded from the computation of the values of S_t in Table 3.4 both for enhancing comparability between past and pre-war results and because census occupational categories for this sector are disproportionately wide.

6 In the firm surveyed there were two extra divisions, egg-processing and animal feed accounting for 18% of the labour force.

7 For a detailed discussion of the secular increase of female relative pay in Italy, see Bettio (forthcoming chapter 5).

8 For more details on some of these cases refer to Bettio (1984, chapters 1, 2 and 7). Hereafter references will be made only to other works discussing the reported cases.

9 Bastianini (1972) and Gigoletti (1980) discuss the case of the chocolate factories. Geroldi (1981) reports on the baking firm.

10 The share of women in cotton textiles decreased from 64.2% in 1970 to

58.8% in 1977 and from 45.7% in 1978 to 45.0% in 1983. The same applies to other textiles and to clothing though in different degrees. For some of the more detailed studies on the impact of innovations in textiles, cotton in particular, see Vittore et al. (1979); Buccellato (1980) and Frey (1979). The latter emphasizes the importance of shifts for de-feminization. Evidence discussed in Cacioppo et al. (1982) throws doubts on the general validity of this interpretation. Finally, the most recent survey on shift-work in textile firms indicate that the introduction of heavy shifts may have played a role in de-feminization but, at the same time, reports instances where this was avoided by assigning night work only to a fixed and voluntary male team, an arrangement well known in textiles since industrialization (see Miani and Palmieri, 1982).

11 On the ceramic tile industry see Giovannetti (1980), FULC (1978), and Russo (1980).

12 The share of women in the whole of the ceramic industry was 32.1% in 1978 and 32.7% in 1983. Its stability in the sub-division of tile production starting from 1975 is documented by Giovannetti (1980) and FULC (1978). Yet technological innovation has been pushing in the opposite direction. According to our calculations based on information collected by Russo (1980), the share of women in a typical tile producer would have gone down from 45% to 32% if (a) the distribution of occupations by sex did not change and (b) the technology of the sixties was entirely replaced by the most advanced technology available in the seventies. Both hypotheses tend to exaggerate the scope for actual decrease, but the result is nevertheless indicative.

13 In electrical engineering and electronics the proportion of women was 35.2% in 1955, 40.2% in 1970 and 40.3% in 1983. Similar trends are evident in footwear and woodworking: for the increasing feminization of woodwork following conversion to mass production techniques see ISRI (1977).

14 These figures refer to a daily production of 400 television sets, see D'Ambrosio (1979).

15 Both cases are discussed by Della Rocca and Vavassori (1984).

16 See Collettivo Operaio Fiat Rivalta, 'Le donne in fabbrica', *Per il Comunismo*.

17 This impression is reinforced if results for Italy are compared with those for the USA and the UK (Humphries and Rubery & Tarling in this volume). The findings for the USA suggest higher incidence of distinctive female vulnerability in manufacturing, despite the fact that clerical workers were included. Results for the USA are not strictly comparable with ours because of the finer level of aggregation of most tested industries in Italy. Nevertheless, the discrepancy is such that it may not be due to problems of aggregation alone. In the UK the number of single manufacturing industries recording higher female instability was not found to be much larger than in Italy at the finest level of aggregation. Yet one could expect such numbers to be higher in Italy since clerical workers were included in estimations for the UK as well.

18 Figures on the proportion of employees on this scheme are based on Banca d'Italia, *Assemblea Generale 1985*, Appendice. The CENSIS report (1985, p. 224) indicates 102,500 employees that had been on the scheme for longer than 1 year in 1984, while manufacturing employees totalled 5306 thousand in the same year.

19 The proportion of seasonal labour among employees was 59.5% for women and 26% for men in 1983 according to ISTAT data.
20 Bettio and Villa (1985, pp. 25–8 and 77–8).
21 The male and female average of 5.1% of part-timers in Italy in 1981 compared with 22.6% in the EEC (9) as a whole.
22 For earlier dualistic interpretations see May (1977) and David (1978).
23 See FLM (1975; 1977) on the engineering industry and Solinas (1981) on the knitwear industry.
24 See the important work of Brusco (1973: 1980) on the characteristics of the informal sector in manufacturing.
25 A recent survey by Brusco and Solinas on labour market flows in the Emilia regions confirms that employment instability is much more a feature of small firms (under 20 employees) and of female employees within them. This, however, does not necessarily imply that feminization is higher in smaller firms. The survey did not collect data on this point. See Brusco and Solinas (1986).
26 Estimates on the numbers of homeworkers vary a great deal. On the basis of the more recent estimate by CESPE and of official figures we have calculated that the ratio of female homeworkers to the rest of female manufacturing employment may be close to 1:2.5 in the early eighties. See Bettio (forthcoming).

REFERENCES

Bastianini, F. (1972), 'Studio pilota basato sull' analisi qualitativa di una situazione di relazioni industriali', B.A. Dissertation, Università degli Studi di Perugia, Perugia.
Bettio, F. (1984), 'The Sexual Division of Labour: The Case of Italy', Ph.D. Dissertation, University of Cambridge. Forthcoming as *The Sexual Division of Wage Labour: The Italian Case* (OUP).
Bettio, F. and Villa, P. (1985), *Le donne nel mercata del lavoro in Italia*, Report commissioned by the Bureau of Women's Equality, EEC Commission, Bruxelles.
Bruegel, I. (1979), 'Women as a Reserve Army of Labour: a Note on the Recent British Experience', *Feminist Review*, no. 3.
Bruno, S. (1979), 'The Industrial Reserve Army, Segmentation and the Italian Labour Market', *Cambridge Journal of Economics*, vol. 3, no. 2, June.
Brusco, S. (1973), 'Prime note per uno studio del lavoro a domicilio in Italia', *Inchiesta*, aprile–giugno.
Brusco, S. (1980), 'Il modello Emilia: disintegrazione produttiva e integrazione sociale', in *Problemi della Transizione*, no. 5.
Brusco, S. and Solinas, G. (1986), 'Changing Status and Unemployment in the Emilian Labour Market', paper delivered at the 1986 International Working Party on Labour Market Segmentation, Cambridge.
Buccellato, A. (1980), 'L'industria cotoniera', *Quaderni di Economia del Lavoro*, vol. 5, nos. 10–11.
Cacioppo, M. et al. (1982), *Ritagliare il tempo*, Edizioni Lavoro, Roma.
CENSIS (1985) XIX, *Rapporto sulla situazione sociale del paese* Franco Angeli, Milano.

Cigoletti, C. (1980), 'Turni e stagionalità in una azienda del settore alimentare', RSO, Milano (mimeo).

D'Ambrosio, M. (1979), *Mutamenti tecnologici e conseguenti variazioni della struttura professionale nell'industria elettronica di consumo*, ISRI, Roma.

David, P. (1978), 'Il ruolo della donna nell'economia periferica', *Inchiesta*, luglio-agosto.

Della Rocca, G. and Vavassori, M. (1984), 'Il lavoro delle donne nella grande impressa: studio di casi', in IRER, *Lavoro femminile, sviluppo tecnologico e segregazione occupazionale*, Franco Angeli, Milano.

Doeringer, P. and Piore, M. (1971), *International Labour Markets and Manpower Analysis* D.C. Heath, Lexington, Mass.

Edwards, R.C. et al. (1975), *Labour Market Segmentation*, D.C. Heath, Lexington, Mass.

Frey, L. (1979), 'Costo del lavoro ed occupazione femminile con particolare riguardo ai settori tessile e abbigliamento', *Economia del Lavoro*, no. 2.

FLM (1975), *Ristrutturazione e organizzazione del lavoro*, SEUSI, Roma.

FLM (1977), *Occupazione, sviluppo economico e territorio*, SEUSI, Roma.

FULC (1978), *Inchiesta sui comparti produttivi, gli addetti e le loro variazioni e la composizione della forza lavoro*, Reggio Emilia.

Furnari, M. et al. (1975), 'Occupazione femminile e mercato del lavoro', *Inchiesta*, aprile–maggio.

Geroldi, G. (ed.) (1981), *Occupazione femminile, ristrutturazione, mobilità: il caso UNIDAL*, Fondazione Seveso, Monza.

Giovannetti, E. (1980), 'Note su salario e qualificazione', Università degli Studi di Modena, Modena (mimeo).

Humphries, J. (1983), 'From the Latent to the Floating: the "Emancipation" of Women in the 1970's and 80's', *Capital and Class*, no. 20, Summer.

ISRI (1977), *L'industria del mobilio in legno*, Roma.

May, M.P. (1977), 'Il mercato del lavoro femminile in italia', *Inchiesta*, gennaio-febbraio.

Miani, G. and Palmieri, S. (1982), *Innovazioni nell'organizzazione del lavoro a Turni nel settore tessile. Italia, Rapporto di sintesi*, Fondazione Europea per il Miglioramento delle Condizioni di Vita e di lavoro, Luxemburg.

Milkman, R. (1976), 'Women's Work and Economic Crisis', *Review of Radical Political Economics*, vol. 8, no. 1, Spring.

Mincer, J. and Polacheck, S.W. (1974), 'Family Investment in Human Capital', *Journal of Political Economy* vol. 82, no. 2.

Oi, W. (1962), 'Labour as a Quasi-Fixed Factor', *Journal of Political Economy*, vol. 70, no. 6, December.

Russo, M. (1980), 'La natura e le implicazioni del progresso tecnico', Università degli Studi di Modena (mimeo).

Simmeral, M.H. (1978), 'Women as the Reserve Army of Labour', *Insurgent Sociologist*, vol. 8, nos 2–3.

Solinas, G. (1981), 'Segmentazione del mercato del lavoro e carriere operaie nell' industria della maglieria e delle confezioni in serie', Università degli Studi di Modena (mimeo).

Vittore, L. et al. (1979), *Tessili e abbigliamento: organizzazione del lavoro, tecnologia e professionalità nelle fabbriche del Veneto*, F. Angeli, Milano.

4 Women's employment in declining Britain

Jill Rubery and Roger Tarling

If women's employment prospects are argued to be adversely affected by economic recession and cutbacks in social welfare provision then Britain could be said to provide a test case. Britain has probably suffered from the most severe recession amongst advanced countries since 1979: manufacturing output fell by 14 per cent between 1979 and 1981 and unemployment rose from around 1.4 million to over 2.5 million over the same period. Unemployment has since risen to 3–4 million[1] and the underlying trend has continued upwards. These economic problems result partly from structural problems with the British economy but have been intensified since 1979 by the Conservative government's policy of strict control of public expenditure to meet monetarist targets. These financial objectives have been bolstered by ideological objectives to return more of the burden of income support and physical care to the family, and by implication, to encourage women to concentrate on domestic labour. If under these conditions women maintain or even advance their labour market position then the argument that women act primarily as a flexible reserve of labour, to be repelled from the labour market in downturns, would appear to have little substance.

A first glance at the evidence for Britain suggests that women have fared relatively well under these adverse circumstances; women's share of employment has continued to rise and by 1984 numbers employed were rising again after the fall which began in 1979 (Table 4.1). Women's unemployment rate rose faster than that of men's in the late 1970s but in the severe recession of the early 1980s it was men's unemployment rate that rose faster and from a higher base. Recent trends are more difficult to interpret because of changes in definition which tended to reduce the measured rate of men's unemployment more than women's, but in any case the overall effect of the recession has been to widen the gap between the unemployment rates from a difference of around 3 percentage points to a difference of around 6, to the disadvantage of men. Moreover, women appear to have largely maintained the improvements in pay differentials relative to men secured during the period of implementation of equal pay legislation in the mid-1970s even though the restructuring of the earnings distribution that has occurred since 1979 has led to a widening of differentials against most disadvantaged groups (see Rubery, 1986, pp. 72–4).

Table 4.1 Trends in men and women's employment and unemployment 1971–84 (Great Britain)

	Employees in employment (June)						Unemployment*	(annual averages)
	Males	All females	Females as % of total	Female full-time employees	Female part-time employees	% share of part-timers in all female employees	Percentage of male labour force unemployed	Percentage of female labour force unemployed
	1971 = 100	1971 = 100		1971 = 100	1971 = 100			
1971	100	100	38.0	100	100	33.5	4.5	1.2
1972	99.2	101.3	38.5	99.7	104.4	34.5	5.0	1.5
1973	100.4	105.8	39.2	101.4	114.7	36.3	3.5	1.0
1974	99.6	108.6	40.1	100.8	124.1	38.3	3.6	1.0
1975	98.6	109.1	40.4	99.2	128.8	39.6	5.4	1.9
1976	97.6	108.9	40.6	98.2	130.1	40.1	7.0	3.1
1977	97.4	110.6	40.9	99.4	131.2	40.0	7.3	3.7
1978	97.6	111.5	41.2	100.3	133.8	40.2	7.0	3.8
1979	98.2	115.0	41.8	102.2	140.4	40.9	6.5	3.7
1980	97.0	114.8	42.0	100.6	142.9	41.7	8.1	4.7
1981	91.5	110.7	42.6	96.7	138.4	41.9	12.7	6.7
1982	88.9	109.0	42.9	95.1	136.6	42.0	14.8	7.8
1983	87.0	108.0	43.2	93.7	136.4	42.3	15.5	8.8
1984	86.5	110.7	43.9	95.7	140.4	42.5	15.5	9.3
1985	87.0	113.0	44.3	97.9	143.0	42.4	15.9	9.9
1986	86.5	114.8	44.8	99.3	145.5	42.5		

Source: *Department of Employment Gazette,* Jan. 1987; Census of Employment, and historical Supplement 1 & 2, Aug. 84, April 85.
* Series based on new basis for unemployment figures introduced in 1982, that is benefit claimants, not those registered for work. Figures prior to 1982 have been adjusted on the basis of estimates to provide a continuous series, and should be treated with caution. The 1983 and 1984 figures for men have been further affected by the change in regulations which did not require men over 60 to register at an unemployment benefit office.

A closer examination of the pattern of employment of women reveals, however, that there has not been a simple linear upward trend in women's employment that was temporarily halted by the recession. Instead there are notable differences in the sectoral and industrial patterns of utilisation of the female labour supply, and these patterns vary both with the cycle and secularly. These differences need to be related to three separate but interrelated factors which in practice jointly determine the overall pattern of change in women's employment: firstly, the sectoral, industrial and occupational pattern of women's employment; secondly, the terms and conditions under which women are employed (that is the differences in hours, pay and employment protection that apply to female labour compared to male); and thirdly, the changes in women's supply-side characteristics (that is in their patterns of participation, labour turnover and acquisition of educational and work-related qualifications). In short we need to investigate whether the changes we observe in women's employment are related to structural change in the economy or to changes in the utilisation of women's labour, whether brought about by the integration of the male and female labour forces or by further exploitation of the differences in male and female labour. The following three sections examine these factors and attempt to disentangle these influences. In the conclusion we consider the net effects of these three influences in the current recession and suggest that their joint impact may be to increase the importance of divisions within the female labour force in the future.

1 SECTORAL, INDUSTRIAL AND OCCUPATIONAL PATTERNS OF WOMEN'S EMPLOYMENT

1.1 Cyclical patterns of women's employment

We use the regression model, developed in our earlier work (see Rubery and Tarling, 1982; introduction to this section; and Table 4.2), to test for whether women have cyclically more volatile patterns of employment or cyclically more stable patterns of employment than men. The first hypothesis of a flexible reserve mechanism is supported if the rate of change in female employment is significantly greater than that in total employment (the β coefficient is greater than one). A significantly lower rate of change in female employment (the β coefficient significantly less than one), provides support for a strong version of the sex segregation hypothesis, namely that women tend to be concentrated in jobs which are primarily considered as 'overheads', and where employment tends not to vary with output.[2]

We tried two versions of the model, one with a time trend t on the right-hand side to test for acceleration or deceleration in the trend change in women's employment share (see introduction to this section p. 9). Where this term was found not to be significant we dropped it from the equation. Table 4.2 presents the results of the estimation for all industries and services, all manufacturing and for 25 industry orders for the period 1959–83. The employment data from 1978 to 1980 were revealed by the 1981 census of employment to have been inaccurately estimated. As a result our current data set includes only an annualised rate of change from 1978–81.[3] Partly to check for the acceptability of annualising the rate of change over the period 1978–81, we ran all the regressions first for the period up to 1978 and then used these results to predict changes in women's employment up to 1983. Comparing actual with predicted results showed a relatively low degree of error,[4] implying that for most industries there was no significant difference in the pattern of adjustment to the major employment reductions in the 1980s over those patterns that were revealed in the period up to 1978.

Table 4.2 The relationship between percentage changes in female employment and total employment by industry order in Great Britain

1959–83[a]

equation: $\log F_t - \log F_{t-1} = \alpha + \beta (\log T_t - \log T_{t-1}) + \gamma t$

where F = number of females employed, T = total number of employees

	$\hat{\alpha}^b$	$\hat{\beta}^b$	$\hat{\gamma}^b$	R^2
All industries and services[c]	0.010* (0.001)	1.064 (0.060)	–	0.93
All manufacturing	–0.011* (0.004)	1.354* (0.096)	0.0011* (0.0004)	0.94
Agriculture	0.054* (0.020)	1.435 (0.291)	–0.0024* (0.001)	0.56
Mining and quarrying	0.027 (0.013)	0.854 (0.248)	–	0.37
Food, drink, tobacco	–0.008 (0.005)	1.459* (0.134)	0.0009* (0.0004)	0.89
Chemicals	–0.002 (0.003)	1.068 (0.129)	–	0.77
Metal manufacture	–0.002 (0.004)	0.948 (0.068)	–	0.91
Mechanical engineering	0.000 (0.002)	1.203* (0.061)	–	0.95
Instrument engineering	–0.004 (0.005)	1.319* (0.140)	–	0.81
Electrical engineering	–0.001 (0.004)	1.619* (0.124)	–	0.90
Vehicles	–0.005 (0.004)	1.151 (0.104)	–	0.86
Metal goods	–0.010* (0.003)	1.256* (0.072)	–	0.94

	$\hat{\alpha}^b$	$\hat{\beta}^b$	$\hat{\gamma}^b$	R^2
Textiles	−0.017*	1.063	0.0010*	0.94
	(0.004)	(0.065)	(0.0003)	
Leather and fur	0.003	1.112	–	0.58
	(0.008)	(0.212)		
Clothing and footwear	0.003	1.024	–	0.84
	(0.004)	(0.101)		
Bricks, pottery, etc.	−0.002	0.940	–	0.67
	(0.011)	(0.147)		
Timber and furniture	−0.000	0.944	–	0.80
	(0.004)	(0.107)		
Paper, printing, etc.	−0.015*	1.398*	0.0011*	0.95
	(0.004)	(0.082)	(0.0003)	
Other manufacturing	−0.018*	1.320*	0.0012*	0.94
	(0.007)	(0.093)	(0.0006)	
Construction	0.035*	0.725*(−)	–	0.65
	(0.005)	(0.120)		
Gas, electricity, water	0.048*	0.334*(−)	−0.0022*	0.50
	(0.009)	(0.195)	(0.0007)	
Transport and communications	0.018*	1.389*	–	0.76
	(0.003)	(0.177)		
Distribution	0.010*	1.037	−0.0010*	0.93
	(0.003)	(0.071)	(0.0002)	
Insurance, banking, finance	−0.001	1.314*	–	0.91
	(0.003)	(0.091)		
Professional services	0.001	1.056	–	0.97
	(0.001)	(0.044)		
Miscellaneous services	−0.006	1.079	0.0006*	0.94
	(0.003)	(0.062)	(0.0002)	
Public administration	0.011*	1.270	–	0.71
	(0.004)	(0.183)		

[a] Data for 1979, 1980 are not available. Changes 1978 to 1981 have been annualised.
    n = 22.
[b] For α and γ, * indicates that the estimate is significantly different from zero at the 5
    per cent level. For β, * indicates that the estimate is significantly different from 1 at
    the 5 per cent level. (−) indicates that β is significantly less than 1. Standard errors in
    brackets.
[c] 1959–84 annual data for all industries and services only. n = 25.
Source: Department of Employment Gazettes, Censuses of Employment, June 1959–78, September
    1981–83.

Not only do the regression results appear to be relatively robust over
the 1980s but in general the results obtained were very similar to those
found in our own earlier work and that of others on Britain (see for
example Bruegel, 1979; Dex and Perry, 1984). That is, there is no
evidence of the flexible reserve army hypothesis working at the aggregate
level but there is support for the hypothesis within specific parts of
manufacturing. If we look in more detail at the results presented in

Table 2 we find that β is significantly greater than one for all manufacturing, seven manufacturing industry orders (food, drink and tobacco, mechanical engineering, instrument engineering, electrical engineering, metal goods not elsewhere specified, paper, printing and publishing, and other manufacturing) and for two service type industry orders, namely transport and communications and insurance, banking and finance. The coefficient β is also significantly less than one in construction and in public utilities. On balance, there appears to be reasonably strong support for the hypothesis of greater cyclical volatility of women's employment in 9 out of 25 industry orders.[5]

However, as noted in the introduction to this section, there are several different types of processes by which women's employment can become more cyclically volatile than that of men's. Employers are not necessarily dismissing female workers in preference to equally suitable male employees. Instead women may be concentrated in more cyclically vulnerable jobs; in jobs which are more prone to technological restructuring;[6] or within an industry women may be disproportionately concentrated in firms which are particularly exposed to the recession, and likely to expand rapidly in the upturn; for example small firms, and subcontractors of all kinds. Finally, within an industry order there are several distinct industries which may have very different patterns of employment change, so that women's cyclical sensitivity may be accounted for by their concentration in industries that have declined or expanded more rapidly than the sector as a whole.

We can test indirectly for this 'aggregation' affect by estimating the same equations at the single industry level. We included over 60 industries (minimum list headings (mlhs) or combinations of mlhs) in this second stage of the analysis. We investigated the component industries of six of the nine industry orders with β coefficients significantly greater than one.[7] We also included most of the industries that were important employment providers for women, to see if any cyclically volatile industries were included in industry orders with β coefficients less than 1. We thus included all industries in textiles, clothing and footwear, divided distribution into retailing and wholesale and public administration into national and local government, and selected out education, health, other professional services, pottery, catering, hairdressing, laundries, drycleaning and other services as all relatively significant employers of women.

Table 4.3 presents the detailed results for all those industries where we found β to be significantly greater than 1. The large number of omissions from the table indicates that the more volatile pattern of female employment change discovered at the industry order level was not generally confirmed at the mlh level, suggesting that to a considerable extent the volatility of female employment is explained by the aggregation effect. Electrical engineering provided the major exception to that conclusion, with 6 industries out of 9 indicating greater volatility

Table 4.3 The relationship between percentage changes in female employment and total employment by industry (mlh) in Great Britain

1959–83[a]

equation: $\log F_t - \log F_{t-1} = \alpha + {}_1\beta(\log T_t - \log T_{t-1}) + (\gamma t)$

where F = number of females employed, T = total number of employees

	$\hat{\alpha}$[b]	$\hat{\beta}$[b]	$\hat{\gamma}$[b]	R^2
Food, drink and tobacco				
Cocoa, chocolate and sugar confectionery	−0.000 (0.003)	1.269* (0.060)	–	0.96
Electrical engineering				
Insulated wire	0.005 (0.008)	1.513* (0.163)	–	0.81
Telegraph and telephone	−0.003 (0.007)	1.335* (0.098)	–	0.90
Radio and electrical components	−0.012* (0.004)	1.377* (0.061)	–	0.96
Broadcast receiving and sound reproducing equipment	−0.014* (0.006)	1.133* (0.062)	–	0.94
Radio, radar and electronic capital goods	−0.014 (0.007)	1.323* (0.122)	–	0.85
Other electrical goods	−0.000 (0.005)	1.287* (0.093)	–	0.91
Textiles				
Weaving of cotton, etc.	−0.019* (0.008)	1.286* (0.099)	0.0017* (0.0006)	0.90
Lace	−0.010 (0.022)	0.552*(−) (0.178)	–	0.33
Textile finishing	0.011 (0.007)	1.391* (0.138)	–	0.84
Clothing and footwear				
Footwear	0.008* (0.003)	1.185* (0.067)	–	0.94
Transport and communications				
Postal and telecommunications	−0.007 (0.005)	1.459* (0.209)	–	0.71
Public administration				
Local government	0.006 (0.006)	1.652* (0.245)	–	0.69

For notes, see Table 4.2.

of female employment. Out of 15 industries included from the food, drink and tobacco industry order, only one cocoa, chocolate and sugar confectionery, had a β significantly greater than 1, and in paper, printing and publishing, other manufacturing, and insurance, banking and finance, no significant results were found. In transport and communications we only included the two industries with a greater than 20 per cent female share of the labour force, and the largest of these, post and telecommunications, did produce a coefficient significantly greater than 1. This industry was almost entirely a public sector industry over the period and our division of public administration also revealed a pattern of significantly greater volatility of female employment in the local government sector. None of the private service industries which we included were found to have β coefficients significantly greater than one. The only other industries which we discovered to have volatile female employment within sectors which did not yield significant results overall were footwear, weaving and textile finishing. The data at the disaggregated level thus provided relatively little support for the operation of a flexible reserve at the micro level, and the relatively strong evidence at the industry order level must be partly accounted for by the concentration of women in more volatile industries.[8] However it is also interesting that there was even less support from this test for the strong version of the sex segregation hypothesis, that is that women's employment is part of fixed overheads. Only two industry orders had β coefficients which were significantly less than one and our detailed investigation at the single industry level revealed only one industry, lace, where women were relatively more stable. Other industries excluded from the analysis might reveal such a relationship but these, by definition, were relatively unimportant employers of female labour as indeed are lace, construction and public utilities. It is in fact in general the case that industries with a low share of female employment have β coefficients close to one, even though the scope for variations in the rate of change of female to the rate of change of total employment is large. Women thus act neither as a minority flexible reserve nor as a protected enclave.

This more detailed investigation of the flexible reserve hypothesis suggests that its influence on trends in women's employment is even more constrained than was evident in our 1981 investigation, and that it is in fact limited to only a narrow range of manufacturing industries and some public sector service industries, where any buffer mechanism must be related to government policy in the recession, and may not therefore be a stable feature of cyclical employment change.

These models also provide some evidence on trends in the share of women's employment relative to total employment. A negative constant term implies a tendency towards a decrease in female employment share. As in our previous results, we found the constant term for most manufacturing industries to be negative, and for most service industries to be positive. However, only four industry orders had a constant term that was stable enough to be significant at the 5 per cent level, and in three of these cases the negative constant was found alongside a positive and significant time trend.[9] These results indicate that within these industries the trend decrease in women's employment share implied by the negative constant was being reduced over time by the time trend. By the latter part of our period the combined trend element of the constant and the time trend was positive in these three industries and in fact for manufacturing as a whole. Nevertheless, as the actual change in total employment has tended to be strongly negative in the recent past in these industries, the combined effect of the trend element and the cyclical element has been still a decline in women's employment share brought about by the large size of the β coefficients in these industries. The only non manufacturing industry to have a positive significant time trend and a negative constant was miscellaneous services.

More of the non-manufacturing industries had positive significant constants, implying a strong positive trend element in these areas, probably associated with a trend growth in clerical employment, for example in construction. However, agriculture, public utilities and distribution all had positive significant constants and negative significant time trends, such that by the end of the period the trend element had become negative in all three industries.

The combination of these cyclical and trend factors is likely to reduce further the significance of the flexibility hypothesis for explaining women's employment in the future. Manufacturing, the sector where there is most evidence of the flexibility hypothesis, is tending to register trend as well as cyclical declines in women's employment share and is in any case declining rapidly as an employment sector, both in absolute terms and relative to services. Thus the importance of these volatile sectors for women's employment is declining over time and we need to examine in more detail the secular trends in women's employment by sector, industry and occupation.

1.2 Secular patterns of women's employment

Differences between sectors and between industries have already been found to be important in the observed cyclical patterns of employment but these become even more apparent when we come to consider the absorption of women into the wage employment system in the post war period. Over the period 1951 to 1981 women increased their share of employment from 34% to 43% but not all industries even maintained their 1951 female share of employment, let alone improved upon it. Table 4.4 shows that most of these declines in shares were in manufacturing industries and that this relative displacement of women had already begun in the earlier part of the period, 1951–65, although the numbers registering a decline rose from 40 to 48 out of 78 in the latter period, 1965–81, despite the strong growth in part-time employment in manufacturing[10] which could have been expected to raise the number

Table 4.4 Changes in women's employment shares by industry and sector in the UK 1951–81 (No. of industries)

	Increase in women's employment in total employment	No change in share	Decrease in women's employment in total employment
Manufacturing			
1951–65	27	11	40
1965–81	24	6	48
Other industry[(a)]			
1951–65	11	4	3
1965–81	15	1	2
Private services			
1951–65	11	3	4
1965–81	14	2	2
Public services[(b)]			
1951–65	3	1	–
1965–81	4	–	–

[(a)] Agriculture, mining and quarrying, construction, gas, electricity and water, transport and communications.
[(b)] Education, health and public administration. All other services are classified as private services.

Source: Tarling (1985). The industries are MLHs or combinations of MLHs on SIC 1968 definition linked on a continuous basis from 1951 to 1981.

of women employed relative to the number of men. In contrast other industries (namely agriculture, construction, utilities and transport and communication), and both private and public services all experienced generally increasing shares of women's employment in both periods. Those manufacturing industries which went against the trend and registered an increased share were largely those with low proportions of female employment, presumably concentrated primarily in clerical occupations which tended to expand relative to other occupations throughout the post war period. Some, such as clothing, were in fact already highly feminized industries which were becoming even more feminized. Similarly in service-type industries some of the major increases in female shares were found in already feminized industries (such as retail distribution) and others in industries where the initial share was extremely low. Only a handful of industries, such as banking and finance, appeared to be moving towards a truly mixed labour force, and even these may eventually become strongly feminized industries instead of integrated ones. The outcome of the big increase in female employment has not therefore been to homogenize the sectoral and industrial employment patterns of men and women; the expansion of female employment in the service sectors and the decline in manufacturing served in general to accentuate differences.[11] The aggregate level of female employment has been boosted by the fact that feminization of sectors has by and large been concentrated in the relatively expanding service sectors and defeminisation has been concentrated in the manufacturing sector which has been declining in relative and absolute terms.

To understand current and potential future changes in women's employment prospects we need to know what have been the processes behind the recent trends in female employment. Has women's employment been maintained and increased in the 1970s and early 1980s simply because those occupations and industries which have traditionally been feminized have increased their share of total employment or have women been increasing their employment shares in a wider range of industries and occupations? Evidence of the latter effect would suggest that the secular trend towards integration of women into the wage economy had not been halted by the creation of massive excess supplies of labour. However it would not tell us whether the overall impact was to accentuate or to modify the differences in the male and female pattern of employment. If the increases in the proportion of females to total employment were concentrated in already feminized sectors then there would be an increase in sex segregation but there would be a decrease if they were concentrated in sectors with low shares of female employment. We therefore need to investigate these questions in several stages.

The main data source that we have used is the Warwick Institute for Employment Research industry by occupation matrices for the 1971 and 1981 censuses, based on Warwick's 25 occupation and 45 industry classification system (Elias, 1985).[12] Changes in both occupational and industrial classifications preclude the use of direct census data and comparisons to earlier censuses. Occupational and industrial concentration of female employment are closely related: in some instances such as clerical work the tendency towards feminization is common across all industries, but in other cases, such as semi-skilled operating jobs, feminization is industry-specific and as a result these types of jobs are often classified as different occupations. It is therefore essential to look at both occupational and industrial segregation and at their interactions to obtain a clear picture of the differences in the allocation of male and female labour. Survey evidence in the UK has found segregation to be much higher at the micro or firm level than is found in aggregate data on industry or occupation classifications so that even these occupation by industry matrices will understate segregation at the workplace level (McIntosh, 1980; Snell et al., 1981; Martin and Roberts, 1984; Craig et al., 1985).

The first stage of our analysis involved the decomposition of women's employment trends into those that could be accounted for by the growth of industries (or occupations) assuming constant proportions of female employment, those accounted for by the changes in female employment shares within industries (or occupations) assuming a constant structural composition of employment, and those accounted for by the interaction between the two effects (see introduction to this section, appendix 2). Table 4.5 presents these results[13] for the 45 industries in the Warwick classification, for the 25 occupational categories, and for the 25 by 45 matrix as a whole, that is taking occupation by industry as the unit for the analysis. Finally we look at the growth versus share effects by sector by aggregating the 45 industries into 4 sectors, manufacturing, other industry, private services and public services.

Table 4.5 Decomposition of the growth of female employment 1971–81 into the growth and share effects (000s)

	Total increase	Increase accounted for by the growth effect	Increase accounted for by the share effect	Increase accounted for by the inter-action effects
1 Decomposition of total employment growth				
(a) Industry divisions (45)	459.32	145.21	270.20	43.92
(b) Occupational divisions (25)	459.32	53.60	329.36	76.36
(c) Occupation by industry divisions (25 × 45)	459.32	22.85	376.80	59.67
2 Decomposition of employment growth by sector Occupational divisions (25) within				
(a) manufacturing	− 641.97	− 677.43	+ 39.77	− 4.31
(b) other industry	+ 61.54	− 21.35	+ 83.72	− 0.83
(c) private services	+ 510.25	+ 323.46	+ 151.22	+ 35.57
(d) public services	+ 529.51	+ 413.97	+ 95.53	+ 20.01

Source: Institute for Employment Research, Warwick, industrial and occupational matrices based on Census of Population data.

The results for the first three analyses in Table 4.5 indicate that changes in women's share of employment within job categories, whether these are industrial, occupational or occupation by industry categories, accounted for a much higher share of total female employment change than changes in the weights of industries or occupations within total employment. Women's employment was not therefore protected simply by favourable employment trends in sectors where women were already concentrated but by increasing penetration of job categories by women. However a consideration of the results by sector, explains the pre-dominance of the share effect. This effect is found to be positive in all four sectors but relatively small compared to the growth effect in each sector (except for other industry). However, the growth element was strongly negative in manufacturing, and strongly positive in private and public services, so that the net growth effect was only small and positive. It is not therefore the case that sex segregation of employment has had only a small impact on overall women's employment trends; instead occupational sex segregation has been a major cause of reductions in women's employment in manufacturing and a major cause of increasing women's employment in services.

It is still notable that the share effect has been positive for all classifications of jobs. This observation is confirmed by Table 4.6 which shows that there has been an increase in the female share in 19 out of 25 occupational categories.[14] However we still cannot tell from these data whether or not the changes in shares are such as to increase or decrease the similarity in the distribution of male and female employ-

Table 4.6   Changes in the share of female employment by occupation 1971–81

Warwick Occupational Categories (Revised)	Females as % of total employment 1971	1981	Change in female share 1971–81
1 Managers, administrators	4.4	8.0	+3.6
2 Education professions	54.9	56.0	+1.1
3 Health, welfare professions	69.5	73.9	+4.4
4 Other professions	15.5	22.2	+6.7
5 Literary, artistic, sports occupations	33.6	40.9	+7.3
6 Engineers, scientists, etc.	1.8	5.6	+3.8
7 Technicians, draughtsmen	9.8	13.8	+4.0
8 Clerical occupations	65.3	71.3	+6.0
9 Secretarial occupations	99.2	98.2	−1.0
10 Sales representatives	11.0	14.7	+3.7
11 Other sales occupations	73.9	78.5	+4.6
12 Supervisors	46.3	55.8	+9.5
13 Foremen	7.7	8.5	+0.8
14 Engineering craft occupations (module)	2.9	2.2	−0.7
15 Engineering craft occupations (non-module)	0.4	0.8	+0.4
16 Construction craft occupations	0.5	1.0	+0.5
17 Other craft occupations	16.2	12.0	−4.2
18 Skilled operatives	42.6	38.8	−3.8
19 Other operatives	24.4	22.4	−2.0
20 Security occupations	7.3	13.0	+5.7
21 Skilled personal service occupations	40.2	42.0	+1.8
22 Other personal service occupations	81.8	83.1	+1.3
23 Other occupations	5.6	7.6	+2.0
24 Armed forces	4.8	6.6	+1.8
25 Inadequately described occupations	41.0	40.4	−0.6

Source: Institute for Employment Research, Warwick, industrial and occupational matrices based on Census of Population data.

ment. To investigate this issue we need to compute indices of dissimilarity for 1971 and 1981. We use the same indices as those in Humphries and Bettio (see Introduction to this section, Appendix 2(ii)); a value of 100 per cent indicates men and women are segregated into completely different occupations or industries, while a value of zero indicates that exactly the same proportions of the male and female labour force are found in each occupation or industry. These simple aggregate indices pose problems of interpretation (Garnsey and Tarling, 1982): in the first place the extent of measured dissimilarity depends on the classification system used, with in general the finer classifications giving rise to higher observed levels of dissimilarity as the effect of averaging is to obscure the existence of both male-dominated and female-dominated areas within a broadly defined category. Changes in the indices also have to be decomposed into the effects of changes in the weights of occupations or industries in total employment (the structural effect), changes in the sex-composition of job categories such as to increase or decrease the over or under representation of men or women (the sex-composition effect), and into the interaction effects between the two.

The results from all four sets of analyses are presented in Table 4.7. It is first important to note that each set of job classifications gives rise to a different absolute level of dissimilarity, with the distribution between industries showing a much lower level of dissimilarity than that for occupations despite a finer classification system. The occupation by industry classification showed the highest level of dissimilarity overall, a result which fits with other findings of a much higher level of segregation at the micro level even though segregation within firms in an industry still cannot be identified from these data. All the changes in the indices over the ten year period were comparatively small, when compared both to past experience in the UK (Hakim, 1981) and in particular to recent experience in the US, and not all were in the direction of greater equality in the distributions.[15] The occupation by industry category registered a decrease in the dissimilarity index but from the highest level; the industrial distribution also became slightly more similar, but the occupation indices registered a positive increase in the index of 1.4 per cent. For all three categories the sex-composition effect was positive, indicating a tendency towards a more uneven representation within job categories for men and women, particularly within occupational job categories. Although women made substantial inroads into several non-traditional female areas, such as 'other professional' and security occupations, these were more than offset by the substantial rises recorded in already feminised occupations such as clerical and other sales work, which account for a much bigger weight in total female employment. Changes in the weights of industries and occupations over the decade tended to reduce the level of dissimilarity

Table 4.7 Indices of dissimilarity

	Index of dissimilarity 1971	Index of dissimilarity 1981	Change in index 1981–71	Structural effect 1981–71	Sex-composition effect 1981–71	Interaction effect 1981–71
1 *Distribution of the total male and female labour forces by*						
(a) Industry divisions (45)	38.45	38.26	− 0.19	− 1.04	+ 0.86	− 0.01
(b) Occupational divisions (25)	53.95	55.40	+ 1.45	− 0.58	+ 2.09	− 0.07
(c) Occupation by industry divisions (25 × 45)	62.94	62.49	− 0.45	− 0.96	+ 0.38	+ 0.14
2 *Distribution of the sectoral male and female labour forces by occupational divisions (25)*						
(a) manufacturing	46.23	45.60	− 0.63	+ 1.36	− 1.86	− 0.13
(b) other industry	63.38	65.93	+ 2.55	− 0.75	+ 5.87	− 2.57
(c) private services	52.41	51.75	− 0.66	+ 0.41	− 0.83	− 0.24
(d) public services	52.80	47.74	− 5.07	− 3.32	− 1.57	− 0.17

Source: Institute for Employment Studies, Warwick, industrial and occupational matrices based on Census of Population data.

in all three categories so that it is the sex-composition within categories which accounted for the tendency towards little change or to increases in dissimilarity over the period.

A somewhat different picture emerges when we consider the indices of dissimilarity by occupation within each of the four broad sectors. Again within the manufacturing and the private services sectors there was only a small decline in the size of the index, but in the public services sector there was a significant decrease in the index of over 5 per cent and in the other industry sector there was a relatively strong increase in the index of 2.5 per cent. However, in contrast to the decomposition of changes in the overall indices of dissimilarity, the sex-composition effect had a negative effect on the index in three of the sectors although it was strongly positive in 'other industry', the sector with the highest initial level of dissimilarity. The overall findings of increased dissimilarity therefore appear to result from the aggregation across sectors. This finding arises partly because occupational classifications are not in fact analytically distinct from sectoral classifications; for example personal service occupations and health and education professionals are strongly concentrated in the service sector. A slight tendency towards a reduction in segregation within individual sectors has thus been offset by sectoral trends which act to increase segregation. Nevertheless, it was only in public sector employment that a sizeable reduction in the sex segregation index was found, and that result was primarily accounted for by changing occupational weights and not by greater similarity in representation within occupations.

Thus the gradual further integration of women into most occupational categories in the 1970s involved further concentration of women in already feminized sectors and occupations. The overall conclusion must be that there was little fundamental change in the level of job segregation by sex even though the pattern of segregation had been reconstructed. If trends in the 1970s are continued into the 1980s then women's employment prospects are dependent both on the maintenance of relatively higher rates of growth in service sector employment and the continuation of the trend towards a higher female share in these sectors.

Table 4.8 shows the sources of employment change by sector between 1971 and 1984. These data confirm that it has been the sectors with a high and rising share of female employment that have been the best providers of jobs in the 1970s and 1980s. Public and private services expanded between 1971 and 1974 and again between 1974 and 1978. Private sector services continued to expand in 1978–81 and 1981–4 although not sufficiently to offset the loss of employment in the manufacturing and 'other industry' sectors. Public service employment declined but only marginally, so its relative stability could be considered a positive contribution to employment protection. However, whereas there was a continued increase in the number of women employed in

Table 4.8   Sources of employment change by sector 1971–84

	Total	All males	All females	Full-time females	Part-time females	Females: Full-time equivalents [a]
1971–4[b]						
All sectors	+ 649	− 60	+ 709	+ 45	+ 664	+ 376
Manufacturing	− 181	− 195	+ 14	− 102	+ 116	− 44
Other industry [c]	− 89	− 110	+ 21	—	+ 21	+ 10
Public services [c]	+ 395	+ 73	+ 322	+ 120	+ 202	+ 221
Private services	+ 522	+ 170	+ 352	+ 27	+ 325	+ 189
1974–8[d]						
All sectors	− 24	− 264	+ 239	− 28	+ 267	+ 105
Manufacturing	− 590	− 321	− 268	− 163	− 105	− 216
Other industry	− 116	− 124	+ 8	+ 8	+ 1	+ 8
Public services	+ 290	+ 40	+ 250	+ 112	+ 138	+ 181
Private services	+ 393	+ 143	+ 251	+ 16	+ 234	+ 133
1978–81[d]						
All sectors	− 888	− 822	− 66	− 195	+ 129	− 131
Manufacturing	− 1048	− 701	− 347	− 264	− 83	− 306
Other industry	− 135	− 162	+ 27	+ 18	+ 9	+ 22
Public services	− 40	− 63	+ 22	− 35	+ 57	− 6
Private services	+ 335	+ 103	+ 232	+ 86	+ 146	+ 159
1981–4[d]						
All sectors	− 540	− 580	+ 40	− 1	+ 41	+ 20
Manufacturing	− 773	− 580	− 193	− 105	− 88	− 149
Other industry	− 252	− 244	− 8	− 10	+ 3	− 9
Public services	− 74	− 13	− 60	+ 5	− 66	− 28
Private services	+ 562	+ 259	+ 302	+ 111	+ 192	+ 207

[a] Part-time jobs for women are counted as half a full-time job for a women.
[b] SIC 1968.
[c] See Table 4.4 for definitions.
[d] SIC 1980.

Source: Department of Employment Gazette and Historical Supplement August 1984, April 1985. *Department of Employment Gazette* January 1987.

private services compared to the number of men even in 1981–4, in the public sector female employment fell absolutely by more than male employment. Women accounted for 85 per cent of the job loss in the public sector, a development which could herald the beginning of a major job loss for women in the public sector as a result of the government's policy of privatisation. As a result many jobs will be switched to the private sector but these can be expected to be provided on worse terms and conditions, and to involve both an intensification of labour and a reduction in services, hence resulting in net job loss (see Chapter 8, this volume).

A closer consideration of the trends in employment demand in private sector services also suggests that these have begun to be less favourable to women than to men. While 302,000 more women were employed in private services in 1984 compared to 1981, almost two thirds of these were part-timers. If we count each part-time job as equivalent to half a full-time job, and many involve much shorter hours,[16] the total increase in employment was only equivalent to 207,000 full-time jobs during a period when male employment, which is still primarily full-time, grew by 259,000. If, we compare changes in absolute employment levels between men and women in terms of full-time equivalents, rather than total numbers employed, we find that the only factor leading to favourable trends for women is their lower share of job loss in industrial sectors and not their relative increase in services. However, part-time working is the only employment form to register a positive rate of growth overall, even though female full-time employment has not declined as rapidly as had previously been estimated.[17] The increase in numbers of women employed may thus be related not only to the industrial and occupational distribution of jobs, but also to the different employment conditions associated with their employment.

2 EMPLOYMENT CONDITIONS AND WOMEN'S EMPLOYMENT

There are three main differences in the terms and conditions under which women are employed: their hours of work, their rates of pay, and their rights to employment protection.

2.1 Part-time employment

Part-time working has been increasing throughout the post-war period and this expansion has been maintained in the 1970s and 1980s, the period for which we have reasonably reliable data on part-time working. The matrices in Table 4.9 show changes in female part-time employment against changes in female full-time employment and against total male employment for industry class groups (SIC, 1980 2 digit). Observations on the diagonal of the matrix imply that changes in female part-time employment are in the same direction as those in female full-time employment or total male employment, whereas observations off the diagonal indicate that female part-time employment changed in a different direction, implying some substitution between categories of workers. In 1971–4 female part-time employment increased in the majority of sectors, but female full-time employment and male employment declined in over half the sectors. Decomposition of these data into sectors reveals that the substitution in the 1971–4 period was concentrated in manufacturing. Sixteen of the 26 industries indicating

Table 4.9   Changes in female part-time employment, by female full-time employment and male employment by industry 1971–84 (nos of industries)

	Female full-time workers											
	71–74			74–78			78–81			81–84		
	+	=	−	+	=	−	+	=	−	+	=	−
Female +	19		26	20	2	6	18	1	3	12	1	4
part-time =	1	1		2	1		2	1	2		1	2
workers −			2	4		21	4		25	8		28

	Male workers											
	+	=	−	+	=	−	+	=	−	+	=	−
Female +	15		30	20		8	16		6	12		5
part-time =	1		1	1		2	2		3	1		2
workers −			2	3		22	2		27	6		30

Source: Employees in employment by SIC 1980 class. *Department of Employment Gazette*, Historical Supplement no. 1, August 1984; no. 2, April 1985. Data for 1971 and 1974 based on Census of Employment for 1971 and 1974, SIC 1968 MLHs regrouped to correspond as closely as possible to SIC 1980 classes. This procedure yielded 49 usuable categories, compared to 56 for 1974–81, and 52 for 1981–4. 1971, 1974, 1978 data are based on June; 1981, 1984 data are based on September.

substitution of female part-time for female full-time, and for male employees were in manufacturing. In each of the following three sub-periods, 1974–8 and 1978–81 and 1981–4, all categories showed similar directions of change within industries, suggesting that growth in part-time employment is more associated with overall growth in the industry than with substitution within a declining labour force.

Case-study and survey evidence also suggests that the main rationale for the widespread introduction of part-time working may have varied across sectors and over time (Robinson and Wallace, 1984; Craig et al., 1985; Beechey and Perkins, 1985; Mallier and Rosser, 1980). The stimulus to part-time working in the 1960s and early 1970s appears to have been the opportunity to generate further supplies of female labour at relatively low wage cost, an employment strategy which was actively encouraged by the national insurance system in Britain. As the labour shortage eased due to recession and technical progress, many of these part-time workers may have been displaced.[18] Elsewhere, particularly in service sectors, part-time working was being introduced increasingly as a means of intensifying labour by concentrating employment into the peak hours of demand and eliminating slack time. Thus part-time working has become a very important part of the way in which British employers have sought to control and to vary their costs of production.[19] Some of these benefits accrue from the shorter hours, as described above, and it is arguable that this provides the single biggest incentive towards the employment of part-time labour, but other benefits derive from the lower rates of pay, the legal avoidance of national insurance payments by both employers and employees and the weaker employment protection laws for many part-timers, as described below.

2.2 Pay

The single most important factor in maintaining the system of job segregation by sex, which in turn underpins the pattern of demand for female labour is the continuing differential between male and female pay rates. Women's low pay is associated with both vertical and horizontal job segregation: they are crowded into the bottom grades of a firm's payment structure,[20] confined to the bottom rungs of occupational career structures and concentrated in lower paying firms. These practices are much more prevalent than the practice of paying different rates in the same establishment to men and women doing the same job and are consistent with the higher level of segregation found at plant and firm level than in aggregate occupational categories.[21] The system of wage regulation in Britain in fact allows for a wide spread of earnings both within industries and between and within occupations, a characteristic which has facilitated the integration of women into the wage economy at low wage rates. Collective bargaining is based primarily on the work-place with the consequence that industry-wide regulation of wages is generally weak and there is no national minimum wage. Women's wages tend to be best protected in strongly unionized firms or in sectors such as the public sector with a strong system of national regulation, or when they happen to be employed alongside men at their actual workplace (Martin and Roberts, 1984). Moreover, case study work including our own has made it clear that these lower rates of pay do not derive from the characteristics of the jobs but from the conditions under which women supply their labour. Exclusion from particular forms of skilled work still prevails, particularly from the types of skilled work which are protected by strong unions or professional associations, but not all women's jobs are low skilled, even though they may be so classified for purposes of job and pay grading.

Support for the proposition that women's pay levels are determined by the social and institutional conditions of their labour supply is provided by the changes that have taken place in women's differentials relative to men's in the 1970s and 1980s. Instead of women's wages rising gradually relative to men's over the post-war period under the impact of rising demand for female labour, women's earnings stuck at around 60 per cent of men's right up until the early 1970s when they rose sharply to over 70 per cent (Table 4.10). These changes are directly attributable to institutional changes in wage determination, most obviously the 1970–75 Equal Pay Act, but perhaps more importantly, the trade unions' policy of implementing this act through raising minimum

Table 4.10 Ratio of hourly earnings of female to male full-time adult employees 1970–85

1970[a]	1971[a]	1972	1973	1974	1975	1976	1977
61.8	63.3	63.4	63.2	65.4	69.7	73.2	74.2

1978	1979	1980	1981	1982	1983[b]	1984[b]	1985[b]
72.9	71.3	72.4	72.6	72.4	75.0	74.2	74.7

[a] These figures include employees whose pay was affected by absence.

[b] Until 1983 male adult employees were those aged 21 or over and female adult employees were those aged 18 or over. From 1983 the definition for males and females is all those on adult rates. The estimate for 1983 on the previous basis was 73.1.

Source: New Earnings Surveys.

wage rates for women to those for men, and the series of incomes policies which provided for the same absolute increases for all workers.[22] These changes resulted from increases in relative wage rates in all industrial classifications. Nevertheless the main impact of these significant increases in women's pay has been to move the distribution of women's pay rates closer to those for male workers, rather than to effect an integration of the two structures.

A common expectation of the impact of the recession was that these relative wage gains, modest as they were, would be reversed under the impact of excess labour supply. Now whereas the prediction of falling relative wage rates for the weaker segments of the labour force has been strongly confirmed for most vulnerable groups (for example youth wages, manual workers' wages and wages for workers at the lowest decile of the earnings distribution) the expected fall in the pay of women full-time or part-time workers relative to men has not taken place. To some extent this finding confirms the argument that the differential between male and female earnings is not sensitive to labour market forces; the new higher rates for women's jobs have been integrated into payment structures so that they are not easily modified or reversed. However, consideration of the whole distribution of women's pay rates, instead of comparisons of full-time adult rates between men and women, reveals a significant deterioration in women's earnings. In the first place there has been a significant deterioration in the youth to adult pay differentials for girls since 1979 (7 percentage points decline in the ratio of females under 18 to females over 18 non manual and manual average earnings (Rubery 1986, p. 73)). Secondly the switch towards a much higher level of part-time working has in fact substantially lowered average female earnings, primarily at the weekly and annual earnings level but also at the hourly earnings level, as part-timers earn on average only about 80 per cent of full-timers hourly earnings.[23] Moreover data on part-timers earnings are much more incomplete than for full-timers and many of the lower paid part-timers are likely to fall outside the scope of official wage statistics. Other sources, such as the records of the Wages Council Inspectorate, suggest that the incidence of low paid employment in at least wages council industries has increased rapidly since the mid-1970s and part-timers and homeworkers are amongst the groups most likely to be affected by these employment practices.[24]

There are thus contradictory tendencies in the development of women's pay in the 1980s: on the one hand they have managed to maintain and consolidate the relative gains of the 1970s, but on the other hand there has been a major expansion of lower paid part-time employment. Divisions within the female labour force are taking on greater significance: these include divisions between full-time and part-time workers, divisions between workers in union-regulated employment and those in unregulated employment, and divisions between adult and young workers, with the young having to bear most of the reductions in wages for full-time jobs and at the same time competing against the supply of older married women for part-time jobs. However the balance of advantage may be subject to serious change once the 1986 Wages Act which removes people from the scope of the wages councils' legal minimum wage regulation has come fully into effect, as this may provide sufficient incentives for employers to hire the young in preference to older part-timers in several major employment sectors for women, including clothing, retail distribution and catering.

2.3 Employment protection

Employment protection has traditionally been provided in Britain through trade unions and state regulation of employment contracts has developed relatively recently, mainly in the 1970s. This protection was not, however, universal and the most important groups to be effectively excluded were many part-time workers (all those that worked less than 16 hours a week),[25] and homeworkers, that is mainly women (Deakin, 1986). Under the Thatcher governments the extent of state-provided employment protection has been reduced again, with some particular adverse consequences for women. For example the lengthening of the period to qualify for protection against unfair dismissal from six months to two years employment with the same employer will effect women considerably more than men because of their larger share of labour force flows. Other provisions that are specific to women, such as maternity leave, have been reduced even though by European standards they were already at a low level.[26]

If the state regulation of employment contracts continues to diminish then there will be less incentive to employ women on a part-time basis to avoid fixed labour costs. It would be wrong, however, to overstate the current importance of these advantages to employers in determining current employment of women. State regulation of employment is relatively weak, and unlike in France or Italy, firms face few legal or regulatory difficulties in, for example, adjusting their labour force to demand. Trade union organisation is a more effective constraint on a 'hire and fire' policy and the increase in women who are employed in unionized plants and who are themselves members of trade unions has probably done more for their employment protection than the state system of regulation. However, it is precisely that system of protection that the current government is trying to break, through its trade union legislation and through its policy of privatization of public sector services. It is the latter policy that will have most direct effect on women because it has been mainly in the public sector that women have secured better terms and conditions for service and manual-type occupations directly through the effect of active union organisation.

Much more important than employment protection per se is the opportunity offered by part-time work to reduce employment costs because national insurance payments are not required for workers earning below a certain amount per week.[27] This means that there is a kind of legalized black economy in Britain, that is a section of the employment system which is not subject to taxation. However, although it is easier for firms in Britain to avoid employment taxes the incentives are not as great as in other countries as the levels of tax are lower.

2.4 Employment conditions and women's employment: a summary

Women's continued employment expansion, temporarily interrupted by the severe recession of 1979–81, cannot be considered evidence for increasing integration and homogenization of the labour force. Increasing employment for women in fact now involves the sharing out of work over a larger number of women, so that the net increase in female labour utilization even in the expanding service sectors is much less than the absolute growth in numbers employed, and at the same time there has been an expansion of very low paid employment with the switch to even more part-time work. Instead of a progressive improvement in both employment opportunities and the terms and conditions of women's employment we may be experiencing a trend towards a more intensive form of labour exploitation for a substantial part of the female labour force.

This trend may be coinciding with changes in the female labour supply towards a more stable, permanent and qualified labour force, and one of the most crucial questions to address is the extent to which women have been able and will be able in the future to affect their position within the wage economy through changes in their labour market behaviour and characteristics.

3 LABOUR SUPPLY CONDITIONS

Even though the demand for female labour, measured by changes in numbers employed, has been stronger than that for men throughout the 1970s and in particular during the recent severe recession, it appears to have been considerably outstripped by the increase in supply, for, on the basis of measured unemployment figures, we find that the unemployment position for women has deteriorated faster than that for men since 1971 (Table 4.1). However, it was in the mid-1970s that women's unemployment rate rose faster than that for men and it is men who suffered a faster rate of increase during the severe recession of 1979 to 1982. Moreover, these figures on unemployment pose several major problems of interpretation. On the one hand changes in the system of national insurance, and women's more permanent involvement in the labour force may have resulted in a higher propensity to register as unemployed, but, on the other hand, married women do not usually qualify for supplementary benefits once their entitlement to unemployment benefits is exhausted and at this point they usually leave the register of the unemployed even if they have no job. The faster rate of increase in measured unemployed amongst men between 1979 and 1982 has been due almost entirely to longer durations of unemployment and not to increased flows into unemployment, but the true duration of women's unemployment is not measured because of these differences in entitlement to benefits.[28] Since 1983 men's unemployment rates have been reduced by rule changes that have effectively taken men over 60 years of age out of the unemployment count. However women's unemployment is likely to be even further underestimated in the future because of the switch to benefit claimants as the basis for measuring unemployed; in the past those not claiming benefits could register as unemployed although there were few incentives to do so. The increasing rate of unemployment for women in the mid-1970s was associated with the cutbacks in the public sector in this period, and although there has been a further expansion in the numbers of women employed in the 1980s, many of those taken into part-time employment were not on the unemployment register. In fact the higher rates of unemployment for women in part reflect the increased divisions in the female labour force, as the young and others seeking full-time, permanent employment compete with those willing to take the part-time and even temporary job openings. One of the reasons in general why female unemployment rates can be expected to rise faster than male rates in a recession is the higher share of young people amongst the female unemployed at all times. However this problem of female unemployment in Britain should be put in perspective: the measured rate of unemployment is still lower than that for men in contrast with the majority of OECD countries, as is the unemployment rate for young women compared to that for young men.

As is implied by the trends in unemployment and employment, the participation rate of women workers has continued to rise. A slow-down in the rate of growth of participation in 1977–9 was at the time taken as evidence of a discouraged worker effect and used to depress predictions of participation in the 1979–81 period which subsequently had to be revised upwards substantially as the discouraged worker effect failed to materialize.[29] In fact there is little evidence of a net discouraged worker effect during recessions in Britain; both added and discouraged worker effects appear to be present, although the inadequacies and inconsistencies of the current instruments measuring participation are such that it is impossible to determine the actual size of the active female population or the extent of voluntary or involuntary abstention from economic activity (Joshi and Owen, 1985, 1987).

The pattern of participation by age still maintains the M-shaped or bi-modal pattern, with the peaks coming in early twenties and again in the forties. This aggregate pattern is often interpreted as implying an individual bi-modal pattern with women making one withdrawal from the labour force to have children and then re-entering on a permanent basis at some point when their children are of school-age. More recent evidence on women's life-time patterns of participation shows this to be too simple an interpretation. It is still true that the majority of women leave the labour force to have children but an increasing proportion are working continuously over the family formation phase. Moreover, even those that quit the labour force to have children increasingly do not wait until they have had all their children before returning to work: many in fact re-enter the labour force in between having children (Dex, 1984; Martin and Roberts, 1984). Nevertheless the factor most likely to lead to low participation is the presence of very young children: this factor is in fact much more important than the number of dependent children as Tables 4.11 and 4.12 make clear. These patterns of participation are related to the system of social organization in Britain; on the one hand the lack of state-provided pre-school care for children and the relative weakness of family networks to provide private child care encourages at least short term withdrawal from the labour market. On the other hand, the low level of family income support which the tax and social security system provides, results in women having to find some means of supplementing family income resources, usually through part-time work, whether or not they have a heavy domestic burden because of the presence of several children (see also Dex and Shaw, 1986). We have already seen that this system of participation appears

Table 4.11 Activity rates of married women by number and by age of dependent children 1961–1981

	1961	1966	1971	1981
No child	33.2	41.4	44.7	45.5
1 child	30.1	39.8	42.8	51.9
2 children	23.2	32.9	38.4	49.1
3 children	18.1	27.7	34.8 ⎱	
4 children	14.9	23.8	30.8 ⎰	40.4
5 or more	10.0	19.1	25.7	
Age of youngest child				
0–4	11.5	17.8	19.9	24.9
5–10	23.8	34.0	40.0	54.4[a]
11–15	33.5	46.1	52.2	67.6[a]
16+	31.1	46.5	53.8	67.5[a]

[a] For 1981 the ages are 5–9, 10–15, and 16–18.

Source: Joseph (1983) and Census of Population 1981.

Table 4.12 Activity rates of married women by number of dependent children by age of youngest child 1981

	0–2	3–4	5–9	10–15	16–18
1 child	25.0	36.8	54.5	66.1	67.3
2 children	19.8	33.9	56.0	70.0	70.9
3 or more children	17.8	30.6	50.8	64.4	63.0

Source: Census of Population 1981.

to fit well with employers' current demand for labour which is favouring part-time work and more mature and experienced labour which is nevertheless prepared to work for low wages. There are thus forces at work in both the spheres of social reproduction and production which are reinforcing and extending women's position as a low-paid and unprotected part of the wage labour force. However to interpret current trends as working towards a mutual coincidence of wants between the social and the productive system may be a serious error.[30]

There is considerable evidence from the responses of women themselves to these trends that they are not themselves willing to accept this type of role in the wage labour market. This evidence includes the dramatic fall in women's voluntary turnover rates in the 1970s (Rubery and Tarling, 1982, figure 1) which has been sustained through the 1980s,[31] indicating a preference for stable permanent employment amongst women unless forced to quit; a very fast rate of increase in the number of women acquiring educational, vocational or professional qualifications as a means of securing entry to better jobs in the labour market;[32] the rapid increase in female trade union membership in the 1970s and the slower rate of decline compared to male trade unionists in the 1980s;[33] the struggles by women against the privatization of public sector services and associated casualization of their work (see Walker this volume). Some of these supply-side responses are likely to widen the divides within the female labour force, in particular between the qualified and the non qualified but this is because most women, under current labour market conditions, are not in a position to secure through their own efforts a better place in the labour market. It cannot, however, be presumed that they are necessarily satisfied with their current job opportunities.

4 CONCLUSION

The resumed upward trend in women's employment in the 1980s cannot be taken simply as evidence that women enjoy relative protection from the recession as this employment growth has been strengthened by the restructuring of industrial and labour market organisation that is being induced by economic recession and by associated government labour market policies. Thus women's employment has been protected and expanded not because women are progressively overcoming their relative disadvantage in the labour market, but because of the continued existence of these disadvantages which causes them to be an attractive source of labour supply to employers for particular types of jobs. This provides a relative advantage in finding employment, although not necessarily either secure or adequately-remunerated employment. It is also the case that women are being increasingly forced into competition with other disadvantaged groups in their traditional employment areas, particularly from young people and the long-term unemployed of both sexes. This competition is being precipitated by the government in both cases: in the case of young people the government has pursued a range of policies designed to lower wages for young people and is now taking the under 21s out of scope of minimum wage legislation; and long term unemployed are being subsidized to take jobs at low wages, traditionally only considered by female members of the labour force (see Chapter 8 this volume). Thus women could lose their dubious advantage of being the most important source of disadvantaged labour supply to British employers, but there is not yet strong evidence of men either being prepared to work for women's wages or to participate in part-time employment, and it is these characteristics of women workers that has done most to secure their relative upward trend in employment in recent years.

There is in fact probably little danger that women in general will be displaced from their established positions in the employment structure. Desegregation of feminized occupations has tended to come about through the upgrading of the pay and status of an occupation and not simply through the existence of excess supply in the male labour market. Any adverse trends in the number of women in employment that may develop are therefore more likely to be associated with the rate of job loss in feminized areas than with direct male substitution. Moreover, women themselves are taking positive action to secure their position in the labour market by becoming more stable and continuous participants in the labour force and by actively increasing their levels of qualifications pre and post entry to the labour market. Under current labour market conditions such supply-side responses by women are only likely to improve labour market opportunities for a minority, and may involve stresses on family organization that many women would consider unacceptable. In these circumstances the likely outcome of the opposing forces from the demand and the supply-sides is likely to be increases in the divisions between different types of female labour, with the employment conditions for the majority deteriorating while an increasing minority acquire more of the characteristics and labour market opportunities traditionally reserved for male labour.

NOTES

1 It is impossible to give exact comparative figures for this later period because of the changes introduced in the way unemployment is measured (in particular the change from a registration to a benefit recipient basis) and the expansion of schemes to take especially the young unemployed out of the employment figures.
2 The flexible reserve hypothesis really has two elements: the first that women are disproportionately displaced from employment and the second that they voluntarily withdraw from the labour market in a recession (the discouraged worker effect). We are only testing for the first effect here. The second is discussed in section 3.
3 The data for 1979 and 1980 have been revised in the light of the 1981 Census of Employment results but are only available for the 1980 Standard Industrial Classification. Our data is based on the 1968 SIC and the changeover in classification is also the reason why our data series finishes in 1983. The exception is the data for all industries and services which is available on a continuous series and has therefore been estimated up to 1984.
4 Taking the distribution of the errors for all three periods together, we found that for both the equations with the time trend and for those without over one third of cases had errors of less than 1 percentage point, and over three quarters had errors of less than 3 percentage points. The larger errors were found to apply in the main to the three year period, 1978–81, and not to the single year changes, and implied that there was some systematic under- or over-prediction in a minority of cases.
5 Two sectors, namely coal and petroleum products and shipbuilding, have been omitted from the analysis because the small numbers of women employed in these industries result in data inaccuracies due to rounding errors.

6 In industries where the rate of change in employment has been virtually consistently negative, some of this restructuring process is likely to be captured in the estimate of the β coefficient.

7 We did not investigate the other three industry orders, either because none of the component industries had a significant share of women's employment (mechanical engineering), or because we felt that the linking of the data for the component industries between the 1958 and the 1968 SIC was unsatisfactory (that is for metal goods not elsewhere specified and for instrument engineering).

8 This conclusion is supported by the distribution of the sizes of the β coefficients for industries within industry orders. With the exception of electrical engineering all the industry orders with volatile female employment were composed of industries which in the main had quite small β coefficients. Indeed only food, drink and tobacco and paper and publishing had any coefficients greater than 1.2 (2 industries out of 15 in food, drink and tobacco and 1 out of 2 for paper and publishing), that is excluding those coefficients that were significantly greater than one and thus included in Table 4.3. However there is some evidence of a change in the equation since 1978 for two industries, narrow fabrics, and more importantly, other business services, which had β coefficients significantly greater than 1 for the period 1959–78. The latter industry still has the highest β of the component industries in the insurance, banking and finance sector and probably accounts for the finding of cyclical volatility at the industry order level.

9 Food, drink and tobacco also had a positive significant time trend and a negative constant but the latter was not significant. Nevertheless similar arguments apply.

10 Between 1951 and 1965 the share of part-time in total female employment in manufacturing rose by 3.7% from 12.2 to 15.9% (2.1% of the increase occuring between 1963 and 1965) but by 1978, when the series finished, it had risen by another 4.3% to 20.2%. (British Labour Statistics yearbooks and historical abstract). There appears to have been relatively little increase in part-time working in manufacturing since 1973: using Census of Employment data, the share of part-time working in manufacturing was 22.2% in 1973 and 22.6% in 1986.

11 The share of manufacturing in total employment was quite similar for males and for females in 1951 at 41.9 and 41.1% respectively but by 1981 only 17.3% of women were employed in manufacturing compared to 35.4% of men.

12 We are very grateful to the Institute for Employment Research for making these data available to us.

13 The net change in female employment recorded by the census is considerably less than that recorded by the Census of Employment for the same period, which is based on employer and not household returns. The discrepancy could be related to multiple job-holding as those with more than one job will be included more than once in the Census of Employment data, but there is no reason to presume that women are more involved in multiple job-holding than men. Probably a more likely cause of the discrepancy is a change in the questions relating to economic activity in the 1981 census (Joshi and Owen, 1985) but there is no reason to presume that this problem biases the results on the pattern of distribution of employment.

14 The pattern of change in the 45 industries is, as we already know, much more mixed. 12 out of the 45 registered little change in the female share (<0.5%), while 22 registered an increase and 11 a decline.

15 This finding supports the work done by Hakim (1981) using the labour force sample survey to estimate changes in occupational segregation since 1971. These results showed a tendency first towards reductions in segregation, followed by a reversal of this trend after 1977, consistent with little overall change over the whole decade.

16 The EEC Labour Force Sample Survey for 1983 gives an average of usual hours for part-timers of around 18 hours, that is less than half the 38 hours for women with a full-time job in the survey. Moreover the share of part-timers with very short hours of working appears to be increasing: 23 per cent of women part-timers usually worked between 1 and 10 hours in 1983, compared to the 13% of women part-timers which worked between 1 and 14 hours in 1979. Note, however, that this earlier data only applied to women whose main job was part-time.

17 The 1984 Census of Employment was not published until January 1987; this census revealed that part-time employment had only increased by 77,000 between 1981 and 1984 whereas previous estimates had indicated an increase of 391,000.

18 The share of part-timers in manufacturing has declined slightly and then stabilized since the mid-1970s but our own survey evidence suggests that some firms were eliminating part-time working at the same time as many smaller firms in particular were increasing their use of part-timers (Craig et al., 1985)

19 There is also some evidence of an increase in the use of homeworking as a means to control labour costs and achieve flexibility, in some traditional industries such as clothing (GLC, 1985) and more importantly in non manual occupations and in some parts of high technology industries (Huws, 1984). However the overall importance of homeworking is still considerably smaller than part-time work, even though the terms and conditions for homeworkers are even less advantageous than for part-timers.

20 These systems of vertical segregation have reemerged after the restructuring of payment structures that was associated with the implementation of the Equal Pay Act. The effect of this act was generally to integrate male and female grading structures with minimum rates set equal to the old minimum rate for male employees. However at the same time many of the male jobs which were previously on the bottom grade were regraded upwards (Craig et al., 1980; Snell et al., 1981; Craig et al., 1985).

21 See Chiplin and Sloane (1979) for a study which shows that lower pay within occupations is a more important source of lower earnings for women than concentration in low pay occupations.

22 There have been attempts to disentangle the impact of the Equal Pay Act and the flat rate incomes policies on women's pay (Zabalza and Tzannatos, 1985), but the debate is somewhat artificial as it is probable that without equal pay legislation women would not have received the same flat rate increases as men.

23 The change in relative weights of part-time to full-time employment has resulted in a fall of at least 2 to 3% in female hourly earnings (based on a weighted average of the respective median hourly earnings in 1984) since

1971, even assuming that NES data on hourly earnings for part-timers are not biased upwards.

24 The share of establishments inspected by a visit from the Wages Inspectorate which were found to be underpaying at least one worker rose from 20 per cent or less in the 1960s and early 1970s to around 35 per cent in 1976, and has remained around that level ever since.

25 New proposals exist to increase the minimum hours requirement to 20.

26 Since 1975 women who have worked 2 years with the same employer are entitled to six weeks paid leave and six months unpaid leave. The requirement that women should be offered exactly the same job has now been modified and very small firms have been exempted from the legislation.

27 In 1986 national insurance payments are paid only when a person earns over £38 per week or £195 a month. A woman on average hourly pay for part-timers could therefore work 14.6 hours per week without any obligation on her or her employer's part to pay national insurance.

28 The likelihood of male workers becoming unemployed (measured as the inflow into unemployment over the year divided by employees in employment) has remained remarkably stable, standing at 23% in 1971 and 22% in 1982, while that for women rose from 12 to 17 per cent over the same period. Similarly the average likelihood of leaving unemployment has dropped much more steeply for women, from a rate of 110 to a rate of 15 per month (outflow over year at monthly rates divided by average unemployment rate in year) compared to the fall in the rate from 51 to 10 for men. However most of this fall took place before 1979 so that the fall for women between 1979 and 82 was from 26 to 15 but for men the fall was from 21 to 10. As a result average duration of unemployment for men almost doubled over this period (4.7 to 9.3 months) but for women it rose by just over 60% (from 3.9 to 6.3 months) (Tarling, 1985).

29 Our earlier work on women and recession used these predictions of female participation that were based on behaviour in 1977–79 (Rubery and Tarling, 1982).

30 There is evidence that many part-timers are actively seeking full-time work (Robinson and Wallace, 1984, p. 39), although many full-timers would find it more convenient to work part-time (Martin and Roberts, 1984). The basic point is that working hours are not mainly determined by supply-side preferences, and women cannot choose the working hours that suit them because of the limited availability of jobs and because only certain types of jobs are available on a part-time basis.

31 In June 1982, just after the severe recession of 1980/81, quit rates in manufacturing had fallen to a very low level of 1.3 (those leaving over a 4 week period as a percentage of the numbers employed at the beginning of the period) for both men and women. Since then women's quit rates have increased more than those for men (2.2 for women in June 1985 compared to 1.5 for men) but these rates are still at an historically low level and below those prevailing even in the late 1970s (data on quit rates in manufacturing is published regularly in the *Department of Employment Gazette*).

32 One of the interesting questions which these findings of Crompton and Sanderson (1985) raise is whether or not these strategies to acquire higher qualifications are likely to be associated with continuous working and career paths, or whether they will be used to improve the labour market

opportunities of women with discontinuous working patterns. The authors suggest that both effects are likely.
33 Female trade union membership rose steadily throughout the 1970s from 2.7 million in 1970 to a peak of 3.9 million in 1979 but still stood at around 3.8 million in 1981. In contrast male trade union membership fell from 9.5 to 8.4 million between 1979 and 1981 (Rubery, 1986).

REFERENCES

Beechey, V. and Perkins, T. (1985), 'Conceptualising part-time work', in B. Roberts, R. Finnigan and D. Gallie (eds), *New Approaches to Economic Life*, Manchester, Manchester University Press.
Bruegel, I (1979), 'Women as a reserve army of labour: a note on recent British experience', *Feminist Review*, no. 3.
Chiplin, B. and Sloane, P (1976), *Sex Discrimination in the Labour Market*, London, Macmillan.
Craig, C. and Wilkinson, F. (1985), *Pay and Employment in Four Retail Trades*, research paper no. 51, London, Department of Employment.
Craig, C., Garnsey, E. and Rubery, J (1985), *Payment Structures and Smaller Firms: Women's Employment in Segmented Labour Markets*, research paper no. 48, London, Department of Employment.
Craig, C. Rubery, J. Tarling, R. and Wilkinson, F. (1980), *Abolition and After: the Paper Box Wages Council* research paper no. 12, London, Department of Employment.
Crompton, R. and Sanderson, K. (1986), 'Credentials and careers: some implications of the increase in professional qualifications amongst women', *Sociology*, vol. 20, no. 1.
Deakin, S. (1986), 'Labour law and the developing employment relationship in the UK', *Cambridge Journal of Economics*.
Dex, S. (1984), *Women's Work Histories: an analysis of the Women and Employment Survey*, research paper no. 46, London, Department of Employment.
Dex, S. and Perry, S. M. (1984), 'Women's employment changes in the 1970s', *Employment Gazette* vol. 92, no. 4, April.
Dex, S. and Shaw, L. (1986), *British and American Women at Work*, London, Macmillan.
Edwards, R. Garonna, P. and Todtling, F. (eds) (1986), *Unions in Crisis and Beyond: Perspectives from Six Countries*, Dover, Mass. and London, Auburn House.
Elias, P. (1985), 'Changes in occupational structure, 1971–81', Institute for Employment Research, University of Warwick, mimeo.
Garnsey, E. and Tarling, R. (1982), 'The measurement of the concentration of female employment', paper for Working Party no. 6 on the Role of Women in the Economy, MAS/WP6(82)3, Paris, OECD.
Greater London Council (GLC) (1985), *The London Industrial Strategy*.
Hakim, C (1981), 'Job segregation: trends in the 1970s', *Employment Gazette*, vol. 89, December.
Hakim, C. (1979), *Occupational segregation: a Comparative Study of the Degree and Pattern of the Differentiation between Men and Women's Work in*

Britain, the United States and Other Countries, research paper no. 9, London, Department of Employment.

Huws, U (1984), 'New technology homeworkers', *Employment Gazette*, January.

Joseph, G. (1983), *Women at Work: The British Experience*, Deddington, Oxford, Philip Allan.

Joshi, H. and Owen, S. (1987), *How Long is a Piece of Elastic? The Measurement of Female Activity Rates in British Censuses 1951–1981*, Cambridge Journal of Economics, forthcoming.

Joshi, H. and Owen, S. (1985), '*Does Elastic Retract? The Effects of Recession on Women's Labour Force Participation*', discussion paper no. 64, Centre for Economic Policy Research, London.

Mallier, A. T. and Rosser, M. J. (1980), 'Part-time workers and the economy', *International Journal of Manpower*, vol. 1, no. 2, pp. 1–7.

Martin, J. and Roberts, C. (1984), *Women and Employment: A Lifetime Perspective*, report of the 1980 DE/OPCS Women and Employment Survey, London, HMSO.

McIntosh, A. (1980), 'Women at work: a survey of employers', *Employment Gazette*, November.

Roberts, B., Finnegan, R. and Gallie, D. (eds) (1985), *New Approaches to Economic Life*, Manchester, Manchester University Press.

Robinson, O. and Wallace, J. (1984), 'Growth and utilisation of part-time labour in Great Britain', *Employment Gazette*, September.

Robinson, O. and Wallace, J. (1984), *Part-time Employment and Sex Discrimination Legislation in Great Britain*, research paper no. 43, London, Department of Employment.

Rubery, J. (1986), 'Trade unions in the 1980s: the case of the United Kingdom', in R. Edwards, P. Garonna and F. Todtling (eds) (1986).

Rubery, J. and Tarling, R. (1982), 'Women in the recession', in D. Currie and M. Sawyer (eds), *Socialist Economic Review 1982*, London, Merlin Press.

Snell, M. Glucklich, P. and Povall, M. (1981), *Equal Pay and Opportunities: a Study of the Implementation and Effects of the Equal Pay and Sex Discrimination Acts in 26 Organisations*, research paper no. 20, London, Department of Employment.

Tarling, R. (1985), 'Employment prospects in the 1990s', Department of Applied Economics, University of Cambridge, mimeo.

Zabalza, A. and Tzannatos, Z. (1985), 'The effect of Britain's anti-discriminatory legislation on relative pay and employment', *Economic Journal*, vol. 95, September.

Part Two
Women, the state and the family

Introduction

There are two main sets of issues which the chapters in this part address. The first is the historical interrelationship between the system of social reproduction and production: changes in the family economy and in state support for social reproduction help to shape the pattern of women's participation in the wage economy, but influences flow also in the other direction, with labour market opportunities shaping family organisation. These issues are considered from a longer term historical perspective, emphasizing the specific country systems of family organisation and state and institutional policy, which evolve out of a particular social, political and economic context.

The second set of issues are more concerned with the present, specifically with the influence of changes in state policy and in family organisation on women's involvement in non wage and wage labour. There is some difference of emphasis between the four chapters, with the Italian chapter concentrating on the first set of issues, and the US and British chapters on the latter, with the French chapter addressing both. These differences are related to the salience of the issues for the four countries: in Italy the main concern is to explain the lower levels of participation of women, and the late change from a declining to increasing participation rate, compared to other advanced countries. This explanation requires an understanding of the interrelationships between the production and social reproduction spheres over the long period. Moreover, in contrast to the US and Britain, there have been no recent sharp changes in state policy of particular relevance to women. Indeed, as it is argued in the chapter, recent changes, for example in women's participation, find their origin in much earlier changes in the family economy which did not immediately feed through to the wage economy because of restricted demand for female labour. France, provides a further contrast for even though it has maintained a basic policy stance of regulating the conditions under which women work, through protection of minimum wages and through strengthening of discrimination legislation, it has adopted social security and tax policies which encourage women to stay at home. In the British and US cases, state policy also appears to have contradictory implications for women, albeit of a different nature from those in France. While encouraging or forcing the family, and therefore women, to take on a higher share of caring work as a consequence of cutbacks in social welfare, both governments have stimulated both the demand and the supply of low paid female labour though their labour market and social security policy. These policies, instead of transforming the 'floating reserve' of female labour into a 'latent' reserve again, have tended to intensify the utilisation of female labour both in and out of the labour market.

Studies concerned with the interrelationship between production and social reproduction run a dual risk of either over emphasizing the 'functionalism' of the country's system of social reproduction, which is identified as responding smoothly to the requirements of the productive sphere, or of over emphasizing the cultural and historical peculiarities of the system of social reproduction, which is then identified as entirely independent of the productive sphere. A more appropriate method-ology, as we have argued elsewhere (Humphries and Rubery, 1984), is to view social reproduction and production as *relatively autonomous*: that is, changes in one sphere will influence the other, but the impact will not necessarily be smooth or predictable, and will certainly be historically specific. It is this type of methodological approach that can be found in all four chapters,[1] and this empirical evidence lends support to the relative autonomy hypothesis in four separate respects.

In the first place, the diversity of systems of social reproduction revealed by the four studies demonstrates the non-functionalist and non-reductionist nature of family and social organisation. No sys-tematic relationship could be identified between the type of social reproduction system and either the participation rate of women or the level of development of the wage economy. The US scored the highest on the latter two points, and had also experienced the fastest rate of change in family organisation away from the standard nuclear family model, but it also had the lowest level of state support for social reproduction. Moreover, ideological and political support for the family is not only strong in systems such as the Italian one, with its extended family networks and reliance on income sharing as a means of social support, but also in a system with a well developed social security system such as France, where state income support for the family is used as an alternative means for bolstering and strengthening traditional family forms.

The second way in which the studies support the relative autonomy approach is in the emphasis placed on the non reversibility of changes in the family economy induced during the expansion phase of the post-second world war economies. Italy provides a particularly interesting example of the non-reversibility hypothesis, for in this country the expansion phase in the wage economy failed to materialize, at least for women, but changes in the family economy were nevertheless taking place, encouraging women to participate in the labour market as they were released from domestic labour through the expansion of the welfare state, and forced into greater reliance on wage income as the children became less a source of support and more a financial burden on the family. These changes have led eventually, after a lag caused by lack of demand, into much higher participation rates for women, a trend which has not been suppressed by the channelling of a large share of this participation into unemployment.

The other three chapters also point to the non-reversibility of changes in the family economy: tax and social security policies in France to encourage women to have larger families and to stay at home are unlikely to have much effect both because they cannot compensate for the loss of the women's earnings, and because of changes in attitudes to work and to the family. The chapters on the US and Britain point to the difficulties that their respective governments have faced in cutting back state social welfare support. It is, of course, the case that many women have been forced, through lack of alternatives, to take on extra caring burdens, but these have not necessarily resulted in a change in labour market participation of women. More importantly, there is a limit to the extent that the state can force the burden of care back on the family because of the increasing instability of families which means that there are more individuals without access to family support. This evidence of non-reversibility can also be interpreted as evidence of a relatively independent dynamic in the structure of social reproduction. Such a dynamic makes responses to state policy difficult to predict: for example in the US the change in welfare organisation could have been expected to reduce women's participation as the reward to working was reduced. The opposite appears to have happened as women work longer hours to escape the poverty trap of welfare. This response may be related to simple work ethic values, but women's increased involvement and integration into the wage economy system may make them more reluctant to become a permanent 'welfare class'.

The existence of contradictions within state policy, and between state policy and family organisations, is pointed to in all chapters, and further supports a 'non functionalist' methodological approach. The conflicts between state policy and family organisation arise from a much slower adjustment in the basic model of the family underlying state policy than exists in reality: governments in all four countries persist in adopting policies based on the assumption that most families have a male bread-winner and a dependent wife. These stereotypes may in part be respon-sible for governments applying inappropriate policies in the field of social reproduction which are ineffective or result in unintended out-comes. However there is also evidence of conflicting objectives within the state. Examples of these contradictions have been outlined above for France, US and the UK. There is, in fact, no real problem in interpreting and understanding these contradictions, if first it is recog-nised that there is no monolithic state, with one set of objectives, and secondly that women are affected by state policy in all areas and activities, and the implications of policy across the whole spectrum for each gender are not necessarily identified, let alone used as a basis for policy formulation. Some policies clearly have specific gender, and indeed 'patriarchal' objectives in mind but the objectives of all policies cannot necessarily always be interpreted from that perspective. The French government's policy decision to include anti-discrimination legislation in its strengthening of labour market control may have been more related to its general political stance on labour market control, while its policy to support women who stayed at home to look after their third child relates to a historical concern with supporting the family and population growth; the two policies do not form part of a fully developed coherent policy to reduce participation.

The fourth theme that emerges from this section to lend support to the 'relative autonomy' perspective is the importance of collective over individualised responses on the part of women if the general position of women in the economy and society is to be improved. These conclusions fit with the view that women's position in the economy is not related to their individual characteristics as workers but to their characteristics as women. Without institutional or collective action to change the ways in which women's work is assessed and rewarded, the majority of women will be confined to low paid employment. These trends are most clearly seen in the US where there has been little improvement in the average pay of women relative to men, despite the rise in participation rates. There is instead a trend towards increasing divergence amongst women as a growing minority obtain access to higher status jobs and professions through education, with little benefit, if at all, for the mass of women still left in undervalued work. In France there is a tendency for the movement to shorter work hours to be used as a means of individualising women's hours, compared to collective agreements on shorter working hours and work sharing in male-dominated firms. The former is a means of deregulating the labour market whereas the latter acts to strengthen solidarity and trade union control. In Britain women's access to collective control is being reduced by the privatisation of much of women's work in the public sector. Italy however provides the best example of the continual tensions that arise out of the benefits and costs of collective control. State and trade union control of the labour market has provided women within the labour market with much greater job security and pay than in other countries, but confines those excluded to participation in the informal sector and to higher levels of domestic labour. There are thus complementarities as well as conflicts between the objectives of protecting and regulating the labour market in the interests of the working class *in general*, and the interests of women in particular. Conflicts arise partly out of the fact that organisation for control takes place in the labour market and tends to act to the detriment of those outside, as well as from the fact that the controlling institutions are dominated by men. Complementarities arise because of the extreme vulnerability of women in the labour market without strong forms of regulation. Moreover, without a commitment to advancement for women through protection and regulation, any potential complementarity between class and gender political action may disappear. If the focus of the latter switches towards the pursuit of competition within an increasingly deregulated system, only the most advantaged from both sexes are likely to benefit.

NOTE

1 These chapters illustrate the type of methodological approach supported by Humphries and Rubery (1984) but the other contributors to the volume cannot be assumed to endorse all the aspects of the relative autonomy approach outlined in the above article.

REFERENCE

Humphries, J. and Rubery, J. (1984), 'The reconstitution of the supply side of the labour market: the relative autonomy of social reproduction', *Cambridge Journal of Economics*, vol. 8, no. 4.

5 Women, the state and the family in the US: Reaganomics and the experience of women

Marilyn Power

Reaganomics is the term used to describe a broad array of policies advocated by the Reagan administration which have the goal of restructuring the United States economy. These policies (which have had varying degrees of success) are intended to 'discipline' labour, redistribute income toward high income individuals and capital, reduce the government deficit, and return many government services and functions to the 'free' market.

Women have been hit directly and disproportionately by the policies of Reaganomics. To understand the impact of Reaganomics on women, and the implications for political activity by women, however, we must remain aware of class and race differences among women. For the purposes of this discussion, women will be divided into three groupings: first, a group of marginalized women in poverty; second, the majority of women workers, who are located in clerical, service, and (to a lesser extent) blue collar occupations; and third, women in professional and managerial occupations, a small number of whom have 'made it' into high status, high income positions. In addition, we must remember that women engage in two types of labour: wage labour and domestic labour. The policies of the Reagan administration have impact on both these areas.

This paper investigates the effects of Reaganomics on women in the United States. We will begin with an overview of women's economic position at present. Next, we will examine the effects of Reagan's cuts in social services, and particularly welfare, on poor women. This section will also examine whether these cuts can be understood as a means of improving the efficacy of the use of poor women as a reserve army of labour. The third section will detail the weakening of enforcement of anti-discrimination and affirmative action rules, particularly with respect to women in the (broadly defined) working class. Fourth, we will discuss the impact of Reaganomics on women's nonwage labour, emphasizing the administration's efforts to 'privatize' social services. Finally, we will speculate about future trends for women in the United States; the effects of some form of economic 'recovery' on women; and the possibilities for growing division and for growing unity among women workers.

In carrying out this discussion, it is important to distinguish the

Reagan administration from the New Right which has emerged as a political force in the United States in the past decade. Reagan has often expressed his sympathy for New Right policies, and we have little reason to doubt his sincerity on this point. Nevertheless, the Reagan administration has made economic restructuring and the re-establishment of United States military and political dominance in the world its priorities. Many of the (deeply sexist) social policies that are the heart of the New Right programme, as a result, have been downplayed by the Administration, much to the dissatisfaction of the neo-conservatives.

Reagan had little choice but to put economic restructuring first. Not only his corporate support, but also his support from the public in general was predicated on his ability to produce an economic recovery. The Reagan administration's attack on women, then, must be understood not only as a reflection of New Right anti-feminism, but more immediately as a part of the Administration's strategy to confront economic crisis.

1 Women in the United States economy

Historically, the expansion of capitalist production in the United States has progressively incorporated women into wage labour. This process has been quite gradual, however, at least until the last half century. In the nineteenth century, only unmarried women commonly performed wage labour, although desperately poor married women and widows did work for wages. Not coincidentally, wage work was more common for black married women than white, but it was not prevalent for either group. There were strong ideological sanctions against work outside the home for married women, and the high birth rate and lack of household amenities meant that domestic labour could in any event absorb most of their waking hours. But additionally, married women were not forced into wage labour because their domestic work included home production which contributed directly to the support of their families (see Power, 1983).[1] The expanding capitalist sector gradually limited women's ability to engage in production for use and exchange in the home and by the early twentieth century, few married women were able to contribute substantially to their families' support through home production. Also at this time, capitalist expansion generated a rapid increase in demand for clerical and service workers. And, concurrently, labour force participation rates among married women began gradually to rise.

Thus we can understand the entrance of married women into the labour force in the twentieth century as the extension of their historic role of support for their families into a new sphere, as their old sphere of home production was progressively eliminated.[2] This movement of married women into wage labour was, of course, not instantaneous, and has, in fact, followed a varying pattern over time.

In the early twentieth century, married women tended to leave the labour force with the birth of the first child, and perform exclusively domestic labour for the rest of their lives. Beginning after World War II, this pattern began to change, as married women began to reenter the labour force in middle age.[3] Women's labour force participation by age took on an 'M' shape, with two peaks and a substantial dip in between. During the 1950s through 1970s, this pattern of labour force participation changed in two important ways. First, there was a general rise in participation by women at *every* age level. And, second, the middle of the 'M' gradually began to disappear, as participation became more evenly spread over age levels. By 1980, the 'M' shape was completely gone, as women's labour force participation remained virtually uniform (and uniformly high) across all the prime working years (see Table 5.1).

As these figures suggest, women are less and less likely to remain out of the labour force when their children are small.[4] Labour force participation among married women, husbands present, with pre-school children (i.e. under 6 years old) climbed from 18.6% in 1960 to 47.8% in 1984 (see Table 5.2). Women with pre-school children and no husband present (a growing proportion of households) had a rate of 54.0% in 1984.

It is clear that women's labour force participation has grown extremely rapidly over the past several decades. From 1972 to 1982, for example, women accounted for nearly 62% of the increase in the labour force. In addition, women are remaining in the labour force for longer periods of time, and are far less likely to drop out even when their children are small. If we understand these trends in the context of the absorption of home production into the capitalist sector, we can see that the entrance of married women into wage labour is neither aberrant nor reversible. Women cannot return in any numbers to full time domestic labour, not because there is not work to do in the home (housework still takes a considerable amount of time), but because that work does not contribute to the support of the woman and her family.

Women's wage earnings have become increasingly important in maintaining the family's standard of living, particularly with the chronic stagflation that began in the 1970s. Money wages failed to keep pace with the rate of inflation, with the result that real wages declined over the period. While real wages fell, however, median family income remained relatively stable over the decade, largely because of the increased participation in wage labour by married women. Thus women's earnings have become necessary to keep family income from falling, although they have not prevented it from stagnating. Women's

Table 5.1 Women's labour force participation rates by age, 1950–85

Age	1950	1960	1970	1980	1985
Total, 16 & over	33.9	37.7	43.3	51.6	54.5
16 and 17	30.1	29.1	34.9	43.8	42.1
18 and 19	51.3	50.9	53.6	62.1	61.7
20 to 24	46.0	46.1	57.7	69.0	71.8
25 to 34	34.0	36.0	45.0	65.4	70.9
35 to 44	39.1	43.4	51.1	65.5	71.8
45 to 54	37.9	49.8	54.4	59.9	64.4
55 to 64	27.0	37.2	43.0	41.5	42.0
65 and over	9.0	10.8	9.7	8.1	7.3

Source: US Department of Labor 1980, p. 4; 1982, p. 152; 1986, p. 154.

Table 5.2 Labour force participation rates for married women, husband present, with children under 18 years

Year	Total	With children aged 6 to 17 years	With children under 6 years
1950	18.4	28.3	11.9
1955	24.0	34.7	16.2
1960	27.6	39.0	18.6
1965	32.2	42.7	23.3
1970	39.7	49.2	30.3
1975	44.9	52.3	36.6
1980	54.1	61.7	45.1
1984	58.8	65.4	47.8

Source: US Department of Labor, 1980, p. 27; 1984.

earnings are particularly important for families in low to middle income brackets and, of course, for families maintained solely by women (see Table 5.3).

While women have become part of the permanent wage labour force, the majority of women workers continue to be segregated into traditional women's occupations, which are characterized by low pay and limited opportunities for advancement. At the same time, women's participation in elite, traditionally male professional and managerial positions has expanded extremely rapidly over the past decade, allowing a small number of women virtually unprecedented access to income, power, and prestige. For example, between 1972 and 1982, women were one-fourth of new physicians and lawyers, one-third of new computer specialists, and two-thirds of new accountants (see Table 5.4). And, at the opposite end of the economic hierarchy, poverty among women has risen, particularly as a growing number of women find themselves raising children alone without adequate employment opportunities or adequate social services.

By 1981, while 15% of all families were maintained by women, 49%

Table 5.3 Earnings of married women, husband present, and of women maintaining families, as percent of family income, 1978

Married women, husband present, wife worked 50 to 52 weeks full-time: family income	*Median percent of family income earned by wife*
Under $10,000	63.6
$10,000 to 14,999	49.8
$15,000 to 19,999	42.3
$20,000 to 24,999	38.6
$25,000 and over	33.4

Median family income in 1978: $25,346

Women with earnings maintaining families, householder worked 50 to 52 weeks full-time, family income	*Median percent of family income earned by wife*
Under $5,000	85.1
$5,000 to 9,999	84.1
$10,000 to 14,999	79.5
$15,000 and over	61.6

Median family income in 1978: $13,219

Source: US Department of Labor 1980, p. 57.

Table 5.4 Entrance of women into traditionally male professional and managerial positions, 1972–82

	Change in Employment 72–82 (thous)	*% Change*	*women as % of workers 1972*	*women as % of workers 1982*	*change women/ change workers*
Occupation					
All occupations	17,824	21.8	38.0	43.5	68.7
Professional and Technical	5,492	47.9	39.3	45.1	57.2
Computer specialists	478	175.1	16.8	28.5	35.2
Engineers	472	42.8	0.8	5.7	17.1
Lawyers and judges	310	96.9	3.8	15.4	27.3
Physicians	158	48.2	10.1	14.8	24.5
Managers and Administrators	3,462	43.1	17.6	28.0	52.1
Bank officials	304	71.2	19.0	37.1	52.1
Accountants	479	67.1	21.7	38.6	63.8

Source: US Department of Labor 1973; 1983.

of all family members who lived in poverty were in families with a female householder. Among black families the percentage maintained by a woman alone rose particularly rapidly, from 28.3% in 1970 to 41.7% in 1981; by 1981, nearly two-thirds of all poor black family members were in families with a female householder (see Tables 5.5 and 5.6).

Table 5.5 Number and percent of family members below poverty line who lived in families with a female householder, no spouse present, by race, selected years 1959–81

Female householder all races	Number (thousands) below poverty*	Percent of all poor family members
1981	15,738	49.4
1980	14,649	50.0
1975	12,268	47.4
1970	11,154	40.9
1959	10,390	26.3
Female householder, white	*Number (thousands) below poverty**	*Percent of all white poor family members*
1981	9,347	43.4
1980	8,569	43.5
1975	7,324	41.2
1970	6,832	39.0
1959	7,115	25.0
Female householder, black	*Number (thousands) below poverty**	*Percent of all black poor family members*
1981	6,081	66.3
1980	5,807	67.7
1975	4,784	63.4
1970	4,213	56.5
1959	2,906	29.3

* Includes female unrelated individuals.
Source: US Department of Commerce, pp. 7–8.

Table 5.6 Percent of families with female householder (no spouse present) by race, selected years 1970–81

Per cent of families with female householder	1970	1975	1980	1981
White	9.0	10.5	11.6	11.9
Black	28.3	35.3	40.3	41.7

Source: US Bureau of the Census 1982–83, pp. 43, 51.

Thus, while the majority of women workers remained mired in traditionally female occupations, there was a developing polarization between a newly-emerging female elite and an expanding (though not new) group of marginalized women on the bottom of the economic scale. This polarization is racial as well, as women entering the elite occupations are disproportionately white, while women (and men) in poverty are disproportionately black.

2 Reaganomics and poor women

Ronald Reagan pledged during his 1980 election campaign to enact sharp cuts in the federal budget (with the exception of military spending, which he promised to increase), and he began his budget cutting immediately upon taking office. The deepest cuts to social services came in the Omnibus Budget Reconciliation Act for fiscal year 1982, which took effect in October 1981. Sixty per cent of the cuts in federal entitlement (income transfer) programmes in that budget came from programmes for the poor. Aid to Families with Dependent Children (AFDC) was cut by approximately $1 billion, Medicaid (medical aid for the poor) was cut by an estimated $800 million, and food stamps by $700 million – around 875,000 people were entirely eliminated from the food stamps programmes (*New York Times*, 21 September 1981). All of the Reagan administration's subsequent budgets proposed additional cuts in programmes for the poor; however, the further reductions were more modest, due in large part to Congressional resistance.

Women, especially nonwhite women, bear the brunt of these cuts in social spending because, as we have seen, they are disproportionately represented among the poor. The Reagan administration claimed that its budget cuts have not removed the 'safety net' of support for the 'truly needy', but for many poor women and their children, basic survival is now in question.

To understand the justification behind the Reagan cuts to poor women, and their possible effects, we will focus specifically on AFDC. AFDC was established initially during the Depression, as part of the 1935 Social Security Act. It was expected at the time that the recipients of AFDC would be mostly widows with small children – a group whom public sentiment viewed with sympathy as deserving of aid. This conception of AFDC continued until the 1960s – in fact, it wasn't until 1962 that families with a father present could be eligible for aid (and then only if he were unemployed or disabled).

But while the conception of the ideal AFDC recipient remained the same, the actual profile of families on AFDC changed sharply, as increasing numbers of divorced, separated, and single mothers joined the welfare rolls. While in 1949 42% of the fathers of AFDC children were dead, by 1963 this proportion had declined to 6%, and by 1979 to 2%. In 1979 nearly 38% of children on AFDC had unmarried parents (Lynn, 1977, p. 73 and US Bureau of the Census 1982–83, p. 343). At the same time, AFDC families were becoming increasingly urban and increasingly black.

The number of AFDC recipients grew extremely rapidly over the 1960s, and somewhat more slowly over the 1970s: in 1960 there were 3 million AFDC recipients; in 1970 9.5 million; and in 1980 11 million (US Bureau of the Census 1982–3, p. 340). This growth was largely the result of the increase in families with female householders, but also (especially during the 1960s) of an increased awareness of the availability of aid among the poor. During the 1970s AFDC payments failed to keep pace with the rate of inflation, so that average monthly payments in real terms had fallen sharply even before the Reagan cuts.[5]

The combination of the growth in the number of AFDC recipients and the changing profile of AFDC families has resulted in considerable public outcry against the programme. The image of the deserving (white) widow has been replaced by the stereotype of the immoral, lazy (black) welfare 'cheat'. Thus, the Reagan administration was on fairly safe political ground in calling for cuts in programmes for poor women and their children. This is especially true as poor women themselves are not politically organized and have little political bargaining power.

The sentiment for cutting AFDC and other income support programmes for poor women has been given further impetus by the so-called 'pro-family' arguments of the New Right. The New Right opposes AFDC because it allows women the option of living separately from men (albeit at a miserably low standard), encouraging women to leave marriages or to refuse to enter marriages in the first place.[6] Additionally, according to New Right author George Gilder, AFDC encourages *men* to break up their marriages: by 'making optional the male provider role'. AFDC demoralizes low income men; they become unmanned, 'cuckolded by the compassionate state' (Gilder, 1981, pp. 140, 148) and are likely to leave their families. Once the man has left, the family is doomed to poverty, since women are inevitably low income earners (due to their instinctual preoccupation with maternity, not because of discrimination). Thus, by allowing women to live separately from men, programs such as AFDC actually *cause* poverty.

Although the Reagan administration would never have openly articulated such controversial views themselves, the New Right ideology provided them with useful support for their social service cuts. It follows from Gilder's argument that welfare cannot play the role envisioned for it by liberals, of easing and aiding the transition out of poverty. Rather, it should be minimal, difficult to attain, for emergencies only. The Reagan administration clearly adheres to this view of welfare. Hence the 'safety net' metaphor: AFDC should be a 'temporary safety net for individuals who have no other means of support', according to Linda McMahon, family assistance chief in the Department of Health and Human Services (*Wall Street Journal*, 21 October 1981).

This view of welfare as a temporary safety net helps explain the focus of the cuts in AFDC: virtually all of the reductions came in aid to women who worked, but who earned so little that they were entitled to supplemental AFDC. Until 1967, any dollar earned from working resulted in a dollar decrease in AFDC payments. However, in that year, in an attempt to encourage poor women to enter wage labour, the '30 and one-third' rule was implemented. This rule allowed a woman to disregard the first $30 per month plus one-third of her remaining monthly earnings when her AFDC benefits were calculated, up to a cut-off level of income determined by each state.[7] The 1981 budget cuts eliminated the 30 and one-third disregard after four months on welfare. Additionally, maximum income for eligibility for AFDC was set at 150% of the state need standard;[8] deductions for work-related expenses and child care were limited as well.

These changes in the AFDC rules removed an estimated 400,000 families with working parents from the AFDC rolls, and cut benefits for approximately 260,000 more.[9] The AFDC cuts not only eliminated the income incentive to work, but, when combined with cuts in food stamp payments and Medicaid, actually seemed to provide a *disincentive* to wage labour. According to estimates by the Center for the Study of Social Policy, in eleven states the 1982 cuts resulted in a situation in which an AFDC family with three members and average earnings actually had *less* disposable income than a comparable family without a working parent; in eleven more the return to working became $10 or less per month. In contrast, in 1981, before the cuts, the *lowest* return to working for such a family was $79 a month (Joe, 1982, p. 15).

In order to evaluate the impact of these cuts, it is important to confront the popular misconception that there are two groups of poor: the working poor and a 'welfare class' of permanently nonworking poor. A number of studies have examined the work and welfare experience of women on AFDC, and they clearly illustrate the falsity of this assumption. At a given point in time, approximately 16% of the women receiving AFDC are working (Joe, 1982, p. 13). Over the course of a year, however, about *half* are employed; over a five-year period, 92% of the AFDC households in Harrison's study had a working member at least part of the time (AuClaire, 1979 and Harrison, 1979, p. 3). Rein and Rainwater used longitudinal data to attempt to measure the existence of a 'welfare class' (which they defined as being on welfare for 9–10 years out of a 10 year period, with welfare accounting for more than half of family income over that period). They estimated that only 9% of the families receiving some welfare during the 10 years would fit this description; the rest spent less time (usually considerably less) on welfare and received an average of only one-third of family income from welfare *during* the years they were on welfare (Rein and Rainwater, 1978, pp. 524–5). In short, the vast majority of women on welfare work for pay. The problem is that they can only find jobs that are temporary and/or extremely poorly paid. Many 'cycle' between periods of total self-support, periods where they require supplementary welfare, and periods of full dependence on welfare, depending on such factors as the state of the economy, the seasonality of jobs, and their own and their children's health. This is an important factor, since loss of AFDC frequently also means loss of the Medicaid card – and one family illness can mean economic disaster for a marginally-employed single mother. Many critics have pointed out the disincentives to work built into these cuts in AFDC. The Administration responded that positive incentives had not worked; what was needed was negative incentives (coercion). They therefore proposed to eliminate AFDC benefits for any parent who 'voluntarily' reduced earnings or quit a job. (Children, however, would still receive benefits, Joe, 1982, p. 23). In addition, the Administration proposed a mandatory 'workfare' programme, in which AFDC recipients who did not hold paying jobs would be required to work part time without pay for government or non-profit agencies. The stated justification for such a programme was that it would provide valuable work experience.[10] The most basic purpose of workfare, however, was to coerce women to enter the labour force. According to a Reagan administration spokesperson, the prospect of having to work without pay would provide incentive to seek paid work (*New York Times*, 29 March 1981). Thus far Congress has refused to make workfare mandatory for the country as a whole; several states, however, have made it mandatory.

This issue of incentives requires closer examination. As usually presented, it is based on orthodox (neoclassical) economic assumptions about human behaviour: that human beings act continuously to maximize their self-interest through rational, informed cost/benefit calculations. Thus women on welfare are seen as calculating the 'tradeoff' costs of work versus welfare, and choosing the mix of the two which exactly maximizes their well-being. Given such a view, it is evident that raising the cost of working (by cutting welfare payments to working women) will inevitably cause women to choose more welfare and less work.

There is, however, ample evidence that these 'rational' calculations are not the only factors determining the work effort of poor women. Poor women continuously express a desire to get off welfare, which they find distasteful and humiliating, and to lift themselves and their families out of poverty through paid work (see Chrissinger, 1980 and Stack, 1975). The damage done by the budget cuts is less to their psychological orientation toward work than to their material conditions. By combining what paid work she could find with welfare and other sources, a woman had the possibility of raising her family above the most abject level of poverty, if not to anything resembling comfort or security. Further, she could *sometimes* parlay the job experience into a path out of poverty, despite the limited job possibilities and lack of child care. The budget cuts destroyed both these opportunities for many women. They sharply reduced their standard of living for working AFDC women and their families, and they may also make it impossible for many women to continue working at all. Working costs money, both for work-related expenses and day care; the Reagan cuts sharply limit the income disregards for both these costs. In addition, there are costs of working which cannot be deducted at all (substitutes for women's work in the home such as laundry services and prepared foods, possibly clothing expenses necessary to retaining a job, etc.). Women who have had their supplemental welfare cut may find these expenses outweigh the return to working. Women who have lost *all* their AFDC and their Medicaid may find themselves quickly on the brink of economic disaster. As a result, some women who currently work may be forced into full dependence on welfare – they may literally not be able to work. On the other hand, given their strong desire to work their ways off welfare, women may respond to the cuts by desperately increasing their work effort.[11]

Arguments can be made, then, that the cuts in AFDC to working women could either increase *or* decrease their work effort. It would seem that this question could be the subject of empirical investigation. It is difficult, however, to obtain conclusive information on the behaviour of women whose welfare payments were cut or terminated. The problem basically lies with a lack of systematically collected data. Information on AFDC case loads is collected on a state-by-state basis, using widely differing methods, and producing different levels of detail and accuracy. The Center for the Study of Social Policy attempted to trace the effects of the budget cuts on AFDC families in ten states, and concluded that the variability of the data made definitive statements impossible. To measure the work disincentive effects of the AFDC cuts, the Center collected information on the proportion of terminated recipients who later returned to the rolls. They found that state estimates varied from a low of around 10% to estimates of 30–40%. The Center commented, 'Because these estimates vary so greatly from state to state, the (budget cut) data can be said to have provided "something for everyone" ' (Center for the Study of Social Policy, 1983, p. 41).[12] Of course, even if accurate data on returnees were available, it would not explain *why* the women returned to the AFDC rolls: did they voluntarily quit work to get back on AFDC or Medicaid, or were they forced out of wage labour by illness or by termination (especially likely because of the deep recession in 1981–2)?

The Center for the Study of Social Policy (1984) participated in an in-depth study of women in Georgia, Michigan, and New York City who were terminated from AFDC because of the Reagan cuts. The women were interviewed twelve to eighteen months after they had lost their welfare benefits, to determine the effects on their families' welfare and on their work behaviour. Although the population of the three study areas varied greatly (for example, Georgia's sample was 80% black and 37% rural; New York City's was 40% black and, of course, 100% urban), their work behaviour was similar in a number of important ways. All three samples showed a strong attachment to the labour force: a majority in each area had worked at least 21 of the 27 months prior to the interview. The majority in each area worked full time (defined as at least 35 hours per week), and virtually all were employed as service or clerical workers. Even though most of the women worked full time, half of those in New York and two-thirds in Georgia and Michigan wanted to work more hours. Clearly, incentive to work was not a problem for these women; the problem was the low wages they received from low-skilled, traditionally female occupations.

Their termination from AFDC greatly increased poverty among these women and their children. One-third of the Georgia sample, and one-half of the Michigan and New York samples reported having run out of food at least once since losing their welfare benefits, and large numbers in each area could not afford medical care for themselves or their children (less than half the women received medical insurance through their jobs). Unpaid bills piled up, and a majority of the women reported that they became ill, anxious, or depressed as a result of their termination from AFDC.

Although many of the women reapplied for welfare benefits, there is no evidence that any substantial number quit working in order to regain their AFDC. On the contrary, 12% of the Georgia sample and 16% of the Michigan sample either increased their working hours on their job or took on an additional job in the period since losing their AFDC (there is no comparable data for New York City). Since a majority of the women in the three areas expressed a desire to work longer hours, it is likely that the percentage increasing their work effort would be higher if more work were available.

This study confirms what more general observation of the behaviour of women on welfare would lead us to expect: given the extremely low level of support offered by AFDC, and the strong preference for work evidenced by women on welfare, these decreases in AFDC payments seem more likely to *increase* than to decrease the work effort of many poor women. To the extent that this is true, the Reagan cuts will increase the effectiveness of the use of poor women as a reserve army of labour.

Women on welfare constitute an important element of the reserve army of labour, and serve the classic roles of the reserve: responding to cyclical and secular changes in the society's need for labour, and acting to depress wages for the 'regularly' employed. When incomes of this poorest group of workers are decreased, it becomes more possible to decrease earnings for other groups of workers. Welfare, or part-time work plus welfare, becomes a less viable alternative to work at the minimum wage; and women forced off welfare will be competing with others (mostly other women) for low-wage, low-skilled work. Historically, skilled and unionized workers have struggled with some success to insulate their wages from those of lower skilled workers. But the employers' historic response of mechanizing, deskilling, and otherwise eliminating union jobs means that eventually the entire wage structure can be affected by depressing wages at the bottom.

Clearly men as well as women are found in the reserve army of labour, and nonwhite people of both sexes are disproportionately represented in this category. Poor women, both white and nonwhite, may be a particularly important surplus labour pool, however, because two of the occupational categories which have been growing fastest in the past decade, clerical and non-domestic service work, are heavily female, and because women accounted for the majority of the increase in total employment.

3 Changes in federal equal opportunity programmes

The Reagan administration acted quickly after taking office to weaken federal commitment to enforcing equal opportunity for women in the labour force. Their actions in this area are consistent with the conservative belief in non-interference in the 'free' market for labour, and in minimizing government regulation of the private sector. It would have been very difficult for the Administration to actually dismantle the equal opportunity apparatus; instead, they have severely marred its effectiveness through cuts in funds, rule changes, and through bringing Justice Department lawyers into litigations in *opposition* to certain civil rights rulings.

The Administration's actions on affirmative action have perhaps been the most significant in terms of their effect on women's employment opportunities. The federal government's affirmative action policy is administered by the Office of Federal Contract Compliance (OFCC) of the Department of Labor, according to guidelines set by the Department. Companies must conform to these affirmative action guidelines in order to qualify for federal contracts. Because federal contracts are so lucrative, and because the OFCC has reviewed companies' *past* hiring practices before awarding federal contracts, the affirmative action guidelines are a potentially powerful tool for reversing past discrimination both in firms with federal contracts and firms hoping for future federal contracts.

The Reagan Administration has been an active opponent of affirmative action from the time Reagan took office. In August 1981, the Labor Department announced a proposed new set of rules for federal contractors which would drastically weaken the affirmative action guidelines. The proposal met with considerable protest, however, and was not implemented. A second attempt to weaken the guidelines in the autumn of 1985 has been similarly unsuccessful to date. Accordingly, the Administration has tried a new strategy of using the Justice Department to attack affirmative action, specifically the use of quotas for the hiring of minorities and women. This use of the Justice Department is extremely ironic: in past administrations over the last fifteen years, the Justice Department has filed lawsuits against municipalities and states for discrimination, resulting in consent decrees which established racial and sexual goals for the hiring of public employees (for example, police and firefighters). It is precisely these consent decrees that the *current* Justice Department is challenging in at least 47 cases. In addition, the Department has been actively supporting appeals by white men claiming reverse discrimination: appeals against past Justice Department rulings. It is apparent that the Reagan Administration hopes to have affirmative action goals and timetables (which are the heart of the effective affirmative action policy) ruled illegal by the courts. In this way Reagan can avoid the direct blame for dismantling affirmative action. However, in June and July 1986, the Supreme Court dealt the Justice Department a major defeat by upholding the use of goals and timetables in hiring and promotion. Despite this ruling, the Reagan Administration's attack on the affirmative action guidelines, coupled with a sharp reduction in the OFCC's budget, gives employers the clear message that affirmative action is a low priority for the Regan Administration, and can be effectively ignored.

It is impossible to measure the exact effects of this change in policy but it is clear that the affirmative action rules have in the past been extremely effective in promoting the hiring of women and minorities by federal contractors. A study by the Labor Department (which the Reagan administration refused to make public) found that companies subject to affirmative action requirements between 1974 and 1980 hired substantially more women and minorities than firms not covered by the rules. Affirmative action also changed the structure of employment for these groups, allowing significantly more women and minorities to move into managerial positions, and also to move from service and low-skilled blue collar positions into skilled production, craft, and white collar jobs (*Washington Post,* 20 June 1983 and *New York Times,* 19 June 1983).

For young working-class women, the ability to move into the skilled crafts which had been traditionally closed to them was probably the most significant effect of affirmative action. And it is probably precisely in this area that the de facto weakening of affirmative action has been most strongly felt. Mechanization and recession have in any case led to declines in the skilled trades, and employer resentment about having to find and train women and minorities for these positions has been most vociferous. The movement of women into management, by contrast, may have taken on somewhat of its own momentum (although the same may not be true for minorities). Firms may be willing to accept women with advanced degrees from respectable business schools without the 'whip' of affirmative action pressure.[13]

4 Reaganomics and Women's Unpaid Labor

Consistent with the conservative belief in severely limiting the role of government, the Reagan administration argued that its cuts in social spending should be compensated for by an increase in 'volunteerism', the voluntary assumption of responsibility for these services by private organizations and individuals. In addition, the family should take on more responsibility for the care of sick, handicapped, and elderly family members.

Both the call for increased volunteerism and for greater family responsibility are of particular significance for women, since women are the primary providers of unpaid domestic and organizational labour. The most recent major study of time use in the United States found that, for families with two children and both parents present, 'homemakers' (including women engaged in wage labour) averaged 6.5 hours per day on housework, while their spouses, averaged 1.9 hours per day (Virginia Agricultural Experiment Station 1981, pp. 38–45).[14] Cuts in federal outlays for social services such as health care could sharply increase women's domestic labour responsibilities. The recent and continuing cuts in Medicare, federal outlays on medical care for the elderly, illustrate this trend.

Medicare expenditures for the elderly have grown extremely rapidly over the past decade, from $7.5 billion in 1971 to $41.8 billion in 1982 (US Bureau of the Census 1982–83, p. 318). This figure does not include Medicare payments for the nonelderly disabled (who have been included in Medicare since 1972), so the *total* federal outlay is even greater. The growth in Medicare expenditures is partially the result of an increase in the number of elderly Americans over the period, and partially the result of increased use of medical services per person; but the most important factor has been the rapid increase in medical prices, which has far exceeded the general level of price increases.[15]

In 1983, in an attempt to stop the rise in Medicare costs, the Federal government changed its payment procedure for hospital care. Instead of simply covering the hospital bills (subject to deductions), Medicare now pays a flat rate for specific illnesses and medical procedures. The Administration is currently attempting to extend this system of payment to doctors' bills as well. This new method prevents hospitals from inflating costs, but it may have negative implications for the elderly and may increase women's domestic labour. Since hospitals receive the standard payment even if their costs are below that amount, there is an incentive to save money on Medicare patients by sending them home as soon as possible. Since the new payment system was set up, the average length of hospital stay by Medicare patients has decreased by two days. This means that more of the nursing of convalescent patients is being done at home – which results both in an increase in women's domestic labour and an increase in private (family) expenditure on medical care for the elderly. Further cuts in Medicare in the next few years may exacerbate this tendency.

Policies such as this change in Medicare may have the effect of *coercing* women into performing more domestic labour. In addition, there have been a number of legislative proposals aimed at providing *incentives* to women to perform more domestic, and less wage, labour. Most of these proposals have been included in an omnibus bill entitled the Family Protection Act of 1981. The Family Protection Act is basically a 'wish list' of New Right antifeminist 'pro-family' legislation, much of which could never pass Congress and is, in any event, unconstitutional.[16] Some parts of the Act, however, are much more viable, and these have been splintered off for separate consideration. Chief among these are tax proposals which would allow tax credits and/or deductions for households containing a dependent aged 65 or older, and a special one year tax exemption of $1,000 for married couples who give birth to or adopt a child. Both of these proposals have positive aspects, of course; but they are written in such a way as to reward only a family structure advocated by the Right. Thus, the tax incentive applies only if the elderly are taken into their kin's households, not if they are helped to continue living on their own. And only *married* couples are entitled to benefits for producing or adopting a child. The bias toward a traditional family structure is made particularly clear in another proposal, which would allow a husband to set up a tax-deductible retirement fund for his homemaker wife, but only if she earns *no* money at all in the course of the year. As the Women's Research and Education Institute noted, even a temporary job at Christmas time (very common among housewives) would make a woman ineligible for this benefit (The Women's Research and Education Institute 1981, p. 15).

The New Right would clearly like to see a return to a patriarchal family structure, in which the economically dependent wife provides care for the sick, the handicapped, and the elderly, functions which are currently provided (to some extent, at least) by the state. The Reagan administration has shared this New Right goal. Nevertheless, very little of this vision has become reality. Most of the Family Protection Act has never been and probably never will be brought to a vote, and there is little evidence as yet of success in returning social services to the family.

There are probably a number of reasons why these plans have reached stalemate. Increased political activism and awareness by women has made even conservative politicians wary of legislation which would be construed as detrimental to the interests of women. The heady atmosphere that produced the Family Protection Act shortly after the first Reagan victory has disappeared as the New Right has faced defeat on many of its key anti-feminist issues (most notably anti-abortion legislation). And economic crisis has diverted attention from issues of social restructuring to issues of economic restructuring.

It is highly unlikely, however, that the New Right plan to return women to the home could have succeeded in any event. As we have seen, married women have become part of the permanent wage labour force. Their paycheques are necessary to the maintenance of the family, and the trend is liable to be toward *more* as opposed to less labour force participation. Economic restructuring based on wage austerity in particular guarantees that fewer and fewer families will be able to make ends meet with only one earner. As a result, there are very stringent limits to the extent to which the state can return responsibility for social services to the family. Women simply are not available, and cannot become available, to take over these tasks.

5 The future: economic restructuring and women

I have argued that Reagan's policies centre around a strategy to restructure the United States economy in response to continuing economic crisis. But can this restructuring work? And what effect would the resulting 'recovery' have on women?

First, we must define what is meant by economic recovery. To Reagan and his advisors, recovery means first and foremost an improved, more profitable investment climate; this should ideally result in more investment in productive capability, increases in productivity, higher growth rates for the gross national product, and an improved international balance of trade – as well, of course, as reduced interest and inflation rates.

Since 1982, GNP has been growing steadily, though slowly, although many economists believe this recovery is due to Reagan's unprecedentedly high deficits rather than his supply-side policies. How have women been affected by the economic growth? The Reagan administration has maintained that the most economically disadvantaged groups in society have the most to *gain* by his recovery programme. I would argue, however, that women, especially poor and nonwhite women, are helped *least* by a conservative restructuring of the economy, and in fact in many cases lose, both relatively and absolutely, by such a 'recovery'.

Note that recovery does *not* necessarily mean low rates of unemployment; in fact, orthodox economists and conservative politicians have revised their estimates of 'acceptable' levels of unemployment ever higher over the past decade, so that unemployment rates of 5–7% (more than 6–7 million people) are considered reasonable. Throughout the period since 1982, unemployment rates have remained stubbornly above 7%. (In the 1960s an unemployment rate of 3–4% was the usual goal, and rates below 4% were achieved in 1966–9 – but never since.) One major argument offered for acceptance of a higher unemployment rate is that *women* are a higher proportion of the labour force now; women are considered to have a 'naturally' higher unemployment rate than men because of their weaker attachment to the labour force.

Thus recovery is consistent with continuing high rates of unemployment. Further, as I have argued, one key basis for Reagan's recovery plan is the cheapening of labour power: the lowering of real wages and weakening of labour's ability to control working conditions. This has already happened to a considerable extent, with a consequent lowering of the standard of living for the working class. Recovery may bring increases in real wages for some, but an enormous amount of ground has already been lost, and rebuilding union power in the face of a hostile government could be slow and painful.

Perhaps more important, many workers, including a large proportion of women workers, are left out of the recovery almost completely. This is because a successful recovery involves a substantial increase in computer-based automation, Automation is likely to have two effects on women workers. First, it tends to deskill work, making it boring and repetitious to perform, and making the worker herself easier to replace and hence more vulnerable. Second, automation results in more output per worker, which can mean that the pool of jobs will not expand as rapidly, or may even decline.[17] In industry, robots are likely to cause an absolute decline in employment, particularly among skilled, unionized blue collar workers.[18] Women are not highly represented among skilled blue collar workers, but in recent years affirmative action pressure on apprenticeship programmes and on employers has helped increase their participation in these relatively high-paying jobs. Clearly this option is being closed off.

It is less clear whether automation will result in an absolute decrease in the number of office workers; however, with increases in office productivity estimated at 200% (*Business Week*, 3 August 1981), the job pool may not expand very rapidly. This factor is of particular significance for women, as over one-third of all employed women are in clerical occupations (See US Department of Labor 1980, p. 10).

While the pool of clerical jobs is not likely to be expanding greatly, and the pool of skilled industrial jobs will probably decline, the number of women needing jobs is likely to increase. The number of women raising children alone continues to grow, and the strategy of 'wage austerity' means that married couple families continue to need two incomes to survive. Where, then, will the jobs come from for these women (and the men displaced from industry)? *Business Week* (3 August 1981) concludes that there will be no employment problem, because employment in service-oriented industries is expected to grow by an estimated 7.5 million jobs over the 1980s, taking up the slack. The United States has become an increasingly service-oriented economy since World War II, and service occupations have grown accordingly in the last ten years, especially in restaurant and custodial work (Leon, 1982, p. 20). But even if service work can expand rapidly enough to employ all the displaced workers (which is questionable), it does not provide a satisfactory alternative to the jobs lost to automation. Service occupations tend to have short hours (one-third of all service workers work part time) (Leon, 1982, p. 24), few chances for promotion, and very low pay. However it is these types of jobs that are increasingly likely to be the only ones available to many women and blacks: already in 1979 62.4% of all service workers were women, accounting for 18.3% of all white women workers and 34.8% of all black women workers (US Department of Labor, 1980, pp. 11, 74).

In short, while the Reagan administration's economic restructuring has resulted in a modest and possibly short-lived recovery, that recovery involves weakened labour unions, wage austerity for industrial workers, and the banishment of a large number of workers, particularly women and nonwhite people of both sexes, to a life of poverty on greatly reduced welfare payments, unemployment, and low-paid, dead-end service jobs. Corporations, corporate managers, certain professionals, and a subset of the working class involved in high skilled 'high tech' industries may prosper, but a large pool of women find themselves pushed out the bottom of such a 'recovery', at best cleaning the offices and cooking the hamburgers for those to whom prosperity has returned.

Class differences among women mean that they have been affected in differing ways and to varying degrees by the Reagan administration's economic policies. Poor women were the most immediately and most severely affected by the budget cuts. Women at the absolute bottom of the job ladder lost some of the pathetically-few opportunities available to pull themselves and their families out of poverty.

Reagan's recovery could mean a deterioration in employment conditions for a majority of women, as clerical work is deskilled and low paid, menial service work becomes the dumping ground for growing numbers of 'surplus' women workers. Finally, a small but significant number of highly educated women may have found that the Reagan economic plan was, in fact, in their interest. This is not to say that women who get a toehold in traditionally male professions or corporate hierarchies are as likely to succeed as men. There is ample evidence of discrimination still in existence at every step along the way. However, this small but articulate minority of women is sufficiently affluent and sufficiently established that Reagan's recovery can directly benefit them, in terms of tax benefits, expanding job opportunities, and even a growing pool of female service workers to care for their children and perform household chores.

Thus we may see a growing rift between the increasingly proletarianized majority of women workers, and an increasingly established minority of highly educated, affluent women with markedly different economic interests. Certain social issues could unite these two groups of women – e.g. reproductive rights – but on issues like budget cuts for social programmes they might well come down on different sides. Eisenstein, among others, has argued that women are increasingly recognizing their unity as a 'sexual class' (Eisenstein, 1982, p. 581); I am suggesting, on the contrary, the continuation of real material class differences among women on the basis of diverging labour market positions. If true, this rift will create a real challenge to the feminist movement in its attempts to achieve social and economic justice for all women.

NOTES

1. Women raised gardens, and tended poultry and milked cows; they baked, preserved, sewed, and manufactured household goods like soap and candles. In addition, women were able to contribute to their families' money incomes through the sale of their produce and wares, and from taking in boarders. As a result, they were able to participate in the support of themselves and their families without engaging in wage labour.
2. This is not to say that home production and wage labour are identical. Wage labour confronts women directly with capitalist exploitation. Perhaps equally important, wage labour takes place outside of and independent from the patriarchal family.
3. There are a number of factors that may have influenced this change. It was probably important that women stopped bearing children earlier, in many cases by the time they were 30.
4. Additionally, the birth rate, which had been extremely high in the 1950s, began to decline in the 1960s and declined sharply in the 1970s.
5. It is difficult to come up with precise figures, because both monthly payments and inflation adjustments vary state by state. However, in *no* case has there been a full adjustment for inflation.
6. It is striking that, despite their belief that the patriarchal nuclear family is the natural and desirable way to live, the New Right seems to feel that women have to be coerced into entering and remaining in such families.
7. At the same time that the 30 and one-third rule was implemented, other, more coercive measures were also introduced, requiring AFDC mothers

of school-age children to search for waged work. Both the incentive and the coercion approaches reflect the changing attitude toward women on AFDC, the view that they were getting a 'free ride' from society.

8. Each state determines an amount of money necessary for a family to meet basic living costs. They vary greatly from state to state, for both political and objective (cost of living) reasons.

9. AFDC records are highly decentralized and haphazardly kept. To this day no one (including the federal government) is exactly sure how many families were affected by the budget cuts, or exactly how much money was saved.

10. However, workfare jobs are not supposed to compete with regular labor market employment, so they are very unlikely to provide competitive skills.

11. This possibility, in fact, corresponds to the Reagan administration's justification for the cuts to working AFDC families, although for quite different reasons. Not only were such families not 'truly needy', but also having their AFDC cut or terminated would 'provide the incentive needed to make the transition from welfare to self-support' (McMahon, 1982). As Piven and Cloward (1982, pp. 38–9), among others, have pointed out, the Reagan economic policies taken as a whole reveal strikingly different beliefs about the behaviour of the poor and the affluent. The affluent are expected to increase their work effort in response to positive incentives (tax cuts); the poor only in response to negative incentives (welfare cuts).

12. The Center study adds that data on returnees was the *least* reliable of all the data generated on the budget cuts (p. 47).

13. The movement of women into traditionally-male professional and managerial positions has been extremely rapid in the past decade. However, it is true that the number of women officials and managers increased 73% between 1974 and 1980 in firms subject to affirmative action rules, compared to a considerably lower 36% in firms not subject to the rules. This discrepancy suggests that my conclusion about momentum continuing the hiring of women at the managerial level may be too optimistic.

14. Not only did men spend considerably less time on housework, but also fully 40% of their 1.9 hours per day was spent on the traditionally male tasks of maintenance of the house, car, and yard. Despite a decade of feminist activity (the data was collected in 1977–8), and despite the increasing labour force participation of married women, men spent virtually no time on basic housework tasks such as dishwashing, housecleaning, and laundry.

15. Medical price increases are estimated to have accounted for more than half the health care spending increase between 1965 and 1980, and three-quarters of the increase between 1975 and 1980 (Feder et al., 1982, p. 274).

16. For example, one provision of the Act would deny federal funds to educational institutions for the 'purchase or preparation of any educational material which tends to denigrate, diminish or deny the role differences between the sexes as it (sic) has been historically understood in the United States.' Quoted in The Women's Research and Education Institute, 1981, p. 19.

17. Automation also *creates* jobs, as workers are needed to produce and service the new machinery. However, employment forecasts indicate that automation in the 1980s is likely to destroy more industrial jobs than it creates. (*Business Week*, 3 August 1981, p. 63.)

18. According to *Business Week* (3 August 1981), robots currently developed or in the process of development are capable of performing the jobs of seven million current factory workers, of whom 45% are union workers.

REFERENCES

AuClaire, Phillip A. (1979), 'The mix of work and welfare among long-term AFDC recipients', *Social Service Review*, vol. 3, no. 4, December.

Center for the Study of Social Policy (1983), *Effects of Federal AFDC Policy Changes: A Study of a Federal-State 'Partnership'*, working paper, Washington, D.C., March.

Centre for the Study of Social Policy (1984), *Working Female-Headed Families in Poverty*, Washington, D.C., March.

Chrissinger, Marlene Sonju (1980), 'Factors affecting employment of welfare mothers', *Social Work*. vol. 25, no. 1, January.

Eisenstein, Zillah (1982), 'Sexual politics of the New Right: understanding the "crisis of liberalism" for the 1980's', *Signs*, vol. 7, no. 3, spring.

Feder, Judith, Holahan, John, Bovbjerg, Randall R. and Hadley, Jack (1982), 'Health', in John L Palmer and Isabel V. Sawhill (eds), *The Reagan Experiment*, Washington, D.C., Urban Institute Press.

Gilder, George (1981), *Wealth and Poverty*, New York, Bantam Books.

Harrison, Bennett (1979), 'Welfare payments and the reproduction of low-wage workers and secondary jobs', *Review of Radical Political Economics*, vol. 11, no. 2, summer.

Joe, Tom (1982), *Profiles of Families in Poverty: Effects of the FY1982 Budget Proposal on the Poor*, working paper for the Center for the Study of Social Policy, Washington, D.C., 25 February.

Leon, Carol Boyd (1982), 'Occupational winners and losers: who they were during 1972–1980', *Monthly Labor Review*, vol. 105, no. 6, June.

Lynn, Lawrence E. Jr (1977), 'A decade of policy developments in the income-maintenance system', in Robert H. Haveman (ed.), *A Decade of Federal Antipoverty Programs*, New York, Academic Press.

McMahon, Linda (1982), In testimony before the House Budget Committee, 14 December, in Center for the Study of Social Policy 1983.

Piven, Frances Fox, and Cloward, Richard A. (1982), *The New Class War*, New York, Pantheon Books.

Power, Marilyn (1983), 'From home production to wage labor: women as a reserve army of labor', *Review of Radical Political Economics*, spring.

Rein, Martin and Rainwater, Lee (1978), 'Patterns of welfare use', *Social Service Review*, vol. 52, no. 4, December.

Stack, Carol (1975), *All Our Kin*, New York, Harper & Row.

US Bureau of the Census (1982–3), *Statistical Abstracts of the United States*.

US Department of Commerce, US Bureau of Census, (1981), 'Characteristics of the population below the poverty level' *Current Population Report*, series P-60, no. 138.

US Department of Labor (1973), *Employment and Earnings*, January.

US Department of Labor (1980), *Perspectives on Working Women: a Databook*, Washington, D.C., October.

US Department of Labor (1982), *Employment and Earnings*, January.

US Department of Labor (1983), *Employment and Earnings*, January.

US Department of Labor (1984), Bureau of Labor Statistics, *News Bulletin*, 26 July.

US Department of Labor (1986), *Employment and Earnings*, January.

Virginia Agricultural Experiment Station (1981), *Family Time Use: an Eleven-state Urban/Rural Comparison*, bulletin VPI-2, Blacksburg, Virginia, December.

The Women's Research and Education Institute (1981), *The Family Protection Act of 1981*, Washington, D.C., July.

6 Women's employment, the state and the family in France: contradiction of state policy for women's employment

Patricia Bouillaguet-Bernard, Annie Gauvin

In the last thirty years, women's employment in France has been through a period of profound change; by March 1985, more than 45% of women of working age were in employment compared to 36% for 1962.

In Chapter 2, we attempted to show how the large-scale entry of women into the labour market in the past thirty years is part of the dynamic of change within the productive system in France. However, the long-term relationships between the increase in female participation and the transformation of the productive system are not the only influences on the nature of women's work. The key position held by women within the family and family structures themselves are also influential factors. The family has undergone equally massive changes in the past thirty years: the falling birth-rate, the growing instability of marriages and the rise in the number of families in which both partners work are all evidence of the radical changes in the relationship between women, the family and employment.

In what ways has the state in France attempted to integrate these profound changes, through the complex and wide-ranging means of intervention at its disposal, including family, social and fiscal policy, as well as economic and employment policy?

Are these policies fundamentally an attempt to accommodate or to apply a brake to the increase in women's employment? Do they really help to reduce the inequalities that exist between men and women both socially and in terms of employment?

These are the questions that we shall be attempting to answer in this chapter, not by analysing the whole range of government policies but those that are central to the position of women in the family and the employment system. These policies will be examined from two main points of view.

(i) Women's work has become a key factor in enabling families to join in market consumption. Women's earnings now constitute an essential element of household income. But has the increase in women's employment tended to increase the inequalities in primary income between families, particularly of those on the lowest incomes? To what extent have family and fiscal policies reduced these initial inequalities and, as a consequence, influenced women's employment?

(ii) The dramatic increase in unemployment in the past ten years has led governments to implement an active employment policy linking together a whole range of complex measures. But the risk of unemployment is unevenly distributed among individuals. Women are particulary vulnerable (see Chapter 2 this volume). To what extent do government policies designed to boost employment take account of this inequality in order to combat it, and to what extent do they encourage a more equitable distribution of employment opportunities between men and women?

1 WOMEN'S EMPLOYMENT, THE FAMILY AND SOCIAL POLICIES
1.1 Women's employment and the family: the direction of change

The last twenty years have seen profound changes in family structures in France. The rapidly rising divorce rate, the increase in the number of young, unmarried couples living together, the fall in the birth-rate and the reduction in the size of the nuclear family are indicative both of changes in the organisation of the family and of the development *of new relationships between women and paid work*. Nevertheless, in the 1980s, couples still represent the predominant form of family structure, accounting for 67% of households in the 1982 census. However, their numbers are tending to fall, while the number of single people is tending to rise. In 1982, unmarried people, widows or widowers and divorced men and women without children accounted for almost one household in four, compared with one in five in 1968.

The number of single-parent families (men or women living alone with their children) has increased rapidly (by 14% between 1975 and 1982) although their share in all households still remains at around 4%. However, this relative stability conceals profound changes in the composition of such households: first, that there has been a sharp increase in the number of single-parent families in which the head of the family is a woman (80% of single-parent families in 1982); and second, that divorce and separation, rather than widowhood, have become the main cause of single-parent families (Courson and de Saboulin, 1985).

The increase in marital breakdown, which reflects these changes, leads to greater and more continuous participation by women in the labour market, with increasing numbers of women being the main breadwinner in the family. The rates and cycles of activity for unmarried women tend in fact to be very similar to those of men. Between the ages of 20 and 45, almost 85% of such women are in employment.

Nevertheless, the most radical changes of the past twenty years concern married women. Since 1968, they have accounted for more than 80% of the increase in female participation. In 1982, almost one in two (and two out of three between the ages of 20 and 40) were active in the labour markets, compared with barely one in three twenty years earlier.

At the same time, there have been profound changes in their employment cycle. The traditional 'bimodal' curve of female employment has disappeared since the 1975 census and been replaced by a curve very similar to that for men; this was confirmed by the 1982 census.

These changes are evidence of the increasing permanence of women's position as wage-earners and of the decreasing dependence of their employment cycle on the family life cycle. Total non-participation in the labour market is becoming rare for women, discontinuous participation is less frequent and continuous participation is becoming established as the dominant form of career path among the younger generations. There are two immediate consequences of this major change in the years between 1975 and 1980.

(i) At the 1982 census, the couple in which both partners work became for the first time the dominant form of household structure, whereas the number of couples in which the man worked and the woman did not had been in continuous decline for 15 years (21% of households in 1982, compared with 34% in 1968).

(ii) The burden of family responsibilities on female participation is declining. The threshold of incompatibility between family and working life is moving from two towards three dependent children.

Of all the social and family factors that affect the level and structure of women's employment, family responsibilities (the number and age of dependent children) undoubtedly constitute the greatest burden (cf. Figure 6.1). Nevertheless, the differences in participation rates among women according to whether they have no children or one or two children have been narrowing considerably for 15 years. The most rapid increase in participation rates has been among married women with one or two dependent children. However, the presence of a third child did not prevent 40% of these women from being economically active in 1982, compared with 30% in 1975.

In France, in contrast to what can be observed in other countries, notably the UK, it is the number of children rather than the age of the youngest child that seems to be the main determinant of the employment pattern of women with children, at least until the second child. It is only from the third child onwards that the age effect plays any significant role, with the participation rates for the women in question rising with the age of the youngest dependent child.[1]

Nevertheless, the extent to which the age of dependent children affects the structure of female participation is indicative of the (dis)continuity

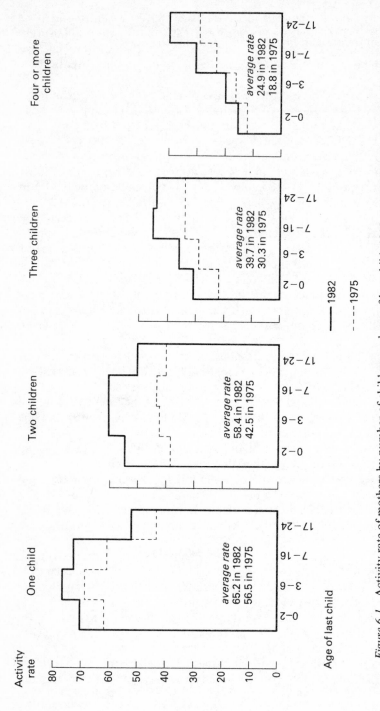

Figure 6.1 Activity rate of mothers by number of children and age of last child, 1982 and 1975 (couples with children).

Source: Derived from J. P. Courson and M. de Saboulin (1985).

of that participation. For women with at least three dependent children, a discontinuous employment cycle remains the norm.

These general trends have not, however, eradicated the differences that exist between the social classes. Among wage earning families,[2] it is the wives of middle managers, technicians and office workers whose participation rates are highest and least sensitive to family constraints. In contrast, the participation of the wives of manual workers is severely constrained by the burden of family responsibilities (discontinuous activity).

There are several factors that determine these class differences: not only household income and the woman's level of education or training, but also the different working conditions of the jobs typically held by women from different social classes (skill level, job status, wage levels, the unpleasantness of the job, the rate of work, travelling time, etc.). The relative flexibility of working hours is a major element in the class differences between the career paths of working mothers (Villeneuve Gokalp, 1985). Opportunities for part-time work when family responsibilities become too heavy a burden,[3] for flexible working hours, for choosing annual holiday periods and also for absence from work for family reasons (to look after sick children or for maternity leave) are all ways in which working mothers can alter their working hours in order to combine their working and domestic lives.

It is the wives of middle managers and of white-collar workers in government departments and state-owned firms who seem to have the most favourable opportunities for adjusting their working hours in order to remain in work. The wives of manual workers, on the other hand, have the least favourable opportunities for remaining in employment when their family responsibilities increase (Villeneuve Gokalp, 1985).

The role of child care

It is widely assumed that the age of the youngest child plays a smaller role in the decision of French women to enter the labour market due to the existence of an established system of child care.

One of the principal characteristics of the French system of child care is undoubtedly the almost comprehensive provision of pre-school education for children from three to six years of age (when they start primary school). In contrast to the situation in other countries,[4] a third of all children aged two attend a nursery school.[5] At three years of age, the figure is 80%. Between the ages of four and six, all but 3% of children go to nursery schools (Desplanques, 1985). The structure of day care for children before they first go to nursery school between the ages of two and three years is very varied.[6] It depends partly on the mother's occupation – in particular, if she is working, whether she is a wage-earner or not – and also on social class.

In 1982, out of a total of 2,372,120 children under three years of age,[7] there were 1,145,600 children under three with two working parents, and 70,700 children in single-parent families, giving in theory 1,216,300 children in need of day care.

The following provision is made for the 2,372,120 children under three years of age:[8]

(i) about 260,000 children attend nursery school;

(ii) 1,300,000 children are looked after by their mothers who may or may not be economically active. If they are, they work at home, in private households, in family businesses or in part-time jobs.[9] This is the case for about 24% of these children whose mother is economically active;

(iii) 475,000 children are cared for by qualified or unqualified mother's

(iv) 175,000 children are cared for by another member of the family (usually the grandmother);

(v) 60,000 children are cared for at home by nannies;

(vi) about 150,000 children are looked after in creches (118,000) or day nurseries (32,000).[10] Creches are themselves divided into two basic categories; state-run creches in which children (78,000 in 1983) are looked after in premises designed for the purpose, and family creches that organise and supervise the care of children (40,000 in 1983) at the home of registered childminders.[11]

It is clear from these figures that only 8.6% of working mothers with a child under three use a collectively organised creche. Most of the children of working class and immigrant families go to nursery school from the age of two or three. Child care before three is usually based on the family, which is less expensive.

In the more affluent classes, children go to school a little later. Before the age of three, more costly forms of child care are often used, e.g. creches or nannies. The financial cost of child care falls unequally on parents according to the income level of the family and to the type of child care. The cost of a mother's help is fixed and borne entirely by the parents, whereas parents sending their children to state creches pay according to their income. Tax deductions for the costs of child care only partially reduce the uneven distribution of costs.[12]

Thus the French system of pre-school child care is extremely complex and has a relative effect on the level of economic activity of mothers of young children. Child care is provided by the public and private sectors, or by a combination of the two, with the public sector clearly offering the lowest amount of provision. The state and collective child care system, because of its very inadequacy, has an anti-redistributive effect (Leprince, 1985). The use of state creches rises with the educational level of the women or if they are social or health-care workers (Desplanques,

1985). This is indicative of the inherent inequality of the system. Even though the state and collective child care system has been expanded (between 1960 and 1983, the number of creche places increased by a factor of 6), provision still does not match needs, particularly in view of the large-scale entry of women with young children into the labour market. The aim of current policy in this area is to diversify the types of provision and to reduce the level of state involvement.

1.2 Women's employment, household income and the effects of social policies

Economic analysis of the supply of female labour within the context of the family has traditionally been based on the financial logic underlying patterns of economic behaviour. We shall follow this tradition to a certain extent by focusing our attention on the following two aspects:
(i) analysis of earned income, which will deal on the one hand with the national minimum wage (the SMIC) and its influence on women's wages and, on the other, with the contribution made by women to household incomes;
(ii) analysis of family policies and tax and social security systems and their impact on women's work.

Women's wages and the influences of the national minimum wage
In 1983, average annual wages for full-time wage-earners was 85,310 F for men and 63,610 F for women (CERC, 1985), that is a relative difference of 25.3%.[13]

It is not easy to interpret this difference, in that it can be explained to a fairly large extent by the unequal distribution between the sexes of qualifications and economic activities. A residual difference due to indirect discrimination (working hours, bonuses, seniority) still persists even if structural effects are eliminated.

The relative difference between men's and women's wages was 36% at the beginning of the 1960s and then fell gradually to 32% in 1968, 28% in 1980 and 26.5% in 1981 (CERC, 1985). It is not easy to determine the extent to which this reduction is due to changes in the labour market and employment structures,[14] or is a direct result of government policies aimed at raising low wages; or indeed to identify whether the existence of a minimum guaranteed wage accounts in part for the smaller differences between men's and women's wages in France than in the UK or the USA.

The principle of a guaranteed minimum wage, the SMIG,[15] was established in France by a law of February 1950, which was passed both in order to establish a bench-mark wage and also in order to guarantee all wage-earners a living wage (indexation of SMIG to the cost of living). The SMIG became the SMIC[16] in 1970, when significant changes were made to the methods of assessing the bench-mark wage. The SMIC is an important instrument of both economic policy (cyclical pump priming) and social policy (raising low wages, reduction of inequalities), since the government has the power to make discretionary increases in addition to those made automatically in line with inflation.[17]

However, in aggregate only a low percentage of all wage-earners are paid at SMIC level; increases in the SMIC during the period 1970–80 only directly affected between 2.5% and 6% in firms with more than 10 employees (CERC, 1985). Nevertheless, this relatively low proportion conceals some wide structural disparities:

The SMIC mainly affects:

(i) *wage-earners in small firms;* in July 1984, 16% of wage-earners in firms with less than 10 employees (artisan firms and shops) benefited directly from rises in the SMIC, compared with 1.9% of wage-earners in firms with 500 or more wage-earners,

(ii) *manual (10.8%) rather than white-collar workers (3.9%),*

(iii) *wage-earners in the hair-dressing and beauty industry (44%), the clothing industry (24.7%) and catering (18.8%),* which are moreover relatively unconcentrated and highly feminised sectors. In contrast, increases in the SMIC affected only 0.2% of wage-earners in the oil industry, 0.7% of wage-earners in the chemical industry and 0.9% of wage-earners in banking and insurance, which are highly concentrated sectors with favourable pay agreements.

It seems clear that the firms in which wages are highly concentrated close to the levels of the SMIC also make great use of female labour and that, as a result, the SMIC is a norm for determining the wages of female rather than male manual workers. In July 1984, 22% of female manual workers were directly affected by rises in the SMIC compared with only 6.9% of their male counterparts (Wagner, 1985).

Since women's wages tend to be concentrated around the level of the SMIC, any policy aimed at raising low wages has an immediate effect on the relative structure of women's wages. The sharp increase in the SMIC in 1968 and the fact that the rate of growth of the SMIC since 1972 has been higher than that of the average hourly wage have contributed towards the rapid narrowing of differences between men's and women's wages since 1968. On the other hand, it is less clear that the SMIC is to blame for the level of unemployment among women, which is higher in France than in other countries.

The existence of a minimum wage is often considered an important factor in wage rigidity in France (OECD, 1985) and to act as a constraint on hiring for the most vulnerable categories of labour in the market (women and young people). The lack of recent studies in the area makes it difficult to assess the pertinence of this relationship. An OECD study of youth employment (OEC, 1983) points to the absence of any perceptible effects of an increase in the SMIC on unemployment and the employment of young people. The conclusions could be expected to be the same as far as women's employment and unemployment is concerned. It is notable that those who benefit from the SMIC are concentrated in small firms (two-thirds of them are in firms with fewer than 50 employees) which, since the beginning of the recession, have been the biggest net creators of new jobs. Furthermore, many of the jobs for women have been created in parts of the service sector such as the public sector which pay wages above SMIC and in practice are relatively unaffected by increases in the SMIC. Any effects that there might be can thus be only very limited at the macro-economic level.

Women's employment and household income
The increase in women's participation rates is part of a process of profound change in social and cultural structures. However, it would be over-simplistic to see this increase merely as a social phenomenon brought about by factors exogenous to the functioning of the economic system.

It is true that opinions on the family and women's work have changed considerably in the past ten years, and the belief that women should not work at all is tending to disappear (Houzel-Vaneffentere, 1985). But the increase in women's employment can be attributed in a more fundamental sense to the extension of 'Fordian consumption model' based on the development of mass consumption and the increasing exteriorisation of domestic activities (see Chapter 2). In this context, the large-scale entry of women into the labour market has become an important factor in the integration of families into a pattern of market consumption (Glaude, 1984). If the importance of the women's income in total household income is taken into account, the predominance of economic constraints (not only financial need but also the desire to improve living standards) in the motivation of women seeking employment becomes clear. A recent survey (CERC, 1985) among more than 4,000 mothers shows that 40% of women wage-earners would stop working if their husband earned as much as their combined incomes and that 22% would work shorter hours (i.e. seek part-time work). However, for 35% of the women questioned, this would not in any way change their working life.

In one sense, the results of this survey confirm the conclusions of empirical tests of macro-economic models of the supply of female labour (Henin, 1985) that reveal that increases in a husband's wage have a negative 'income effect' on the participation rate of the wife.

According to the statistical data available in France, this negative income effect is, however, subject to two threshold effects:
(i) *A family threshold:* participation rates for women with three or more children are not very sensitive to the husband's income level. The

family responsibilities effect predominates over the income effect in the structure of economic activity.

(ii) *An income threshold:* the negative elasticity of the supply of married female labour relative to the husband's earned income is observed only above a certain minimum income threshold.[18] Below this threshold, the relationship appears to be relatively insignificant (Charraud, 1978; Lollivier, 1984; CERC, 1985). Thus for high-income families, the wife's work and earnings provide a secondary job and additional income, whereas for low-income families the two wages are a necessity. This threshold effect shows clearly the interaction of other variables, particularly the socio-occupational variable.

Differences in participation tend to reduce inequalities in income within and between socio-economic groups. In higher economic groups women's participation is concentrated at younger age levels as a means of maintaining standards of living in the early years of married life; participation falls as husband's income rises, so that there is a relatively low differential in the senior managerial class between families where the wife works and where she does not. In the manual worker classes women's wage income is a permanent essential element in family income as becomes clear from comparisons of household incomes where the wife does and does not work. Incomes where the wife does work are 52% higher in households where the husband is a manual worker, 64% higher where he is a shop worker, 74% where he is a skilled worker and 94% higher where he is an office worker (CERC-INED, 1981). These differences arise from the greater similarities in male and female earnings in these categories and from the tendency for couples to belong to the same occupational groups. Inequality is thus increased within socio-economic groups but reduced between groups as a recent survey (CERC-INED, 1981) found that the family of a skilled manual worker where both partners work had a similar income to that of a teacher's family where the wife did not.

Earned income is not, however, the same as disposable income. The transition from one to the other immediately raises the problem of the effect of fiscal and family policies on the reduction (or otherwise) of these initial inequalities and thus, as a consequence, on female participation rates.

The effects of family, social and fiscal policy on women's work
On average, taking into account family allowances, income tax and the cost of child care, 76.5% of the woman's earnings is available as disposable income (CERC-INED survey). This rate is 73.4% in the families of managers and 78.2% in families in which the husband is an office or manual worker. In the case of families where the wife does not work, disposable income is on average 10% greater than earned income. In the case of families where the mother works, disposable income is

2.5% lower than earned income (CERC-INED survey). Progressive increases in taxation, methods of allocating family benefits and the link between child care arrangements and social class are all partial explanations of the rates of return from women's earned income. In reality, the effects of three systems are interacting here: the financial assistance to families linked to family policy, the system of social security and the tax system. The systems have their own underlying logics: protection of the family, increasing the birth rate and the redistribution of wealth. However, they concern us here both because of the obvious impact that these systems can have in encouraging or discouraging women to work and on the legitimacy of women's wages and also because of the impact of social transfers and redistribution on family incomes. The degree of consistency that exists between the aims and means of these policies is debatable, as is the degree of consistency between the various policies (IRES, 1983). For example, family allowances apply more to large families[19] and to low-income families.[20] On the other hand, the main beneficiaries of the tax advantage linked to the system of tax relief in respect of dependants used to calculate an individual's income tax are average-sized families with high incomes.

This obviously concerns the principle of redistribution, but whether or not this redistribution is horizontal (family with or without children) or vertical (families on high and low incomes), it also incorporates the question of women's work: households in which both partners work have a higher income; working mothers have on average fewer children than those who do not work.

This is a vast and complex issue, of which we shall attempt to analyse only a few strands.

Financial assistance to families and family policy

Any analysis of family policy must be based on two aspects: government statements on the family on the one hand, and the nature of the various family allowances and the conditions under which they are allocated on the other. Policies on the family are part of an overall economic context, linked either to social policy objectives or to objectives connected with conditions in the labour market (shortages or surpluses of labour).[21] Examination of successive economic plans shows that real concern with increasing the birth rate (First Plan, 1946–53) gave way to an attempt to solve the problem of labour shortages through the increased use of female labour (Third Plan, 1958–61) and then finally to a recognition of the reality of women's entry into the labour market (Sixth Plan, 1971–5). This outlines the general framework within which family policy was drawn up.

The origin of family policy in France is the 'model of the family' and the idea that a worker should be entitled to an income supplement because he is raising children. This idea is characteristic of the family movements that developed out of social catholicism (IRES, 1983). The principle originally suited the various social actors, including the employers, both because it reduced pressure from workers for wage increases and also because it was an effective means of stabilising and controlling the labour force.

One of the instruments of family policy during the 1950s and 1960s, in addition to maternity and child allowances, was the single wage allowance (for families in which only one of the partners was a wage-earner while the other was economically inactive).[22] The single wage allowance was the subject of much debate during this period. Its underlying principle was fundamentally 'familialist', since it might well have encouraged women to stay at home. However, the majority of women were not economically active and the level of the allowance gave it symbolic rather than practical value, which meant that it was a relatively inefficient allowance.

.The value of the allowance was increased in 1972 and made subject to a means test. The nature of it was altered and it became more redistributive in character. From 1970 onwards, in response to a reduction in the means available, governments gave priority to greater selectivity in family allowances, both according to needs (families with specific needs) and according to means. At the same time, more women were entering the labour market, and this tendency grew stronger, partly in response to the nature of the jobs being created. As a result, the right of mothers to work was gradually recognised.[23] In this context, family policy constituted an element of incomes and social policy, with family allowances being increasingly integrated into the system of social transfers.[24]

In 1977, the single wage allowance was replaced by the family income supplement, which was designed to guarantee 'a minimum family income' and was paid whether or not the wife was working. For some observers (Lenoir, 1985), it reflected renewed concern about the fall in the birth rate and the re-emergence of the 'familialist' ideas of the 1950s. The new allowance was indeed paid to families with children under three, or with three or more children. The means test, by which the allowance was awarded, changed according to whether the household had one or two incomes,[25] but nevertheless at a certain income level operated a greater dissuasive effect on women's employment than the single wage allowance ever had. This effect is an illustration of the reorientation of family policy towards measures designed to encourage couples to have a third child.[26]

When the socialist government came into power in 1981, this element of family policy was at first played down, but the 'familialist' ideas underlying policy orientation were strongly reaffirmed by an increase in the levels of family allowances and changes in the conditions of entitlement (according to the number of children). This took place in the context of a programme for economic recovery. Since 1983, austerity policies have again left their mark on family policy. This is reflected by a policy of selectivity,[27] with measures designed to increase the birth rate, and is illustrated by the reform in January 1985 of the family allowance system. The so-called 'young child allowance' was introduced (this was a merger of the maternity grants and family income supplement), together with a 'bringing-up' allowance.

This latter allowance is awarded on the birth or adoption of a third child to the parent who stops working in order to bring up the child.[28] It is paid for two years and is worth 1,000 F per month. The purpose clearly is to encourage couples to have a third child. But it also encourages women to return to the home, since it is the change from two to three dependent children that imposes the severest constraints on the decision either to enter the labour market or to stay at home and bring up children. The level of the allowance, taken in conjunction with the progressive increase in other family allowances when the third child arrives, softens the effect of the reduction in disposable income when the second income is lost. This is all the more true since the new allowance is targeted basically at families with modest incomes (Droit Social, 1985).[29]

There has been neither continuity nor any radical change of direction in family allowance policy since the beginning of the crisis: the emphasis of such policies has continuously shifted between the principles of redistribution, support for the family and encouraging an increase in the birth rate. A study by the Caisse Nationale des Allocations Familiales showed that the categories that have gained most from the increase in family allowances since 1970 are low-income families with three or four children; families with two children, two wage-earners and high disposable income; and young couples with a child under three, two incomes and average disposable income. This is a very disparate spread of beneficiaries and does not reveal any penalisation of working mothers. Nevertheless, very recent developments and the establishment in 1985 of the 'bringing-up' allowance indicate that these conclusions may have to be qualified. This new allowance is a symbolic step towards a 'mother's wage', which would constitute a major blow to the legitimacy of women's work and wages (Maruani, 1985).

The social security and tax systems and women's work
The social security and tax laws were drawn up at times when the situation considered to be the norm, or which it was intended to make the norm, was one in which the husband worked and the wife did not. The present systems are thus based on the patriarchal notion of the family, according to which it is the man's responsibility to provide for his family. There is no recognition in these systems of women's right to work and they are one factor in discouraging women from working

outside the home. The basic unit of social organisation according to this view is the married couple in which the man is head of the family; as we shall see, this leads to two forms of discrimination: between men and women, and between working women and those who stay at home (Henniquau, 1984).

The question of social security has already been touched upon in the discussion of financial assistance to families. Family allowances are an integral part of the system of social security payments, accounting in 1984, for 13.7% of all such payments (Comptes de la Nation). Moreover, the existence of means testing makes these payments part of a principle of vertical redistribution peculiar to the social security system. This also concerns the areas of health, employment and provision for old age.[30]

The social security system in France is an occupational insurance system that also covers dependants. Under the sickness insurance system a working woman is insured in her own right, and like any other worker she pays contributions.[31] A woman who does not work and who stays at home is deemed a 'rightful claimant', whether she is married or, since 1978, living with a man. In this case, there are no specific contributions for the 'rightful claimant'. It is here that the discrimination between working and non-working women lies. A minimum number of hours must be worked in order to be covered under the scheme (200 hours per quarter or 120 hours per month). In certain cases, the hours worked by part-time workers are too few to qualify for cover.[32] Most of those affected are women.

Under the Old Age Insurance system, two types of cover are provided based on an accounting model that assumes that each family has only one economically active person. From the age of 60, the contributor is entitled in his own right to a pension of 50% of his wages provided that the period of contribution is at least 37 years. If the contributor dies, the spouse is entitled to a reversionary pension, provided that he/she has reached the age of 55, has been married for at least 2 years or has one or more dependent children. This pension is equal to 52% of the pension to which the contributor had been entitled. The conditions attached to the reversionary pension (marriage, widowhood and low wage earnings) means that the beneficiaries are almost exclusively women.[33]

To the extent that pensions reflect career paths and that women have lower earnings and shorter working lives, the system obviously produces inequalities between men and women.[34] In order to reduce the inequality associated with an interrupted working life, two years' contributions have, since 1975, been credited for each child. This measure has undoubtedly had a real, if partial, impact. The system still discriminates between men and women, and between working and non working women. In 1975 the pension of a women manager was only 38.5% of

. that a male manager and that of a forewoman 66.4% of that of her male counterpart. In 1975 the widows of managers were entitled on average to a reversionary pension 41% higher than the pension acquired by a woman manager through her own contributions (Henniquau, 1984).

The French system of income tax for private individuals is based on the concept of the 'fiscal household', which may be one person (unmarried, widowed or divorced) or a married couple, with or without dependents (basically children or handicapped people). The income coming into the household is added up in order to assess the tax liability. The tax is progressive[35] and is calculated according to the system of tax relief in respect of dependants.[36] In the case of a married couple, if the two partners have the same income, the system is neutral for them in comparison to what it is for two single people.

The problem for married women arises out of the inequality in earnings and the system of tax relief in respect of dependants. The greater the difference between the incomes of the two partners, the more they profit from the tax relief.[37] In this latter case, the discrimination with respect to the woman's work is the greatest. Indeed, if the woman does not work, the higher the husband's earnings the greater the tax relief will be.[38] The family is thus retained as the basic unit of taxation at a time of growing autonomy for women as they enter the labour market on a large scale. This reveals once again the contradictions that social forces are probably not ready to resolve. A plan for changes to the tax system was drawn up in 1982 at the request of the prime minister; if it had been implemented, separate taxation would have been introduced, but it was never made public. 'Separate taxation affects the financial unity of the family, the subordination of women's work, the real and symbolic power of the head of the family and the hierarchy implicit in the greater value attached to men's work'. In short, it attacks the power relationships between men and women (Maruani, 1985).

Working women pay taxes and social security contributions from which they do not receive the total benefit (cf. the system of family allowances). Women who do not work have a tax advantage, free social security cover and benefit from family allowances.

If a balance sheet is drawn up for the contributions paid throughout the working life for women on the one hand and couples on the other (Eckert, 1983), the results are conclusive. The skilled female manual worker needs five children to recover her outlay, while semi-skilled and unskilled women workers need to have four children. Olivia Eckert, who carried out this study, concludes: 'by working and making social security contributions, women acquire rights which they never enjoy'.

Nevertheless, social security payments are not equal to a second income. Thus there is no element in social policy that is aimed explicitly at sending women back to the home, or preventing them from leaving it in the first place. However, certain systems interacting in often complex ways may well dissuade women from working. They may penalise women's work. They may be anti-redistributive. They are based on a clear differentiation in male and female roles between the world of work and the home and family, which is itself reinforced by the inequality inherent in conditions of employment.

2 GOVERNMENT JOB CREATION MEASURES AND THEIR EFFECTS ON THE ENTRY OF WOMEN INTO THE LABOUR MARKET

Since the end of the 1970s, successive governments, faced with the dramatic rise in unemployment, have increased the number of job creation measures, piling one on top of the other without always stopping to consider the overall coherence of the system thus created. The result is that the structure of job creation schemes in France is now extremely complex, since it includes both:

(i) general and specific measures aimed at target categories (young people, women, the long-term unemployed, the older unemployed), sectors in which the restructuring currently taking place is accompanied by massive job losses (sectoral plans) and regions that are particularly badly hit;
and

(ii) supply side measures (training programmes, early retirement schemes), measures to improve the demand for labour and thus create jobs and measures to improve the functioning of the labour market (compensation for unemployment, improvements to the state employment services such as ANPE and AFPA[39]).

In view of this extreme complexity, it would be unrealistic to claim to be presenting an overall picture of the place of women within the whole range of measures. Instead we concentrate on those measures that currently constitute the main planks of government policy on job creation and those that are aimed exclusively at women.

From this point of view four measures are of particular interest. They include two general measures (the system of unemployment benefit and the job sharing policy) and two specific measures (those designed to help young people enter the labour market and those aimed at promoting equality between men and women in the world of work).

2.1 Unemployment benefit: the unequal functioning of the French system

As in most other Western countries, there has been a rapid increase in unemployment in France in the past ten years. In 1985, 2.4 million people were registered unemployed, just over 10% of the working population (Heller, 1985). Although women were not the first to be hit by rising unemployment (see Chapter 2), women form the largest single category of those affected. In March 1985, 50% of unemployed people were women, whereas they account for only 42% of the working population. Involuntary job losses (redundancies, loss of insecure jobs) are the main element in the rise in both male and female unemployment.

Already disadvantaged in the labour market, women are doubly disadvantaged with respect to unemployment benefit. Fewer women are entitled to benefit, and average benefit rates for women are significantly lower than for men.

There are no specific discriminatory rules against women that give rise to this uneven distribution of unemployment benefit. The inequalities inherent in the funtioning of the labour market are reproduced in the functioning of the unemployment benefit system or the national insurance scheme whose own internal rules reflect the functioning of the employment system.

Ever since its belated introduction in 1958 the French system of unemployment benefit has provided unequal treatment and benefits. Reforms in 1967 and 1979 were designed to reduce, if not eliminate, the inequalities arising from the system's selective coverage of the population, variable benefit rates and entitlement periods. The effect of these reforms was to bring a higher percentage of the population within the scope of the benefit system, so that by 1981 61% of unemployed women and 69%of unemployed men were receiving benefit compared to 36% and 40% respectively in 1973. Indeed from 1979 until 1982 the French system of unemployment benefit was one of the most generous in Europe (Euvrard, 1982) but this improvement in benefits coincided with a massive increase in unemployment which threatened to destabilise the financial basis of the system.

In 1982, the government, followed by the trade unions and employers in 1984, adopted a series of measures intended to cut back the system. These measures included restricting the period of entitlement to the period of contribution to the system (1982), reductions in benefit rates, restricting benefit rights by extending the minimum period of contribution and the application of more restrictive conditions of access to the 'solidarity allowance' for single women with family responsibilities (1984). The cuts particularly affected one of the categories hardest hit by the worsening in general employment conditions: workers in insecure jobs, a high proportion of whom are adult women and young people.

Not only are women and young people disadvantaged in terms of benefit rates and period of entitlement to benefit, they also constitute, within the framework of the new system, the largest population of unemployed people not covered by the system. The signs of the current worsening in unemployment protection for women can already be observed. In September 1984, one unemployed woman in two was drawing no unemployment benefit, either under the unemployment insurance scheme or under the so-called 'solidarity' scheme (Dejean and Revoil, 1985).

The consequences of these cutbacks in social security are to accentuate the concentration and reproduction of cycles of precariousness among the most marginalised groups of unemployed in the labour market. In the current employment situation, a lower level of protection for the unemployed means less protection from being thrown back on the secondary segment of the labour market and, as a consequence, less protection from the risk of recurrent unemployment (Bouillaguet-Bernard and Outin, 1984).

2.2 Work sharing: the different effects for men and women

Since 1981, the work sharing policy has been one of the main planks of government employment policy. The term 'work sharing' is taken to mean any form of reduction in working hours with the aim of reducing unemployment (or its rate of increase).

The French work sharing policy is based on two principles:
(i) the principle of legal constraints (the 39 hour week, the 5th week of paid holiday and lowering of the normal age of retirement to 60);
(ii) the principle of 'contractual persuasion' (the so-called 'solidarity contracts' aimed at encouraging early retirement and additional reductions in working hours).

Initially, the main emphasis was on encouraging reductions in working hours. These measures did not have the anticipated effect (Michon, 1985, and Commissariat General du Plan, 1984). So from 1984 onwards, there was a shift of emphasis towards encouraging flexibility in working time as well as reductions in working time (Elbaum, 1984).

Case studies of firms (see Boisard et al., 1985; Michon, 1985 and Commissariat Général du Plan 1984) have revealed differences in the ways in which working time reductions have been introduced, differences which are not apparent from macro statistics. These differences are related to the principal motives behind the change, and to whether or not it involved male or female workers. Working time reductions might be introduced out of legal necessity, to further social welfare, to defend jobs or to increase efficiency. Where the main motive was to defend jobs in the context of falling production, the volume of employment for men tends to be reduced through short-time working or early retirement, but for women it is reduced through the introduction of part-time work. When the aim is to increase efficiency, there are differences again in the treatment of male and female employees. In male-dominated manufacturing firms, productivity gains are ensured by the extension of shift working to increase utilisation of equipment, and by moves to monthly or annual working time to adapt employment to levels of activity. These measures have been introduced along with partial or full compensation for loss of wages. In female-dominated sectors shift working with both reduced hours and reduced wages is often introduced.[40] These changes in working hours are even more common in services where the aim is to adapt labour hours to maximise contact with the public.

Thus the ways in which working hours are adjusted or reduced when the workers in question are mainly men affect total working hours[41] and the collective employment form. For women, on the other hand, reduced working hours and wages are more usually introduced, sometimes with irregular working hours or part-time work; in this case, therefore, a particular employment form and contract is established.

Moreover working hours can be more easily individualised with a female work force. The aim of the second phase of the work sharing policy, after 1984, was to encourage not simply the reduction of but also increased flexibility in working hours. The latest measures explicitly encourage part-time work (Elbaum, 1984). Two simple observations can be used to justify this argument. Firstly, part-time work has for several years played a crucial role in the creation of new jobs (Perronet and Rocherieux, 1985). Secondly, an assessment of the measures taken clearly shows that employment forms with reduced hours and wages are one of the main ways in which work sharing and flexibility can be combined.[42]

The majority of part-time workers are women.[43] Despite the increase in part-time working, this job form has retained its essential characteristics: highly feminised, low skill levels and mainly in the service sector. According to statistics and statements by employers and trade unions, however, there has been some movement towards making part-time work a more standard and more permanent job form.[44]

Thus we are dealing here with general measures to boost employment that are based on a specific form of employment and therefore on a particular category of labour, which runs the risk of being disadvantaged thereby. The development of reduced and individualised working hours, the so-called flexi-time[45] does not currently affect the whole of the labour force. It is undeniable that while firms regard the introduction of more flexible and shorter working hours as ways of making more flexible use of their labour force, this development is indicative of the need for women to reconcile the constraints of family responsibilities with their working lives.

The diversification and individualisation of working hours may well lead to new inequalities, reinforce traditional family roles and extend the forms of discrimination that operate within the employment system.

2.3 The place of females in schemes for helping young people to enter the labour market

Youth unemployment in France is, together with Italy, the highest in Europe; the unemployment rate for under 25s was 26 per cent in March 1985. As a result of the scale of the problem, there have been a series of different schemes introduced to alleviate youth unemployment, with ten in existence in 1984/85. These schemes fall mainly into two types: those where firms enter into a contract with the state to offer employment or training to young people in return for partial or full exemption from social security payment;[46] and secondly those offering vocational training[47] to young people, funded out of public funds and only indirectly linked to employment in firms, even though some schemes offer work experience. Young people in the first type of scheme have the status of employee, and in the latter of vocational trainee. Girls are under-represented on the first type of scheme, which are also the most effective schemes for job creation. In 1982–3 they only accounted for 41% of young people on employment-training contracts and 24% on apprenticeship contracts (Huet, 1984), at a time when they accounted for 60% of young people seeking work. Moreover the percentage of girls in these schemes has continued to fall even though government policy has been to increase their access to such schemes.[48] Representation in the vocational schemes is more equal but these are not directly linked to firms and are consequently less effective at job creation. These findings reveal that if firms are allowed to influence the operation of these policies they will result in unequal treatment for women.

Moreover the sexual division of labour is being reproduced within these schemes (Bouillaguet-Bernard et al., 1985) as girls are confined to jobs and training courses that reproduce the stereotypes of men's and women's jobs (Gadrey-Turin, 1985).

This raises the question of whether the policies for occupational equality between men and women include schemes that are more effective in encouraging women's employment.

2.4 Occupational equality policies

An examination of the effect of government policies on women's employment must consider the legislation that both introduced anti-discriminatory measures and attempted to encourage the entry of women into the labour market. Indeed the introduction of legislation aimed at increasing occupational equality between men and women is still the government programme that has done most to establish the right of women to work (Maruani, 1985).

Taken chronologically, the laws that define the right of women to work developed first to protect that right, particularly the right to combine working and motherhood, and then second to give women autonomy (in 1907, married women were given control over their own wages, in 1920 they obtained the right to trade union membership without the authorisation of their husband and in 1965 they obtained the right to work without the authorisation of their husband). Since 1946, legislation has gradually introduced a logic of occupational equality. The law of 22 December 1972 established the principle of equal pay for men and women for 'the same work or work of equal value'.

The law of 4 July 1975 prohibited any sexist considerations or reference to family situations in offers of employment, and made it illegal to refuse a job to or dismiss anyone on grounds of sex, 'unless there is a legitimate reason'.

Finally, the law of 13 July 1983 on occupational equality[49] corrected certain shortcomings in the earlier legislation and introduced a change of perspective into the legislative framework. The new law replaced the defensive principle of non-discrimination with the positive principle of equality in employment, training, promotion, wages, etc., and did away with the loophole provided by the 'legitimate reason' clause. A restrictive list of jobs reserved for one or other of the sexes was drawn up and a precise definition of 'work of equal value' was put forward: 'work requiring from wage earners, a comparable range of vocational knowledge established by certificate, diploma or practical experience, of skills derived from the experience acquired, of responsibilities and of physical or mental stress'.

The law also promoted equality of opportunity, taking into account the disadvantages accumulated by women and the need to redress the balance of socially and historically unequal situations by means of positive discrimination in favour of women.

The law not only created the conditions for establishing equality of opportunity but also established the means for exercising the new rights. Firms with more than 50 employees have to draw up annual reports on the relative situation of men and women. They are submitted to the works councils and then sent on to the Factory Inspectorate. The areas to be covered by law are as follows: general conditions of employment, hiring, training, promotion, qualification and classification, working conditions and actual pay levels.

Firms may introduce temporary measures that discriminate positively in favour of women, for example in the areas of recruitment and vocational training. In order to do this, they have the option of implementing 'Vocational Equality Plans' for which they receive financial assistance from the state.

Finally, the law introduced new opportunities for trade unions and factory inspectors to take legal action in the case of discriminatory offers of employment, hiring practices or dismissals.

This legislative framework seems to offer certain guarantees of actual change and strengthens the trend towards equality of treatment for men and women at the work place (Sabourin, 1984).[50] However, these changes will only prove effective if there is mutual agreement between both sides of industry on the schemes to be implemented (Laufer, 1984). Beyond the conditions established by the law, the egalitarian dynamic must become incorporated into firms' employment strategies.

Since July 1983, about ten Equality Plans have been negotiated and signed. Others are currently under discussion. The reports on the relative situations of men and women are an undeniably useful way of gathering information and keeping firms under scrutiny. However, they are only the initial instrument in a procedure that must be voluntarist if the objectives of equality are to be achieved. While the law prevents all forms of direct discrimination, the persistent economic crisis has led to the appearance of new forms of discrimination to add to the existing types of indirect discrimination which are very difficult to fight against. Among these types of indirect discrimination, mention should be made of the discrimination linked to the systems of unemployment benefit and to the logics of work sharing which, by increasing the amount of part-time work, introduce new ways of ensuring that women remain in an inferior position within the employment system.

3 CONCLUSION

During the thirty years of high growth (1945–75), the question of women's work was at the heart of the contradictions between, on the one hand, the objectives of family policies that were dominated by a concern to support the family unit and to increase the birth rate and, on the other, employment policies that encouraged the development of women's work as an answer to the labour shortages that threatened to compromise the pattern of strong and regular economic growth.

With the collapse of the French economy and the large-scale destruction of jobs in manufacturing industry, there has been a radical change in the issues surrounding women's work.

Despite the large amount of public money that has been spent, the government has not succeeded in bringing down unemployment and has only just been able to slow down the rate at which it is increasing. There might therefore be a great temptation for the government to encourage women to withdraw from the labour market.

In fact, the French government does not have a unified or deliberate policy aimed at sending women back to the home, or at keeping them there in the first place, nor is it developing selective employment policies that would encourage men to re-enter into the labour market while discouraging women from so doing.[51]

The legitimacy of women's work and the right of women to work are gains which for the moment remain undisputed, at least as far as the general principles are concerned. It is, however, necèssary to point out the existence of flagrant contradictions between the general principles that affirm the right of all people to work, the employment creation schemes that help to worsen the already inferior position of women in the labour market and the social security systems which, without actually being a brake on women's participation, continue to confer tax advantages, as well as free social security benefits and family allowances on mothers who remain at home.

We have identified a range of examples of such contradictions in policy. These include the relative exclusion of women from state employment promotion schemes, which were aimed at helping the most disadvantaged groups, such as women, but which in fact have tended to recreate the inherent inequalities of the labour market system. The work-sharing programme has encouraged the development of individualised working hours and thus stimulated the growth of part-time work, but this employment form has remained exclusively female. This trend is therefore likely to result in further compartmentalism between men's and women's work, with women alone bearing the financial burden of work sharing. Finally, the change in the family allowance system has both established a new concept, of an allowance payable for a baby and not for a family, which breaks the link between social welfare payments and the traditional family. At the same time, a 'bringing up' allowance was introduced specifically for women on low income levels who leave work to bring up a third child. By paying a certain category of economically active women, however small in numbers they may be, to interrupt their working lives, the notion of a 'household income' is confirmed (which reinforces the idea of the top-up income), and divisions are created between different groups of women.

Thus our examination of the whole range of policies and their contradictory logics leads to the conclusion that there is a diversity of strategies with regard to women. In the crisis, the female labour force has not been treated in an homogeneous way. The fact that most women work means that this is no longer possible. On the other hand, the legitimacy of an uninterrupted working life and of stable employment is being undermined.

The reinforcing of inequalities is based on the characteristics of the various categories of women: social classes, family forms and family responsibilities. The coherence of state intervention, through social and employment policies, in women's work, is perhaps to be found in the creation of these differences.

NOTES

1 The link between this observation and methods of child care for young children will be examined more closely in the next section.
2 The structure of female employment in the non-wage-earning categories (farmers, artisans, shop-keepers, self-employed) is somewhat unusual. Participation rates by age for married women exceed 70% and are not very sensitive to family responsibilities. This unusual structure is linked to the characteristics of their employment. It is mainly non-waged, part-time work (help in the family business). The fact that they live and work in the same place gives the women great flexibility in the organisation of their working and domestic lives.
3 There is a significant relationship between the rates of part-time working among women and the number of children: in 1980, 15% of married women aged between 20 and 54 with less than two children rising to 21% for women with two children and to 30% for women with three or more children. In P. Laulhe, 'La montée du chômage féminin', *Economie et Statistique*, October 1980, no. 126.
4 Compulsory schooling starts at 6 in France.
5 Data from the 1982 census.
6 The age at which children start nursery school depends on various factors: the month of birth, local policy on day care, social class.
7 Population census.
8 These figures are taken from the Family Survey, carried out by INSEE in 1982 among a sample of 4,000 women as part of the census and from Ministry of Health data from 1983.
9 Almost 16% of economically active women with a child less than three years old work between 15 and 29 hours a week. A third of these women look after their own children.
10 Day nurseries do not look after children for the whole day.
11 There are also creches organised by parents based on the principle of developing private initiatives.
12 Since 1980, the social security contributions paid by parents for the mother's help that they employ have subsequently been reimbursed by the Child Benefit Office. Since 1984, child care costs have been taken into account in the calculation of income tax if parents use a registered form of child care (creches or mother's help) (Leprince, 1985).
13 Relative difference: $\dfrac{\text{men's wages} - \text{women's wages}}{\text{men's wages}} \times 100$.
This is an average difference that varies according to qualifications (Bughin and Payen 1985).
14 In particular the entry of women into sectors and skill areas where they have traditionally been few in number (see Chapter 2). Moreover, the reduction in the gap between men's and women's wages is part of the more general trend towards a narrowing of the wages hierarchy. Having been considerably widened between 1950 and 1967, due partly to the relative shortage of managers, the wages hierarchy has since narrowed considerably. The ratio of the average earnings of a senior manager to those of a manual worker increased from 3.3 in 1950 to 4.5 in 1967, falling back again to 3.5 in 1980 (Willard, 1984).
15 Salaire Minimum Interprofessional Garanti.

16 Salaire Minimum Interprofessionel de Croissance. In July 1985, it was fixed at 26.04 F per hour, i.e. 3,728 F (net) per month.

17 The SMIC is subject to an automatic increase by decree as soon as the price index rises by 2% or more.

18 Which the authors of the CERC-INED survey estimate to be between 6,000 F and 7,500 F a month for 1984 for working mothers. Lollivier (1984) estimates it at three times the SMIC.

19 The family allowance rate increases with the number of children.

20 Housing benefit and family income supplement are both subject to means tests.

21 'For women, family policies are also employment policies' (Maruani, 1985, p. 79).

22 The same applies to the allowance paid to mothers looking after children at home, which was simply the counterpart of the single wage allowance for wives whose husbands were economically active but not wage earners.

23 At the same time there was a dissociation within government institutions between questions specific to women (viz. the establishment in 1975 of the post of Secretary of State for women's affairs) and those relating to the family (dealt with by the Ministry for Social Affairs).

24 As early as the mid-1960s, the share of income tax relative to family allowances in all social transfers to families was beginning to increase.

25 The income ceiling giving entitlement to family income supplement is fairly low – which excludes all but a minority of women from receiving it.

26 Other similar measures include sharply increased maternity grants for children after the second one and households with at least three children are entitled to additional tax allowances (measures implemented in 1980).

27 This selectivity is based on three fundamental criteria: the number of children, the age of the family and of the children and income.

28 Since 1977, it has been possible, at the end of the statutory maternity leave, for one of the parents to take unpaid leave from their job in order to bring up the child with the guarantee that the job would be held open for them.

29 It is precisely among these families that the women most frequently interrupt their working life.

30 Employment and unemployment benefits will be dealt with in Section 2.

31 Social security contributions amount to 18.2% of total wages; employers' contributions account for 12.6% and employees' contributions for 5.6%.

32 Until 1984, moreover, contributions did not increase beyond a certain maximum wage level, which meant that contributions were a relatively greater burden for lower-paid workers. This unequal system has been abolished.

33 There may exist very complex partial cumulation rules between entitlement in own right and derived entitlement. In order to be entitled to a reversionary pension, earned income at the time of application must be lower than the SMIC.

34 The difference in cumulative wages between men and women over the ten best years of earning is about 33% (relative to women's wages). A women's working life is on average 10 years shorter than that of a man (interruption of economic activity, work in the 'black economy').

35 The progressive tax system is based on the view that it is the standard of living and not total income that must be established, particularly if the standard of living is high. The calculation is carried out in the following

way: the household income is divided by a number of portions or shares that increase with the number of people in the household. A sliding scale is then applied to the resultant total, which gives the tax payable per share. The total tax liability is calculated by multiplying this figure by the number of shares.

36 The number of shares is calculated according to the following rule: one share for each married partner (or per adult in the case of single people) and one half share for each child; an additional half share is granted to families with three or more children and also to certain other categories, including people over 65 and single parents.

37 I.e. two shares are applied to the sum of two incomes rather than one share being applied to each of the incomes.

38 For the purposes of simplification, we are disregarding the effect of the number of children and isolating the impact that more directly penalises women's work.

39 Agence Nationale pour l'Emploi and Association pour la Formation Professionnelle des Adultes (National Employment Agency and Association for Adult Vocational Training).

40 The banning of night work for women acts as a constraint.

41 With partial or total compensation for wages lost.

42 The introduction of part-time working means that for temporary peaks of activity the same work force can be retained but working hours increased by the use of overtime. For the work force, this combines irregular working hours with fluctuating earnings.

43 More than 86% of part-time jobs are held by women; 20% of women are part-time workers.

44 Employers obviously reserve part-time work for women and working mothers, particularly in the service sector. For their part, the trade unions cannot protest against what is now a social reality, but simply expose the problems and ambiguities associated with part-time work.

45 The term flexi-time is often misleading. Variable working hours, weekend working, split shifts and reduced working hours often lead to constantly changing schedules for individuals. This has the effect of increasing time constraints rather than relieving them if family life and working life have somehow to be reconciled.

46 These schemes include the apprenticeship contracts (1971), the employment/training contracts (1975), the qualification or adaptation contracts (1984), support to 'intermediate' firms (1985).

47 These schemes include the 16–18 (1982) and 18–21 (1982) schemes, the Work Initiation scheme (1984) and the 'stages jeunes volontaires' (1982).

48 During the 1983–84 campaign, only 38% of the young people on employment-training contracts were women (Guasco 1985).

49 This law is known as the 'Loi Roudy'.

50 Cf. the directives of the EEC.

51 These comments refer to the Socialist governments under Mitterand. This paper was written before the election of a conservative government.

REFERENCES

Amat, F. (1985) 'Les mesures en faveur de la formation et de l'emploi des jeunes de 1977 à 1985', *Revue Formation et Emploi*, no. 9 Jan. Mar.

Bloch-Michel, C. and Picard M. (1980), *Le contrat Emploi-Formation, portée et limites d'un dispositif d'aide à l'insertion des jeunes*, Service des Etudes et de la Statistique, Ministère du Travail, Jan.

Boisard, P. Bouillaguet-Bernard, P. and Letablier, M. T. (1985), *Les effets de la politique de partage du travail sur les emplois tenus par les hommes et les femmes*, Communication à la Commission Emploi du Conseil Supérieur pour l'Egalité Professionnelle, Oct.

Bouillaguet-Bernard, P., Gauvin, A. and Prokovas, N. (1985), *La place des femmes dans les dispositifs des politiques d'emploi au sein de la Communauté Economique Européenne*, Rapport pour la Communauté Economique Européenne, Déc.

Bouillaguet-Bernard, P. and Outin, J. L. (1984), 'Le nouveau régime d'indemnisation du chômage face aux transformations de l'emploi: l'éclatement de l'économique et du social', in 'Le chômage éclaté', *Critiques de l'Economie Politique*. Sept.

Bughin, E. and Payen, J. F. (1985), 'La disparité des salaires des hommes et des femmes', *Travail et Emploi*, no. 23, Mar.

Canceil, G. (1985), 'L'effet redistributif de l'impôt direct et des prestations familiales', *Economie et Statistique*, no. 177, Mai.

CERC (1985), 'Mères de famille: coûts et revenus de l'activité professionnelle', *Document du CERC*, no. 75.

CERC (1985), 'Les revenues des Français: la croissance et la crise – 1963–1983', *Document du CERC*, no. 77.

Charraud, A. (1978), 'Activité féminine et famille: aspects socio-économiques', in *Données Sociales – INSEE*.

Commissariat Général du Plan (1984), 'Aménagement et réduction du temps de travail', *La documentation française*.

Courson, J. P. and Saboulin, M. de (1985), 'Ménages et familles: vers de nouveaux modes de vie', *Economie et Statistiques*, no. 175, March.

Dejean, G. and Revoil, J. P. (1985), 'Les chômeurs non indemnisés au 30 Septembre 1984', in *Bilan de l'Emploi 1983 – Dossiers Statistiques du Travail et de l'emploi*, nos. 12–13, Ministère du Travail, de l'Emploi et de la Formation Professionnelle, Sept.

Desplanques, G. (1985), 'Modes de garde et scolarisation des jeunes enfants', *Economie et Statistiques*, no. 176, Apr.

Droit Social (Special Issue) (1985), *Regard sur les prestations familiales*, May.

Eckert, O. (1983), 'Activité féminine, prestations familiales et redistribution', *Population*, May–June.

Elbaum, M. (1984), 'La politique de l'emploi en 1984' in *Bilan de l'Emploi 1984, Dossier Statistiques du Travail et de l'Emploi*, nos 12–13, Sep.

Euvrard, F. (1982), 'L'indemnisation du chômage en France et à l'étranger', *Document du CERC*, no. 62.

Gadrey-Turpin, N. (1985), 'Le dispositif 16–18 ans, une chance de qualification pour les filles?', *Revue Consommation*, no. 1.

Glaude, M. (1984), 'Diversité et cohérence des budgets', in *Données Sociales*, INSEE.

Goupil, A. and Trimouille, F. (1982), 'Le contrat emploi-formation en 1980;

un processus de sélection et d'adaptation de la main-d'oeuvre âgée de 16 à 26 ans', *Travail et Emploi*, no 13, Jul–Sep.

Guasco, G. (1985), 'Les contrats emploi-formation', in *Bilan de l'emploi 1984, Dossiers Statistiques du Travail et de l'Emploi*, nos. 12–13 Sep. Ministère du Travail.

Heller, J. L. (1985), 'Emploi et chômage en mars 1985', *Economie et Statistique*, no. 183, Déc.

Henin, P. Y. (1985), *Un aperçu des résultats économétriques relatifs aux explications de l'offre de travail et du chômage*, Group de Travail 'Emploi – Chômage, INSEE, Mar.

Henniquau, L. (1984), 'Protection sociale et fiscalité: une législation sexiste!' *Cahier No 8 du Club Flora Tristan*, Mar.

Houzel-Vaneffenterre, Y. (1985), 'La famille se transforme, les opinions se nauncent: 1978–1983', *Revue Consommation*, no. 1.

Huet, M. (1984), 'L'impact des politiques d'emploi menées depuis 1981 sur la situation socio-professionnelle des femmes', *Travail et Emploi*, no. 21 Sept.

IRES (1983), 'La protection sociale', *Dossier* no. 1, Nov.

Journal Officiel de la République Française (1985), *Droits nouveaux: Egalité professionnelle entre les hommes et les femmes*.

Laufer, J. (1984), 'Egalité professionnelle, principes et pratiques', *Droit Social*, no. 12, Dec.

Lenoir, R. (1985), 'La politique familiale et la femme depuis 1945', *Cahiers de l'APRE*, no. 1, Feb.

Leprince, F. (1985), *L'accueil des jeunes enfants: les actions des comités d'enterprise et des associations parentales*, Laboratoire d'Economie Sociale, Etude réalisée pour la Caisse Nationale des Allocations Familiales, Dec.

Lollivier, S. (1984), 'Revenu offert, prétentions salariales et activité des femmes mariées: un modèle d'analyse', *Economie et Statistique*, no. 167, Jun.

Lolliver, S. (1985), 'Une évaluation récente des revenus fiscaux des ménages', *Economie et Statistique*, no. 177, May.

Maruani, M. (1985), *Mais qui a peur du travail des femmes*, Syros.

Michon, F. (1985), *Succès et échecs d'un traitement social du chômage: l'expérience française d'une politique contractuelle de partage du travail*, Cahier du Séminaire d'Economie du Travail, no. 85.

OECD (1983), *'Effets du salaire minimum sur le marché du travail des jeunes en Amérique du Nord et en France*, Etudes spéciales, Jun.

OECD (1985), *Perspectives Economiques: France*, Rapport, July.

Perronet, F. and Rocherieux, F. (1985), Temps partiel féminin: principal statut des emplois créés après la crise' in *Bilan de l'Emploi 1984, Dossiers statistiques du travail et de l'emploi*, nos. 12–13, Sep.

Sabourin, A. (1984), *Le travail des femmes dans la CEE*, Economica, Paris.

Villeneuve Gokalp, C. (1985), 'Incidences des charges familiales sur l'organisation du travail professionnel des femmes', *Revue Population* no. 2, Mar–Apr.

Wagner, J. J. (1985), 'Les salariés au SMIC en Juillet 1984', *Dossiers Statistiques du Travail et de l'Emploi*, no. 17, Ministère du Travail, Nov.

Willard, J. C. (1984), 'Les salaires', *Données Sociales*, INSEE.

7 Women, the state and the family in Italy: problems of female participation in historical perspective

Francesca Bettio

1 INTRODUCTION

Compared to other countries, Italy has experienced a late growth in female participation, reversing the steady decline which prevailed until the late 1960s. Moreover, 'hidden' forms of participation have remained very important, their dynamism being revived by the growth of a modern, 'informal' or 'submerged' sector with greater resilience to stagflation.

However the recent increase in participation has led to higher unemployment accounting for about half of the rise in measured female participation, a result partly caused by the recent stagnation in aggregate labour demand, at least in the 'official' sector of the economy. To understand this pattern of participation, and to identify whether the potential growth of female labour supply is likely to be curbed by unfavourable demand conditions, we need to adopt an historical perspective. This paper for this reason makes reference back to the beginning of this century.

Models of long term female participation proposed for other countries provide a poor fit for the Italian case. Orthodox interpretations, following Mincer (1962), favour comparison between the substitution effect of rising female wages and the income effect, the dominance of the former being taken to explain the behaviour of the main category of growing female participation, i.e. married women. Some Marxist analyses also depend on wages, but in this case wages in relation to men's wages. Beechey (1977) identifies the driving force behind the postwar attraction of cheaper female labour to be the fall in the rate of profit. For Humphries (1983), instead, relaxation of sex-linked segmentation accounts for the increasing competitiveness of female labour and, hence rising employment, especially over the late post-war period.

Wages seem to be of doubtful importance for explaining the pattern of participation in Italy. Considerable increases in relative female pay occurred long before as well as after the upward turn in the participation rate. In fact real wages for women rose but with occasional reversals before the end of World War Two, but have risen consistently since.[1] Whatever the specification chosen for wages, their movements do not correlate with the pattern of aggregate female participation, nor even with that for married women separately, whose participation rate, in contrast to the aggregate female pattern, stopped declining around the 1930s. Yet, even this growth in participation was extremely modest until the late 1960s. Hence, married women's response to rising female wages (in real terms) was disconcertingly slow, even if in the expected direction.

Approaches which explain participation by institutional factors and labour market segmentation seem more promising. Sex-typing of occupations breaks the link between wages and levels of employment and participation is thus tied strictly to the occupational distribution of aggregate demand for labour (Oppenheimer, 1970; Boserup, 1970). But while we share with these approaches both the rejection of the 'wage hypothesis' and the alternative formulation of a sex-segregated labour demand, we do not consider it valid to reject all supply-side influences on the determination of the participation rate (Humphries and Rubery, 1984). For example, this kind of approach would not be able to explain different trends in participation between married and non-married women.

What follows proposes a three-way analysis that focuses on sex-typing on the demand side, key modifications to the economy of the family on the supply side and the welfare state as the mediating agent; that is, the agent increasingly called upon to coordinate the reproduction of labour and its participation in production. The discussion is organised accordingly. The first part of the paper deals with the importance of sex-typing for the pattern of participation and, in particular, with current obstacles to the full integration of female labour. The second part deals with the role of the family and of the state. Future prospects and the impact on female labour of current employment policies are discussed in the final section.

2 THE LABOUR MARKET: THE IMPACT OF SEX-TYPING ON PARTICIPATION OVER THE LONG TERM

If sex-typing is rigid in the long term, changes in female employment will be explained simply by changes in the industrial and occupational composition of demand (the growth effect: see introduction to section one, p. 12). If sex-typing or the share of female employment within occupational or industrial categories is variable over the long term, then employment may not be determined by the size and structure of demand and supply-side factors may be playing some role. However the interpretation of the share effect (that is the growth in female employment attributable to changes in sex ratios, assuming a constant structure of demand) as an indication solely of supply-side changes is problematic, not least because any statistical occupational category includes a number of different occupations, with different patterns of sex-typing, so that changes in the share may be the result of demand-side changes in the relative importance of female or male dominated occupations.

With these provisos, we will attempt to use this type of decomposition[2] to analyse the changes in the participation rate in Italy. Here we are explaining changes in percentage of women employed, and not absolute levels. Thus a negative growth effect here implies that the employment growth associated with changes in the structure of demand was not sufficient to maintain a constant proportion of the female population in employment, and conversely a positive growth effect implies that changes in population alone without an increase in the participation rate would not have been sufficient to match the demand for female labour under stable sex-typing of industries and occupations. The data on participation rates includes some of the unemployed, that is those with previous work experience, so that this growth effect may include a small supply-side element, but the number of unemployed is relatively trivial. The share effect is, as mentioned above, also likely to include demand as well as supply-side influences, the more so because we have had to use industry and not occupational breakdowns because of the lack of standardisation between censuses. Particular caution must be attributed to the 1971–81 results because they had to be constructed on a 9 industry instead of a 65 industry classification which was used for all the other results.[3]

Results are summarised in Table 7.1. It appears that over the first half of the century – 1901 to 1951 – 78% of the decrease in the female rate of participation is attributable to the growth component. In fact between 1951 and 1971, the growth component would, alone, have caused a decrease larger than the actual decrease. Its impact is partly offset by the tendency of the share component to increase participation but the growth effect remained dominant. The growth effect also dominates change in each inter-census period with two exceptions: the results for 1931–6 quinquennium when the campaign of Abyssinia temporarily reversed the negative trend and the results for the 1911–21 decade which may be due to the unreliability of the 1921 census.

As noted, the decreasing trend in participation was finally reversed during the seventies. Between 1971 and 1981 the female rate exclusive of unemployed first entrants (as in Table 7.1) increased by 4.6 percentage points, the full rate by 7.1 points, from 19.6 to 26.7. The rise continued into the 1980s according to the Labour Force Sample Survey: from 26.5 in 1981 to 27.8 in 1984. Definitions of activity are not strictly comparable between the two sources, but this is likely to affect the precise magnitude of the change rather than its direction.

The decomposition of the increase between the two latest censuses

Table 7.1 Contribution of the share and growth effects to inter-census variations in female activity rates[a]

(a) *Activity rates*

1901	1911	1921	1931	1936	1951	1961	1971	1981
37.1	35.1	33.5	30.2	31.6	23.5	20.4	18.4	22.9

(b) *Change in activity rates*

Inter-census period	Change in participation rate[b]	Growth effect[b]	Share effect[b]
1901–11	−1.9	−3.0	+1.1
1911–21	−1.6	−0.5	−1.1
1921–31	−3.3	−3.1	−0.2
1931–36	+1.5	+0.2	+1.3
1936–51	−8.5	−5.1	−3.4
1951–61	−2.8	−3.5	+0.7
1961–71	−2.0	−2.6	+0.6
1971–81	+4.6[c]	+1.5[c]	+3.1[c]
1901–51	−13.9	−10.9	−3.0
1951–71	−4.8	−6.0	+1.2

[a] Activity rates as a percentage of the total female population.
[b] Growth effect + share effect = change in activity rate. See appendix for statistical formula.
[c] Based on 9 entries breakdown instead of a 65 breakdown for all other inter-census variations.

Source: See Bettio (forthcoming), Appendix 1 for all years between 1901 and 1971. Data for the 1971–81 comparison are taken from ISTAT, Banca Dati sul XII Censimento della Popolazione.

yields somewhat novel results. Both the share and the growth effects are positive, i.e. both contributed to increasing participation. Moreover, the share effect accounts for almost 70% of the increase against the 30% of the growth effect. Admittedly, because of the use of more aggregate data the growth effect is likely to be underestimated and conversely for the share effect, since the higher the aggregation the more the share effect is influenced by variations in the composition of activities classified under the same entry. In other words, the post-1970s shift towards a service economy might be responsible for the growth of female employment more than our test reveals, as was common experience earlier on in more mature economies. Notwithstanding, these results raise the possibility that supply factors were strongly behind the reversal of the trend.

Summing up, female participation in Italy was over a long period tied to the sectoral distribution of aggregate labour demand because of persistent sex-typing. As a result, a negative trend prevailed until the seventies. Thereafter, the relatively greater feminization of the growing service sector partially removed obstacles to the expansion of female activity; but only partially, because the growth in participation on account of the changing structure of demand alone would have been rather limited. In all probability the driving force behind the reversal of the trend came from factors on the supply side whose impact, even though feeble, was discernible even before the 1960s. Because of the hypotheses embedded in the previous tests and the ambiguous interpretation of the share effect this conclusion requires, however, independent assessment of developments on the supply side.

3 THE SUPPLY SIDE OF FEMALE PARTICIPATION: FAMILY AND INSTITUTIONAL DEVELOPMENTS

During the period of declining participation the explanations offered in Italy oscillated between the progressive withdrawal of female labour into domestic production or their withdrawal into areas of employment not covered by official statistics, mainly seasonal work or homework (Vinci 1974; Furnari et al., 1975; May 1973 and 1977; Frey et al., 1976; Padoa Schioppa, 1977). Withdrawal was seen as voluntary or involuntary depending on the perspective of the author. The parallel growth of female participation and unemployment during the last and the current decades came almost as a surprise and is taken to signal a turning point in the behaviour of female labour (Del Boca and Turvani 1980; Leoni, 1984).

Both current and earlier views are somewhat at odds with facts. The first oddity surfaces as soon as one distinguishes between married and non married women, since the decline in participation is associated with the latter who least fit the withdrawal explanation. This leads to the second oddity. Married women's participation showed a stable or mildly rising trend even before the post-war period, which puts in a different light the leap in their participation since the 1970s. It becomes an accentuation of an underlying and long-standing, if inconspicuous, tendency rather than a new qualitative development. Since, moreover, married women contributed the most to the recent growth of female activity, continuity offers a more fruitful perspective on the whole pattern.

Indeed, the long term opposing trends for the married and the non married components do not require different explanations: instead they can be seen as two sides of the same coin. Both are traceable to a fundamental development affecting the economy of the family, namely the decreasing value of the offspring as contributors of income and services to the original nucleus. The spread of welfare provisions like education, health care and security schemes for the elderly form a significant part of this development. The related modifications in the economy of the family changed both the constraints on and the convenience of paid work for married women through their influence on fertility, while at the same time entailing a reduction in the activity of single women.

This is the core of the argument developed in this section. We will first document the different participation trends by age and by marital status and link them to the pattern of fertility and the institutionalisation of welfare provisions.

3.1 The changing age profile of female labour

In Italy, as elsewhere, women in the extreme age groups – younger than 21 and older than 54 – consistently reduced their rates of activity, a development common to male labour as well (Table 7.2). The trend is traceable to the turn of the century, although its effects became more obvious in the post-war period. But, whereas for men central age groups have retained the primacy they always had, central age groups have only recently taken on major importance for women, since female activity rates continued to peak in the younger age groups until just before World War Two, in spite of the trend decline. The shift in the age profile of female and male labour alike has affected all sectors of the economy. Indicative of the situation for women is the case of industry where younger age groups have now completely lost their traditional pre-eminence. While in 1911 41.9% of all female industrial labour was aged below 21, only 12.5% was aged below 20 in 1981.

The modifications of the age structure of the active propulation unmistakably reflect shifts in the supply of its constituent segments. The underlying factors bear obvious connections to institutional developments: on the one hand the banning of child labour and the expansion of education, on the other, increasing provisions for retirement. The first restrictions on child labour date from 1886. Compulsory primary education for children was introduced one year later. Of course, both provisions were only gradually enforced, but the proportion of school children in the population aged 10 and 14 increased from 28.0% for men and 22.8% for women in 1901 to 65.1 and 53.3%, respectively, in 1931 and to 73.6% and 73.3% in 1961 (Vitali, 1970, p. 217 for 1901 and 1931; Census of Population, 1961). In the 1960s the legal working age was raised to 14 years of age. For older children – 14 to 18 years of age – the rate of school enrolment was already relatively high in 1966, 40.6% for men and 29.7% for women and grew to 54.6% and 51.1% respectively, in 1978–9 (Livraghi, 1984, p. 142).

The first compulsory insurance schemes covering retirement were implemented in 1919 for wage labour. As a result the proportion of

Table 7.2 Activity rates by sex and age group (over total population). 1911–1981

Age groups	Women						Men	
	1911[a]	1936[a]	1951[b]	1961[a]	1971[a]	1981[a]	1911[a]	1981[a]
0–9	0.0	0.0	0.0	0.0	0.0	0.0	0.0	0.0
10–14	31.5	18.6	12.1	6.7	0.0	0.0*	53.0	0.0*
15–20	52.6	49.8	34.1	36.4	30.7	16.8*	89.9	23.2*
21–24	} 42.7	47.2	36.5	37.1	38.9	44.6*	} 95.8	60.5*
25–29		} 35.7	30.5	28.4	32.3	50.4		} 89.7
30–34								
35–39	} 35.4	} 29.5	27.6	26.7	29.8	42.8	} 96.9	} 95.4
40–44								
45–49	} 32.9	} 24.8	24.8	23.7	28.3	33.3	} 94.0	} 88.9
50–54								
55–59		} 20.0	16.1	14.9	13.4	14.0		} 50.6
60–64								
>65	26.7	11.5	7.1	5.1	3.2	1.9	81.4	6.8
0–∞	29.0	24.0	20.2	18.8	18.4	22.9	66.2	49.4

[a] Excludes unemployed first entrants.
[b] Includes unemployed first entrants.
* A slight inaccuracy arises for 1981 since the first four age groups specified by the latest census are: 0–9, 10–13, 14–19 and 20–24.

Source: Reconstructed from Population Censuses, and Robotti (1978, p. 95).

pensioners among the elderly increased steadily though at a very slow rate for women at first. Taking only non active men above 65 to give an indication of the trend, the share of pensioners among them increased from 21.2% in 1911 to 34.3% in 1931 to 81.7% in 1961 (census data).

The growing weight of the central age groups consequent on declining activity of the extreme groups was not only far more accentuated for women, but in their case was also closely linked to the changing balance between the married and the non married.

3.2 Married and non married female participants

An expanding share of married women among female participants is traceable back to the first census that distinguishes activity by marital status, that of 1931. Notably, this development also appears to be fairly independent of the structure of demand, as married women's participation increased equally in all the sectors (Table 7.3), and there were divergent trends in the participation of the married and the non married (single, widowed, divorced).

The interpretation of available figures on the participation of these two components (Table 7.4) is, however, less than straightforward, partly due to problems of reliability and comparability, partly because

Table 7.3 Share of married women among active females, by sector. 1903–1984

Sector	1903	Proportion of married women (%)				
		1931	1936*	1961*	1971*	1981*	1984
Agriculture (1)	—	33.4	43.0	63.6	76.5	82.7	82.5†
Industry (2)	24.1ª	18.2	23.5	31.3	45.2	62.5	62.8†
Other activities (3)	—	19.1	24.1	35.5	44.7	63.6	64.0†
Total (1, 2, 3)	—	24.2	32.7	42.8	53.3	65.6	66.0†
Unemployed (first entrants) (4)	—	—	0.4	2.4	8.1	19.9	10.2
Total active population (1, 2, 3, 4)	—	24.2	31.9	41.5	50.4	59.1	60.7

ª Employees only (excludes self-employed) up to 55 years of age. MAIC (1905), Prospetto XXIV, pp. 54–5 reports a value of 27.5% for workers aged 15–55. The figure of 24.1 takes into account workers younger than 15 included in the sample (Prospetto IV, pp. 19–20) assuming that none of them were married.
* Married and legally separated.
† Unlike census data unemployed who previously held a job are excluded.

Note: Since figures are taken directly from censuses as well as other sources, allowance must be made for a degree of non homogeneity.

Source: Reconstructed from: Population Censuses; ISTAT, *Rilevazione delle forze di lavoro, media 1984*; MAIC (1905).

it must be set in historical context.[4] Though the rate of activity of married women was not separately recorded prior to 1931, the comparison between their 1931 census share of industrial employment and that reported by the 1903 ministerial survey (Table 7.3) suggests that their participation probably declined as well as that of the non married during the first thirty years of the century. Although the 1931 census data is of limited reliability this result is not unlikely, because of the rising importance of industry during the first decades of the century, which provided employment for young unmarried women. Service employment may have come to offset this tendency later on.

While the above hypothesis remains conjecture, the Abyssinia campaign around 1936 provides strong grounds for believing that the rate of activity of married women was higher in that year than in 1931, though perhaps not to the extent suggested by Table 7.4 – 20.7% compared to 12.0%. If the increase in 1936 is indeed accounted for by war conditions, then the slight fall recorded for 1961 could well be interpreted as a return to normality and not as the result of a negative trend. In fact, the comparison of the rate in 1961 to that in 1931 (18.3% and 12.0%, respectively) would suggest a rising trend interrupted by the exceptional interlude of 1936. This latter and less conservative interpretation finds support in subsequent developments, since between 1961 and 1971 the participation of married women continued to rise

Table 7.4 Activity rates of married and non-married women, 1931–1984†

	1931	1936	1961	1971	1981	1984
Status						
Married	12.0	20.7*	18.2*	21.1*	30.9*	32.9
Non married[a]	22.6	26.1	19.4	16.0	15.7	18.3
All	18.6	24.1	18.8	18.4	22.9	25.7

† From original census data and exclusive of unemployed first entrants.
* Married and legally separated.
[a] Non married include divorced, widowed and single women.

Note: Values for the activity rate of all women differ here from those of Table 7.1 because the latter refer to the standardized series from Vitali (1970). Figures for 1931 in this table must be discounted for a higher degree of underestimation compared to the others. Finally, figures for 1984 are taken from the current Labour Force Sample survey and are not, therefore, strictly comparable with census figures.

Source: Population Censuses and ISTAT, *Rilevazione delle forze di lavoro, media 1984.*

despite the slight decline in aggregate female participation. The rising trend has become obvious over the past and current decades.

In sum, it is around the 1930s that the pattern for married women became distinct from that of non married women. Doubts may remain as to whether a minor increase or overall stability characterised the period between the 1930s and the 1950s, but they do not lessen the contrast with the pattern of activity of non married women whose rate fell decisively from the beginning of the century until well into the early 1970s.

3.3 The changing economy of the family

The same factors which were significant in explaining the decreasing participation of single women have also changed the economic context for married women's participation. The lower participation of older age groups (men and women) has been accompanied by a slow growth in forms of income insurance, whereas falling activity of the young entailed a net reduction of family earnings, frequently in association with rising expenditure on education. On both these counts family income has become progressively less dependent on contributions from children, but increasingly reliant on those from parents. Growing participation of married women can be seen, we argue, as a response to decreasing contributions from children to the family, monetary and in kind, and thus related to the same developments that play a part in the falling activity of single women.

These developments reflect the modification that the family economy undergoes with the transition to a market system. Schematically, in pre-capitalist, agrarian societies the family is often the unit of production. Family members supply the necessary labour resources, so that control over reproduction and allocation of family labour is a key issue. As the labour market gains ground and commodity production is increasingly located outside the family, it is no longer possible for the family to generate either control over income earned by children or control over their services. There follows a potential decline in the value of the offspring to the family economy; potential so long as the alternative of children remaining tied to the original nucleus and pooling their income (earned outside) and their labour (for household production) continues to offer a solution for organising material survival acceptable to all concerned. The translation of potential into actual decline depends on the specific historic conditions in which the family operates.

In their historical study of European families during the nineteenth and twentieth century, Scott and Tilly (1978) locate the main factor that brought about the decline of the value of the offspring to the family in the individualistic drive inherent in a capitalist system, compounded by the increasing geographical mobility consequent on the dislocation of commodity production from the family. In their accounts children first started retaining part of their earnings and eventually severed financial links with the original nucleus by anticipating the formation of their own. Obligations in kind (e.g. assistance to parents in their old age or in sickness) can be assumed to have been also reduced as a consequence. In short, values about traditional children–parental obligations changed paving the way to the modern family. (See Amsden (1980) for review of Scott and Tilly (1978).)

Allegedly, the process began to interest Italian families (in the north) around the turn of the last century. However, we believe that if the study of the process of change in the family economy is carried on further into this century a different factor might appear relevant. The data reviewed earlier suggest that in Italy the size of the decline in the activity of the young was such that it could not fail to alter, on its own, the economic position of children in the family. The phenomenon, we have seen, is linked to institutional developments such as the ban on child labour as well as the setting up of a system of public education. There was a parallel growth in forms of insurance for the unwaged, the sick and the elderly in particular, at first through charities and later taken over by the state.[5] Gradually these further undermined the need to secure inter-generational financial links and child–parental obligations in general. Links and obligations have by no means disappeared to this date. They are in fact stronger in Italy due to traditional inadequacy of overall welfare provisions and may have been recently reinforced by the growth of unemployment. Nevertheless they lack the earlier cogence and exist within irreversibly altered parent-child relations. The significance of institutional developments for modifications in the family economy arise from the need to secure coordination between production and reproduction. The transition from a family to a wage labour system means that institutions external to the family are progressively called to take upon themselves the coordination earlier provided by the family. In this role the state or, more broadly, social institutions become an integral part of the functioning of the labour market.

When traditional sexual roles are accepted (and we stress the implication of this premise) and when children pool their resources within the family, at least while unmarried, it can make sense for married women to give priority to reproduction both from their own point of view and that of the overall family welfare. Priority is turned into a stark choice when reproduction and rearing are difficult to combine with labour market participation on account of prevailing material conditions for childbirth and childrearing, for example if labour market participation cannot be combined with breastfeeding, at a period when the latter is essential for children's health. The declining value of children to the family economy weakens this priority to the detriment of fertility and in favour of higher participation in the labour market.[6]

If then, as we maintain, the link between the observed modifications in the age profile of the active population and the emergence of a distinct trend for married women is to be found in the changing economy of the family, we should next find a correspondence between these modifications and the pattern of fertility.

3.4 The pattern of fertility

The relation between fertility and work of married women must first be studied on a cross-section basis, where it emerges more directly. According to local surveys throughout the post-war period working wives recorded lower fertility than housewives with the significant exception of women engaged in agriculture and waged homework. Indeed, married women working in agriculture tend to be the most fertile, followed by housewives (whose incidence is higher in non-agricultural households) on a par with homeworkers.[7] Notably, this order is independent of the level of family income. A recent national survey provides the information that participation of married women tends to fall with every additional child. The proportion of couples with wife working was 39.8% for the first child in 1984 and fell progressively with the number of children to 20.0% for couples with five children or more.[8]

Progressive withdrawal into 'inactivity' as the number of children increases for wives outside agriculture or the homework sector suggests that priority is given to reproduction when the time and location constraints imposed by, for example, work in industry make it difficult to combine work and rearing. The lower fertility of non-agricultural workers may reflect the weakening of the priority given to reproduction because of decreasing value of children for non agricultural households, as well as reflecting the presence of the said constraints. Thus, overall, cross-section data give support to the interpretative framework proposed earlier and its application to the analysis of the pattern of fertility over time, which is crucial to the arguments developed here.

Declining fertility can be observed in Italy from the early nineteenth century, before the industrial revolution got under way. Until the early twentieth century, however, the decline was restricted to the wealthier population groups. It is only between the twenties and the thirties that the negative trend accentuated and the decline became pervasive until assuming dramatic proportions in the late post-war period. This emerges from time series data (Table 7.5a) but especially from cohort data based on the 1961 census (Table 7.5b).

Table 7.5 Patterns of fertility in Italy, 1862–1981

(a) *Birth rate 1862–1981*

Years	1862– 71	1882– 91	1902– 11	1912– 21	1932– 41	1951– 61	1961– 71	1971– 81
Births/ 000	37.4	37.2	32.2	27.2	23.0	18.0	18.2	13.6

(b) *Average number of children per married woman by occupation and educational attainment, 1961 Census*

	Occupation				Educational attainment		
	Agri- culture	Other activi- ties	House- wife	Total	Illiter- ate	Primary	O levels to gradu- ates
Before 1886	4.50	3.05	4.39	4.38	5.07	3.97	2.33
1887–91	4.52	3.13	4.17	4.17	5.04	3.74	2.13
1892–96	4.35	2.89	3.82	3.82	4.83	3.47	2.14
1897–1901	4.42	2.75	3.72	3.73	4.88	3.45	2.16
1902–06	4.39	2.63	3.57	3.58	4.91	3.34	2.12
1907–11	4.13	2.37	3.30	3.30	4.71	3.04	2.07
1912–16	3.69	2.21	3.03	3.01	4.44	2.81	2.05
1917–21	3.27	2.01	2.77	2.72	4.22	2.60	1.98
1922–26	2.82	1.75	2.46	2.40	3.74	2.31	1.81
1927–31	2.26	1.40	2.04	1.98	3.08	1.92	1.47
1932–36	1.60	0.89	1.48	1.42	2.24	1.36	0.96
1937–41	0.97	0.49	0.94	0.89	1.43	0.87	0.55
1942 onwards	0.51	0.37	0.60	0.57	0.80	0.55	0.35
Total	3.06	1.70	2.71	2.64	4.26	2.43	1.67

Sources: Table (a) is based on Livi Bacci (1980, p. 65) and ISTAT, *Annuario statistico italiano.* Table (b) is reproduced from Livi Bacci (1980, p. 296).

The first and generalised drop in fertility immediately follows the already sizeable reduction of child and juvenile labour and just precedes the stabilisation (if not the increase) in the participation of married women. Thus, the expectations raised by our reference framework are confirmed, albeit indicatively since data do not allow any more meaningful statistical elaboration.

Other features of the pattern of fertility, namely its pace of decline and the role of education, are also compatible with our framework. Fertility decreased at a similar pace for all women, irrespective of whether and where they worked (Table 7.5b). But one would also expect that the value of children decreased across households. For even in agricultural households, schooling reduced the contribution of children, as did increasing prospects of employment or migration elsewhere. As for education, although the pace of the decline was similar between wives of different educational attainments (Table 7.5b) the spread of education nevertheless fuelled the process. It worked both ways, by reducing the activity of children and by providing the motivation and knowledge to control fertility.[9] Consistently lower fertility for better educated women brought out by Table 7.5b underscores this point and suggests that welfare provisions towards mass education were an important accelerating factor.

Thus the shape and timing of demographic patterns are consistent with the contention that changes within the economy of the family that began consolidating around the 1930s bore a part in shaping the pattern of female participation, especially by differentiating between married and non married women.

3.5 The sexual division of labour as a brake on female labour supply

There still remains an unresolved puzzle which is central to the relation between factors on the demand and on the supply side, as well as their respective impact on participation. Namely, given that changes within the family economy that favoured progressive integration of married women into the labour force are traceable back to the 1930s, why is it that these changes had such a weak influence over the forty years or so that followed, i.e. up to the late 1960s? For, however significant in qualitative terms, the increase in the rate of activity of married women was at best inconspicuous until recently.

Our answer is that the negative employment prospects which we have already attributed to a sex-segmented demand for labour not only inhibited over a long period married women's full response to these modifications in the family economy but they may even have slowed down the process of change by helping to retain traditional family roles and organisation. Inhibited is the word, for the potential increase in the supply of married women did eventually take place, partly spurred on by a growth in demand for female labour that was, however, too restricted to absorb fully the growing supply.

Insufficient demand exercised a restraining influence even on the supply of single women, which as noted, decreased steadily until the 1970s. Factors like education and earlier retirement cannot, in fact, explain the decline that also affected single women of central age groups. Had employment prospects been more favourable, rising participation of these groups might, conceivably, have offset declining participation of extreme groups.

It was the reversal of the trend in the demand for female labour around the late 1960s that brought to the surface the full potential of women's supply. The behaviour of female unemployment underscores

Table 7.6 Female and male unemployment over the post-war period

(a) *Unemployment rates at peaks and lows, 1960–84*

	1960	1963	1966	1967	1973	1974	1984
Women	7.4	5.7	8.9	8.7	11.6	9.6	17.1
Men	4.8	3.1	4.7	4.1	4.2	3.6	6.8

(b) *Female unemployment by status (%)*

Status of unemployed	1960	1974	1984	Share of married women 1984
Previously holding a job	19.6	9.3	14.9	42.0
First entrants	33.8	41.3	45.0	10.2
Others*	46.6	49.4	40.1	60.1
Total (%)	100.0	100.0	100.0	34.9
Total (000)	494	589	1377	481

* Others include housewives, student, retired and others in search of a job.

Source: Based on ISTAT, *Annuario di statistiche del lavoro.*

this point (Table 7.6). After the peak of post-war expansion around 1960–63, female unemployment rose unremittingly, growing further apart from male unemployment. The pace accelerated in the 1970s with the result that between 1970 and 1984 women have contributed the most to the growth of unemployment (63.3%) while also contributing the most to the net increase of the total labour force (83.1%).

The accelerating pace as well as the growing disparity vis à vis men owes little to redundancies induced by the recession. Partly on account of the Cassa Integrazione that disguises potential redundancies as employment (see Chapter 3) the shares of females who are unemployed as a result of job loss was low to start with (19.6% of all female unemployed in 1960) and lower still in 1984 (14.9%). The recession affected matters insofar as it reduced demand even further in relation to an expanding supply.

Yet there is an oddity. While married women were especially prominent in expanding the female as well as the total labour force, they remained underrepresented among the unemployed. Wives alone accounted for 65.7% of the net expansion of the aggregate labour supply between 1971 and 1981 (census data) while their share of female unemployment remains much lower than their share of female participants: 34.9% against 60.7%, respectively. In order to explain this oddity the distinctive stickiness of the 'official' labour market must be brought into the discussion.

The official and the informal labour market in Italy identify two segments characterised, respectively, by the strictness and the looseness of institutional regulations and control, be they of fiscal, legal, trade union or even statistical nature (see Chapter 3). In the official market, i.e. that for which available data is based, both voluntary and involuntary turn-over declined beginning with the seventies and has hardly picked up in the 1980s, thus slowing down new entries more than the shrinking employment opportunities warranted.

In particular, dismissals decreased as a proportion of employees in response to both mounting opposition by unions and progressive extension of the Cassa Integrazione in order to avoid mass redundancies (see Chapter 3). Quits declined largely as a consequence, for the risk involved in job changing increased as employers became reluctant to recruit when the related rigidities could not be avoided. Employment in fact grew more in small firms and in the informal segment of the economy. For women, under the rising pressure of their supply, the risk involved in quitting became even greater and their voluntary exit turn-over rate fell even more sharply.[10] Thus married women increased their participation mainly through prolongation of their stay in the market, with the consequence of shifting the burden of unemployment on to young first entrants.

Summing up, while the decline in demand relative to the growth of female population lasted it was only partly met by an independent decrease in supply, the latter being restricted only to segments of single women. At the same time it prevented new potential supplies from surfacing, mainly married women. The recent reversal of the demand trend is finally bringing to light the full supply potential even though the increase so far has been modest and has met with recessionary conditions which have hindered the materialisation of this supply into actual employment. The resulting unemployment has been born disproportionately by young, unmarried females due to the increasing rigidity of the official labour market in Italy.

3.6 The unperceived participation of married women

Why did the potential growth of female supply remain a latent supply in Italy for so long compared to other industrialised countries, given that sex-based segmentation is as common elsewhere? The reasons are partly substantive, partly statistical. Three factors stand out for their importance, namely, the pattern of development, the resilience of the family and the specific characteristics of labour market institutions in Italy.

The pattern of development played a substantive role. Because Italy was a comparative late comer to industrialisation, the negative repercussions on female participation of the decline of agriculture and other traditional, family based activities, lasted well into the post-war period, whereas the growth of services has been and still is slow to develop.

Distinctive family patterns and labour market institutions sustained instead extensive 'irregular' employment in the informal sector, especially for married women. The related problems of statistical coverage bias international comparisons of female participation.

This last point needs to be developed in full. Partly as a result of the protracted importance of agriculture, the average size of households is still larger in Italy than it was, say, in the UK in 1961, despite a process of secular decline. The respective figures are 3.2 members in 1984 against 3.1 in 1961 in the UK.[11] In particular, households consisting of more than one nuclear family were especially common among Italian share-croppers, retaining a sizeable, if declining, share of total households throughout the post-war periods. They accounted for 22.4% of all households in 1951 and 11.2% in 1981. In addition, where the development of the nuclear family is still recent the tradition of close family ties still remains.

It is thought, following Paci (1980) that such tradition and family structure offered fertile ground for the growth of those small scale, but often modern, industrial and service ventures that make up the fabric of the informal economy. Part of the labour and the initial capital often came from within the extended family network, as indicated by the spread of these ventures in localised, traditionally agricultural and share-cropping areas. Flexible utilisation of wage labour was both the condition for survival and the strength of the informal network of firms in that they provided an alternative to an increasingly rigid labour market that was attractive for both employers and employees. The same flexibility also made it easier to mobilise segments of the female population through homework and other discontinuous forms of employment.

Given the distinctively large proportion of the informal segment in Italy, two alternative inferences can be drawn for the pattern of female participation. According to the first, a substantial growth in the supply of married women might have taken place, via the informal sector, before the 1970s, undetected by national sources. If this was true, sex-segmented demand would have inhibited supply much less than suggested by the recorded slow growth in the participation of (married) women. Persisting in this line of reasoning, one could find support for it in the much flatter age-specific participation profile of women in Italy (Table 7.2),[12] for the resumption of work after childbearing could be substantially disguised within the informal economy. Since in many countries the return to work after childbearing was historically associated with increasing female participation, the invisibility of the same pattern in Italy could have masked an equally invisible increase.

Despite its appeal, this line of reasoning is unconvincing on a number of points. First, the argument has dubious claims to generality, since the informal sector blossomed in parts of the country only. Also, as a modern phenomenon it only took on considerable importance by the late sixties. Since then, moreover, official statistics have not been altogether insensitive to this development. If we take two of the core areas of the informal economy – Marche and Emilia – census data record an increase in the proportion of married women among active females of 81% and 75.3% respectively, between 1961 and 1971 against the average, national figure of only 44.5%. Also the same regions and others equally involved in the development of the informal economy show the highest rates of female activity according to the latest census.[13] Finally, the invisibility of bi-modality in the age specific participation profile of Italian women owes as much to comparatively higher risk of a strategy of discontinuous participation in a stickier labour market.

As an alternative, it could be hypothesized that the degree of underestimation of female participation has remained largely unchanged over the decades due to two mutually offsetting tendencies. On the one hand there was the decline of agriculture and other traditional activities where women's work is known to have always been underestimated. On the other hand, a modern informal sector grew in the post-war period. Put differently, discontinuous work in, say, agriculture might just have been replaced by, for example, industry-related homework or by seasonal work in the tourist trade, all being largely impermeable to official statistics. One needs, moreover, to mention that homework was always widespread in Italy. It received explicit encouragement under the fascist regime, in opposition to 'regular' participation of wives. And, although encouragement was not followed by explicit action, it gave firms more freedom to resort to this arrangement.

The difference with other countries might then be put as follows. Whereas elsewhere traditionally 'unperceived' forms of participation became increasingly visible through institutionalisation of part-time or temporary work, the opposition that these arrangements encountered in Italy favoured the persistence of older forms, albeit in a modern context, that continued to go undetected. Hence the observed differences with Italy in the timing of the rise in the participation of married women, as well as in rates of female activity, in Italy are partly a product of statistical coverage.

4 PROSPECTS AND POLICIES

There are two possibilities for the near future. If there is significant growth in total employment the pressure of women's supply may well rebound on demand, leading to a relaxation of sex-based segmentation, for women represent the main potential source of expansion of the labour force. Recent years witnessed several instances in this direction, but their impact was limited (see Chapter 3). This outcome is less probable under the alternative of slowly growing or shrinking employment, even if the foreseeable expansion of the services at the expense of the remaining sectors is discounted. In this case the excess supply of women may favour, beside unemployment, further expansion of the informal economy.

So, problems for the 1980s remain largely those of the 1970s, namely, too few jobs and even fewer 'good' jobs. Unlike in other countries long affected by the recession/stagnation, these problems are more serious in their implications for the emancipation of female supply than for cutbacks in income and wages. This point is important for evaluating current policies affecting women and calls for a re-consideration of the interrelations between the family, the state and labour market institutions in this particular respect.

In the Italian context, both union and government wage and income strategies sharpened the divide between 'protected' labour in 'regular' employment and those out of it, leaving the family to compensate for the resulting disparities between members of the two groups. Even workers in the non-official segment or the self-employed who are better off on a number of counts – and this is not uncommon among men – may still need to rely on other family members, for institutional 'guarantees' are not available to them. The context is the same for male and female labour but implications are sharper for the latter.

Throughout the post-war period in the 'official' labour market wage indexation helped to prevent a fall in real wages even under stagflation. It also contributed to decreasing male-female differentials to levels unprecedented in the EEC and in most other industrialised countries (see Chapter 3). Although there are signs of differentials widening again after 1983, this trend is unlikely to assume major proportions. On the income side, the Cassa Integrazione cushioned the consequences of the recession of the 1970s and the 1980s for those already in employment, including women. Hence, overall, female income from employment does not compare as unfavourably to that of men as in other countries. The female to male income earning ratio was 74.3 in 1983 for employees working the whole year and had risen from 70.0% in 1975. (See Banca d'Italia, *Bollettino*, January 1977 and July 1984.)

Against this favourable position in the formal sector must be set the not infrequent underpayment of labour in the informal sector and the growing weight of unemployed not eligible for any subsidy for being completely out of work. Both problems are far more serious for women and the former is certainly underplayed by the quoted figure on relative income from employment.

Compensation between 'protected' and 'unprotected' segments thus falls on the family, reinforcing its resilience under recessionary conditions. In the vast majority of families – 72% to 88% depending on income groups – members pool all incomes towards common utilization. Also, financial links are not uncommon between non cohabiting kins. This is fortunate in a situation where one family out of 10 has at least one member in the household unemployed.[14] But if this avoids impoverishment, it might nevertheless retard a choice of self-sufficiency on the part of women.

The family system is in fact integrated into welfare expenditure in general with contradictory implications for female participation. At purchasing power parity, per-capita welfare expenditure was the third lowest in Italy within the EEC9 in 1981, which is not a particularly low position given that per-capita income in Italy is about 12% lower than the EEC9 average and that welfare expenditure tends to rise in relation to GNP.[15] Nevertheless, although in Italy deflationary policies were milder than elsewhere and did not reduce welfare expenditure on the most important items (Table 7.7), families still have to step in heavily to complement services being provided.

Aggregate welfare provisions increased by 37% at 1970 prices between 1975 and 1982 against a population increase of 2.7%. Yet, the instance of the national health service illustrates how inadequate provisions still are in important areas. Despite the service being free for all, the percentage of cases in which families resorted to the private sector varied in 1984 from 43% for examination by specialists to 28% for mental health treatment, 22% for tests, down to 9% for examinations by general practitioners. And, of course, statistics are silent on the amount of ancillary assistance by the family and the very time consuming procedures required by the national health service.

As far as women are concerned, this system of family welfare organisation cuts both ways. On the one hand the task of compensating for the inadequacies of social services falls mainly on them, since sex roles are still rather well defined. This makes the burden of a working wife harder and discourages participation. On the other hand, services by older parents or other family members frequently make the choice of

Table 7.7 Social expenditure 1975–1982 at 1970 prices

1975 = 100

Items	1982
Total	137
NHS	153
Social insurance of which:	146
Pensions	168
Work related sickness	105
Unemployment	113
Maternity allowance	124
Family allowances	70
Others	112
Social assistance of which:	117
Invalidity and social pensions	145
Other income subsidies	50
Services in kind	168
of which:	
Nurseries	194
Boarding schools, homes for the sick and the elderly	163
Direct assistance services	87

Source: Based on ISTAT, *I conti della protezione sociale*, supplemento al *Bollettino mensile di statistica* no. 28, 1985.

work possible. Some figures may, again, be illustrative. Beyond the task of housework that still falls overwhelmingly on wives, women are called in the majority of cases (61%) to assist kins and relatives in need. At the same time, to give just an example, in 64% of cases children below 10 are minded by grandparents, often not living in the household, when they are not at school or with their parents and cannot be left on their own.[16]

On the whole, closely knit family ties have redistributed the benefits of non deflationary, albeit selective and often inadequate, social and income policies to groups like women that suffer severely from deficient expansion of employment or are overrepresented among the least protected labour market members. The price is dependency on the family that may hinder the process of emancipation under way.

The main priority remains, therefore, increasing 'good' employment opportunities for women. Little has been done so far in this respect and measures under implementation are not very promising. Over the last ten years only two policy provisions were aimed specifically at female employment; the 1977 Equal Opportunities Act that formally abolished any remaining form of discrimination; and a reduction of employers' social security contribution for every job held by women (1978). The reduction was modest but, more importantly, acted as a subsidy to employers of traditional female industries like textiles rather than as an incentive to additional female employment (CERES, 1979). Most other measures implemented were aimed at reducing unemployment, but despite higher female representation there, women benefited modestly, if at all.

It was hoped that the merging of the official unemployment queues, previously distinguished by sex, that followed implementation of the 1977 Act would favour women who invariably ended up at the top of the merged queue. But, although, *de iure* all hirings go through the official employment agency (Ufficio di Collocamento), *de facto* only 12–13% of regular hirings and an even smaller share of total hirings respect the order of the official queue (Ichino, 1982, p. 21). In the remaining cases the agency rubber stamps private deals between employers and candidates who are temporarily added to the queue, or else employers pick and choose from the queue, alleging specific skill requirements. So, abolition of the distinction on the basis of sex favoured women in a limited number of cases, often under the condition that unions of the hiring firms closely supervised procedures (see Chapter 3). Starting from 1983 the possibility of selection independent from the queue order was enhanced, thus cancelling the nominal advantage of women.

The first attempt to introduce a youth training scheme in 1977 to counteract the growing problem of youth unemployment was largely a failure, with only 6.6 per cent of those eligible taken on, and these mainly in the public sector. However there was no evidence of a sex bias in recruitment (ISFOL, 1980, Tables 16 and 18). In 1983 a more flexible youth training policy was introduced, providing firms with greater choice in selection: small industrial firms have made widespread use of the scheme but only 31.8 per cent of those hired have been women. (Rassegna di Statistiche del Lavoro, no. 1–2, 1984, p. 11.)

Provisions aimed at furthering flexibility of the labour market are being progressively heralded as appropriate answers to unemployment, female unemployment in particular. This outcome and future implications are, however, uncertain at best. Work sharing schemes (*contratti di solidarieta'*) were first introduced in 1984. The response was poor since some 8000 employees only were involved after one year of implementation, and these predominantly women (CENSIS, 1985, p. 199). A far more important provision was the liberalization and regulation of part-time work in 1984. As expected, the vast majority of part-time contracts signed since implementation have involved women: specifically, 80% of them between 1984 and April 1985 and mainly in the service sector (ISFOL). So far, however, contracts being signed represent a too minute proportion of employees to warrant even informed guesses about their future incidence. Although, theoretically, regulation of part-time work could represent a step towards bringing to the surface, under some institutional protection, hidden segments of female labour, in actuality its liberalisation may favour marginalisation of parts of the currently protected segment of female employment if employment prospects remain moderate.

5 CONCLUSION

The pattern of female participation over time reflects the interplay between three main factors. The rigidity of sex-typing made participation dependent on the occupational and sectoral distribution of demand, with the shift towards industry and away from agriculture favouring a protracted decline, and that, more recently, towards the services favouring an increase. At the same time modifications in the economy of the family altered the priorities of married women in favour of participation while reducing participation by single women. While demand remained unfavourable it partly spurred on the autonomous reduction in supply of non married women, and partly retarded the potential growth of the supply of married women. The full potential emerged as soon as the trend in demand was reversed. However these trends in women's employment have been further threatened by the recession. The welfare state has served to coordinate this historical process of mutual interaction between supply and demand. Schooling, medical care, provisions for retirement and all other measures for that coordination between reproduction and use of labour that the state is increasingly called upon to guarantee were all important for changing both the constraints and the convenience of paid work for married women.

While these same factors are common to other countries, their combination in particular time periods and their forms may differ, thus producing different results. Since Italy is somewhat of a late comer, demand turned in favour of women comparatively recently. More importantly, this turn occurred while the country was caught, like others, in the recession, with the consequence that the emerging female supply risks being choked by unemployment. But perhaps not only by unemployment, for another important difference with other countries lies in the fact that the recession hides dynamism in the informal sector, which is providing alternative and invisible sources of employment to women. Elsewhere the equivalent to informal female employment has been long institutionalised through part-time and more flexible employment contracts.

There is therefore a high risk in Italy that the pressure of female labour supply under uncertain demand prospects will fuel the expansion of irregular employment or the development of part-time work in the formal sector as a means of marginalising the currently protected segments of female employment.

Family ties have remained closer in Italy, partly because the late emergence of a movement towards economic activity and relative independence for married women from the family was recently constrained by the international recession. A stronger family, and the wage indexation and non deflationary policies of the state have helped to cushion the impact of unemployment and widespread irregular employment of women. The most dramatic problem thus remains poor prospects for the expansion of overall employment opportunities with a sufficient degree of institutional protection. In this respect policies already implemented or under implementation are largely inadequate.

APPENDIX
COMPONENTS OF THE DIFFERENCE
BETWEEN TWO ACTIVITY RATES

Define:

F_t as total female population, year t

$T_{i,t}$ as total active population (male and female) in sector i, year t

$W_{i,t}$ as female active population in sector i, year t

$p_{i,t} = W_{i,t}/T_{i,t}$ as the proportion of women in sector i, year t

then

$$A_t = \sum_i (T_{i,i}, p_{i,t})/F_t$$

is the female activity rate in year t.

The difference between two rates $(A_1 - A_0)$ can be decomposed as follows:

$$A_1 - A_0 = \sum_i (T_{i,1}/F_1 - T_{i,0}/F_0)((p_{i,1} + p_{i,0})/2) +$$
$$\sum_i (p_{i,1} - p_{i,0})(T_{i,1}/F_1 + T_{i,0}/F_0)/2)$$

where the first term on the right hand side captures the effect of the sectoral distribution of participants and the second the impact of variations in the proportion of women within each sector, respectively, growth and share effects.

A three components formula specifying a residual effect beside the growth and share effects would be more rigorous (see Kitagawa, 1955). For the purposes of this paper the advantage of a neat allocation of change outweighs the disadvantage of loss of rigour, particularly because it was shown elsewhere (Bettio, 1984, ch. 8) that results are practically equivalent using either formula.

NOTES

1 Relative female wages since around 1850 are analysed by Bettio (forthcoming), ch. 5. Since relative female wages almost never fell and increased dramatically during and after World War Two, the post-war rise in real aggregate wages was even more accentuated for women from the start. Leoni (1984) has also noted the weak correlation between real wage increases and female participation over the post-war period.

2 See the appendix to this chapter for the formula decomposing the change into growth and share effects. Note that under this formula there is no interaction effect because of the use of the average of the beginning and end years as the basis for standardisation.

3 Industrial breakdowns of all censuses between 1881 and 1961 were standardised by Vitali on the basis of a 65 entries code that follows the 1961 classification of economic activities. It was possible for us to extend the standardisation to the 1971 census but not to that of 1981 due to major alterations to the 1981 industrial classification. For the details of the standardisation of 1971 see Bettio (forthcoming), Appendix 1.

4 Caution is needed for interpreting the data in both Tables (7.3 and 7.4). Particularly problematic in Table 7.3 is the comparison between the 1903 share of married women in industry and that of 1931. Unlike the latter, the former refers to employees below the age of 55. The absence of the self-employed tends to underestimate the 1903 figure in relation to that of 1931, whereas the shorter age interval pulls in the opposite direction. Both sources of bias are likely to be minor because of the small number of self-employed females in industry and of female employees older than 55. Regarding Table 7.4, the main problem is how much one should take account of underestimation of female activity in the original census data. If activity rates for the whole female population in Table 7.4 are compared with the corresponding rates in Table 7.1, the underestimation is evident for all census years included in Vitali's reconstruction of standardised and corrected series (i.e. values up to 1961 reported by Table 7.1). A strong degree of underestimation is evident particularly for 1931. We are, however, interested in broad trends rather than the precise magnitude of change. So, although we cannot even know which category of women were underestimated the most (but the married are more likely), we need to assume that the downward bias for married and non married women taken separately stood in largely the same proportion in all census years. Having done that, comparison of the original values with those of the standardised series gives an idea of how much to discount for underestimation.

5 Limited forms of compulsory medical insurance were introduced starting from 1898. In the post-war period they were extended to common sickness and to the dependants of employees. In the 1970s everybody was given free access to the national health system.

6 The new home economics (see Schultz, 1974) treats the declining value of children in terms of them coming to represent 'consumer goods' rather than 'consumer durables', low fertility and high participation being associated with the latter status. However, the said paradigm takes the institutional and historical conditions that determine the passage from one status to another as 'givens' rather than seeing them as the inevitable counterpart of the transformation of the family consequent on the spread

of the labour market. In so doing it ignores the basic point. Moreover, the value of the mother's time, as expressed by the prevailing wage rate for women is seen as an essential co-determinant of fertility and participation, whether children are consumer goods or durables. Under different assumptions we have shown that the level of female wages is dependent on the role of married women within the family (Bettio forthcoming, ch. 1), i.e. on the degree to which reproduction and rearing take priority over incomes earning. Then rising female wages may not be independent of declining fertility, i.e. the very phenomenon they are supposed to explain.

7 The most articulated survey is a locality study and refers to 1972. See Bielli et al. (1973). Federici (1968) had earlier reached similar conclusions on the basis of the 1961 census.

8 Figures are taken from the results of a survey conducted by ISTAT: *Indagine sulle strutture ed i comportamenti familiari*, Rome 1985. Children living in the family are considered so that the values do not strictly measure fertility. However, the fall in activity of married women as children increase is even clearer for younger couples with whom children almost invariably live together in the same household.

9 It is an established fact that fertility could be controlled well before the introduction of contraceptives in the sixties and that education helped to increase control. See Livi Bacci (1980).

10 See Carmignani (1980) for an analysis of turn-over until the middle 1970s. Bettio (forthcoming), ch. 9 examines in detail male–female differences in turn-over rates.

11 Figures for Italy are taken from ISTAT, *Indagine* ... op. cit. Those for the UK are based on census.

12 The bimodality was just evident in 1961 on the basis of five instead of ten years age interval as in Table 7.2 and had disappeared completely by 1981.

13 In the region of Marche, for example, the rate of female activity referred to the population 14 and over and inclusive of all unemployment was 36.9 in 1981 compared to the national average of 32.8. According to a survey of some districts of Marche (Canullo and Montanari, 1978, p. 156) the same rate was equal to 48.1 in 1976. While this signals underestimation by the census, the survey was too restricted for figures based on it to be representative. Moreover, attention was paid to irregular work to a degree that no census ever could.

14 See ISTAT, *Indagine* ... op. cit., prospetti 5.4, 8.2 and 8.3. See also Arangio Ruiz (1985), fig. 5.

15 See ISTAT, *I conti della protezione sociale*, supplemento al Bollettino Mensile di Statistica no. 28, 1983, fig. 19.

16 See ISTAT, *Indagine* ... op. cit., prospetto 8.6 on child minding and Donati (1985, p. 9) on the use of the private health sector.

REFERENCES

Alessandrini, P. (ed.) (1978a), *Lavaro regolare e lavoro nero*, Il Mulino, Bologna.

Alessandrini, P. (ed.) (1978b), *Struttura della forza lavoro e sviluppo economico* Il Mulino, Bologna.

Amsden, A. H. (ed.) (1980), *The Economics of Women and Work*, Harmondsworth, Penguin.

Arangio Ruiz, M. G. (1985), *Le forze di lavoro nella famiglia*, mimeo, Convegno 'La famiglia in Italia', Roma, 29–30 Oct.

Beechey, V. (1977), 'Some notes on Female Wage Labour in Capitalistic Production', *Capital and Class*, no. 3, Autumn.

Bettio, F. (1984), 'The Sexual Division of Labour: the Italian Case', Ph.D. Dissertation, University of Cambridge, forthcoming as *The Sexual Division of Wage Labour: the Italian case*, OUP.

Bielli, C. et al. (1973), *Fecondita e lavoro della donna*, Istituto di Demografia, Università degli Studi di Roma, Roma.

Boserup, E. (1970), *Women's Role in Economic Development*, St Martin's Press, New York.

Canullo, G. e Montanari, M. G. (1978), 'Lavoro regolare e lavoro nero in alcuni comuni delle Marche', in Alessandrini, P. (1978a).

Carmignani, f. (1980), 'La mobilità del lavoro nell'industria italiana', in Pinnarò, G. (ed.).

CENSIS (1985), *XIX Rapporto sulla situazione sociale del paese*, Franco Angeli, Milano.

CERES (1979), 'Il costo del lavoro femminile', *Economia del lavoro*, no. 2.

Del Boca, D. and Turvani, M. (1980), *Women at Work in Italy: The Changing Pattern of Female Participation*, mimeo, Conference on 'Economic Policies of Female Labour', Rome, 9–11 December.

Donati, P. (1985), *Famiglia, servizi e reti informali*, mimeo, Convegno 'La famiglia in Italia', Rome 29–30 Oct.

Federici, N. (1968), 'The Influence of Women's Employment on Fertility', in Szabady, E. (ed.).

Frey, L. et al. (1976), *Occupazione e sottoccupazione femminile in Italia*, Franco Angeli, Milano.

Furnari, M. et al. (1975), 'Occupazione femminile e mercato del lavoro', *Inchesta*, Apr.–May.

Humphries, J. (1983), 'From the Latent to the Floating: the Emancipation of Women in the 1970's and 80's', *Capital and Class*, no. 20.

Humphries, J. and Rubery, J. (1984), 'The Reconstitution of the Supply Side of the Labour Market: the Relative Autonomy of Social Reproduction', *Cambridge Journal of Economics*, vol. 8.

Ichino, P. (1982), *Il collocamento impossible*, De Donato, Bari.

ISFOL (1980), 'Legge 285: riflessioni e proposte', *Quaderni di Formazione*, no. 69.

Kitagawa, E. M. (1955), 'Components of a Difference Between Two Rates', *Journal of the American Statistical Association*, vol. 50, no. 272.

Leoni, R. (1984), 'L'offerta di lavoro nel ciclo di vita. Un 'applicazione al mercato del lavoro in Italia' in Schenkel, M.

Livi Bacci, M. (1980), *Donna, fecondità e figli*, Il Mulino, Bologna.

Livraghi, R. (1984), *Segmentazione dei mercati del lavoro e scelte professionali*, Franco Angeli, Milano.

MAIC (Ministero dell'Agricoltura, dell'Industria e del Commercio) (1905), *La donna nell'industria italiana*, Tipo'grafia Bertero, Roma.

May, M. P. (1973), 'Mercato del lavoro femminile: espulsione o occupazione nascosta?' *Inchiesta*, Jan.–Mar.

May, M. P. (1977), 'Il mercato del lavoro femminile in Italia', *Inchiesta*, Jan.–Feb.

Mincer, J. (1962), *Aspects of Labour Economics*, National Bureau of Economic Research, New York.

Oppenheimer, V. (1970), *The Female Labour Force in the United States: Demographic and Economic Forces Governing its Growth and Changing Composition*, Population Monograph Series no. 5, University of California, Berkeley.

Paci, M. (1980), 'Struttura e funzioni della famiglia nello sviluppo capitalistico periferico', *Inchesta*, Jan.–Feb.

Padoa Schioppa, F. (1977), *La forza lavoro femminile*, Il Mulino, Bologna.

Pinnarò, G. (ed.) (1980), *Lavaro e redditi in Italia 1978–1979*, Editori Riuniti, Roma.

Robotti, L. (1978), Tassi di attività e sviluppo economico in alcuni paesi indutrializzati. Un'analisi storica', in Allesandrini, P. (ed.) (1978b).

Schenkel, M. (1984), *L'offerta di lavoro in Italia*, Marsilio Editori, Venezia.

Schultz, T. W. (ed.) (1974), *Economics of the Family: Marriage, Children and Human Capital*, National Bureau of Economic Research, Chicago.

Scott, J. W. and Tilly, L. A. (1978), *Women, Work and the Family*, Holt, Rinehart & Winston, New York.

Szabady, E. (ed.) (1968), *World Views on Population Problems*, Akädemiai Kiadò, Budapest.

Vinci, S. (ed.) (1974), *Il mercato del lavoro in Italia*, Franco Angeli, Milano.

Vitali, O. (1970), *Aspetti dello sviluppo economico italiano alla luce della ricostruzione della popolazione attiva*, Istituto di Demografia, Università di Roma, Roma.

8 Women, the state and the family in Britain: Thatcher economics and the experience of women

Jill Walker

During the 1960s and 1970s both Labour and Conservative governments failed to arrest the decline of the British economy. While the Labour government of 1974–9 struggled to balance their economic policies between the monetarism of the IMF initiative and the 'Social Contract' with the unions which had formed their election platform, the right of the Conservative party was debating the 'Social Market Strategy' (Gamble, 1982). The election of Mrs Thatcher as leader of the party signalled a shift in the dominant thinking of the party, which was endorsed in the 1979 election manifesto.

'Thatcherism' recognised that there was something fundamentally wrong with the economy, and that a radical alternative to the consensus Keynesian politics of the post-war era was required. The New Right politics required a transformation of the social relations of production, and of the role of the state in economic, labour market and social policy. On the macro level, Keynesian notions that the government could select target rates of unemployment and output and engineer the result through demand management, were rejected. Government macro-economic policy should concentrate on controlling the money supply to achieve price stability. However, government action on the *micro* level of labour market and social policy *can* affect the 'natural rate of unemployment'. The post-war Keynesian welfare state was seen as a major impediment to the operation of the market (Minford, 1983).

This chapter will examine the implications of this restructuring of state economic, social and labour market policies for the position of women in the system of production and reproduction.

It is often assumed that Thatcherism requires a reversal of any economic advances that may have been achieved by women in the post-war period: a reduction in paid employment and a return to unpaid labour in the family. But are these necessarily the implications of the new economic policies and can the changes of the post-war era be so easily reversed? Before examining these questions, I will first set them in the context of the post-war changes in family structures, and the role of the state in social and labour policies.

1 THE POST-WAR BACKGROUND

1.1 Changes in family structure

The traditional nuclear family has changed quite substantially in the post-war period. The proportion of households composed of a married couple and dependent children has fallen from 38% in 1961 to 30% in 1983, as Table 8.1 indicates. Correspondingly, more people are living alone or in single parent households. The proportion of households made up of single people, both pre- and post-retirement, has increased from 11% to 24%; and the proportion of households made up of single parents with dependent children from 2% to 5%. The increase in divorce and separations accounts for most of the rise in single parent households, but more and more single mothers are choosing to bring up their own children rather than have them adopted.[1]

Furthermore, within the nuclear family there have been substantial

Table 8.1 Households by type, Great Britain (%)

	1961	1971	1981	1982	1983
No family					
One person					
− under retirement age*	4	6	8	8	8
− over retirement age*	7	12	14	15	16
Two or more people					
− One or more over retirement age*	3	2	2	1	1
− all under retirement age*	2	2	3	2	2
One family					
Married couple only	26	27	26	27	27
Married couple with 1 or 2 dependent children	30	26	25	24	24
Married couple with 3 or more dependent children	8	9	6	6	6
Married couple with independent children only	10	8	8	8	8
Lone parent with at least 1 dependent child	2	3	5	4	5
Lone parent with independent children only	4	4	4	4	4
Two or more families	3	1	1	1	1
	100	100	100	100	100

* 60 for females, 65 for males.

Source: *Social Trends* 1985, Table 2.5, p. 33.
Data for 1961, 1971 and 1981 are taken from the 10 per cent sample analyses of the Population Censuses. Data for 1982 and 1983 are from the General Household Survey.

changes occurring. In particular, the proportion of married women participating in paid employment, including those with small children, has increased substantially, as Table 8.2 indicates. The proportion of married women defined as economically active increased from 26% in 1951 to 57% in 1981. According to the 1982 'Women and Employment Survey', 60% of married women, excluding full-time students, defined themselves as working either full or part-time, and a further 5% were unemployed. Of those women defined as 'economically inactive', 14% still did some regular or occasional paid work, such as child minding, mail order agent or outwork. Even among married women with children under five 27% were working, and a further 4% were unemployed (Martin and Roberts, 1984).

Table 2 Labour force participation rates by sex, and by marital status for women, England and Wales, 1901–81. (%)

	Men (aged 15*–64)	All women (aged 15*–54)	Married women (aged 15*–59)
1901	96	38	10
1911	96	38	10
1921	94	38	10
1931	96	38	11
1941	—	—	—
1951	96	43	26
1961	95	47	35
1971	92	55	49
1981	90	61	57

* 16 for 1981.

Source: Hakim 1979, Table 1, p. 3.
Census 1981, National Report Great Britain, Part II, Table 2, pp. 54–6.

Most of these women entered low paid 'women's jobs', often utilising the skills of domestic labour such as sewing, cooking and cleaning; and often with little or no trade union or legal protection (Hakim, 1979). A notable feature of women's employment in the UK has been the high proportion of women working part-time, or at hours which can be fitted in around domestic commitments. According to the 1981 census, while 87% of economically active men worked full time in 1981, only 58% of economically active women, and only 47% economically active married women were in full-time work. The Women and Employment Survey found significant variations in the arrangement of working hours for women with young children. The proportion of women working a 'standard day' was highest among women with no children – 82% of women under thirty without children working full time – and lowest amongst women with children under five – 53% of those working full time and 7% of those working part time. For women with children under five working part time, 38% worked evenings, the time when young children can most easily be left with their fathers, and a further 6% worked nights, which for most women would probably be followed by a day of childcare and housework. For women working full time with children under five, 10% were working nights.

Entry to paid employment on these terms, where primary responsibility for child care and domestic labour still rests with women[2] has not raised women from economic dependence on men. Most married women still earn less than their husbands and tend to move with their husband's job even if this means giving up their own job. Elias calculated that although the proportion of married women earning the same or more than their husbands has increased it was still only 8.0% in 1977, compared to 3.6% in 1968 (Elias, 1983). Average full-time weekly earnings of women covered by the 1984 New Earnings Survey were only 66% of those of men.

However, families are becoming more dependent on women's earnings as a major source of household income. Data from the Family Expenditure Survey (FES) indicate that for all households the importance of wives' income from wages and self-employment has increased from 7.9% of total household income in 1965 to 11.3% in 1983, while the contribution of the head of household fell from 58.9% to 50.9%. In households where a married woman was working, her contribution to household income in 1983 was 19.5% and 27.4% respectively, according to whether dependent children were present or not, compared to 61.9% and 50.0% for their husbands. For single parents, the importance of women's earnings is even greater. In 1983, single parents' earnings made up 36.3% of household income, and 49% of lone mothers covered by the Women and Employment Survey gave their earnings as a major source of income. The survey also indicated that the earnings of married women do not generally constitute 'pin money'. Thirty per cent of married women and 48% of non-married women in paid employment stated that their main reason for working was to earn money to buy basic essentials such as food, rent or mortgage. For non-married mothers the figure was 78%. Of married women in paid employment, 40% said they would have to give up a lot in order to manage financially without their earnings, and a further 14% said they would not be able to manage at all. The Central Policy Review Staff (CPRS) estimated that the number of families living in poverty would increase three to four times without the earnings of married women (CPRS, 1980).

1.2 The growth of the welfare state

During the last forty years the state has taken over an increasing responsibility for the production and reproduction of labour power: both via the direct provision of services such as housing, child care,

care of the elderly, health services and education; and indirectly via income support mechanisms of contributory and non-contributory benefits for the unemployed, poor, sick, disabled and pensioners. Table 8.3 indicates that total government expenditure on the 'Welfare State' increased from 15.1% of GDP in 1949 to 21.1% in 1979, an increase in real expenditure from just under £16 million to over £57 million. The services provided fell well short of need, creating long waiting lists for housing, hospital treatment, etc., and they also failed to provide people with any real control over the provision of services. The basis of provision hinged on the maintenance of the nuclear family as the basic unit for the production and reproduction of labour power, where married women are assumed to be financially dependent on their husbands as the main bread winner and families continue to be a major source of welfare services (Wilson, 1977).

Table 8.3: Government expenditure on the welfare state 1949–79 (£m and %)

	Education	National Health Service	Personal social services	School meals, milk and welfare foods	Social security benefits	Housing	Total
1949							
£m (1980 prices)	2,762	3,865	215	593	5,326	2,915	15,845
£m per 1,000 population	0.05	0.08	0.004	0.01	0.1	0.06	0.3
% of GDP	2.6	3.7	0.2	0.6	5.1	2.8	15.1
1959							
£m (1980 prices)	4,985	4,450	299	519	8,238	2,515	21,007
£m per 1,000 population	0.10	0.09	0.01	0.01	0.2	0.05	0.40
% of GDP	3.6	3.2	0.2	0.4	6.0	1.8	15.3
1969							
£m (1980 prices)	9,512	7,139	952	651	14,508	4,698	37,452
£m per 1,000 population	0.17	0.13	0.02	0.01	0.26	0.09	0.68
% of GDP	5.1	3.8	0.5	0.4	7.8	2.5	20.2
1979							
£m (1980 prices)	11,980	11,012	2,337	643	23,251	7,995	57,218
£m per 1,000 population	0.21	0.20	0.42	0.01	0.42	0.14	1.02
% of GDP	4.4	4.1	0.9	0.2	8.6	2.9	21.1

Source: Calculated from the *Annual Abstract of Statistics*, various years.

Married women were eligible for contributory benefits in their own rights, but until recently were encouraged to opt out by paying the reduced rate of National Insurance. They were not independently eligible for non-contributory benefits such as Supplementary Benefit, Family Income Supplement or Invalid Care Allowance.[3] Family Allowance and later Child Benefit[4] were an important source of non-means tested independent income for all mothers. For the growing number of single parents, most of whom are women, social security payments of one form or another constitute a major source of income: 46% of average income in 1983 for those families covered by the Family Expenditure Survey; and 97% of lone mothers covered by the Women and Employment Survey gave child benefit as a major source of income, while 49% also gave supplementary benefit as a main source.

While the provision of services increased vastly during the post-war period, it was certainly not universal, and domestic labour has continued to be a major source of provision for the care of children, the elderly and the disabled. Some care for children under five is provided by the state through local authority social services and education departments, who run full-time day nurseries and provide full- and part-time places in nursery schools and classes. State provision of education and day care for under fives increased from 276 thousand places in 1966 to 612 thousand in 1983, but as a proportion of children under five years this was still only 17.5%, and many of these were in 'rising five' classes in schools. Private schools, nurseries, play groups and registered childminders together provided a further 623 thousand places (*Social Trends*, 1985, p. 45). Since many of these places are only part-time, some children will be covered by more than one type of provision, while the majority of children have none. The CPRS estimated that in 1978/79 unregistered child minders provided between 100 and 300 thousand additional places. The scarcity of state provision has meant that informal arrangements with family and friends continue to provide the major source of child care. Ninety-seven per cent of women in paid employment covered by the Women and Employment Survey used a relative, usually the husband or grandmother, or a friend or neighbour to provide all or part of their day care requirements for pre-school children; while only 6% used a state-provided day nursery, creche or nursery school/class. Only 30% of the women paid for the care of pre-school children, and the average payment was £8.70 per week. The limited nature of state sector child care, and the reliance on informal family networks is probably a major factor in explaining the high percentage of part-time work in the UK and the high percentage of women working evening and night shifts when children can be left with their fathers.

Similarly, despite increased state provision, care of the elderly and disabled still falls heavily on the family, and within the family it is mainly women who take on the responsibility (Rossiter and Wicks, 1982). The state provides support to the elderly and disabled both through the direct provision of residential care and financial support in private residential care; and through social security payments and support services, such as meals-on-wheels,[5] home helps, district nurses and day centres, to those living with their families or alone. However, contrary to popular belief, in 1982 only 2.3% of those over 65 were living in some form of residential accommodation.[6] According to CPRS, in 1976 69% of the elderly lived alone or with their spouse, 12% lived with their children and 13% in other types of household, while only 6% lived in residential or hospital accommodation. For the elderly and disabled (most of whom are elderly) who have children or other relatives the majority of care is still provided within the family. According to the CPRS, one in five of all the elderly with children are living with a son or daughter, as do the majority of the disabled who have children. A study by Hunt found that in 1965 10% of working women and 13% of non-working women were responsible for the care of at least one elderly or infirm person, and she suggested on the basis of a survey of home helps two years later that between the ages of 35 and 64, one in two housewives could expect at some time or other to give help to an elderly or infirm person (Hunt, 1968; 1970). For 1980, the Women and Employment survey found that 13% of working women and 15% of non-working women (excluding full-time students) were providing care for sick or elderly dependents. Nineteen per cent of these women felt that their paid work had been affected by caring responsibilities, over half of whom said it prevented them from going out to work, and the others were restricted in hours or other ways. For married women, 15% were providing such care, and they are not eligible for the Invalid Care Allowance to compensate for lost earnings. Relatives are also an important source of social contact and support for the elderly, even when they are not living in the same household. In 1976, over half of the elderly received visits from relatives at least once a week. Overall, about 40% of the elderly receive help from visiting relatives, while only 9% had received a visit from a home help in the previous six months, and $2\frac{1}{2}$% had received meals on wheels (CPRS, 1980).

To summarise, while provision of State services and income support schemes have increased considerably during the post-war period, it is important to see this in perspective: the 'Welfare State' is built around supporting the nuclear family as the major unit for the production and reproduction of labour power, with domestic labour, mainly performed by women, continuing to provide the majority of care and support for children, the disabled and the elderly. It should also be pointed out that health and welfare services are provided via local authorities and the National Health Service (NHS), which means that levels of service provision have varied greatly across the country.

1.3 The state and women's employment

The expansion of state welfare services also involved a vast expansion of women's employment. Women form the majority of workers in the health service and in local authority education and social services, as Table 8.4 indicates: in 1984 they comprised 79% of National Health Service workers; 86% of local authority health and social service

Table 8.4 United Kingdon public sector employment mid-1984 (millions)

	Total	Male total	Full-time	Part-time	Female total	Full-time	Part-time
Total public sector	6.83	3.56	3.45	0.11	3.26	1.82	1.44
Public corporations	1.61	1.36	1.36	0.01	0.25	0.21	0.04
Central government	2.34	1.00	0.97	0.02	1.34	0.86	0.48
– HM Forces	0.33	0.31	0.31	—	0.02	0.02	—
– NHS	1.22	0.26	0.24	0.02	0.96	0.54	0.42
– Other	0.79	0.42	0.42	—	0.36	0.30	0.06
Local authorities	2.88	1.21	1.12	0.08	1.68	0.76	0.92
– Education	1.43	0.40	0.34	0.06	1.02	0.43	0.59
– Health and social services	0.37	0.05	0.04	—	0.32	0.12	0.20
– Police	0.19	0.14	0.14	—	0.05	0.03	0.01
– Other	0.90	0.62	0.60	0.02	0.28	0.17	0.11

Source: Economic Trends March 1985.

workers; and 71% of education workers. Many of these women work part-time: 44%, 63% and 58% respectively. Between 1961 and 1976, total employment in these three sectors expanded from just over $1\frac{1}{2}$ million to more than 3 million, as Figure 8.1 indicates. Complete series broken down by sex are only available for the local authority sector, but here the expansion of employment was clearly concentrated among women, and especially part-time women, as Figure 8.2 indicates. Employment of part-time women expanded by over 300% between 1952 and 1976, compared to only 30% for full-time men.

Within the state sector women are concentrated in 'women's jobs', often performing similar tasks as they had previously been doing (and continued to do) in the family: caring for the sick, the old and children, cooking meals and cleaning. The concentration of women by major service category in local authorities is shown in Figure 8.3, with women outnumbering men in both education and social services, but only very few women being employed in construction and transport. The jobs they occupy are both manual and non-manual. Manual jobs are mainly low paid and low status with little prospect of promotion. School meals staff and cleaners, for example, are both on the bottom of the national pay scale for manual workers, and mostly do not receive additional bonus payments. Bonus pay was received by only 10.2% of female manual workers in local government in 1984, and made up only 1.2% of their average pay, compared to 68.9% and 16.1% for men (*New Earnings Survey*, 1984). In 1972, the local authority management consultants, LAMSAC, drew up a model bonus scheme for the school meals service (LAMSAC, 1972). Its implementation, however, was limited because authorities found that women were already working at levels which would earn bonus (Cunnison, 1983).

For non-manual workers, the vast majority of women are concentrated in low grade, low paid clerical posts with very limited access to training and promotion (Alexander et al., 1982; Crompton and Jones,

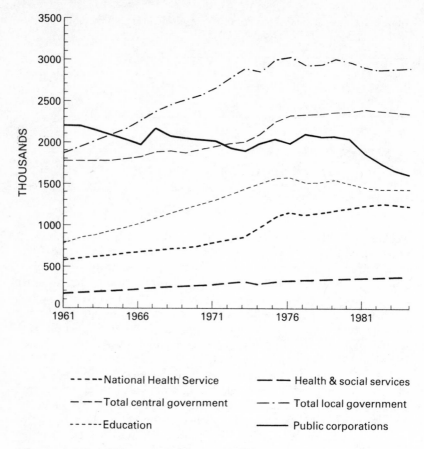

Figure 8.1 UK public sector employment 1961–83

Source: *Economic Trends*, various years.

1984). Where women have gained access to professional jobs in the public sector, such as teachers and civil servants, they have remained overwhelmingly concentrated in the lower grades, and career structures are not compatible with taking time off to have children. In 1979, for example, women made up 59.6% of scale 1 secondary teachers in England and Wales, but only 16.5% of head teachers (*Statistics of Education*, 1979). However, public sector jobs did provide women with more secure jobs than those in the private sector, and they were more likely to belong to a union and be covered by formal collective bargaining agreements. White collar workers also gained equal pay in advance of legislation.

The post-war period also saw the state taking a bigger role in relation to protection of the labour market at large. Workers were given legal

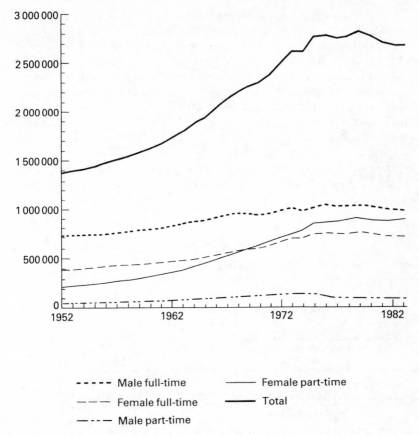

Figure 8.2 Local authority employment excluding police by sex and status, UK 1952–84

Source: Department of Employment.

rights relating to contracts of employment, redundancy and unfair dismissal; some protection was afforded from unsafe working conditions by health and safety legislation; and some groups gained minimum wage protection through the wages councils, the Fair Wages Resolution and Schedule 11 of the Employment Protection Act (see below, section 3.3). These measures should have been particularly important for women, who were concentrated in small firms and secondary jobs, and were generally less likely to be members of trade unions or protected by collective bargaining agreements. But much of the legislation relating to individual rights at work did not cover part-time workers until 1975, and then only if they worked over 16 hours per week. Since 34% of women work part-time, the legislation was limited in its impact. In 1980 there were still 36% of women in employment not covered by the legislation, either because their hours were too short or because they had not been in the same job for long enough (Martin and Roberts, 1984). Minimum wage legislation has traditionally been resisted by the trade unions, who argue that it inhibits the development of voluntary collective bargaining, but the wages councils that do exist are particularly important for women – they make up three quarters of the workers covered (Low Pay Unit, 1983). During the 1970s there were new initiatives relating to equal pay, sex discrimination and statutory maternity leave, although employers managed to circumvent many of the provisions by re-organising the division of labour and payment systems (Snell, Glucklich and Povall, 1981).

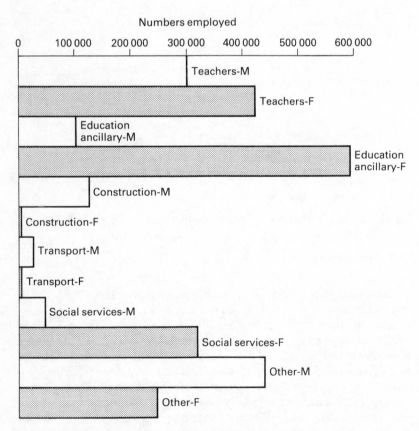

Figure 8.3 Local authority employment by service and sex, 1984

Source: Department of Employment.

2 THATCHERISM AND WOMEN

For most of the post-war period there was a consensus in British politics which supported expansion of the welfare state and government intervention in management of the economy. The expansion of state expenditure, particularly in the areas of welfare spending, was checked in 1976 as a result of the mounting economic crisis and the intervention of the IMF. But changes in state policy were limited by the corporatist basis of the Labour government. In 1979, however, a new Conservative government was elected, committed to a radical re-structuring of state economic and welfare policies, aimed at reversing the downward trend in profitability and growth of the economy. How does this change in approach relate to the position of women in the system of production and reproduction? This has to be looked at within the overriding priority of government policy – to restore the profitability of British capitalism.

The UK has not seen the upsurge of moral majority politics that has taken place in the US, and the government has remained neutral on the issue of abortion. Anti-abortionists launched a campaign after the 1983 election, but a rally they held in London was scarcely noticed. Despite the comments of some Tory MPs,[7] there has been no explicit attack on the right of women to paid employment. Rather, there has been an indirect attack by emphasising their responsibility in the family:

> ...the role of the housewife in a family was and remains the most important thing (Thatcher, 1982b).

> The home should be the centre but not the boundary of a woman's life (Thatcher, 1982a).

This approach has been carefully tied up in the rhetoric with the notion of choice and freedom:

> Improving family life is one of our principal objectives and that is reflected in the work of our ministers and officials. In particular we are determined to give individuals and their families more choice and more freedom to exercise responsibility, and to improve the efficiency of welfare services. (Thatcher, 1983).

It is a rhetoric with great appeal to people who feel alienated from the bureaucracy of the welfare state which is supposed to serve their interests, and which they are paying for through taxes.

As Mrs Thatcher indicated, this approach links up with the government's desire to reduce state expenditure on welfare services and social security – to 'take the state out of people's lives' – and encourage the family to take up those responsibilities. This line of thinking is explicit in the work of the Family Policy Group (FPG), a secret group of senior cabinet ministers whose papers were leaked to the *Guardian* newspaper in February 1983. The FPG's purpose was to 'ensure that all the government's domestic policies help to promote self-respect and a sense of individual responsibility' (Lister, 1983, p. 15). Its discussions revolved around 'an interconnected ideological trinity of family, private market and voluntary sector' to which responsibility was to be shifted from the state (Wicks, 1983). They considered 'what more can be done to encourage families – in the widest sense – to reassume responsibilities taken on by the state, for example responsibility for the disabled, elderly, unemployed sixteen year olds' and how to 'encourage mothers to stay at home' (Lister, 1983). A junior minister, Rhodes Boyson said that the government has no intention of increasing provision for the under fives, because women should stay at home to look after them. The government's 1983 public spending plans were based on the assumption that the percentage of three and four year olds entering education via nurseries and 'rising five' classes in schools would fall to 36% by the mid 1980s, compared to 40% in 1981.

But we have seen that this view of 'the family' contained in Tory rhetoric is not 'the family' in which most people live. Only 14% of households covered by the 1982 General Household Survey were composed of a male bread-winner with dependent wife and children, and for most families, both married couples and single parents, women's earnings are an essential contribution to family income, often keeping them out of poverty. The FPG was not totally naive to these changes, however, and considered 'adjusting tax and benefit allowances to see if families might be better rewarded' (Wicks, 1983). Given the constraints of the government's macro economic policy on expenditure, any such changes would have to be achieved by savings elsewhere. The government has recently announced plans to abolish the married man's tax allowance, which does not discriminate between men with wives in and out of paid employment, and to replace it with a single *transferable* personal allowance, giving a direct incentive for married women to stay at home.

The government's approach to state intervention in economic and social policy is not so much a withdrawal of the state, but rather a transformation of its role: withdrawing its supportive role in social and labour market policy, but increasing the repressive role, for example in relation to 'social security scroungers', trade union legislation and policing. However, the valid territory of state 'policing' is not a subject of total agreement among the philosophers of the New Right. While 'right to life' groups want to increase the powers of the state in relation to restricting access to abortion and contraception, and overriding parents' wishes relating to deformed babies and life-support, one of the Prime Minister's advisors, Ferdinand Mount, saw this as a betrayal of Tory promises to roll back the state; and the Secretary of State for Education, Sir Keith Joseph, wanted to maintain the existing situation against an alternative of 'irresponsible parenthood' feeding into the 'cycle of deprivation' (Davis, 1983).

The reduction of public expenditure, and thereby employment, also fits neatly with the government's policy in relation to the labour market. They want to 'free up' the labour market from the interference of trade unions and state protective legislation, and allow a 'market clearing wage' to eliminate unemployment. The public sector is seen as a particular obstacle to this policy because of the high levels of unionisation and formal systems of collective bargaining:

'In my opinion the trade union problem is Britain is almost exclusively concentrated in the nationalised industries and the public sector. If Mrs. Thatcher or successive governments are successful in reducing the size of the public sector, I think you will simultaneously and without very great difficulty, reduce the trade union problem that you face.' (M. Friedman in Dimbleby, 1981)

Again, however, there is something of a contradiction here for women. The type of low paid 'secondary' employment, unfettered by trade union or legal protection, which the government is seeking to promote relies, at least in part, on the exploitation of women's position as primarily responsible for domestic labour in the family, and relatively lacking in independent access to the social security system. If the expansion of employment is to be based on this segment of the labour supply, how are they also to provide the caring role that is expected of them by the government's family policy?

3 THE EFFECT OF STATE POLICIES

Rhetoric is one thing, but policy is another – what has the government actually done to affect the position of women in the system of production and reproduction, and with what results? We can look at government policies in three dimensions: provision of state services and state income support mechanisms; the state as a direct employer; and state intervention in the labour market at large.

3.1 Provision of state services and income support

Cuts in government expenditure have not been evenly applied across the whole spectrum of government expenditure. As Table 8.5 shows, the cuts have fallen primarily in the areas of 'social consumption', that is those areas concerned with the reproduction of labour power, to which women, in their role as primary domestic labour, have a specific relation. Expenditure on housing, education and school meals have all

Table 8.5 Functional analysis of total government expenditure 1974–1983 (1980 prices)

	1974	1977	1980	1983
			Indices	
Defence and external relations	100.0	102.4	107.9	113.2
Roads and transport	100.0	57.8	52.6	58.8
Employment and industry	100.0	60.0	108.6	89.0
Agriculture, forestry, fishing and food	100.0	52.7	51.0	60.7
Housing	100.0	71.9	65.8	46.3
Environmental services	100.0	78.4	89.4	88.0
Police, prisons, law courts, parliament	100.0	103.6	116.0	133.7
Education	100.0	101.3	99.1	98.0
School meals, milk and welfare foods	100.0	96.2	70.0	60.6
NHS	100.0	104.5	114.2	121.1
Personal social services	100.0	106.6	124.1	128.2
Social security benefits	100.0	114.7	123.4	144.3
Other	100.0	102.6	98.7	89.4
Total	100.0	93.8	100.8	103.1

Source: Calculated from *National Income and Expenditure, 1984.*

been cut, while expenditure on health and personal social services have failed to keep pace with the rapidly growing demands on them. In particular, the number of old people and especially the very old, is growing rapidly: the number of people aged 75 and over is expected to grow from 3.3 million in 1981 to 4.1 million in 2001; and the number of people aged 85 and over from 0.6 million to 1.1 million – almost double in 20 years (*Social Trends*, 1985, p. 20). These people form the most expensive age group in terms of welfare service requirements: in 1980–81, costs of health and social welfare were £220 per head for the total population, but £1,005 per head for those over 75 (Wicks, 1983). As welfare services are cut in relation to needs, a larger share of responsibility for meeting those needs will inevitably fall on the family, and the voluntary sector or other private provision, or else be left unmet.

Between 1979 and 1982, the number of children under five in England[8] increased from 2,696 thousand to 2,811 thousand, yet Local Authority provision of day nursery facilities has failed to keep pace as Table 8.6 shows. Only in Inner London and the West Midlands did the number of daycare places rise. Large variations in levels of provision exist between different local authorities, and changes in provision mean that the dispersion has increased. Ten local authorities do not provide any day nursery places at all, and while others have cut places drastically, such as Trafford who cut places from 320 to 190, others have sub-

Table 8.6 Local authority day nursery provision, England 1979–83

Area	1979/80		1982/83	
	Average number of children cared for per day	Population under 5 years ('000)	Average number of children cared for per day	Population under 5 years ('000)
Non-metropolitan counties	6,357	1,691	6,117	1,762
Tyne and Wear	708	67	570	70
Outer London	3,252 ⎱	392	3,148 ⎱	411
Inner London	3,779 ⎰		4,451 ⎰	
West Midlands	1,788	164	1,980	172
Merseyside	1,640	92	1,573	95
South Yorkshire		n.a.		
West Yorkshire	1,024	128	950	134
Greater Manchester	2,864	162	2,774	167

Source: National Council for One Parent Families and the National Childcare Campaign; *Regional Trends* 1982 and 1985.

stantially increased provision, such as Brent from 553 to 703. Local authorities have been a focus of struggle around cuts in public expenditure, with central government taking more and more controls over local authorities in order to enforce cuts and radical local councillors in some areas defying central government wishes and increasing levels of provision. The way that local authorities are planning for future provision is indicated by the fact that the number of staff employed on the relevant grade for nursery nurse trainees fell from 4138 in 1974 to just 56, most of whom are in London, in 1983 (figures supplied by the National Childcare Campaign).

Cuts in local authority provision mean increasing pressure on voluntary and other private provision, as well as on the family and its own support networks. However, the National Childcare Campaign (NCC) found that 49 of England's 104 local authorities responsible for social services have reduced grants to voluntary groups to provide play groups, mother and toddler groups and child minders, the biggest reductions being 87% in Cleveland, 66% in Barking and 63% in Bradford. Local authorities reducing grants tended to be the same as those who were reducing their own provision. Other local authorities have substantially increased grants to the voluntary sector, for example Bromley which increased grants by 167%, and Sheffield by 233%. In many areas, then, voluntary child care groups are being squeezed between coping with increased demand displaced from local authority provision, and cut backs in their grants (Raphael and Roll, 1984). The people performing the voluntary work are almost universally women – in 1981 7% of women aged 16 and over, and 19% of those aged 25–34 provided voluntary help for play groups, as compared to less than 0.5% of men (*Social Trends*, 1984).

One area on which the government has particularly focussed cuts in public expenditure has been the school meals service. School meals have been provided by local authorities at subsidised prices and regulated nutritional values since the 1944 Education Act. For children of families on social security or low incomes they have been provided free. They provide a direct substitute between paid and unpaid female labour power. Under the 1980 Education Act, the government released local authorities from any statutory responsibilities except to provide free meals to children in families on social security. Expenditure was expected to fall by £200 million, almost one half. The result has been increased prices combined with cuts in both the quantity and quality of school meals provided, and an increase in unpaid domestic labour. While the proportion of children taking school meals fell from 64.1% in 1979 to 48.2% in 1980, the proportion taking packed lunches prepared at home increased from 12.6% to 27.0% (Department of Education and Science annual school meals census). Some schools have also brought in parents to help run the school meals service on a voluntary basis. For children in receipt of free meals, for whom they may form an important part of their diet, the stigma of receiving them has increased as in many schools they form the majority or only children eating school meals. (Bisset and Coussins, 1982). In consequence the take up of free meals fell from 11.9% of school children to 9.9% between 1979 and 1980 (Department of Education and Science annual school meals service) and in April 1988, many families will lose their right to free meals altogether when local authorities lose their discretionary power to provide free meals to low income families just above the social security threshold (Byrne and Pond, 1985). For women, these cuts involve both an increase in unpaid domestic labour and the financial costs of lost subsidies and unclaimed free meals, the latter particularly concentrated on single parents.

Turning to the care of the elderly, state provision has remained static against the increasing numbers of old people. Between 1981 and 1983 places in homes provided by local authorities increased from 121.7 thousand to only 122.3 thousand (*Social Trends*, 1985, p. 119). Since the alternative of family care supported by the Family Policy Group is not a real one, there has been a rapid growth in private and voluntary sector provision – from 65.2 thousand places to 76.2 thousand. Much of this increased provision is being paid for indirectly by the state through social security payments to old people unable to afford the fees – such payments increased from £34 million in 1982 to £90 million in 1983, prompting the government to impose a ceiling on the fees that it will reimburse. To the extent that local authorities have been able or willing to shift the burden of caring for the elderly onto families and the 'community', it means an increased burden of unpaid labour on women, either looking after their own relatives and neighbours, or through participation in organised voluntary help. Many local authorities, under pressure from increased central government financial constraints on the one hand, and increased demands for help from the elderly on the other hand, have looked to more formally organised 'community care' schemes, utilising voluntary labour, to provide a cheaper alternative to residential care. A recent study by the Department of the Environment found that costs ranged widely, but averaged around £4,000 per person per year, compared to £5,000 for sheltered housing, £6,000 in an old people's home and up to £20,000 in hospital (Tinker, 1984). What these figures conceal is the level of informal help. Families were by far the largest source of help for personal and domestic tasks, and paid carers also provided a lot of unofficial help; again in practice this unpaid help is provided mainly by women. Meanwhile, the amount of non-residential services provided by local authorities have also failed to keep pace with the growing demands placed on them; only 8% of people aged 65 and over had a home help in 1982, compared with 9.6% in 1979, again placing an increased burden on the family (Health and Personal Social Service Statistics, 1982).

The rising numbers of old people have also put increasing strains on the National Health Service. According to the Commons Select Committee on Social Services, real spending on the health service has only increased by 7.2% in the last five years, and only 4% in the hospital service. Yet demographic changes and technological advances have increased demand in the same period by 6.8% even by the DHSS's own figures. Between May 1979 and December 1982, 109 hospitals were closed, involving the loss of 6,709 beds in the health service, and there were a further 146 partial closures, involving 1201 lost beds (figures provided by the Confederation of Health Service Employees). Despite this loss of beds, and a loss of 11,400 employees, the number of in-patient cases treated in 1983 were up 5% on 1982; day cases were up 15% and out-patients visits 2.5% up. What this means is that more patients are being sent home early to be cared for by their families, principally by women.

The situation with state income support mechanisms is somewhat complicated. Table 8.5 indicates that there has been a substantial increase in real levels of social security spending, increasing by 26% between 1980 and 1983. This represents the outcome of several different trends: firstly there are increasing numbers of people unemployed and dependent on income from social security; secondly, as direct service provision is cut and increased charges raised, more people are forced to claim social security benefits to pay for services such as housing or old people's homes; but thirdly, there have been cuts in the coverage and rates of social security benefits, which have limited the increased expenditure, and led more and more poor people to depend on handouts from private charities.

So far the government has restricted itself to administrative reforms and adjustments to the coverage and rates of social security benefits. In the former category, the burden of administering sick pay was shifted to employers and the administration of housing allowances unified and shifted to local authorities. Reductions in entitlement to benefit have included the abolition of earnings-related unemployment benefit, and making school leavers and people who 'voluntarily' quit jobs ineligible for benefit. Women's access to unemployment benefit has been threatened by the introduction of a requirement to show adequate child-care arrangements before qualifying as 'unemployed'. Access to housing benefits has also been reduced for those on low incomes: 2,260 thousand claimants lost benefit as a result of the changes during the introduction of the new scheme, and over two million more will lose as a result of cuts in April and November 1984 (*Hansard* col. 404–SW, (28.4.83) and col. 150 (14.2.84)). Rhodes Boyson, as Social Security Minister, was energetic in plugging 'holes' in the Social Security system: he reversed decisions to pay for medical aids for the sick and the disabled, to pay the unemployed if they had been getting holiday pay or pay in lieu, to pay students supplementary benefit under certain conditions, to pay grants to the single homeless for cookers and beds, and he enforced the deduction of the value of gifts of firewood and food parcels from claimants' benefits (Golding, 1984).

Many of these changes are limited in terms of the numbers of people effected but they are often the poorest members of society, the majority of whom are women. One such change has been the reduction of clothing grants to people on supplementary benefit. Before 1980, extra payments for clothes and shoes were made to nearly one fifth of all supplementary benefit claimants, and nearly half of single parents (Raphael and Roll, 1984). The 1980 Act replaced the administrative discretion of local officers and severely restricted the conditions for receiving clothing grants, to cases where the need has arisen 'otherwise than by normal wear and tear', or to cases where it is the 'only means by which serious damage to the health and safety of any member of the assessment unit may be prevented'. As a result, payments fell from 355 thousand in 1980 to 71 thousand in 1982, while the number of people living on supplementary benefit increased from 4.4 million to 7 million. These cuts have resulted in rapidly rising applications to private charities for clothing grants. Birmingham Voluntary Services Council, for example, reported that applications for clothing grants had increased by 60% between 1982/3 and 1983/4. The number of clothing grants awarded by the Family Welfare Association increased from 72 in 1979/80 to 323 in 1982/83, most of the increase being for children's clothes. In 1982/3, 254 grants for childrens' clothes were made, covering

1,701 children, an average of just over £5 per child, hardly adequate to meet needs.

The reduction in social security spending resulting from cuts since 1979 has been estimated at £8,000 million. In contrast there have been income tax cuts worth £5,500 million, 20% of which have gone to the richest 0.4% of the population (*Hansard*, 4 April 1985, col. 709–710, quoted in Byrne and Pond). For those people affected, many of whom are women, especially single parents, who are unemployed or earning low wages, these cuts make them even more vulnerable to exploitation in the secondary labour market, forcing them to take on additional employment such as homeworking or part-time work that can be fitted in around domestic responsibilities, but at low wages.

Yet despite these cuts, as unemployment rises and government provision of subsidised housing and homes for the elderly falls, the number of people dependent on social security, and particularly on means tested benefits, continues to rise, increasing levels of government expenditure. This prompted the government to introduce more substantial reforms of the social security system described as 'the most substantial examination of the social security system since the Beveridge report'. The aim of the review was stated to be rationalisation at zero cost, but the Secretary of State made it clear that reductions in expenditure would be preferable (Byrne and Pond, 1985, p. 2).

The reviews are characterised by three features: reducing public expenditure; sharpening labour market incentives, and encouraging low wage employment; and shifting the emphasis in social security benefits further away from universal benefits and increasing the emphasis on means testing, reasserting notions of the 'deserving' and 'undeserving' poor.

The reforms involve a concentration of power in the hands of the Seceretary of State who will in fact be responsible for determining the detailed provisions of the legislation. The notion of deserving and undeserving poor is further reinforced by the new 'Social Fund' which will replace social security claimants' rights to single payments for special or urgent needs with discretionary payments, preferably in the form of loans, with no right of appeal.

The major features of the reforms, to be implemented in 1987 and 1988, are the replacement of Supplementary Benefit (SB) by Income Supplement (IS); the replacement of Family Income Supplement (FIS) by Family Credit (FC); substantial cuts in entitlement to Housing Benefit; a watering down of the State Earnings Relation Pensions Scheme (SERPS); the abolition of Maternity Grant and replacement of the Maternity Allowance by Statutory Maternity Pay (SMP); and reduced entitlement to widow's pensions.

Women's entitlement to benefits will be particularly affected by new rules for eligibility. The SERPS is now to be calculated on the basis of *lifetime* earnings rather than the best twenty years, hitting women with discontinuous work histories. The maternity grant of £25 is being abolished and replaced by a means tested grant of around £75 from the social fund. Entitlement to the new SMP is to be based on criteria of continuous employment with the *same employer*, something which many women's employment histories, characterised by short term jobs in the secondary labour market, will fail to satisfy. Widows will only be able to claim the full widow's pension from age 55 instead of 50, a change which the government justified on the basis that 'far more women are now able to support themselves through work' (*Labour Research*, July 1985, p. 183). This underlines the contradictory messages for women in the government's economic and social policy. On the one hand they are to be encouraged to stay at home and look after their families, but at the same time cuts in benefits make this more difficult, and where women lose their access to a male bread winner they are encouraged *not* to stay at home and become dependent on the state. The unifying theme is the reduction in public expenditure seen to be necessary to revive the fortunes of British capital.

Another feature of the reforms has been the link with labour market policy, aiming to encourage the take up of low paid jobs by youth and adult males, the likely implication of which is a substitution of these groups into traditional areas of women's employment. The new IS replaces the old short and long term SB rate with a system of *age* related personal allowances, plus various premiums. According to the government's estimates, of the 3.3 million households now on SB 1.7 million will suffer a reduction in benefits, most of whom will be youth and pensioners (*Labour Research*, February 1986, p. 19). The aim of the revised structure is clearly to deal with the problem of youth unemployment by sharpening 'incentives to work'. The new FC scheme had a similar aim for fathers which unlike FIS would be paid direct to fathers in their pay packets. It was the probability that this would encourage the growth of low wage employment subsidised by the government that attracted the Prime Minister to the scheme (*Economist*, 28 June–4 July 1986). A backlash by Tory women and opposition from employers, however, eventually forced the Secretary of State to reverse this proposal and pay the FC direct to mothers. Therefore the government has made it clear that the value of child benefit will not keep pace with inflation and that resources are to be switched into the means tested FC scheme. This represents a significant loss in access to independent income for all mothers.

3.2 The state as a direct employer

Table 8.5 showed how cuts in public expenditure have been concentrated in the areas of 'social consumption', such as education and housing. These are the areas where women's employment in the public sector is concentrated, as Table 8.4 indicated, as teachers, school dinner ladies, cleaners, home helps, nurses, etc. – the 'caring' jobs involved in the production and reproduction of labour power. The effects of this squeeze on finance have been both macro and micro. In macro terms there have been cuts in employment or a failure to increase employment in line with demands on the service; and in micro terms there has been a change in public sector financial systems and a corresponding shift in the nature of the social relations of production.

Looking first at the incidence of job loss, only local authorities provide a complete series of data broken down by sex, but this sector covers a large proportion of expenditure on 'social consumption'. It is a highly labour-intensive sector, with 70% of expenditure going on wages and salaries, which means that significant reductions in expenditure can only be achieved by reducing employment (Local Authorities' Conditions of Service Advisory Board, 1981). The incidence of employment change will be the outcome of a process of interaction of several factors: central government political priorities expressed through grants and other controls over local government; local government's political response; the structure of production, and the incidence of technical change; differences in the labour supply situation and trade union organisation of different groups of workers; and the competitiveness of private sector provision. Table 8.7 indicates the incidence of employment change across services and between male and female workers in local authorities between 1979 and 1984. Overall men have lost more full-time jobs and proportionately more part-time jobs than women. Women have lost more part-time jobs absolutely, but for both men and women job losses have been concentrated among full-time workers.

The concentration of women's employment in education and social services, which was illustrated in Figure 8.2, will itself result in an uneven incidence of employment change between men and women. While education has suffered severe cuts, reflecting in part falling school rolls and changes in the school meals service, employment in social services has actually increased, largely due to the increasing demands placed on services for old people. On the other hand construction, which is predominantly a male area of employment, has been cut severely, reflecting heavy cuts in capital expenditure on housing, which is under fairly close central government control, and changes in the system of financing construction which has meant an increasing proportion of work going out to private contractors. Table 8.8 shows the results of shift-share analysis applied to these employment changes in

Table 8.7 Employment change by sex, in full time and part time categories, and by major service, local authorities, Great Britain, 1979–84

	Males				Females				Total	
	Full time No.	%	Part time No.	%	Full time No.	%	Part time No.	%	No.	%
Teachers and lecturers	−13,602	−5.0	−4,854	−10.3	−18,105	−5.4	+2,625	+2.4	−33,936	−4.5
Education ancillary staff	−2,510	−2.9	−501	−2.5	−34,086	−22.3	−40,942	−7.9	−78,039	−10.0
Construction	−24,440	−16.0	−113	−52.6	−338	−11.6	+69	+15.3	−24,822	−15.9
Transport	−735	−2.8	+34	+66.7	−706	−23.9	+12	+3.2	−1,395	−4.7
Social services	+3,847	+9.8	+564	+17.2	+4,141	+3.6	+15,831	+8.5	+24,383	+7.1
Other services	−26,116	−5.8	−4,245	−19.9	+4,772	+3.2	+6,226	+6.8	−19,363	−2.7
Total	−63,556	−6.2	−9,115	−9.9	−44,322	−5.9	−16,179	−1.8	−133,172	−4.8

Source: Calculated from the 'Form L42' data provided by the Department of Employment.

Table 8.8 Shift-share analysis of employment change for male and female employees local authorities, Great Britain, 1979–84

| | Expected change | Actual change | Components of change | | |
			Overall trend	Structural	Differential
	(1)	(2)	(3)	(4)	(5)
Male					
Full time	− 55,842	− 63,556	− 49,398	− 6,444	− 7,714
	(− 5.4%)	(− 6.2%)	(− 4.8%)	(− 0.6%)	(− 0.8%)
Part time	− 4,485	− 9,115	− 4,406	− 79	− 4,630
	(− 4.9%)	(− 9.9%)	(− 4.8%)	(− 0.1%)	(− 5.0%)
Female					
Full time	− 26,573	− 44,322	− 36,215	+ 9,642	− 17,749
	(− 3.5%)	(− 5.9%)	(− 4.8%)	(+ 1.3%)	(− 2.4%)
Part time	− 46,435	− 16,179	− 43,592	− 2,843	+ 30,256
	(− 5.1%)	(− 1.8%)	(− 4.8%)	(− 0.3%)	(+ 3.3%)

Source: Calculated from the 'Form L42' data provided by the Department of Employment.

order to net out the effects of women's employment concentration by service category. Full-time women have lost jobs *more* rapidly than would be expected, as have both full and part-time men, but part-time women have lost jobs *less* rapidly. How can this pattern be explained?

According to data from the Joint Manpower Watch survey manual workers have lost jobs more rapidly than non-manual workers across all service categories but there is no information on manual and non-manual categories by sex (Walker, 1985). Non-manual workers constitute a relatively 'fixed cost' in the structure of production compared to manual workers; they have so far been relatively immune to the impact of technical change; their numbers have actually *increased* as a result of central government imposing new responsibilities and regulations on local government; and they have not been the subject of such extensive reorganisation of the labour process and bonus schemes as manual workers. However the expansion of non-manual employment has been overwhelmingly part-time. Over the same period, 1979–84, full-time non-manual employment fell by − 10,458 (− 1.0%), while part-time non-manual employment increased by + 16,545 (+ 15.7%). This expansion was almost certainly concentrated among female workers. Similarly the falls in manual employment were − 78,301 (− 16.8%) for full-time workers, but only − 32,456 (− 5.1%) for part-timers.

Secondly, it is male manual workers in local government who have a strong history of tight trade union organisation and job control, and who succeeded in establishing bonus schemes which increased earnings without increasing managerial control. Female manual workers mostly belong to trade unions but do not have the same history of activity, and only 10% compared to 69% of males were covered by bonus schemes in 1984 (New Earnings Survey, 1984). Their jobs have been characterised instead by their close social relations of consumption and high rates of self-exploitation. However, in the changed economic and political environment of the 1980s, the balance of power in the local government labour process has moved significantly in management's favour. There has been a widespread re-organisation of production and bonus schemes in areas such as construction and refuse collection, increasing productivity and cutting jobs. These changes have predominantly effected male manual workers, where the scope for increased productivity was greatest.

Thirdly, the service categories identified by the data are quite broad, and there have been significant variations within these categories. For example, among teachers and lecturers there are more women in the school sector, but more men in the further education sector (Wilkinson and Jackson, 1981). The latter, especially evening classes, has been subject to more severe cuts in expenditure and employment, reflected most strongly in the loss of part-time male jobs.

What comes out most strongly from Table 8.8 is the substitution of part-time for full-time employment that has occurred, with the result that women's jobs have fallen less than men's. Part-time employment constitutes a distinct segment of the labour market, related to both demand and supply side factors. Employers may use part-time labour power because the pattern of output demand is concentrated at particular times of day, as for example with recreational or transport services. But for many jobs the use of part-time employment is to allow the utilisation of an increased female labour supply, bringing in married women whose domestic commitments limit their alternative employment opportunities. In the context of financial restraint and uncertainty, part-time labour power provides a cheap and flexible labour supply. Although part-time workers earn pro rata full time rates in local government, if their weekly earnings are low enough employers do not pay National Insurance, and the vast majority of part-time workers are excluded from the local government superannuation scheme. Furthermore, the use of a labour supply with limited alternative job opportunities means that women employed are often over qualified and their productivity frequently higher than could be obtained from a full-time worker. The absence of rigidly fixed hours of employment provides flexibility in the future utilisation of labour power to meet changes in financial and/or market conditions. Part-time workers who work less than sixteen hours per week are not generally protected by legislation covering redundancy and unfair dismissal.

The data in Table 8.8 only indicate that there has been an overall substitution of part-time for full-time employment, that local authorities expanding employment have particularly employed part-timers, while those cutting employment have concentrated on full-timers. However, regressing changes in part-time employment on changes in total employment *across* local authorities has indicated that this substitution is also taking place at the level of the *individual* local authority. Furthermore, this process is common to both Conservative and Labour controlled local authorities (Walker, 1985).

The 'protection' of female job opportunities in local authorities, then, is not so simple. It represents an erosion of the better paid and more secure full-time jobs, both male and female, and the substitution of relatively casualised and dead-end part-time women's jobs. This substitution may be seen as part of a wider *micro* level change in the organisation of public sector labour markets. The Thatcher government has transformed the traditional role of the public sector as a 'model employer'. Traditionally it has been the role of the public sector to act as a 'good' employer, with fair remuneration and conditions of employment negotiated through the well established collective bargaining procedures of the 'Whitley' councils, with formal encouragement to trade union membership. Under the new political regime, the public sector is still to act as a 'model' for the private sector, but now it is in acting as a 'tough' employer, bringing down the level of wage settlements, reorganising the labour process in favour of increased managerial control and productivity, and activating the new employment legislation against trade union activity. Public sector labour markets are to be made directly subordinate to market criteria of profit and loss which is seen as essential for the success of the monetarist economic experiment (Congdon, 1982). Through the introduction of specific 'cash limits' on wage expenditure the government has attempted to reproduce a 'jobs versus pay' trade-off in the public sector. The level of public sector wage settlements has effectively been brought down to the lower quartile of settlements generally through this policy (Walker, 1985).

One example of the casualisation of public sector employment is the school meals service. Not only has service provision and employment been cut, in many cases remaining jobs have been put onto a casual employment basis, with no permanent contract or fixed hours, cuts in pay and the abolition of retainer payments during school holidays, directly contravening the national pay agreement. These moves are being sanctioned at national level, as the following advice to local authorities indicates:

> The national employers have now stated that individual authorities may feel it impossible to adhere to these conditions of service. In the present economic circumstances their relevance is being increasingly questioned and a number of authorities have sought to introduce different conditions for their staff. As holiday and

retainer pay account for an extra 10–11 weeks pay in addition to the normal pay for 38 school weeks any amendment of these provisions could result in considerable savings. (Chartered Institute of Public Finance and Accountancy, 1984, para 20.10.16)

In other areas the government has directly 'privatised' public sector employment, as with British Telecom or ancillary services in local government and the National Health Service. In the latter case, the government has legally required health authorities to seek tenders for cleaning, laundry, catering and other ancillary services, and is currently drawing up similar legislation to cover local authorities, while some have brought in private contractors already. These contracting industries rely almost exclusively on the employment of part-time married women at low rates of pay and unprotected by either legislation or trade unions (Sullivan, 1977; Advisory, Conciliation and Arbitration Service 1980; Craig et al., 1980). By contracting out these services, employment is separated from the wage structure and trade union protection of the Whitley councils. Labour power can be employed on lower rates of pay, casualised conditions of employment and increased rates of exploitation. For example, when Birmingham City Council handed over the cleaning of schools to Servisystem, hours worked per week fell from 12,662 to 7,685, by a combination of staff reductions and reduced hours per worker, pay fell from £2.24 to £1.71 per hour, and there was no sick pay or superannuation and holidays were reduced from 23–25 plus statutory days to 20 plus statutory days. A similar story can be told for other cases. Other local authorities and health authorities have used the threat of privatisation to impose inferior conditions on the direct labour force, a process re-inforced by compulsory tendering.

3.3 Regulation of the labour market at large

The government has ostensibly pursued a policy of 'freeing-up' the labour market from state intervention. What this means in practice is an attempt to divide the labour market, to expand the secondary (predominantly female) sector at the expense of relatively well organised (and predominantly male) primary sector workers in the private and state sectors, and to constrain but not abolish trade unions.

The government has passed progressively more limiting legislation relating to the degree of legal immunity offered to trade union action, and has introduced the right not to belong to a trade union. Strikes which are deemed to be sympathy strikes, inter-union strikes or 'political' strikes have been outlawed, and compulsory ballots introduced for 'legal' strike action. Damages caused by such illegal action are now recoverable from trade unions in the civil courts. Rather than trying to eliminate trade unions, they are being forced to operate under increasingly constrained conditions, where the leadership is pressed into policing the rank and file (Moore, 1982).

A large part of the secondary labour market relies on the exploitation of women's position in the family, which limits their employment opportunities outside the home, and their access to trade union organisation, re-inforced by their limited access to social security benefits such that there is no floor to wages. Thus women's employment is concentrated in small firms, especially in the service sector, in part-time jobs and home-working. Only 38% of women compared to 64% of men are unionised. For these jobs minimum wages and employment protection legislation are particularly important, establishing some limits to the exploitation of women's disadvantaged position in the labour supply. The Thatcher government has been gradually dismantling these limits.

On minimum wages, Schedule 11 of the Employment Protection Act through which the 'going rate' for a trade could be imposed, and the Fair Wages Resolution, which covered government contracts, were both abolished. In the latter case, there is evidence, at least in the case of local authorities, that Fair Wages clauses were inserted in contracts and enforced by the majority of employers (Thomson and Ingham, 1983). Wages Councils, which are the only form of statutory minimum wages in the UK, cover nearly three million workers, mostly employed in areas with limited trade union organisation, for example catering, hairdressing and clothing. Enforcement of minimum wages has been reduced, and the Government has intervened to delay the implementation of increase orders. In 1983 only 120 wages inspectors were employed to check for abuses in payment, compared to 150 in 1978, while the number of complaints regarding illegal underpayment have increased by 10%. Almost ten thousand establishments were found to be underpaying their workers, but civil proceedings for recovery of arrears were taken against only five employers, and criminal proceedings against only two (Labour Research, February 1985).

In 1986 the government introduced legislation to reduce the coverage of the Wages Councils. They are now only to set a single hourly rate plus overtime rate, and are no longer able to regulate other conditions of employment, except to set an upper limit on lodgings deductions. This opens the way for employers to further reduce employment benefits for the mainly female labour force in these industries. However, a further change is the withdrawal of young workers under 21 years from the scope of the councils. The obvious intention of this provision is the substitution of youth for female labour power.

Similarly, enforcement of health and safety legislation has been cut – the factory inspectorate has been reduced from 4,500 to 3,700, the number of visits from 285,000 to 267,000, and there have been fewer enforcement notices and prosecutions. Legislation on unfair dismissal and redundancy has also been watered down: the qualifying period for protection from unfair dismissal has been increased from six months to a year, and two years for firms employing less than twenty employees; tribunal proceedings have been made more difficult, and there is no minimum compensation; compulsory consultation over redundancy has been abolished.

Rights to maternity leave have also been reduced – more written procedure is required to qualify, the right to return to the same job has been removed, and there are no rights for workers in firms employing less than six workers. EEC directives to improve legislation relating to Equal Pay and protection for part-time workers have been resisted and only implemented in the weakest possible way.

In 1986 the government published further proposals for the de-regulation of the labour market, with particular implications for women concentrated in secondary labour market jobs. The qualifying period of employment for the legal right to a statement of reasons for dismissal is to be increased from six months to two years; women employed in firms of less than ten workers would lose their right to return to their jobs after maternity leave; and part-time workers would have to work 20 hours per week if they have been in a job two years, or 12 hours after five years to qualify for most employment rights.

State intervention in the labour market is only to be removed, however, where it provides protection to workers from the excesses of exploitation. Other government intervention, which promotes the expansion of low wage unregulated employment has been increased. The Manpower Services Commission (MSC) has been vastly expanded, and runs a variety of schemes which subsidise cheap labour. The Youth Training Scheme (YTS) replaced the old Youth Opportunities Programme, and the number of young people covered expanded from 162 thousand in 1978/79 to 543 thousand in 1982/83 (*Social Trends*, 1985, p. 71). They were paid an allowance of only £25 per week in 1983, and the theoretical training requirements have been only loosely enforced. The Young Workers Scheme (YWS) in operation between 1982 and 85 provided employers with a subsidy of £15 per week for each worker employed, but only if they were paid less than £42 per week.[9] Other MSC schemes include the Community Programme and Voluntary Projects Programme, which encourage participation of private sector voluntary organisations in promoting low paid employment. Employers in both the private and public sectors have used these schemes at least in part to substitute for their regular labour force. An Institute of Manpower Studies study found that 94% of jobs supported by the YWS would have existed anyway, and even the government puts the figure at 67% (*Labour Research*, March 1986, p. 10). Women have so far made up just under 50% of entrants to youth schemes, but less than 25% of entrants to adult schemes (*Social Trends*, 1985, p. 71), the latter mainly attributable to requirements that entrants are drawn from the long term *registered* unemployed. Data needs to be collected on which workers are being replaced by these MSC schemes, but it seems likely that many of them are substituting youths and long-term unemployed men for women in less secure and 'unskilled' secondary jobs.[10]

Another aspect of increasing State intervention has been the direct promotion of the small firm sector of the economy. This has included financial support through improved loan facilities, etc., relaxation of industrial relations legislation as applied to small firms, and the setting up of 'enterprise zones', in which firms are exempted from taxation and many legal restrictions, and which particularly encourage small firms.

The government policies of 'de-regulating' the labour market encourage the expansion of employment forms traditionally dominated by women, but as the pressures of male unemployment rise, and the numbers of primary sector male jobs diminish, many men may be forced to accept jobs in the secondary sector, as in the case of MSC jobs.

4 CONCLUSION

In conclusion, the Thatcher government's policy in relation to the family and paid employment is a two pronged attack: cuts in state welfare services and income support mechanisms seek to shift the burden of caring and financial support for individuals onto the family; and state intervention, or lack of it, in the labour market of both the private and the public sectors, acts to remove any 'floors' that exist to wages and conditions, to erode the control of organised labour, and to promote the expansion of low-wage, unregulated secondary employment. But there is a basic contradiction between these two policy strands: on the one hand women are expected to take on a growing burden of domestic labour, and on the other hand the government is trying to expand the very segment of the labour market which relies on exploiting women's disadvantaged position in the labour supply. Most families are dependent on women's earnings as a vital source of family income, and as male unemployment rises and state income support is cut, more women will be encouraged to take on such low paid work. What this means is an increasing amount of both paid and unpaid labour for women, and increased levels of stress on 'the family'. Furthermore, most families do not correspond to the 'ideal' imagined by Tory philosophers, and this imposes structural limits to the extent to which it is possible to shift responsibility for caring and income support onto 'the family' – there may be no such family to step in, or they may be quite unable to take up the work.

NOTES

1 The number of children adopted fell from 25,000 in 1967 to less than 15,000 in 1977, and more than half of these were adoptions where at least one adopter was a parent (Central Policy Review Staff, 1980).
2 54/55% of women covered by the Women and Employment Survey in full time paid employment, and 76/77% of those working part time, did all or most of the housework.
3 Supplementary Benefit is a means tested benefit for people out of employment; Family Income Supplement is paid to families where the head of the household is in employment but earns a low wage; Invalid Care Allowance is paid to people other than married women who have caring responsibilities for sick or disabled people. However, as a result of a recent European Court ruling, the government will soon be forced to make married women eligible for the latter benefit.
4 Family Allowance was a small cash payment paid direct to mothers for every child after the first child. Child Benefit replaced both the family allowance and the child tax allowances: it is still a cash payment direct to mothers but is now paid for every child including the first.
5 Hot meals delivered to people's homes.
6 In 1982 local authorities directly provided 122,100 places for people aged 65 and over, and a further 17,800 via voluntary and private homes. Other voluntary and private homes provided 51,600 places, many of which would be indirectly state financed via social security payments (*Social Trends*, 1984). The total number of people aged 65 and over in 1982 was 8,467,000.
7 Patrick Jenkin, for example, said in October 1979, 'I don't think mothers have the same right to work as fathers. If the good lord had intended us to have equal rights to go out to work, he wouldn't have created man and woman' (Rimmer, 1983, p. 19).
8 Excluding South Yorkshire.
9 These rates were subject to slight alteration during the period of operation.
10 The recently introduced top-up earnings scheme, which pays £20 per week for six months to any long term unemployed person taking a job for under £80 per week, explicitly recognises that some financial incentive is necessary if even the most disadvantaged men are to be persuaded to take jobs at women's pay rates.

REFERENCES

Advisory Conciliation and Arbitration Service (1980), *The Contract Cleaning Industry*, ACAS, London.
Alexander, M., Cooper, D. and Dean, R. (1982), *Women in Local Government: The Neglected Resource*, Local Government Operational Research Unit, Reading.
Bisset, L. and Coussins, J. (1982), *Badge of Poverty*, Child Poverty Action Group, Poverty Pamphlet No. 55, August, London.
Byrne, D. and Pond, C. (1985). 'A (Dis)credit to the Family?' *Low Pay Review* no. 23, Autumn.
Central Policy Review Staff (1980), *People and their Families*, HMSO, London.

Central Statistical Office, *Health and Personal Social Service Statistics,* annually, HMSO, London.

Central Statistical Office, *Social Trends,* annually, HMSO, London.

Chartered Institute of Public Finance and Accountancy (1984), *Financial Information Service Vol. 20: Education,* CIPFA, London.

Congdon, T. (1982), 'Why has monetarism failed so far? 2: The Public Sector problem', *The Banker,* April, pp. 34–49.

Craig, C., Rubery, J., Tarling, R., and Wilkinson, F. (1980), *Industrial and Staff Canteens,* EEC Case Studies in Labour Market Segmentation, mimeo.

Crompton, R., and Jones, G. (1984), *White-Collar Proletariat: Deskilling and Gender in Clerical Work,* Macmillan, London.

Cunnison, S. (1983), 'Participation in Local Union Organisation. School Meals Staff: a case study', in Gamarnikow E. et al. (eds), *Gender, Class and Work,* Heinemann, London.

Davis, T. (1983), 'Feminism is Dead? Long Live Feminism', *Marxism Today,* October, pp. 14–18.

Department of Education and Science (1979), *Statistics of Education Volume 4 – Teachers,* HMSO, London.

Department of Employment, *Family Expenditure Survey,* annually, HMSO, London.

Department of Employment, *New Earnings Survey,* annually, HMSO, London.

Dimbleby, D. (1981), 'The Monetarist Experiment: a half-term report on Mrs. Thatcher's progress by Hayek and Friedman', *The Listener,* 12 March.

Elias, P. (1983), 'The Changing Pattern of Employment and Earnings Amongst Married Couples', *EOC Research Bulletin.*

Gamble, A. (1982), 'The 1982 Budget', *Capital and Class,* vol. 17, pp. 5–16.

Golding, P. (1984), 'Living beyond the lens', *New Statesman,* 25 May.

Hakim, C. (1979), *Occupational Segregation,* Department of Employment Research Paper No. 9.

Hunt, A. (1968), *A Survey of Women's Employment,* HMSO, London.

Hunt, A. (1970), *The Home Help Service in England and Wales,* HMSO, London.

Labour Research Department, *Labour Research,* monthly, LRD, London.

Lister, R. (1983), 'Family policy: alternative viewpoints – Forward', *Poverty* No. 55, August, pp. 15–18, Child Poverty Action Group, London.

Local Authorities' Conditions of Service Advisory Board (1981), *Evidence to Inquiry into Civil Service Pay,* LACSAB, London.

Local Authorities' Management Services and Computer Committee (1972), *Manual for LAMSAC Works Study Based Incentive Scheme for Local Application in the School Meals Service,* LAMSAC, London.

Low Pay Unit (1983), *Who Needs the Wages Councils?,* LPU Pamphlet No. 24, London.

Martin, J. and Roberts, C. M. (1984), *Women and Employment,* HMSO, London.

Minford, P. (1983), *Unemployment Cause and Cure,* Martin Robertson, Oxford.

Moore, R. (1982), 'Free market economics, trade union law and the labour market', *Cambridge Journal of Economics,* vol. 6, no. 3, pp. 297–315.

Raphael, T. and Roll, J. (1984), *Carrying the Can: charities and the welfare state,* Child Poverty Action Group and Family Welfare Association, London.

Rimmer, L. (1983), 'Family Trends', *Poverty* No. 55, August pp. 18–24, Child Poverty Action Group London.

Rossiter, C. and Wicks, M. (1982), *Crisis or Challenge? Family Care, Elderly People and Social Policy*, Study Commission on the Family Occasional Paper No. 8, London.

Snell, M. W., Glucklich, P., and Povall, M. (1981), *Equal Pay and Opportunities*, Department of Employment Research Paper No. 20.

Sullivan, J. (1977), *The Brush Off*, Low Pay Pamphlet No. 5, Low Pay Unit, London.

Thatcher, M. (1982a), *Women in a Changing World*, text of a speech to the Institute of Electrical Engineers, July 26.

Thatcher, M. (1982b), Interview, *Sunday People*, November.

Thatcher, M. (1983), *Hansard*, 3 March.

The Government's Expenditure Plans 1983–84 to 1985–86 vol. 12, Cmnd 8789, HMSO, London.

Thomson, A. W. J. and Ingham, M. (1983), *Dimensions of Industrial Relations in Local Authorities*, University of Glasgow, Department of Management Studies, mimeo.

Tinker, A. (1984), *Staying at Home*, HMSO, London.

Wicks, M. (1983), 'Enter right: the Family Patrol Group', *New Society*, 24 February, vol. 63, no. 1058, p. 297.

Wilson, E. (1977), *Women and the Welfare State*, Tavistock, London.

Walker, J. (1985), 'Central Government Policy and the Local Authority Labour Market in England and Wales 1979–1984', doctoral thesis, University of Cambridge.

Wilkinson, G. and Jackson, P. M. (1981), *Public Sector Employment in the UK*, Public Sector Economics Research Centre, University of Leicester.

Part Three
Women and recession:
a comparative perspective

9 Women and recession: a comparative perspective

Jill Rubery

The focus of the two main sections of this book has been on the changing position of women relative both to that of men and to the past experience of women within each country taken separately. Comparisons between the countries have so far only been made indirectly, and it is to the issue of comparative analysis which we now turn.

This organisation of the book follows in part from the origins of the research presented here: the country chapters are derived primarily from independent research by the authors and are not the results of a comparative research programme. However, this ordering also fits with our methodological approach to inter-country comparative analysis. There are two extreme positions on the main function of comparative research. On the one hand neoclassical economists seek a general or universal model of behaviour which is applicable over time and between countries. Country-specific differences then arise out of institutional or cultural differences in the parameters to the model, and in their effect on the functioning of markets. At the other end of the spectrum is the 'societal' approach to comparative analysis, associated primarily with social scientists at LEST.[1] The approach rejects the universalist position (see for example Lydall, 1968; Phelps Brown, 1977), which emphasises deviations from some hypothetical norm instead of 'bringing to light different types of societal coherence' (Maurice et al., 1984, p. 232). Under this perspective societal factors do not create 'imperfections' but structure the whole system of economic and social organisation. Moreover, as 'social relations neither develop nor do they combine in the same way in two different societies' (Maurice et al., 1984, p. 233), one aspect of societies should not be singled out for cross-country comparisons, as this would obscure the different ways in which parts of a society interrelate. Applying this approach to women's employment means that we need to understand the ways in which the system of industrial, labour market and family organisation interrelate[2] and the role of the society's political and social values in maintaining these relationships before we could expect to make sense of the differences between countries in the position of women.

This type of comparative methodology fits with the non deterministic approach to the analysis of industrial and social systems advocated by the Labour Studies Group at the Department of Applied Economics, of which the author is a member (see Wilkinson, 1983; Craig et al., 1982, 1985). One difference between the approach we have adopted and that of the LEST, is the greater weight attached by the latter to boundaries between countries in determining divisions between forms of social and economic organisation. Legal, political and economic policy boundaries normally coincide with country boundaries, but within countries there are regional and sectoral patterns of organisation which could be considered to be relatively independent 'productive systems' (Wilkinson, 1983), deserving analysis in their own right. However, as our prime concern in this book is in fact to distinguish different *country* systems, this criticism of the LEST's approach to within country differences can be left on one side. More important for this project is the question of the forces for change which appear to operate across national boundaries, even if the form of response to such forces remain nation-specific. Internationalisation of markets and of supplies of technology provide common forces for change in the industrial system, and thus provide a cross-national influence on the labour demand structure. On the 'supply side', the increased importance of the state and the decreased importance of domestic labour in the family economy are providing pressure towards change in women's role which are common across all countries, even if, as the chapters in this book make clear, there is no universal model of the family economy emerging out of these changes. Potentially even more important for the development of cross-national pressures for change is the internationalisation of social and political ideas and values. It is impossible to quantify the influence of, for example, feminism on changes taking place in women's role in any particular country, but it is clear that some effect must be attributed to these sets of ideas which are recognised and discussed internationally.

However, although no society can be regarded as an isolated, internally coherent and protected system, there is a need to redress the balance of the debate in comparative analysis which so far has tended towards the universalist type, stressing the similarities in women's role even if a neoclassical framework is not explicitly adopted (for example Paukert, 1984; OECD, 1985). Our approach here is thus to emphasise the current differences in women's role in the four countries, to relate these differences to a country-specific system of economic and social organisation, and to stress the differences as well as the similarities in each country's response to current recessionary conditions.

A further caveat must be made. In order to make clear the differences *between* countries, there is a danger of overstressing the integration, coherence and apparent 'harmony' between the organisation of industry and employment on the one hand, and the social organisation and structure of the labour supply on the other. The social reproduction sphere, as has been argued elsewhere (Humphries and Rubery, 1984), is *relatively* autonomous of the production system, so that no smooth accommodation between supply and demand side structures can be assumed or expected, particularly in periods of rapid change, such as we are experiencing in the 1980s. Thus, for example, women may take up the low paid or insecure jobs offered for want of alternatives but their aspirations for improved employment opportunities may mean that this represents only a temporary and unstable accommodation between demand and supply side structures.

The material we will use for this comparative analysis is based primarily on that provided in the chapters in the book, supplemented by ideas and information drawn from other secondary analyses and from consideration of statistics in readily available international sources. It is not based on a comparative research programme, and some of the hypotheses and explanations of observed phenomena must therefore be considered speculative, and requiring detailed investigation. The purpose is to point to the wealth of material that already exists which demonstrates the need for the kind of 'system approach' that we are advocating, for the understanding of the evolving position of women in different societies.

Our discussion of these comparative issues in this chapter is organised into three main sections. The first is concerned with the characteristics of the jobs that women do, and compares systems of job segregation, pay differentials and employment contracts. This characterisation of women's jobs enables us to locate, in the second section, the role of women in the restructuring of the economy, in cyclical and secular industrial restructuring, and in the system of labour market regulation. In the third section we examine how organisation of labour supply, including the role of the family and state welfare organisation in social reproduction, interrelates with the structure of employment opportunities. In the concluding section we attempt to compare the impact of different systems on women's economic and social position, and consider the potential impact of current pressures for change in economic and social organisation within the four countries.

1 WOMEN'S JOB CHARACTERISTICS

1.1 Job segregation

Women's employment in all four countries was characterised by high levels of occupational and industrial segregation by sex, however measured. Moreover, although both Italy and the US show evidence of a declining level of job segregation, it is only in the US where this trend is related to a more equal representation of men and women within occupational categories and is not simply the result of structural changes in the shares of female or male-dominated occupations. Job segregation has persisted in a period characterised by major changes both in the participation rates of women and the structure of industries and occupations. Far from stagnation in the sexual division of labour there has been the recreation of equivalent levels of segregation around higher rates of female participation and new job structures. For example in Britain where there has been little overall change in job segregation indices in the 1970s women had nevertheless increased their share of 19 out of 25 occupational categories between 1971 and 1981 (see Chapter 4, Table 6) but the overall effect has been to retain the same level of over-representation and under-representation of women within occupations because of the rapid increases in women's share in already feminised occupations. Likewise in the Italian paper examples are given of two-way processes of substitution which result in the reconstruction of sex-typing of occupations around new technologies. In France women have been mobilised in large numbers into the labour force but have been employed in jobs, typified by their routinised and repetitive nature, and tight supervisory controls (Dutoya and Gauvin, 1987). In the US the relatively greater breakdown of sex-typing of occupations has, as we discuss below, not been accompanied by significant improvements in women's relative pay. Confinement to particular occupational or industrial categories is often cited as the cause of women's low pay, but entry into male-dominated occupations may not be sufficient to secure higher pay (Meehan, 1985) for women if, once women make entry into these jobs, opportunities exist either to create new divisions in pay and status within occupations or to downgrade the status of the occupations overall.

This observation suggests that there may be conceptual as well as empirical problems in comparing patterns of job segregation between countries. Broad occupational or industrial categories only provide relevant analytical divisions when there is relative homogeneity within these categories with respect not only to the *content* of jobs but also to the pay, status and longer term employment opportunities that they confer on the holders. In countries such as Italy where there are effective industry-wide pay agreements, or France where industry agreements structure the system of differentials and method of payments, these types of categories may have more relevance than in the UK and the US, where there is more emphasis on plant and company-based payment structures, and extremely weak forms of control of pay in small and non union establishments. In the US divergence of pay between plants may in part explain the relatively low earnings of women compared to men in all occupational categories. To understand how job segregation acts to exclude women from higher paying jobs, one has to know the relevant divisions within the economy between 'good' and 'bad' employment positions. The form of these divisions is likely to be related to the pattern of collective bargaining and labour market regulation within the economy and not simply to technical divisions between jobs. There are in fact even more fundamental problems in comparing patterns of job segregation between countries because of differences in the ways jobs are organised between countries. This factor became clear from the LEST's comparative work on technically similar French and German factories which found differences in job structures and hierarchies related to differences in the educational system, cultural values and social expectations prevailing in the society in which the system of work organisation was constructed. As the skills, training, and responsibilities associated with occupations may vary considerably between countries, occupational distribution does not even give clear cut evidence on women's relative place within the technical let alone the social division of labour.

A further difference arises between the French and the Italian chapters on how the function of job segregation or sex-typing of occupations is to be interpreted. For Bettio, the prime determinant of the employment position of women is the relatively rigid system of sex-typing of occupations. It is this sex-typing that structures the demand for women and has tended to suppress the potential female labour supply in the post war period. Although there is a gradual process of restructuring and recreation of the sexual division of labour around new occupational structures, the dominant characteristic of the sexual division of labour is that of continuity within change. In contrast the starting point for the French paper is the use of female labour reserves in the process of industrial restructuring: in practice this process has often been complementary to the pattern of job segregation, as employment change in the 1960s and 1970s was associated with the rationalisation, routinisation and deskilling of large areas of manufacturing, and with the expansion of the service sectors. These types of jobs were traditionally open to female employees, and thus the sex segregation system complemented the process of mobilisation of female labour reserves. However, Bouillaguet-Bernard and Gauvin not only recognise the potential constraints of the pattern of segregation on the utilisation of female labour; but also, point to instances where this pattern has broken down under the process of restructuring: variable proportions of female labour are found in unskilled manual jobs, with higher proportions in the newly located plants. Moreover, more recently female labour reserves have been used to change the conditions of employment, more specifically to reduce its security and guaranteed hours of work. Both processes have mobilised female labour reserves not to homogenise the labour market but to reconstruct it around a new set of divisions in which differences in female labour supply conditions play a major role.

An important question is whether these two approaches are competitive or complementary. They could be considered competitive in the sense that one uses the Marxist reserve army theory as the analytical basis, and the other uses the persistence of sex-typing to question the validity of the reserves of labour approach; or they may be complementary positions which differ simply because of the different economic and social contexts that are being analysed. For example in Italy the trade unions have effectively resisted the use of cheap labour reserves, such as women, to reconstruct the division of labour within the formal economy (Bettio, 1984; Brusco et al., 1986), but in France the expansion of employment opportunities and the weak control that the unions exercise over the labour process have provided conditions in which female labour reserves could be mobilised to restructure employment. Possibly even more striking than these differences in analytical starting points is the similarity in outcomes: the continual recreation and reconstruction of sex-segregated patterns of employment.

The hypothesis that differences in trade unions can influence the structure of job segregation and the way in which female labour supplies are mobilised can be extended to the US and Britain. A plausible interpretation of the pattern of utilisation of female labour in the US is that the weak system of employment regulation at both the plant and the industry level has facilitated the use of female labour in the restructuring of the economy towards a low wage economy in a wider range of industries and occupations; that is job segregation or sex-typing of occupations at the aggregate level has not been an essential prerequisite for employers to take advantage of the lower wages at which women are available on the labour market.

Britain also provides an interesting contrast with the Italian case. In both instances trade union policy and strategy is associated with the maintenance of custom and practice and resistance to 'flexibility' in labour organisation; but whereas in Britain union strength has traditionally been based on strategies of job demarcation and differentiation, in Italy trade union strength has developed around strategies of equality and solidarity (Brusco et al., 1986). Both strategies tend to rigidify the status quo, but whereas in the UK the breakdown of job segregation by sex is identified as a means of weakening unions, in Italy, unions have not used segregation by sex as a basis for organisation and in recent years have sometimes actively favoured desegregation, provided these changes take place within their broad strategy of control and are not part of a managerial deskilling strategy.

1.2 Pay differentials

We have already argued that the structure of pay differentials may be closely related to the structure of job segregation prevailing in a country. However it is not only the *form* but also the *level* and *rate of change* in pay differentials that varies between the four countries. Table 9.1 shows that in all four countries, women's pay is on average significantly lower than that of men's, and even in the country with the highest ratio of female to male pay, Italy, Bettio argues that the differential is still sufficient even within the formal economy to maintain incentives to employ women in their customary jobs and to encourage the substitution of women for men when jobs are restructured by technological change.

The other point of similarity between the countries is that women's pay has increased on average relative to men's since the 1960s. Because of differences in data coverage and availability it is not possible to use a consistent set of data for all four countries to assess the level and changes in women's relative pay. However by taking the data that is available on hourly, weekly and annual bases (summarised in Table 9.1) it is possible to build up a reasonably consistent picture of differences between countries. In 1970 women in Italy and France were better paid relative to their male counterparts than women in the US and the UK. Since that point there has been no tendency towards convergence in relative pay, with ratios for women's pay relative to men's tending to rise relatively fast in the UK and Italy, and more slowly in France and the US.

The most likely explanation of these differences both in levels of female to male pay and in rates of change lies in the different systems of labour market organisation and regulation in the four countries, rather than in differences in women's attributes or characteristics as workers or indeed in their job opportunities relative to men's. The higher rates of pay for women in Italy and France can probably be attributed to the more effective control of low pay in these countries, at least within the formal sector. In France low pay is primarily controlled through the national minimum wage (the SMIC). In Italy the high ratio, and rate of increase in women's to men's pay has been brought about not through a specific policy to reduce male/female differentials (Bettio, 1984) but by the general egalitarian policy of the trade unions implemented effectively through strong local and centralised bargaining machinery (Brusco et al., 1986).

In contrast in Britain the change in the female to male ratio that was achieved in the early 1970s was directly related to the implementation of the Equal Pay Act. Trade unions have not pursued *general* policies of equalising wage rates, so this change represented a once and for all improvement in the relative pay of women's jobs to men's jobs, and not a continual and gradual movement towards equality.[3] Equal pay and employment discrimination legislation in the US, is potentially stronger than that in Britain as its enforcement is backed by a US government agency (Dex and Shaw, 1986). However in practice it appears to have had less impact on women's wages, which may be due

Table 9.1 Women's earnings as a percentage of men's earnings 1970–1984

Year	Hourly earnings				Weekly earnings				Annual earnings			
	US	France	Italy	Britain	US	France	Italy	Britain	US	France	Italy	Britain
1970			74.2	63.0	62.3			54.3		68.0(1968)		
1971				63.7	61.7			55.6				
1972		78.4		64.5	63.1			55.9				
1973		78.8	78.3	64.2	61.7			55.1				
1974		78.0		65.8	60.8			56.4			68.8	
1975		78.7	78.7	70.4	62.0			61.5	59.6			
1976		78.2		73.5	62.2			64.3	60.2			
1977		78.3		74.0	61.9			64.9				
1978		71.9		72.5	61.3			63.3				
1979		79.2		71.5	62.4			62.1				
1980		79.2	83.2	71.8	63.4			63.3	60.2	72.0		
1981		80.4	83.2	72.8	64.6			65.1	59.2	73.5		
1982	68.2	80.1	83.9	72.0	65.0			64.1	61.7			
1983		80.6		72.3*	65.6			64.9*	63.7	74.7	74.3	
1984		80.7		71.7*				64.3*				

Sources:

US: hourly and weekly — Mellor (1982) Full-time female to full-time male median weekly earnings, adjusted for hours worked 1982. 1970–1978 May, 1979–1982 annual averages.
annual — Statistical Abstract of the United States (1982, 1985) median annual earnings, year round full-time workers.

France: hourly — ILO Yearbooks of Labour Statistics (1982, 1985, table 16). Average hourly earnings, excluding employees in extractive industries, electricity, gas, water, public sector and private domestic services.
annual — Average annual earnings for full-time wage earners (CERC 1985, quoted in Bouillaguet-Bernard and Gauvin, p. 169, this volume).

Italy: hourly — OECD (1986, table III.1) average hourly earnings in industry.
annual — Banca d'Italia, Bolletina no. 4, 1976, and nos 3–4 Dec., 1974, quoted in Bettio (forthcoming).

Britain: hourly and weekly — New Earnings Survey (1970–84). Average hourly/weekly earnings of full-time males aged 21 or over and full-time females aged 18 or over.* 1983 and 1984 data are based on full-time employees on adult rates, but adjusted to link with previous data base.

to the fact that it was implemented at the level of individual plants and could not be used as a basis for a generalised upward movement in minimum rates for women because of the absence of effective collective bargaining machinery at the industry, sectoral or national level. In Britain the increase in women's pay was achieved primarily through trade unions ensuring that the 'unisex' payment structures established to fit the Equal Pay Act provisions were based on a minimum rate equal to that previously paid to men and not on the women's minimum rate (Craig et al., 1980). These changes, which changed the ratio of pay between different jobs, were undoubtedly more significant than the increases which women received because they were doing exactly the same jobs as men (Snell et al., 1981; Craig et al., 1985). In the US the individual claims within single plants or companies have brought about major changes in individual companies personnel policies but could not provide the basis for more general changes in the ratios between men's pay rates and women's pay rates because of the more fragmented system of pay bargaining and restriction of trade union influence on pay to the minority of organised plants. Even current improvements in women's pay may be being achieved more through the downgrading of men's pay under deindustrialisation and 'roll back' agreements, than through the upgrading of women's pay (see Chapter 1 this volume, Harrison et al., 1986).

The hypothesis that it is forms of wage regulation that determine differences in the male/female ratio is not dependent upon the observation of very great differences in these systems in the four countries. The country ratios do not provide a priori support for the neoclassical view that differences in the skills, human capital or work experience of women in the four countries are sufficient to explain women's relative earnings or indeed that differences in pay ratios are in any way systematically related to differences in these human capital variables. For example, it could be argued that because in France and Italy women are more likely to work through the phase of childbearing and rearing than in Britain, they may earn higher pay because they add to their work experience and prevent the depreciation of their human capital, but women in the US also take a shorter period out from work than women in Britain with no clear benefit to relative pay levels (see also England, 1982; Dex, 1985 for critique of human capital depreciation theory).

There also appears to be no systematic relationship between the organisation of family income and resources and women's pay ratio between countries. In France because family budgets are increasingly geared to two incomes, with women working full time or with state family benefits effectively substituting for women's earnings in large families, women may be less vulnerable to pressure on their wages, on the grounds that they are only working for 'pin-money'. However, in

Italy women are even higher paid when employed but the majority of families are still geared to a system of income generation where most women are not employed in the formal sector and at most supplement family income through relatively low wage employment in the informal sector. In the US there is probably the highest dependency on women's income, both because of the progressive decline in real wages which increases the need for multi-participation if standards of living are to be maintained, and because of the high and increasing proportion of female-headed households. However these conditions have not led to women escaping from the 'pin-money' wage bracket, and as a consequence more and more women are living in poverty as their wage income is not sufficient to sustain themselves or their families (Humphries and Rubery, 1984; Chapter 5 this volume).

1.3 The employment contract and flexibility

The third distinguishing characteristic of women's employment is found in the contractual arrangements under which women are often employed. Differences in employment contracts range from the daily or weekly hours, the length of contract, the level of job security and other forms of employment protection, and the legal or official status of the contract. These variations in contractual conditions may be associated with other characteristics of the employment status such as working from home, or working for other family members.

The evidence suggests that these differences in employment contract are of major importance for women's employment in all four countries, but more particularly in Britain, France and Italy, than in the US. Moreover the form of variations in the employment contract differed significantly between countries. In Britain the most important dimension of differentiation was hours of work; in France it was the length of contract, but with part-time work contracts increasing in significance in the 1970s and 1980s[4] and in Italy the informality of employment status, often associated with homeworking.

These different dimensions of variation between women's employment and the standard or 'normal' contract related in turn to the type of legal, institutional and customary regulation of employment which prevails in the country concerned. In France the importance attached to the development of fixed-term contracts, a development in which women and youth labour are disproportionately involved, has arisen out of the much stronger job protection afforded by common law to the employment contract. In Britain the importance attached to part-time work arises out of legal and institutional encouragement to part-time work, through the exclusion of some low-paid part-time work from all employment taxes, and some employment protection, compared to

Table 9.2 Part-time working by industry and by sex, 1981 (% of total employment)

Industries	USA	France	Italy	UK
Manufacturing	3	0.9	5.1	6.6
Wholesale distribution	5	1.8	2.7	10.4
Retail distribution	23	12.9	8.2	39.2
Credit institutions	5	4.5	0.2	7.7
Insurance	5	5.0	0.4	7.9
Women's share of part-time employment (%)	70	85	64	94

Sources: Petit (1985 p. 169). Based on Eurostat (1984), 1981 Labour Costs Survey; OECD Employment Outlook, September 1983. Note that the scope of the Eurostat survey was limited to firms with 10 or more employees.

France and Italy where employment taxes tend not to be related to hours worked (see Table 9.2). This legalised 'black economy' of part-time work in the UK (in the sense that employers of part-time workers are in effect legally subsidised by other employers) contrasts with the situation in Italy where small firms can more easily avoid social security taxes, which has encouraged the development of the informal small firm and outworking economy (Brusco, 1982). In the US the relatively low level of employment regulation and taxation in general could explain in part the somewhat lower significance of part-time work and short-term contracts for women workers although part-time working is still much higher than in France and Italy. In the US part-time work and temporary work can be used to avoid the expensive non-wage benefits provided at the company level to full-time employees, including medical insurance. Despite these incentives, part-time work has been growing in retail and personal services, and has declined steeply elsewhere (Applebaum, 1985) and temporary work, although growing fast, is still at a low level compared, for example, to France. The higher and increasing share of men in part-time work in the US is probably related to the use of a youth and student labour force for casual and part-time work, and possibly also to the lack of a comprehensive social security system for unemployed men.

There are also country-specific differences in the relative importance of *women* in these variable or flexible employment contracts. Part-time work in Britain is overwhelmingly female, but short term contract work in France and the informal economy in Italy involve a significant number of men, even though women are disproportionately represented. One explanation of these differences is the availability of alternative sources of 'secondary' labour supply to provide flexibility; thus youth labour is important in short-term contract work in France (45% of short term contract workers are under 25), and the widespread use of student and youth labour in the US in part-time work could explain its reduced significance for women.[5] Another explanation is that these forms of employment contract do not necessarily result in low income for the worker. In Italy where there are well-established networks of small firms, men can participate in the informal and subcontracting sector by selling their labour services to a wide variety of firms and thereby achieve a high weekly income (see Chapters 3 and 7, this volume; Brusco, 1982).

It is men's general unwillingness to offer their labour on a short-time or variable basis that explains the dominance of women, especially married women, in these types of contractual arrangements. Women often do not have access to social security support, or at least not on a full-time job equivalent basis, and they may face domestic and discrimination constraints on their employment choices. All these factors help to explain why, in all four countries, women could be expected to be more likely than men to offer their labour on more variable terms and conditions than applies to the standard labour contract. The different pattern of flexible employment forms between countries are not therefore likely to be related simply to differences in employees' preferences. There are also institutional constraints which limit employers' opportunities to offer contracts to potential part-time or temporary workers. Trade union opposition to, and legal constraints on part-time work in Italy and in France have probably played a greater role in constraining the development of such employment forms than differences in employee preferences. Part-time work has recently been legalised and regulated in Italy although it is still at a very low level even compared to France where part-time work has been growing rapidly from a low starting point (Garnsey, 1985). In both countries trade unions are not now as able to restrict the growth of part-time employment, possibly in part because as the female labour force expands the problems involved in combining domestic commitments with full-time wage-work become more apparent, thereby increasing the demand for part-time work on the supply-side.

These trends are also related to demand-side pressures, and in particular to pressure to reduce fixed employment costs under recessionary conditions and uncertain and variable product markets. In Britain the acceleration in the growth of part-time work has probably been associated as much with the reorganisation of service sector production (see Table 9.2) to minimise labour hours and intensify the pace of work, as with the advantages of lower employment taxes and the availability of a cheap labour supply. Similarly in France the growth of contract employment agencies and fixed-term contracts was associated as much with managerial strategies to externalise jobs with variable demand or with specialised skills, as with strategies to reduce employment protection for disadvantaged workers (Michon, 1981). In Italy the continued expansion of the informal sector has not been based simply on the opportunities offered to reduce costs; these advantages have helped the informal sector develop in many areas into an efficient and dynamic system of industrial organisation with the ability to compete internationally and even to generate new products (Brusco and Sabel, 1981). However, it is easier to find examples of the influence of demand-side factors in determining the types of employment contract used in particular countries than to explain the reasons why similar demand-side influences do not arise in all countries leading to similar pressures on employment forms. For example, is the explanation of the decline in part-time working in the financial sector in the US in the 1970s, compared to the increase in the UK, simply to be found in differences in the extent of installation of automatic banking services, or are there different systems of work organisation being developed around similar technologies and market conditions?

Part of the reason for women's involvement in some types of 'non-standard' job forms is that these involve a closer integration of paid work with family or home organisation, and therefore permit women to combine income-generating work with their domestic role. Home-working and acting as informal family helpers are the two most important forms of 'non-standard' job forms which have this characteristic. Family helpers are a much more important category in France and Italy than in the US and the UK, and even in these two countries their relative significance has declined rapidly under the impact of declining agriculture and family-based forms of production, particularly in the service sectors (Bouillaguet-Bernard et al., 1981). However, home-working has in some respects taken over from family agricultural work in Italy (see Chapter 7, this volume), and its importance as an employment form has certainly been increasing in Britain and in the US, particularly associated with new technology and non-manual employment (Huws, 1984). It is interesting again to note the combined influence of family organisation and demand-side influences on these trends. In Britain there is evidence of a growth in homeworking in clothing trades, as a consequence of the shift away from factory production to small-firm and family-based production within the ethnic communities. On the other hand part of the growth of homeworking is also associated with technological changes which facilitate the organisation of non-manual work on a home basis, and with demand pressures again to minimise fixed employment costs. In Italy the growth of homeworking can be seen to have reinforced women's role in the family at a time when the changes in social reproduction would otherwise tend to weaken women's ties with domestic production. However this may only be a temporary phenomenon for individual women if women who have been mobilised first as homeworkers, begin to participate later in the formal economy (see Chapter 7, this volume). It could also be argued that in other countries there is a much more limited informal sector simply because of the integration of 'flexible' or 'marginal' employment forms into the formal economy, a process which has not yet happened in Italy. However the variable incidence of homeworking, part-time and temporary working in the four countries suggests that the existence of a large flexible or marginal employment sector is not an inevitable characteristic of an employment system.

2 WOMEN'S ROLE IN INDUSTRIAL RESTRUCTURING AND LABOUR MARKET REGULATION

2.1 Industrial restructuring

Women may play a specific role in either the process of cyclical employment change or in the longer term process of restructuring of the employment system or in both. An example of the first type of role is the buffer or flexible reserve hypothesis; that women are drawn into the labour market at high demand and expelled in periods of low demand. This theory of women's labour market experience was extensively explored in the first section of this book. The results showed some degree of similarity between countries, with the buffer or flexible reserve mechanism found to some extent in manufacturing, but only very occasionally in services. However, closer examination of the evidence found that these results were not amenable to simple interpretation.

In the first place the existence or not of a buffer mechanism appeared to be strongly related to the structure of job segregation. Thus, in industries where women provided a relatively high share of production jobs but did not dominate the labour force, they were likely to act as a buffer because they were concentrated in the more labour intensive parts of production, where it was easier to adjust employment to variations in demand. Where women filled primarily clerical jobs, they were unlikely to fulfil a buffer role (see Chapter 1 Table 1.5 this volume, and Rubery and Tarling, 1982). One consequence of the concentration of the buffer function in particular types of women's jobs but not *all* women's jobs, is that if these jobs are subject to technological displacement, or indeed demand displacement as the manufacturing sector shrinks, the buffer will itself decline in importance over time. Moreover, in Britain and Italy we found evidence to suggest that the buffer role might arise more out of variations in inter-industry employment over the cycle than from variations in women's employment *within* individual industries.

There is therefore no evidence to suggest that women universally take on a buffer role on the wage labour market system. Indeed it has been widely argued that women have been relatively protected from cyclical restructuring by the secular trend towards service sector employment, a trend which has tended to accelerate in periods of low demand as a result of a more rapid rate of reduction in manufacturing. This trend

Table 9.3 Employment distribution by sector

	Share of total employment			Share of females in total employment by sector		
	1963	1973	1983	1963	1973	1983
Agriculture						
USA	7.1	4.2	3.5	19	18	20
France	20.2	11.3	8.0	—	15[a]	17
Italy	27.2	18.3	12.4	34	33	35
UK	4.4	2.9	2.7	16	21	18
Industry						
USA	35.1	33.2	28.0	21	23	26
France	39.6	39.5	33.8	—	25[a]	25
Italy	37.6	39.2	36.1	25	22	24
UK	46.4	42.4	33.6	25	25	23
Services						
USA	57.8	62.6	68.5	44	48	52
France	40.2	49.3	58.2	—	48[a]	51
Italy	35.2	42.5	51.5	33	33	39
UK	49.2	54.6	63.8	44	49	52

[a] 1975 figures.

Sources: OECD (1985) *Labour Force Statistics* 1963; Petit (1985; table 6.8) based on OECD (1985) for USA, Italy, UK and EUROSTAT, Employment and Unemployment, Luxembourg 1985 for France.

is evident in all four countries, as Table 9.3 indicates. These data also show the higher ratio of women's employment in services in all four countries, but whereas the ratio of female employment in manufacturing is relatively similar in all four countries, only France, Britain and the US have similar ratios of women in services (after allowing for the higher share of part-time work in services in Britain), at just above 50 per cent, but Italian women have a much lower ratio of around 40 per cent. Thus, although the persistence of a high share of female employment in services in recession is undoubtedly related to a relatively rigid pattern of sex segregation, it is clear that this pattern can and does vary between countries. These differences in patterns of sex segregation also appear to be associated with differences in the rewards and status associated with job categories. For example, financial services work has higher pay and status, and a lower share of female employment in Italy than in the other three countries (Petit, 1986, p. 174, table 6.4). Nevertheless, even in Italy, if the dominant trend is towards services, then the demand for female labour is likely to rise rather than fall, although within services it may be female jobs such as typing and filing jobs which become most prone to displacement by technological change, as has been the case with women's jobs in sectors of manufacturing.

The role of women in the restructuring process is not adequately measured in terms of net outcomes. We also need to look at the share of women in labour market flows, as the creation of new jobs, or the absorption of new labour supplies is likely to have a much more significant impact on the shape of the employment system, than if change is brought about within an existing job which continues to be filled by the same employee. From this perspective, we can see that the role of women in restructuring is likely to differ quite markedly between countries. Two factors are important here. The first is the system of labour market regulation and industrial organisation, which influences the rate of job destruction and job transformation. In the Italian system the trade union and legal controls on redundancies, plant closures and on internal restructuring result in limited flows into and out of the official employment sector, whereas in the US there are low job tenure ratios (OECD, 1983) and relatively high rates of labour mobility. However the second factor, that is the net growth in employment, is probably even more important in providing a central role for female labour reserves in the restructuring in the US and France. Table 9.4 shows that between 1963 and 1983 net employment grew by 47 per cent in the US and by 9.5 per cent in France compared to a 2 per cent growth in Italy and a fall of 3.5 per cent in Britain. Mobilisation of male labour reserves from agriculture were also more important in Italy in restructuring in the earlier period than female reserves. However even in Britain where there is a net decline in employment, latent reserves of labour are still being used to transform the structure of employment, as a large share of the expanding part-time jobs are being filled by women from outside the labour market.

Women have thus continued to serve as a flexible labour reserve, at the same time as women in general have progressively become more stable and continuous employees, with a much reduced tendency to quit the labour market. The compatibility of these two arguments arises from the continued existence of a latent reserve of women in domestic or relatively unstable wage work, which allows new labour supplies to be mobilised whilst women already in the labour market have become permanent members of the wage labour force, even if some of them are still called on to act as a floating reserve. Under such conditions divisions within the female labour force are likely to intensify.

2.2 Labour market regulation and restructuring

The system of labour market organisation structures the position of women in the economy from two perspectives. In the first place it determines the extent of *inequality* in the labour market; in the second place it determines the *form* of these labour market divisions, and thereby whether or not women or other disadvantaged groups are the most likely group to fill these disadvantaged slots in the system. This latter issue is of course in turn influenced by the social structure, but it

Table 9.4 Population, participation and employment

1980 = 100	Males and females 1963	1973	1980	1983	Females 1963	1973	1980	1983
Total population								
USA	83.1	93.0	100	103	82.1	92.8	100	103.0
France	88.7	96.7	100	101.6	89.0	96.5	100	101.6
Italy	90.8	97.1	100	100.7	89.2	96.3	100	100.8
UK	95.2	99.8	100	100.1	95.6	99.9	100	100.1
Total labour force					*As % of total labour force*			
USA	68.0	84.0	100	104.3	33.2	38.0	41.9	42.8
France	86.0	94.2	100	101.3		36.7	39.8	40.9
Italy	94.7	92.8	100	102.8	29.8	29.5¹	33.3	34.3
UK	93.8	95.5	100	99.8	33.3	36.6	39.2	39.6
Total employment					*As % of total employment*			
USA	69.1	86.1	100	101.6	34.1	38.5	42.4	43.7
France	90.5	93.0	100	99.1		36.9	39.4	40.6
Italy	98.4	94.0	100	100.2	30.0	28.7¹	32.2	32.8
UK	97.4	99.0	100	94.0	34.0	37.6	40.2	41.6
Labour force as % population					*Labour force as % population of working age*			
USA	39.0	43.0	47.7	48.3		52.7[a]	61.3[a]	63.4[a]
France	42.1	42.3	43.4	43.3		51.2[b]	55.6[b]	56.1[b]
Italy	42.8	38.8¹	40.2	41.0		29.0[c]	39.2[c]	40.2[c]
UK	46.9	45.6	47.6	47.5		56.1[a]	60.1[a]	59.8[a]

Source: OECD (1985), *Labour Force Statistics 1963–83.*

¹ Break in series.   [b] 15+   [c] 14+
[a] 16+

cannot be taken that the former is independent of the system of labour market organisation (for an opposing perspective see Berger and Piore, 1980, ch. 1). For example in the US the importance of illegal immigrants in occupying casual and low paid jobs does not arise inevitably out of the US's proximity to less advantaged countries but because of an unregulated labour market system which facilitates the exploitation of these types of workers.

In effect the *form* of labour market organisation and regulation will influence which social groups suffer labour market disadvantage. Thus economies with a rigid or protected job structure will tend to pass the burden of unemployment disproportionately onto the groups which dominate the flows onto the labour market, primarily the young and women returning to work after child care. France and Italy have overall higher levels of youth unemployment, which is consistent with their more protected employment systems. However this factor does not explain why young women in Italy and France have higher unemployment rates than young men whereas in the US and Britain the rates are similar (Table 9.5). This phenomenon again has to be explained by the system of integration of labour into the employment system: it may be that for example sex-typing of occupations is already important for young workers in Italy whereas in Britain, and possibly the US, at least some young males and females start off on relatively similar jobs with sex segregation occurring at a later stage in the life cycle.[6] In Britain the apprenticeship route into employment has been disproportionately restricted by the recession which may also account for the appearance of relatively favourable trends for young women. In the US the high rates of unemployment for young people of both sexes may be associated with the higher ratios of young people going into higher education

Table 9.5 Unemployment rates by sex and age

		Males		Females	
		1973	1983	1973	1983
Youth unemployment					
US	16–24	9.0	17.1	11.2	15.6
France	15–24	2.9[1]	17.0	5.4[1]	25.5
Italy	14–24	12.5[1]	27.0	12.8[1]	38.0
UK	16–24	3.9[1]	25.8	2.1[1]	19.9
Unemployment rate for total labour force					
US	16 and over	4.0	9.6	6.0	9.2
France	15 and over	1.5[1]	6.2	3.1[1]	10.6
Italy	14 and over	3.0[1]	6.6	4.7[1]	14.9
UK	16 and over	3.0[1]	14.1	0.9[1]	8.9

[1] Break in series.

Source: OECD (1985), *Labour Force Statistics 1963–83.*

in the US. That part of the population which does enter the labour market at a young age is therefore likely to be relatively more disadvantaged, and to include an even higher share of minority racial groups, than is the case for the same age groups in Britain. Moreover, young people in higher education intersperse their studies with short periods in the labour market, thus giving rise to a labour market segment for young people based on relatively unstable employment.[7]

Systems of labour market regulation can be characterised as relatively rigid or relatively flexible or 'fluid' systems. Italy tends to be associated with the former type of system, with high levels of job and pay protection for those in employment and a consequent exclusion of a large share of the female labour supply from the formal labour market (Bruno, 1979, Brusco et al., 1986). Britain and France can be seen to hold middle positions with the US at the other end of the spectrum, offering relatively open access to employment (Ashton, 1986) at lower pay and job protection to women workers.[8] These 'characterisations' need, however, to be qualified: in Italy the rigidity of the formal sector has contributed to the emergence of a large flexible but informal employment sector. Within the more 'fluid' US labour market there exists 'protected' internal labour market systems associated with large companies.

Systems of labour market regulation can be characterised along another dimension; whether employment conditions are regulated on a national or industry-wide basis or on a firm or workplace basis. It is arguable that the latter form of organisation provides the greatest opportunities for strong trade union control over the labour process but that the consequence of this form of organisation is to expose the remaining parts of the employment system to unregulated terms and conditions of employment. Only in Italy are both work-place and national systems of regulation successfully combined, and even this regulation applies strictly to the formal economy. In France there is a relatively strong system of national regulation of low pay through the SMIC, which has increased faster than the rate of inflation and average earnings in the first half of the 1980s, and legally enforceable industry agreements effectively regulate systems of wage payment and conditions of employment. Trade unions have, however, failed to establish strong industry-level bargaining in pay and despite recent reforms, remain weak at the plant and company level. In the US the influence of trade unions is confined through legal restrictions and by political weakness to a minority of companies where they have achieved recognition. There is no industry-wide regulation of pay, and the national minimum wage is set at a low level and has been kept stable in money terms, declining in real terms in the 1980s. This system therefore provides much more scope for paying low wages to women workers. Britain traditionally falls in between these types of systems, with the strength of trade unions at local level used to provide some protection at the industry and national level. However the British system could be argued to be moving more towards the American model, partly because changes in the 1960s and 1970s strengthened the institution at the local level and weakened them at industry-level, but more importantly because recent government policy has been specifically designed to restrict trade unions' control of terms and conditions of employment outside the specific plants in which they are recognised. These policies include legal restrictions on industrial action outside the place of work, the abolition of the legal procedure for imposing the 'going rate' of pay on firms in a specific industry, and on firms working on government contracts, and the weakening of the wages councils which set legal minimum wages in poorly organised sectors. In addition the government is reducing the effectiveness of national organisation in the public sector by contracting out public sector service work to the unregulated private sector (see Chapter 8 this volume).

All of these policies in the UK have specific consequences for women's employment. In fact the role of women in the labour market restructuring that is associated with recessionary conditions will be dependent on the type of labour market regulation that is being fostered by government policy. Deregulation of the labour market has been actively fostered by the state in Britain and the US but in Italy and France, where the state has taken some action to encourage flexibility, these measures have often taken the form of regulating at the same time as legalising and institutionalising forms of flexible employment.[9] Moreover some responses of the state have been to strengthen regulation of the labour market, for example the wage indexation policy in Italy and the raising of SMIC above the rate of price and wage inflation in France. In Britain government policy has been to foster directly 'deregulated' employment and low wages and to resist any international policy towards regulation of flexible employment forms. In the US the pre-existing legal framework provided a suitable framework for the growth of a low wage economy, backed by a government policy stance even more firmly opposed to trade union regulation than that in the UK. We can therefore identify common pressures towards a change in the system of wage employment or in the 'rapport salarial', but there is no evidence that these common pressures will result in a convergence of forms of labour market organisation, as the political and social context plays a central mediating role in determining the institutional response to these pressures.

3 LABOUR SUPPLY AND SOCIAL REPRODUCTION

3.1 Labour supply

There appears to have been a fairly general tendency in advanced countries towards a changing shape in the pattern of female labour market participation over the life-cycle (Paukert, 1984). The 'traditional' pattern of a high participation rate in the early stage of the life cycle, followed by a steady decline had given way first of all to an M-shaped or bi-modal pattern of participation, but more recently this curve has flattened out so that there is no longer any strong tendency towards decline in participation in the 20s and 30s age bracket for women. The four countries that we are concerned with here fit these trends to some extent (see figure 9.1): in France and the US the M shape has now virtually disappeared giving a relatively flat pattern of participation over prime age ranges, but in the UK an M-shaped pattern still prevails, although the dip in the 20s and 30s bracket has been moderated. The Italian participation rate pattern seems to be adjusting from the traditional pattern to the flatter age profile without the intermediate stage of an M-shaped pattern. However, it still retains the characteristic of a relatively high participation rate amongst young women and a relatively low participation rate in the older age ranges, giving rise to an overall participation rate of only 40 per cent compared to 56 to 63 per cent for France, Britain and the US.

The changes in the aggregate pattern of participation are often taken to be indicative of changes in individual participation patterns of women: from participation pre-childbirth only, to discontinuous participation, giving way in turn to continuous participation. Moreover the similarity of trends between countries is taken as indicative of similarities in the relationship between family formation and participation accross countries. Evidence from the four countries casts doubts on both assumptions. In the first place cross-sectional patterns of participation confuse life-cycle and cohort variations in participation (Paukert, 1984, p. 30). Thus for example in France the earlier M-shaped pattern arose primarily out of a general upward shift in participation rates amongst the younger age cohort and not from a marked reduction in participation for the middle-age range, compared to participation rates of that cohort at younger ages.

Apart from these problems, the aggregate data do not provide a good guide either to individual patterns of participation or to the relationship with family formation. For example in Britain the two-entry pattern of participation is still the most common one for individuals but now applies only to a minority of women (Dex, 1984). More women are becoming continuous workers, and even more importantly, more women are returning to work in between births. This phenomenon of

Figure 9.1   Female activity rates by age

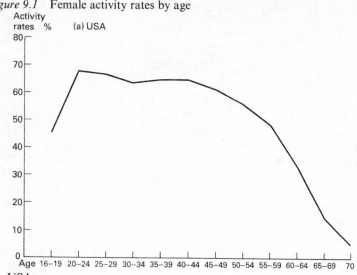

(a) USA

Source: 1980 Census data, *ILO Labour Yearbook*

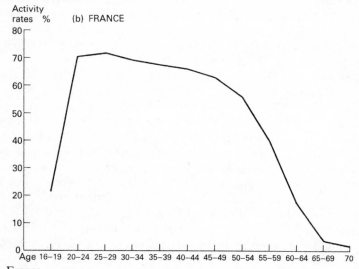

(b) France

Source: EEC Labour Force Sample Survey 1983

multiple flows into and out of the labour market will not, however, necessarily show up in aggregate data. The US and France indicate patterns of relative continuity in participation but it is likely that more US women take short breaks out from the labour market than in France where maternity leave provision is more universal. In Italy the tendency for some women to remain in work over the period of childbirth, partly

Figure 9.1 (cont'd)

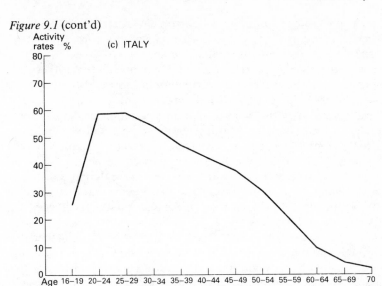

(c) Italy

Source: EEC Labour Force Sample Survey 1983

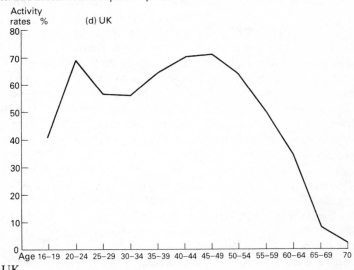

(d) UK

Source: EEC Labour Force Sample Survey 1983

as a result of the difficulties of re-entering the official labour market if they quit, is again not evident from the data, as their behaviour is swamped by that of the mass of women who tend to be excluded from the formal sector and fail to re-enter at a later stage, partly because of the rigidities of the recruitment system.

Moreover, although it is the case that patterns of participation are related to domestic responsibilities, the specific way in which child care affects participation varies significantly between countries. In the UK, it is age of the youngest rather than number of children that affects women's participation but it is larger numbers of children, rather than their age, which leads to lower participation in France. (See Chapter 4, Table 4.12, this volume, Chapter 6, Figure 6.1, this volume.)

These diverse patterns of participation in relation to demographic characteristics can be related to differences in the pattern of childcare and in the sources of income available to females (Chapter 6, this volume). Although in each of the four countries mothers still take on the major responsibility for childcare, there are different sources of childcare support and substitute childcare available to mothers. France has by far the most developed state creche and nursery facilities, often available on a full-day basis. These facilities are more widespread for pre-school children than babies; access to state or private childcare for very young children is much higher for the middle than for working class mothers with the result that it is middle class women who are able to maintain their commitment to employment on a full-time basis and thus retain seniority and status. In Britain state child care facilities are not available for most mothers until the children are of school age, so that the period between child birth and school is too long to be bridged by alternative systems of child care. Moreover the lack of state and indeed private facilities makes part-time work a more feasible option for women in Britain, thereby encouraging them to leave their full-time job at the time of child birth. Research shows that women make very little use of paid childcare in Britain, so that husbands provide the most important source of alternative childcare, followed by grandmothers (Martin and Roberts, 1984). However, extended family networks are much less important in Britain than in Italy where the family provides the support network necessary to allow a minority of women to remain in full-time employment over the family formation phase but the women who provide this support are themselves confined to a mixture of domestic and informal wage economy work (Chapter 7, this volume). In the US there is less reliance on the family than in Britain and much more extensive use of private childcare provision, a system which can only partly be related to the tax concessions on costs of childcare (Dex and Shaw, 1986). More women return to full-time work in the States than in Britain so that this private childcare has to be provided on a full-day basis.

Women's participation is likely to be related to income need as well as to alternative childcare provision. It is notable that it is in France that participation rates fall when there are larger numbers of children, and that it is here that the state provides increasing family income subsidies for larger numbers of children. In large families in France disposable income is considerably higher than gross income for many income groups, and this subsidy system increases sharply with the third child so that it can partially substitute for women's wage earnings in working class families. In Italy the system of family income sharing and the opportunities for earnings in the informal sector provide some support for individuals and families, in particular women, who are excluded from the formal labour market. However, this may be more a means by which families and women adapt to constraints than a preferred system of generating and distributing family income. In Britain there is limited state income support for the family compared to France; the high participation rate of women with several children may thus be associated with increasing income needs in large families. In the States, the initial absence of state support for the cost of child-rearing may be one factor encouraging higher participation of women, and on a full-time basis. The high cost of paying for higher education of children in the States may also be associated with higher participation amongst older age groups.

Labour supply patterns are also influenced by trend factors in the structure of the economy on the one hand and in the structure of the social reproduction system on the other. In the US, for example, declining real wages for men may have bolstered female participation rates. The increase in the number of women who are head of household, and the increase in the number of men and women with more than one family must also keep up the pressure on individuals and families to participate in employment (Chapter 5, this volume; Humphries and Rubery, 1984). In Italy the changing economy of the family, related to increases in the income dependency of children on the parents could have been expected to increase the participation of women in employment, had it not been for the demand-side constraints on job opportunities caused by the slow growth of the service sector and the rigid sex-typing of occupations (Chapter 7, this volume). More recently this pressure from the supply-side has shown itself through the rapid increase in female unemployment even during periods of relatively fast expansion in female employment.

Demand-side factors can in general be expected to structure both the level and form of participation; whether participation is based on part-time or full-time work, or on continuous or discontinuous phases of employment must be dependent on the system of employment organisation. These demand factors can, and indeed have, suppressed the available labour supply in the short and the longer term. However while it is evident that there are still 'suppressed' areas of labour supply that can indeed be mobilised to fill new job opportunities (as for example the part-time jobs expansion in Britain), it also appears to be more difficult to 'suppress' supplies of female labour that are already in wage employment. There is indeed little evidence in any of the four countries of voluntary withdrawal from the labour market under the impact of reduced employment opportunities (see Joshi and Owen, 1985; Chapter 1 this volume) and the discouraged worker/added worker hypothesis is becoming increasingly irrelevant for explaining participation patterns. The form of family organisation is itself in a process of change, which if anything has been accelerated by the recession, such that the rate of divorce and the share of single person and single parent households have been increasing in all countries, although starting from very different levels. These demographic changes, combined with the increased reliance by multi-person households on multi-earnings to achieve their standard of living makes the notion of choice between participation and non participation irrelevant for many individual women in all four countries, although the persistence of income sharing in families in Italy provides more scope for non participation than the unstable and fragmented family system in the US.

Other evidence also suggests that in all four countries, women are not simply behaving as temporary 'added' workers to improve family living standards but are in fact pursuing strategies to consolidate their individual positions in the labour market and to improve the terms on which they compete with men. For example, women have reduced their voluntary labour turnover by reducing movements between jobs and indeed out of the labour force, increased their propensity to register as unemployed and raised their level of general and vocational qualifications. It is through this latter strategy that women appear to be making most progress in entering male-dominated professions, and in all four countries there is evidence of increased employment of women in jobs requiring qualifications. These supply-side strategies appear to be increasing divisions within the female labour force, between those already in work and those seeking work, and between those with qualifications and those without.

3.2 State welfare provision

The common assumption has been that the development of state welfare provision has been a major factor in the change in the pattern of organisation of social reproduction from the stereotype of a male breadwinner and a female domestic labourer to more unstable patterns of family formation involving multi-participation in the labour market. Thus the 'new right' has claimed that state support encourages men to abandon their family responsibilities and women to concern themselves more with their own careers than the welfare and care of their children and husbands (see Chapters 5 and 8 this volume). These views are expressed within individual countries and evidence of a rising trend in welfare provision within countries is taken as evidence to substantiate the argument.

However, the striking fact that emerges from comparisons across countries is the lack of any association between *levels* of state welfare provision and either family structure or female participation rates. Thus the US has experienced the fastest rate of breakdown in traditional family organisation and the highest female participation rates against a background of very limited state welfare support. There are extremely restricted rights to income maintenance for those not in the labour market, no universal state health service and very limited state childcare support, whether in the form of nurseries, school meal provision, income supplements or support for higher education. Thus the only real way in which women can reduce their 'caring' burden, is through the purchase of privately provided services and goods or through changes in the sexual division of labour. State welfare provision is much more developed in Britain and France, although the form of provision varies between countries. The emphasis on childcare provision in France, for pre-school children and for children on school holidays, clearly has a more direct impact on women's job opportunities than, for example, the higher subsidies for further education in Britain. However, while childcare facilities encourage participation, the taxation system in France provides strong disincentives to participation. In Italy state provision of health and caring services has expanded to levels comparable to similar European countries, thereby reducing caring burdens on the household, but the system of state income provision for those out of work is still extremely restricted. In practice income maintenance is only available to those already in employment, who are then protected from unemployment by the 'cassa integrazione', which pays workers a percentage of their income while they are effectively laid off. Those out of employment entirely are effectively dependent on the family. This system increases the divisions between those in work and those out of work, and in practice between young and old and men and women, as women and youth predominate in the latter category.

In the US until the Reagan administration's changes to the welfare system, the policy was to encourage claimants to combine state welfare provision with labour market participation. It was considered desirable not to create a subclass of people solely dependent on welfare but to encourage people to continue to participate without loss of welfare rights. These opportunities have been abolished by the Reagan government, thereby forcing a choice between welfare or participation. The choice so far appears to have been towards higher participation, involving working for longer hours and on low wages rather than opting for dependency on welfare. This pattern is against predictions based on 'rational economic man' and suggests that there is no simple relationship between welfare rights and participation. The dominance of the work ethic, or simply the desire to find some long term route out of poverty might explain this phenomenon in the US, but similar responses would not necessarily be found elsewhere. Also specific to the US is the link between welfare and access to free medical care: this system tends to pull labour market participation downwards but health care has limited impact on labour market participation in other countries.[10] Restrictions on welfare provision are tending to increase the availability of labour, mainly female, for low paid employment, but the increase in single parent families and people past retiring age means that on balance dependence on welfare is not likely to diminish. Strategies to return the burden of income support to the family will not necessarily be successful under changing conditions in the family structure.

In fact while there appears to be no direct relationship between *levels* of welfare provision and women's family and labour market roles, there does appear to be a similar pattern of resistance to the dismantling of state support systems and the transference of burdens to a family system which is not necessarily able or willing to absorb these functions. For example the contraction of state provision for the sick and the old in the UK is certainly constraining some women's labour market participation and forcing them to take on the role of carer. But the likely outcome of these cutbacks is that there will be a general deterioration in the care provided for the sick and the old as women find themselves either unwilling or unable to provide family-based care.

Cutbacks in state provision not only affect the conditions under which women supply their labour but also affect the demand for female labour, and the terms and conditions under which women are employed. The state is less likely to employ women at rates below national minima, and may provide more secure and stable employment than in the private sector. Thus women in Britain, where there has been the most active policy of cutting state provision, face the prospect of a reduced demand for their labour and of worsening terms and conditions as much of the work is transferred to private contractors, and this competition is used to intensify work and reduce labour costs within the public sector (see Chapter 8 this volume).

4 CONCLUSIONS: PROSPECTS FOR WOMEN UNDER DIFFERENT 'SYSTEMS' OF ECONOMIC AND SOCIAL ORGANISATION

The countries included in this study cover a wide spectrum of different forms of economic and social organisation, which in turn offer different sets of opportunities and constraints on women in their efforts to combine employment with domestic roles. There is no means of providing a unique 'ranking' of these systems, according to whether they are 'good' or 'bad' for women. Societies which offer more flexible employment forms, providing opportunities to combine domestic with wage work, may also offer lower pay and status, associated with these types of employment (for example, part-time work in Britain; informal sector work in Italy). Opportunities to maintain employment continuity and status over the family formation phase (for example, in France and Italy), have to be set against disadvantages of taking on full dual burdens of domestic and wage labour, or may only be taken up because of the availability of family assistance based on unpaid female labour. Reliance on state welfare provision may provide a more equitable basis for women to enter the labour market, but where this provision is linked, as in France, to strong state support for the ideology of the family and motherhood, it has contradictory impacts on women's labour market and social roles. It is also not possible or desirable to assess these 'systems' by reference only to the direct effects on women. For example the transformation of the wage system, or the 'rapport salarial', towards a low wage, high participation economy would tend to increase the supply of jobs for women, both absolutely and relatively, but the associated increase in total labour effort for the same standard of living, and accompanying decline in social provision as the effective tax base falls, would have an impact on the quality of life for both sexes (see Chapters 1 and 2 this volume).

Under current recessionary conditions it becomes even more imperative to locate the changes in women's labour market and social roles within the broader perspective of the restructuring of the economic and social system. Special attention must be paid to the restructuring of the system of labour market regulation. Differences in these systems of regulation underlie the variations we have observed in the labour market position of women between countries: moreover it is women's association with low pay and flexible employment forms that make them vulnerable to being used as part of a 'deregulation' strategy.

The system of labour market regulation will condition the impact of forces for change which arise from both the production and the social reproduction spheres. In all countries women are taking steps to become more permanent, more stable and better-qualified employees. These changes in behaviour can be interpreted in part as a response to the contraction of labour market opportunities and labour market flows but they also form part of a longer run transformation of women's employment patterns. Even though these developments are *relatively autonomous* responses from the 'supply-side' their outcome will depend on how these labour supply characteristics affect labour market structure. For example, if the effect of increased qualifications for women is to 'feminise' sections of the qualified labour market, then unless the pay and conditions in these sections are protected through collective action, it is probable that over time these types of jobs will be downgraded, in much the same way as clerical work has been downgraded over time. Alternatively if the 'qualification' expansion results in a minority of women entering primarily male type jobs, then this could provide a relatively effective 'escape-route' for middle class women, detracting attention from the expanding area of low paid female employment. The consolidation of women's position as permanent members of the wage earning labour force at a time of shrinking employment opportunities (at least in Britain, France and Italy) is also likely to add to the demand-side pressures for an expanded, flexible and low paid labour force.

The maintenance and indeed increase in demand for female labour through the recession has been related not to the disappearance of differentiation between male and female labour but to its continuation and in many respects its intensification. This differentiation is centrally related to differences in the terms and conditions of employment under which women are employed, for even the pattern of job segregation that prevails within a particular country can be related to the historical development of job and pay hierarchies which determines which jobs are categorised as low paid and low status female jobs. There is evidence in all countries of an increase in female employment specifically related to the shorter hours, lower pay, or more 'flexible' contracts associated with women's employment.

The demand-side trends are thus related both to sectoral change and to pressure to change the system of labour market regulation. These pressures may in part emanate from the 'obsolesence' of existing forms of labour market organisation but even where the main aim is to establish more appropriate job structures and working arrangements, the cost pressures under which firms operate mean that in practice 'transformation' is associated often with 'downgrading' of terms and conditions of employment. The most obvious example here is part-time working, which may be being introduced primarily to economise on labour hours but is also often associated with reductions in hourly pay rates even if productivity per labour hour is increasing. In some countries, such as the US and Britain these pressures are being actively fostered by governments, but even where governments have been more concerned to defend or regulate the transformation of systems of labour market regulation, the impact of these 'deregulating' pressures have been modified rather than eliminated. Women in all countries share a relatively disadvantaged labour market position based on the assumption of income dependency, often reinforced by unequal access to social security, and their prime responsibility for domestic tasks. The extent to which this 'disadvantage' is modified in the labour market is crucially related to the system of labour market regulation. It is for this reason that priority must be given to defending systems of labour market regulation and to establishing them on the broadest possible basis, to include typical 'marginal' groups such as part-time workers.[11] Changes in attitudes to women's labour market and family roles alone are unlikely to be sufficient to ensure that these potential social changes will be backed up by real improvements in access to resources and opportunities for women unless these changes take place within an effective framework for regulating and improving terms and conditions of employment in the labour market.

NOTES

1 Laboratoire d'Economie et de Sociologie du Travail, Aix-en-Provence. See review of the LEST school by Rose (1985).

2 This societal approach has links to the French 'regulation' school; each phase of capitalist development requires a different set of social, institutional, market and production conditions which interrelate in an historically-specific and country-specific form (Boyer, 1979).

3 There has been a further amendment to the Equal Pay Act in the 1970s providing for equal pay for work of equal value. This amendment, however, is likely to be taken up piecemeal at particular plants and establishments, as it is only within the same firm that such claims can be made. It is therefore unlikely that this amendment will have a generalised impact on women's pay except if it is taken up by trade unions in the public sector where the sheer size of the single employer increases the importance of a case under the equal value amendment.

4 In 1980 2.37 million interim contracts were concluded during the year (Michon, 1982, p. 36) whereas in 1981 1.46 million employees worked part-time (Garnsey, 1985).

5 In 1983 there were just over 3 million part-time employees aged 16–19, a very similar number to those in full-time employment in the 16–19 age bracket. Under 19s accounted for over 20 per cent of total part-time employment (*Handbook of Labour Statistics*, US Department of Labor, 1985).

6 In addition to there being specific demand for males, for example into apprenticeships, and for females into clerical work.

7 It is notable that in the US there is very little difference in median weekly earnings for part-timers between men and women, particularly for under 25 year olds, suggesting that the student population of both sexes provides a low paid labour market segment.

8 Although the average relative terms and conditions of women's employment in the US are probably less favourable than in the UK, women in the US are less prone to downgrading of pay and occupation after childbirth, a factor which may be associated with a more open access system (Dex and Shaw, 1986).

9 Since the change in France in 1986 to a conservative government, there has been a change towards active encouragement of flexibility without regulation.

10 In France, however, high social security payments for the self-employed limit the growth of self-employment and encourage participation by wives in their own right. Access to free health care is linked to social security payments in France.

11 It is arguable that systems of regulation, whether voluntary or legal, can never be universal and that women will always be dominant amongst excluded groups (Deakin, 1986). It is still, however, important to minimise the size of these excluded groups.

REFERENCES

Applebaum, E. (1985), 'Alternative workschedules of women', Temple University mimeo.

Ashton, D. (1986), *Unemployment under Capitalism*, Brighton, Sussex, Wheatsheaf.

Berger, S. and Piore, M. J. (1980). *Dualism and Discontinuity in Industrial Societies*, Cambridge, CUP.

Bettio, F. (1984). 'The sexual division of labour: the Italian case', doctoral dissertation, University of Cambridge.

Bettio, F. (forthcoming), *The Sexual Division of Wage Labour: the Italian Case*, OUP.

Bouillaguet-Bernard, P., Gauvin-Ayel, A. and Outin, J. L. (1981), *Femmes au Travail Prospérité et Crise*, Série: Sciences Economiques, Recherches Panthéon-Sorbonne, Université de Paris 1, Economica.

Boyer, R. (1979), Wage formation in historical perspective: the French experience, *Cambridge Journal of Economics*, vol. 3, no. 2.

Bruno, S. (1979), 'The industrial reserve army, segmentation and the Italian labour market', *Cambridge Journal of Economics*, vol. 3, no. 2.

Brusco, S. (1982), 'The Emilian model: productive decentralisation and social integration', *Cambridge Journal of Economics*, vol. 6, no. 2.

Brusco, S. and Sabel, C. (1981), 'Artisan production and economic growth', in F. Wilkinson (ed.), *The Dynamics of Labour Market Segmentation*, London, Academic Press.

Brusco, S. Carinci, F. and Villa, P. (1986), 'The state, the unions and the labour market. The Italian case, 1969–84', in G. Sziraczky (ed.), *The State, the Trade Unions and the Labour Market: Possibilities of and Limitations to Intervention*, Institute of Economic Studies 27, vol. 1, Hungarian Academy of Sciences.

Craig, C., Garnsey, E. and Rubery, J. (1985), *Payment Structures and Smaller Firms: Women's Employment in Segmented Labour Markets*, research paper no. 48, London, Department of Employment.

Craig, C. Rubery, J. Tarling, R. and Wilkinson, F. (1980), *Abolition and After: the Paper Box Wages Council*, research paper no. 12, London, Department of Employment.

Craig, C. Rubery, J., Tarling, R. and Wilkinson, F. (1982), *Labour Market Structure, Industrial Organisation and Low Pay*, Cambridge, CUP.

Craig, C. Rubery, J., Tarling, R. and Wilkinson, F. (1985), 'Economic, social and political factors in the operation of the labour market', in B. Roberts et al. (eds.), op. cit.

Deakin, S. (1986), 'Labour law and the developing employment relationship in the UK', *Cambridge Journal of Economics*.

Dex, S. (1984), *Women's Work Histories: an Analysis of the Women and Employment Survey*, research paper no. 46, London, Department of Employment.

Dex, S. (1985), *The Sexual Division of work: Conceptual Revolutions in the Social Sciences*, Brighton, Sussex, Wheatsheaf Books.

Dex, S. and Shaw, L. (1986), *British and American Women at Work*, London, Macmillan.

Dutoya, C. and Gauvin, A. (1987), 'Assignment of women workers to jobs and company strategies in France', in R. Tarling (ed.), op. cit.

England, P. (1982), 'The failure of human capital theory to explain occupational sex segregation', *Journal of Human Resources*, vol. 17, no. 3.

Garnsey, E. W. (1985), 'A comparison of part time employment in Great Britain and France', *VII Conference of the International Working Party on Labour Market Segmentation*, vol. 2, Universidad de Santiago de Compostela, July.

Harrison, B; Bluestone, B. and Tilly, C. (1986), 'Wage inequality takes a great U-turn', *Challenge*, March/April.

Huws, U. (1984), 'New Technology Homeworkers', *Employment Gazette*, January.

Humphries, J. and Rubery, J. (1984), 'The reconstitution of the supply side of the labour market: the relative autonomy of social reproduction', *Cambridge Journal of Economics*, vol. 8, no. 4.

Joshi, H. and Owen, S. (1985), *Does Elastic Retract? The Effects of Recession on Women's Labour Force Participation*, discussion paper no. 64, Centre for Economic Policy Research, London.

Lydall, H. F. (1968), *The Structure of Earnings*, Oxford, OUP.

Martin, J. and Roberts, C. (1984), *Women and Employment: A Lifetime Perspective*, report of the 1980 DE/OPCS Women and Employment Survey, London, HMSO.

Maurice, M. Sellier, F. and Silvestre, J. J. (1984), 'The search for a societal effect in the production of company hierarchy: a comparison of France and Germany', in P. Ostermann (ed.), *Internal Labor Markets*, Cambridge, Mass., MIT Press.

Maurice, M. Sellier, F. and Silvestre, J. J. (1986), *The Social Foundations of Industrial Power*, Cambridge, Mass., MIT Press.

Meehan, E. M. (1985), *Women's Rights at Work: Campaigns and Policy in Britain and the United States*, London, Macmillan.

Michon, F. (1981), 'Dualism and the French labour market: business strategy, non-standard job forms and secondary jobs', in F. Wilkinson (ed.), *The Dynamics of Labour Market Segmentation*, London, Academic Press.

Michon, F. (1982), 'La segmentation du marché du travail français: faits et analyses economiques 1968–81', Séminaire d'économie du travail mimeo, Université de Paris 1.

OECD (1984), 'The importance of long-term job attachment in OECD countries', *Employment Outlook*, September.

OECD (1985), *The Integration of Women into the Economy*, OECD, Paris, France.

Paukert, L. (1984), *The Employment and Unemployment of Women in OECD Countries*, Paris, OECD.

Petit, P. (1986), *Slow Growth and the Service Economy*, London, Frances Pinter.

Phelps Brown, H. (1977), *The Inequality of Pay*, Oxford, OUP.

Roberts, B. et al. (eds) (1985), *New Approaches to Economic Life*, Manchester, MUP.

Rose, M. (1985), 'Universalism, culturalism and the Aix group: promise and problems of a societal approach to economic institutions', *European Sociological Review*, no. 1.

Rubery, J. and Tarling, R. (1982), 'Women in the recession' in D. Currie and M. Sawyer (eds), *Socialist Economic Review 1982*, London, Merlin Press.

Snell, M. Glucklinch, P. and Povall, M. (1981), *Equal Pay and Opportunities:*

a Study of the Implementation and Effects of the Equal Pay and Sex Discrimination Acts in 26 Organisations, research paper no. 20, London, Department of Employment.

Tarling, R. (ed.) (1987), *Flexibility in Labour Markets*, London, Academic.

Wilkinson, F. (1983), 'Productive Systems', *Cambridge Journal of Economics,* vol. 7, nos. 3/4.

Index

absorption: of women workers;
France, 59–62; UK, 108–10; US,
26–7; *see also* historical change in
the participation of women
AFDC (Aid to Families with
Dependant Children): 146; and cuts
in, 146–52; and incentives to work,
148–51
Aglietta, M., 51
Alexander, M. et al., 226
Amsden, A. H., 200
Appelbaum, E., 39, 40, 263
Arangio Ruiz, M., 215
Ashenfelter, C. and Heckman, J., 45
Ashton, D., 271
AuClaire, P. A., 148
automation of production processes:
and displacement of women; Italy,
86–8: and restructuring the
economy; US, 157–8

Barron, R. D. and Norris, G. M., 4
Bastianini, F., 96
Battagliola, F., 58
Bednarzik, R. and Klein, D., 22
Beechey, V., 4, 191
Beechey, V. and Perkins, T., 118
Beller, A., 35
Berger, S. and Piore, M. J., 270
Bergmann, B. et al., 43
Bergmann, B. R., 4
Betson, D. and Van der Gaag, J., 43
Bettio, F., xiv, 9, 82, 96, 98, 213, 214,
215, 258, 259, 264
Bettio, F. and Villa, P., 98
Bielli, C. et al., 215
bi-modality of participation: (cross-
country comparison) 273; France,
165–7; Italy, 206–7; UK, 124–5;
US, 142–3
Bisset, L. and Coussins, J., 234

black women: and lone women
households; US, 144: and poverty;
US, 144–5
Bluestone, B. and Harrison, B., 39
Boisard, P. et al., 180
Boserup, E., 192
Bouillaguet-Bernard, P., Gauvin-
Ayel, A. and Outin, J. L., xiv, 50,
52, 68, 265
Bouillaguet-Bernard, P., Gauvin, A.
and Prokovas, N., 182
Bouillaguet-Bernard, P. and Germe,
J. F., 56, 60, 62
Bouillaguet-Bernard, P. and Outin,
J. L., 180
Bowen, W. and Finnegan, A., 3, 21,
22, 23
Boyer, R., 59, 60, 284
'bringing up' allowance, 175, 185
Bruegel, I., 3, 4, 9, 75, 104
Bruno, S., 96, 271
Brusco, S., 98, 263, 264
Brusco, S., Carinci, F. and Villa, P.,
258, 259, 271
Brusco, S. and Sabel, C., 265
Brusco, S. and Solinas, G., 98
Buccellato, A., 97
Buchin, E. and Payen, F., 186
'buffer' hypothesis, 3, 4, 5, 15, 16, 17,
35: evidence of (cross-country
comparison), 10, 266–8; Italy, 92–
5; US, 26–7, 30–3
Byrne, D. and Pond, C., 234, 237

Cacioppo, M. et al., 97
Cain, G., 22
Cain, G. and Dooley, M., 45
Canullo, G. and Montanari, M., 215
capitalism, development of; France,
51, 59–62, 163, 171; Italy, 199–200;
US, 141–2

288   *Index*

Carmignani, F., 215
'cash limits', 243
Cassa Integrazione, 90–1, 204–5, 208
Central Policy Review Staff, 221
CERC, 169, 171, 172
Cezard, M., 49, 69
Charraud, A., 172
childcare: (cross-country comparison), 276; France, 167–9; UK, 124–5, 223, 232–4
child labour, in Italy: importance to family economy, 199–201; laws, 196
Chiplin, B. and Sloane, P., 129
Chrissinger, M. S., 149
Cigoletti, C., 96
collective bargaining; *see* unions
Congdon, T., 243
contract labour, in France, 70
Courson, J. P. and de Saboulin, M., 164
Craig, C., Garnsey, E. and Rubery, J., 110, 118, 129
Craig, C., Rubery, J., Tarling, R. and Wilkinson, F., 129, 244, 254, 260
Crompton, R. and Jones, G., 226
Crompton, R. and Sanderson, K., 131
cross-country comparison: women and recession, 253–85
Cunnison, S., 225
Currie, E., Dunn, R. and Fogarty, D., 40, 43
cyclical influences: estimation of effect on women's employment; France, 62–9; Italy, 75–80, 89–91, 95; UK, 102–8; US, 23–7, 43: on labour supply, US, 19–23: model for estimation of, 9, 12: on restructuring; Italy, 85–9: on women's employment, 8, 10

D'Ambrosio, M., 97
Danziger, S., 43
David, P., 98
Davis, T., 231
Deakin, S., 121, 284
deindustrialisation: evidence of; US, 39–42; hypothesis, 39
Dejean, G. and Revoil, J. P., 180
Del Boca, D. and Turvani, M., 195

Della Rocca, G. and Vavassori, M., 97
deregulation of the labour market, 138–9, 272, 282; France, 138; UK 243–8
Desplanques, G., 167, 168
Dex, S., 124, 261, 273
Dex, S. and Perry, S. M., 104
Dex, S. and Shaw, L., 124, 259, 276, 283
Dimbleby, D., 231
'discouraged worker': effect, 6, 21, 277–8; UK, 124; hypothesis, 3
discrimination: in the labour market, 58; and affirmative action; US, 140, 152–4; and anti-discrimination legislation; France, 138, 182–4; Italy, 210–1; UK, 228: in social security and tax laws; France, 176–8; *see also* sexual division of labour
Doeringer, P. and Piore, M., 3, 11, 13, 75
domestic labour: UK, 221, 231–2, 247: historically; Italy, 195–6, 199–201: and relation to the market, 51–2; US, 141–2
domestic production; *see* domestic labour
Donati, P., 215
dual labour market: operation of; UK, 244–5, 247–8: theories, 3, 84: theories and the informal sector; Italy, 94
dual wage families: France, 62, 165; UK, 158
Duncan, O. and Duncan, B., 11, 34
Dutoya, C. and Gauvin-Ayel, A., 57, 256

Eckert, O., 177
economic 'recovery': France, 175; US, 140, 156–9
Edwards, R. C. et al., 75
earnings, *see* wages
economy of the family, *see* domestic production
economic plans: France, 173, 175
Education Acts, 234
Eisenstein, Z., 159
Elbaum, M., 180, 181
elderly, care of; UK, 223–4, 234–5
Elias, P., 110, 221

employment: estimates of changes in by industry; France, 62–9; Italy, 77–80; UK, 102–15; US, 23–7, 28–34, 40–1: estimates of changes in public sector; UK, 224–7, 229, 239–44: estimates of changes in by sector, cross-country comparison, 267–8; Italy, 76–7, 92; UK, 115–17: rates by sex, cross-country comparison, 269–70; UK, 100–2, 107–8; US, 17–20, 21; *see also* absorption; participation
employment conditions: UK, 117–23; France, 56–9, 71: cross-country comparison, 257–8, 262–5, 282: *see also* labour management policies
England, P., 261
equal opportunity: Act 1977; Italy, 210–11: programmes; US, 152–4: France, 183–4
Equal Pay Act: France, 183; UK, 100, 119–20, 228, 259, 261
Euvrard, F., 179
Eymard-Duvernay, F., 69
Eymard-Duvernay, F. and Salais, R., 54

Fair Wages Resolution, 245
Family Credit Scheme, 237–9
family organisation: and effects on women's labour supply, 135; France, 136, 163, 164–7; Italy, 136, 195, 199–201, 206, 209–10, 212–13; UK, 219–21; US, 136, 280: non-reversibility of changes in, 136, 277–8
family policy in France: family allowance, 174–5, 176; family income supplement, 173; and increasing the birth rate, 173–5, 184
Family Policy Group, 230
Family Protection Act 1981, 155–6; and tax credits, 155
family structure; *see* family organisation
Feder, J., 160
Federici, N., 215
feminisation of industries: Italy, 84–7; UK, 109–10, 115–16; *see also* segregation

fertility: changes in, Italy, 201–3
Fields, J., 22
flexible labour force: women as, cross-country comparison, 264–6, 267–9; France, 58–9, 69–70; Italy, 85, 95; *see also* reserve army of labour
FLM, 197
France: restructuring of employment, 7–8, 48–73, 255–72, 282–3; women, the state and the family, 135–9, 163–90, 273–82
Frey, L., 97
Frey, L. et al., 195
Friedman, M., 231
FULC, 97
Furnari, M., 75, 195

Gadrey-Turpin, N., 182
Gamble, A., 218
Garnsey, E. W., 264, 283
Garnsey, E. and Tarling, R., 113
Gaspard, M., 54
Geroldi, G., 96
Gershuny, J., 40
Gilder, G., 147
Giovannetti, E., 97
Glaude, M., 171
GLC, 129
Golding, P., 236
growth effect: decomposition of changes in employment into, 11, 12, 28, 213: estimates of; Italy, 79–80, 91, 193–5; UK, 110–12; US 29, 32–3
Guasco, G., 188

Hakim, C., 113, 129, 220
Harrison, B., 148
Harrison, B. et al., 261
Heller, J. L., 179
Henin, P. Y., 171
Henniquau, L., 176, 177
hidden unemployment: UK, 123; US, 21
high employment status women: in the US, 143–4, 154, 158–9
Himmelweit, S. and Mohun, S., 4
historical change: in the participation of women, 136; France, 50, 59–62; Italy, 191–9, 203–13; UK, 220; US,

historical change – *contd*
140–1: in the reserve army of
labour, 6, 50; France, 54–6: in the
social structure; France, 50, 164;
Italy, 199–203; UK, 219–21: in the
welfare state; UK, 221–4; *see also*
capitalism, development of
homework: cross-country
comparison, 265–6; France, 168;
Italy, 94–6, 206–7; UK, 245
homogenisation of the labour force:
UK, 122
housework: traditional division of by
sex, 44; Italy, 209; US, 142, 154
Houzel-Vaneffentere, Y., 171
Huet, M., 56, 68, 70, 182
Humphries, J., xiv, 6, 9, 15, 23, 25,
26, 75, 191
Humphries, J. and Rubery, J., xii, 17,
136, 139, 192, 254, 262, 277
Hunt, A., 224
Huws, U., 129, 265

Ichino, P., 211
'income effect' on wives' participation
rates, 191; France, 171–2
Income Supplement Scheme, 237–8
income and women's participation:
cross-country comparison, 262,
276–7; household: France, 171–3;
Italy, 209; UK, 221, 230
index of dissimilarity, 11, 13, 34;
estimates of: Italy, 81; UK, 113–
15; US, 35
informal sector: Italy, 8, 92–6, 191,
205–9, 212, 265; UK, 122, 262
insecure jobs: women's employment
in, 4–5, 58; France, 69–71, 179;
Italy, 94–5; UK, 243–8
International Working Party on
Labour Market Segmentation, xii
IRES, 173, 174
ISRIL, 97
Italy: sex segregation and
restructuring, 7–8, 74–99, 255–72,
282–3; women, the state and the
family, 135–9, 191–217, 272–82

job creation schemes: France, 178,
180–2; Youth Training Scheme
(YTS), 246; Young Workers
Scheme (YWS), 246–7

job segregation, *see* segregation
job skills: France, 56–7; Italy, 82–3,
90; UK, 119; US, 143, 145–6, 152,
153, 157; *see also* high employment
status women
Joe, T., 148, 149
Johnson, J., 15, 20
Johnson, B. and Waldman, E., 43
Joseph, G., 11, 21, 34, 35, 125
Joshi, H. and Owen, S., 124, 129, 278

Kergoat, D., 57
Kitagawa, E. M., 28, 213
Klein, D., 43

labour intensity: of feminised
processes, Italy, 82, 85–9, 90
labour management policies: France,
49, 56; *see also* 'rapport salarial'
labour turnover rates: France, 54–5;
Italy, 205
Labourie-Racape, A. et al., 54
Laufer, J., 184
Laulhe, P., 186
Lawrence, R., 39
Ledrut, R., 56, 66
Lenoir, R., 174
Leon, C. B., 158
Leoni, R., 195, 214
Leprince, F., 168, 186
Lettelier, B., 63
Lister, R., 230
Livi Bacci, M., 202, 215
Livraghi, R., 196
local labour market: characteristics of
and influences on employment, 54
Lollivier, S., 172, 187
lone mothers: France, 164–5; UK,
219, 221, 223; US,143–5: and
poverty; US, 147–8, 158
Low Pay Unit, 228
Lydall, H. F., 253
Lynn, L. E., 146

McIntosh, A., 110
McMahon, L., 160
Magaziner, I. and Reich, R., 42
Mallier, A. T. and Rosser, M. J., 118
Marc, N. and Marchand, O., 48
Marchand, O., 69
Margirier, G., 69

Martin, J. and Roberts, C., 110, 119, 130, 220, 228, 276
Maruani, M., 175, 177, 182, 187
mass consumption; *see* capitalism
maternity leave: changes in rights to in the UK, 246
Maurice, M. et al., xiii, 253
May, M. P., 98, 195
Medicaid (medical aid for the poor), 146, 149, 150
Medicare (medical care for the elderly), 153–5
Meehan, E. M., 256
Miani, G. and Palmieri, S., 97
Michal, M. G., 55
Michon, F., 54, 56, 63, 180, 264, 283
Milkman, R., 3, 15, 75
Miller, R., 15, 34
Mincer, J., 3, 191
Minford, P., 218
minimum wage agreements: and effects on women's wages, France, 169–71, 259; *see also* wages councils
Molinie, A. F. and Volkoff, S., 57
Moore, R., 245

National Health Service, 235
neoclassical: assumptions, 149; theories of pay differentials, 261; theories of segregation, 4
New Right, the, 278–9; UK, 218, 230; US, 141, 147, 155–6
Niemi, B., 15, 20
'non-functionalist' methodological approach, 136–7
nuclear family, *see* family organisation

occupational equality: laws in France, 182–4
OECD, 15, 171, 254, 268
OFCC (Office of Federal Contract Compliance): affirmative action policy, 152–4
Oi, W., 3, 75
Old Age Insurance Scheme, *see* pension schemes
Omnibus Budget Reconciliation Act 1982, 146
Oppenheimer, V., 192

Paci, M., 206

Padoa Schioppa, F., 195
participation: econometric models of, 22; life-time pattern of, cross-country comparison, 273–6; France, 164–7; Italy, 196–9, 206–7; UK, 124–6; US, 141–3: rates for married women; Italy, 193–9; US, 142–3: rates by sex, cross-country comparison, 269; France, 48–50, 55; Italy, 196–7; UK, 220; US, 17–20, 21–2; *see also* historical change in participation
part-time work: France, 70, 168, 180–1, 185; Italy, 93, 211, 212; UK, 117–19, 120–3, 125, 220–1, 223, 227–8, 245–7: cross-country comparison, 262–4, 268, 282–3: in public sector; UK, 225, 241–4
Paukert, L., 63, 254, 273
pension schemes: France, 176–7; Italy, 196–7
Perronet, F. and Rocherieux, F., 181
Petit, P., 267
Phelps Brown, H., 253
Piven, F. and Cloward, R., 160
Podgursky, M., 20
political activism by women, 138, 156
Pommier-Pennef, F., 54
poverty: among women in the US, 143–52, 158
Power, M., xiv, 141
'privatisation': of public sector; UK, 243–4, 280: of social services; US, 140, 154–6
public expenditure: Italy, 91, 209–10: cuts; UK, 222, 228, 231–9; US, 146–56
public sector employment: UK, 116–17: changes in; UK, 224–7, 229, 239–44; *see also* Thatcher government

Raphael, T. and Roll, J., 234, 236
'rapport salarial', 7–8, 59–62, 69–70
Reagan Administration: and cuts in social services, 146–56
Reaganomics: 140; *see also* Reagan Administration
Rein, M. and Rainwater, L., 148
relative autonomy of social reproduction, 136–9, 254–5, 281

reserve army of labour, 4, 6, 258, 268:
evidence of; UK, 100, 104, 107–8:
women as; France, 52–3, 55–6, 62–
3, 67, 71; Italy, 75; US, 140, 151–
2; *see also* flexible labour force;
historical change in
restructuring: of labour organisation;
France, 63; UK, 126: cross-
country comparison; 268–72, 281:
of the productive system, cross-
country comparison; 257, 266–9;
France, 48; Italy, 75, 85–92
Richardson, E., 44
Rimmer, L., 248
Robbotti, L., 197
Robinson, O. and Wallace, J., 118,
130
Rose, M., 283
Rossiter, C. and Wicks, M., 223
Rubery, J., 100, 120, 131
Rubery, J. and Tarling, R., xiv, 3, 9,
23, 25, 26, 75, 102, 125, 130, 266
Russo, M., 97

Sabourin, A., 184
Salais, R., 52, 53, 55, 66
scale effect: decomposition of growth
effect into, 11, 12, 28: estimates of;
US, 29, 32–3
school meals services: cuts in
provision of; UK, 234, 243–4
Schultz, T., 214
Scott, J. W. and Tilly, L. A., 200
sectoral: development; France, 51, 52,
58: distribution of women's
employment; France, 48, 52–3, 68–
9;·UK, 115–17, US 23–6, 31–4: *see
also* 'buffer' hypothesis
secular trend influences: model of, 9,
12: on women's employment, 8;
Italy, 92; UK, 108–17; US, 17–21,
43; *see also* historical change in the
participation of women
segmentation: evidence of; France,
53–4; US, 35–7: hypothesis, 15, 16,
27–8, 34, 37, 75, 192; *see also*
segregation
segregation: and effects on
participation, historically; Italy,
192–5, 203–5, 212: evidence of,
cross-country comparison, 255–8,
266–7; Italy, 81–5, 89–92, 95–6;

UK, 107, 110–17, 126–7:
hypothesis, 3, 4, 5, 74, 102, 191: in
informal sector; Italy, 93–6, 208:
and pay; UK, 119–20: and
restructuring; Italy, 85–9; *see also*
segmentation
service sector: increase in size of;
France, 48, 51–3, 58; Italy, 194–5;
UK, 158
sex-composition effect:
decomposition of changes in sex-
segregation into, 11, 13, 35:
estimates of; UK, 113–15; US, 36
sex-typing; *see* segregation
sexual division of labour, 58–9, 83–5,
256: and job creation schemes;
France, 182: and restructuring;
Italy, 88–9, 203–5
Shapiro, D. and Shaw, L. B., 20
share effect: decomposition of
changes in employment into, 11,
12, 28, 213: estimates of; Italy, 79–
80, 192–5; UK, 110–12; US, 29-31,
32–3
sickness insurance scheme: in France,
176
Silvestre, J. J., 63
Simmeral, M. H., 75
single parents; *see* lone mothers
skill; *see* job skills
Smith, J., 43
Smith, R. E., 45
Snell, M. W., Glucklich, P. and
Povall, M., 110, 129, 228, 261
social hierarchy: influence on job
segregation, 83–4, 89
social reproduction: 51, 62, 192:
cross-country comparison, 272–
83; interrelationship with system of
production, 124–5, 135–9, 200–1,
218; Thatcher rhetoric and, 228–
31; Thatcher policies and, 232: the
welfare state and; UK, 221–2
social security: benefit entitlements;
France, 136–7, 174–80, 185; UK,
123, 222–3, 236–7: expenditure;
UK, 235–6, 237: and recent
reforms; UK, 237–8
social structure; *see* historical change
socio-economic class: and
participation of women; France,
167, 172

Solinas, G., 98
Stack, C., 149
standard of living: AFDC cuts and, 150: effects of wage and employment changes on; France, 62, 171; US, 40–3, 44, 142–4, 157: and participation, 279
state policy: and effects on women's labour force participation, 135, cross-country comparison 268–72; Italy, 135, 196–7, 200–1, 208–12; France, 135, 169–85; UK, 135, 218–48; US, 135, 146–56
Sternlieb, G. and Hughes, J., 40, 43
structural effect: decomposition of changes in sex-segregation into, 11, 13, 35; estimates of, UK, 113–15, US 36
substitution: hypothesis, 3, 5, 15, 16, 27–8, 34–5, 37: evidence of; France, 56, 71; Italy, 85–9, 92; UK, 117–18, 242, 246–7; US, 31–2, 35–7: evidence of in 1930s; Italy, 66
Sullivan, J., 244

Tarling, R., xii, 109, 130
Taylorism, 57, 61, 86, 90
taxation and effects on women's participation: France, 173, 175–8, 185; UK, 230: redistribution effects; France, 173, 176–7
Thatcher, M., 228, 229
Thatcher government: as a direct employer, 239–44; and domestic labour, 221–4, 228–39; and economic policies, 218; effects on women's employment, 219–21, 224–8, 239–48; and employment protection, 121–2, 126, 244–8; and privatisation of the public sector, 116–17, 122, 138; and rhetoric, 228–31
Thelot, J. C., 53
Thomson, A. W. J. and Ingham, M., 245
Thurow, L., 43
Tinker, A., 235

unemployment: effect of economic restructuring on; US, 157–9: rates by sex, cross-country comparison, 270; France, 48, 56, 63–5, 179;

Italy, 204–5; UK, 100–1, 123–4; US, 17–21: rate for women; Italy, 191, 211, 213: of young people; Italy, 211; France, 49, 171, 182; UK, 238; *see also* hidden unemployment
unions: and employment policies, cross-country comparison, 257–8, 264, 271–2; Italy, 84, 86, 90–1, 92–3; UK, 121–2, 244–5: and pay agreements, cross-country comparison, 256–7, 259–62: and wage differentials; Italy, 84–5, 93; UK, 119–20, 242
United Kingdom: women's employment and recession, 7–8, 100–32, 255–72, 282–3; women, the state and the family, 135–9, 218–50, 272–82
United States of America: women's employment and restructuring, 7, 15–47, 255–72, 282–3; women, the state and the family, 135–9, 140–62, 272–82
unstable jobs, *see* insecure jobs

Vandelac, L., 71
Villeneuve-Gokalp, C., 167
Vinci, S., 195
Virginia Agricultural Experiment Station, 154
Vitali, O., 196, 199, 214
Vittore, L., 97

wages: changes in, US, 40–2, 144; hypothesised variations over the cycle, 37; pay differentials, cross-country comparison, 258–61; France, 169–71; Italy, 208; UK, 100, 119–21; US, 37–9; women's lower wage demands, 83–4, 94; *see also* standard of living
Wages Act 1986, 121
Wages Councils, 228, 245
Wagner, J. J., 170
Waite, L., 23
Walker, J., xiv, 241, 243
weight effect: decomposition of growth effect into, 11, 12, 28; estimates of, US, 29–30, 32–3
welfare state, the: Italy, 192, 195–6, 212; UK, 222–4; expenditure on,

welfare state, the – *contd*
  Italy, 209–10; UK, 222, 231–9; and
  social reproduction changes, cross-
  country comparison, 278–80; *see
  also* historical change in the
  welfare state
Wicks, M., 230, 232
Wilkinson, F., xii, xiii, 254
Wilkinson, G. and Jackson, P. M.,
  242
Willard, J., 186
Wilson, E., 222

Women's Research Experiment
  Station, 154
work sharing policies: France, 180–1
  185; Italy, 211: and reductions in
  working hours; France, 180–1
Woystinsky, W., 55

Yanz, L. and Smith, D., 15, 20
'young child allowance', 175

Zbalza, A. and Tzannatos, Z., 129